謹んで古稀をお祝いし　花見忠先生に　捧げる

執筆者一同

花見忠先生　近影

花見忠先生古稀記念論集
LIBER AMICORUM FOR
PROF. DR. TADASHI HANAMI

労働関係法の国際的潮流

NEW TRENDS OF LABOUR LAW IN INTERNATIONAL HORIZON

 信 山 社

は し が き

　本書は『労働関係法の国際的潮流』と題しているが，花見忠教授の古稀を祝賀して編まれた記念論文集である。花見教授は2000年2月にめでたく古稀を迎えられるが，この間期せずして後輩や門下生の間から記念論文集の計画が提案され，このような運びとなったものである。

　途中，花見教授のこれまでの研究活動にふさわしいものにするために，教授と親しい外国の研究者にも呼びかけたところ，続々と寄稿者があらわれ，結局約半分が外国の研究者の論文になった。なかでもブランパン，ヴァイス，ヘプルなど錚々たる学者が，多忙な中で力作を寄せてくれたのは，花見教授のこれまでの研究業績にたいする国際的評価を物語るものであろう。

　論文は「雇用平等及び労働環境法」と「雇用政策と労働法の新潮流」の2部にまとめられているが，全体としては雇用保障，雇用平等，災害補償，紛争処理，労使関係など広い領域に及んでいる。もちろん，これらの領域は，花見教授のこれまでの研究関心と無関係ではない。

　わが国では，大学教授は20代は研究，30代は教育と研究，40代半ばからは教育・研究のほか学内行政にもたずさわるのが普通である。花見忠教授もおおむねこのような途を歩まれ，上智大学では法学部教授として教育・研究のほか，大学院法学研究科長や法学部長を歴任された。今年（1999年）の春同大学を退職し名誉教授となられ，教育からはリタイヤされたものの，研究の面では，現在日本労働研究機構の研究所長，国際労使関係協会の会長として，国内的にも国際的にも第一線に立ち，行政面では中央労働委員会の会長という要職をつとめ，人一倍の活躍をされている。

　われわれ執筆者一同は，花見教授がこのバイタリティを今後も長く発揮され，国内および国際学会のすべての研究者に大きな影響を与え続けられることを祈ってやまない。

　最後に，出版事情の困難な折りであるにもかかわらず，われわれのこの風変りな計画を支持し，本書の刊行を実現して下さった信山社，とくに無理な

はしがき

要求をいつも暖く受入れて頂いた同社の渡辺左近氏に，心からの謝意を表したい。

  1999年12月25日

編 者
山口浩一郎
渡辺　章
菅野和夫
中嶋士元也

目 次

A 雇用平等及び労働環境法
Work enviroment in social dimension

セクシュアル・ハラスメントと使用者の責任　山川 隆一
The Employer's Liability for Sexual Harassment in the Workplace
Ryuichi YAMAKAWA

　はじめに………………………………………………………………… 3
1　わが国における問題処理の状況……………………………………… 4
　(1) セクシュアル・ハラスメントの法的位置づけ………………… 4
　(2) 使用者責任をめぐる問題処理の状況…………………………… 6
　　(a) 法的構成……………………………………………………… 6
　　(b) 不法行為責任(1)――加害者の責任を基礎とするもの……… 6
　　(c) 不法行為責任(2)――管理者の責任を基礎とするもの……… 8
　　(d) 債務不履行責任……………………………………………… 8
　　(e) 使用者責任をめぐる課題……………………………………10
2　アメリカにおける使用者責任………………………………………10
　(1) セクシュアル・ハラスメント法理の概観………………………10
　(2) 使用者責任をめぐる問題処理の状況……………………………11
　(3) 最近の合衆国最高裁判決…………………………………………12
　　(a) Ellerth 事件と Faragher 事件………………………………12
　　(b) 両判決の意義…………………………………………………15
　(4) 日本法との比較……………………………………………………16
　　(a) 使用者責任の法的位置づけ…………………………………16
　　(b) 「職務の範囲内」と「代理関係の利用」……………………17
　　(c) 使用者の免責…………………………………………………17

目　次

3　日本法の検討 …………………………………………………18
(1) 使用者責任の法的構成 ……………………………………19
(2) セクシュアル・ハラスメントと「事業ノ執行ニ付キ」…………20
　(a) 民法715条の解釈における「事業ノ執行ニ付キ」……………20
　(b) セクシュアル・ハラスメントについての準則 ………………22
　　① 上司によるセクシュアル・ハラスメント ………………22
　　② 同僚によるセクシュアル・ハラスメント ………………24
　(c) 使用者の措置による免責の可否 ……………………………25
　　① 民法715条1項但書 …………………………………25
　　② 「事業ノ執行ニ付キ」の解釈 ……………………………27

おわりに ……………………………………………………………29

日本との比較で見る東・東南アジアの女子労働の現状と法制度
香川孝三

Present Situation and Legal System on Female Workers in East and South-East Asia

Kozo KAGAWA

はじめに ……………………………………………………………31
1　東・東南アジア諸国の女子労働に関する実態 …………32
(1) 女性の労働力率の増加 ……………………………………32
(2) 女性の年齢別の労働力率 …………………………………34
　(a) M型の国 …………………………………………………34
　(b) 台形型の国 ………………………………………………35
　(c) 初期年齢ピーク型の国 …………………………………38
(3) 男女間の賃金格差・管理職に占める女性の割合 …………40
2　東・東南アジア諸国の女子労働法制 ……………………41
(1) 包括的な男女雇用平等にかかわる法律が制定されている国……42
(2) 包括的な男女雇用平等にかかわる法律が制定されようとしている国………………………………………………………46

(3)　包括的な男女雇用平等法はないが，それを目指している国……47
　(4)　男女雇用平等に関する法律も法案も存在しない国……………49
お わ り に…………………………………………………………………51

イタリアにおける雇用平等の展開と現状　　　山口浩一郎
Development of Equal Employment Opportunity in Italy
Koichiro YAMAGUCHI

　1　保護から平等へ ……………………………………………………55
　2　賃金の平等──同一労働同一賃金の原則 ……………………57
　3　待遇の平等──差別の禁止 ………………………………………59
　4　セクシュアル・ハラスメント ……………………………………61
　5　間接差別の問題 ……………………………………………………62
　6　アファーマティブ・アクション …………………………………64
　7　平等委員会と平等アドバイザー …………………………………67
　8　訴訟と立証責任 ……………………………………………………69
　9　現状と課題 …………………………………………………………71

健康配慮義務に関する一考察　　　渡辺　章
A Remark on the Employer's Liability to Care for Employee Health
Akira WATANABE

は じ め に…………………………………………………………………75
　1　安全配慮義務の意義および基本的性質について …………75
　2　健康配慮義務の意義および基本的性質について …………78
　3　健康診断をめぐる問題………………………………………………84
ま　と　め…………………………………………………………………95

目 次

脳血管疾患・虚血性心疾患の業務上外認定に関する裁判例
──「共働原因」と「相対的に有力な原因」── 小 畑 史 子

Recognition of Brain and Heart Disease as Resulting from Employment
──"Combined Effect" and "Superior Effect"── Fumiko OBATA

1 問題提起 …………………………………………………………97
2 検 討 …………………………………………………………103
  (1) 「共働」原因,「相対的に有力な」原因の意味 ……………103
  (2) 業務と並列される対象 ………………………………………107
  (3) 最有力な第三の原因の存在 …………………………………111
3 結 論 …………………………………………………………113

職業性疾病・作業関連疾病と安全配慮義務 中嶋士元也

Gesundheitsschutz und Fürsorgepflicht Shigeya NAKAJIMA

はじめに ……………………………………………………………115
1 安全配慮義務論の今日的段階 …………………………………118
2 職業性疾病・作業関連疾病における措置義務 ………………120
  (1) 疾病の態様 ……………………………………………………120
  (2) 義務の一般的範囲 ……………………………………………120
  (3) 義務の具体化・類型化 ………………………………………122
    (a) 疾病の防止段階 ……………………………………………122
      ① 労働安全衛生法令を遵守すべき義務 …………………122
      ② 安衛法令上の規定を斟酌して措置する義務 …………123
      ③ 安衛法令と契約上の権利義務 …………………………125
    (b) 疾病の増悪回避段階 ………………………………………127
      ① 健康診断の結果を告知すべき義務 ……………………127
      ② 増悪回避義務 ……………………………………………127

(4) 因果関係・義務違反の事実 …………………………………130
　　(a) 疾病の防止段階の因果関係 ………………………………131
　　　① 「業務」と「発症」との因果関係の争点……………131
　　　② 義務違反の事実と発症との因果関係 ………………133
　　(b) 増悪回避段階の因果関係 …………………………………136
　　　① 因果関係の個数 ………………………………………136
　　　② 義務の履行の中核 ……………………………………136
　　　③ 循環器系疾患死の場合 ………………………………137
　　(c) 択一的損害惹起の因果関係 ………………………………140
　(5) 帰責事由・義務の軽減・過失相殺 ………………………140
　　(a) 帰責事由と義務の軽減及び過失相殺との関係 …………141
　　(b) 帰責事由と業務の社会的有益性 …………………………143

B 雇用政策と労働法の新潮流
Employment policy and labour law

米国企業における苦情処理 ADR と社内オンブズパーソン
菅 野 和 夫
Grievous Procedures and Corporate Ombudspersons in the US Corporations
Kazuo SUGENO

はじめに …………………………………………………………147
1 米国企業における苦情処理 ADR の発達 …………………148
　(1) 苦情処理 ADR とは…………………………………………148
　(2) 苦情処理 ADR 発展の現象…………………………………149
　(3) 苦情処理 ADR 発展の要因…………………………………150
2 企業内苦情処理 ADR の内容 ………………………………152
　(1) 概　観 ………………………………………………………152
　(2) H 社のケース ………………………………………………153

目　次

　　(3)　P社のケース …………………………………………156
　3　企業内苦情処理制度の一種としての社内オンブズパ
　　ーソン ……………………………………………………160
　　(1)　社内オンブズパーソン（Corporate Ombudsperson）の概観……160
　　(2)　A社のケース …………………………………………164
　　(3)　UT社のケース ………………………………………167
　　(4)　P社のケース …………………………………………171
　　(5)　ハラスメントのひとつの解決方法としての社内オンブズパ
　　ーソン …………………………………………………173
　おわりに──日本の個別労使紛争解決制度への示唆 ………175

裁判所の論理・労働委員会の論理
　　──JRバッジ事件の場合──　　　　松　田　保　彦
Logics at Courts and Commissions
　　──In JR-Union Badge Wearing Cases──　　Yasuhiko MATUDA

　はじめに ……………………………………………………179
　1　国労バッジ事件における論点……………………………179
　2　国労バッジ事件における裁判所と労働委員会の判断
　　の概要 ……………………………………………………180
　　(1)　JR東日本事件…………………………………………180
　　(2)　JR東海（新幹線）事件 ………………………………181
　　(3)　JR西日本事件…………………………………………182
　3　バッジ事件における裁判所の論理と労働委員会の論
　　理……………………………………………………………183
　　(1)　職務専念義務違反の成否と組合バッジ着用行為の違法性
　　　　──裁判所の論理 ……………………………………184
　　(2)　組合バッジ着用行為の正当性と職務専念義務違反の成否

viii

──労働委員会の論理 ……………………………………185
　　(3) 組合バッジ着用行為の違法性とそれに対する不利益措置の
　　　当否 ……………………………………………………………186
4　裁判所の論理と労働委員会の論理の調整に関する試
　　案 …………………………………………………………………187
　　(1) 就業規則違反の組合活動に対する措置の妥当性 …………187
　　(2) 職場内組合活動の評価基準の客観性 ………………………188
　　(3) 組合活動に対する不利益措置における動機の競合 ………190
お わ り に ……………………………………………………………191

Re-examination of Employment Security in Japan in Light of Socio-economic Structural Changes
Takashi ARAKI

1. Introduction ……………………………………………193
2. Features of Regulations on Employment
   Security in Japan ……………………………………195
   2.1. Case Law Protection for Regular Employees …196
   2.2. Limited Protection for Non-regular Employees
        with Fixed-term Contracts ……………………199
   2.3. Characteristics and Current Issues of
        Employment Security in Japan ………………200
      2.3.1. High Protection for Regular Employees
             against Economic Dismissals ……………200
      2.3.2. Remedies for Abuse of the Right to
             Dismiss ………………………………………202
      2.3.3. Lack of Transparency and Effectiveness …203
      2.3.4. Combination of High Protection for

目　次

　　　　　Regular Employees and Low Protection
　　　　　for Non-regular Employees ················204
3. Structural Changes Affecting Employment
　　Security ··204
　　3. 1. Individualization and Diversification of
　　　　　Employees in a Changing Labor Market ······205
　　3. 2. Socio-economic Changes Surrounding
　　　　　Employers ··206
4. The Practice of Long-term Employment:
　　The End or Modification? ····························207
5. Employment Security as a Key Concept
　　Governing Employment Relations ················209
6. Merits and Demerits of the Current
　　Long-term Employment System ···················210
　　6. 1. Demerits of long-term Employment ················210
　　　6. 1. 1. Demerits for individualized and
　　　　　　　diversified Employees ···························210
　　　6. 1. 2. Demerits for Employers ···························214
　　　6. 1. 3. Demerits for Society ································214
　　6. 2. Merits of the Long-term employment System ···215
　　　6. 2. 1. Incentive to invest in human capital ······215
　　　6. 2. 2. Cooperative Labor and Employment
　　　　　　　Relations with high Morale ···················215
　　　6. 2. 3. Employment Security and Protection of
　　　　　　　Terms and Conditions of Employment ···216
7. Increased Employee Mobility and Challenges

x

for Japanese Labor Law ……218

Guidelines for Multinational Enterprises, Forever?

Roger BLANPAIN

Introductory remarks ……221

I. FACTORS INFLUENCING THE WORLD OF WORK ……222

  A. The globalization of the (market) economy ……222

    1. No boundaries ……222

    2. Rigid policies ……223

    3. Less room for social policies ……223

  B. The demographic explosion ……224

  C. Information technologies ……224

    1. From Fordism to Gatism ……224

    2. Tertiarisation ……226

    3. Externalisation ……229

    4. Outsourcing ……229

    5. Chains of SMEs ……230

    6. Industrialisation of services ……231

II. RELEVANCE OF THE GUIDELINES ……233

  A. Objectives and spirit ……233

  B. Content ……237

  C. Binding character and follow up ……239

CONCLUDING ……240

Employment versus Self-Employment: The Search for a Demarcation Line in Germany.

Manfred WEISS

目　次

1. THE CONCEPTUAL FRAMEWORK ……………241
1. 1. THE CATEGORIES ………………………………241
1. 2. THE PRINCIPLE OF UNIFORM TREATMENT OF THE EMPLOYMENTRELATIONSHIP …242
1. 3. THE DEMARCATION LINE BETWEEN 'EMPLOYEE-LIKE' AND 'OTHER SELF-EMPLOYED' PERSONS ………………………246
1. 4. THE DEMARCATION LINE BETWEEN 'EMPLOYEE' AND 'SELF-EMPLOYED PERSON' ………………………………………250
2. THE NEED FOR REFORM ………………………251
2. 1. THE ATTEMPT OF REDEFINTION OF THE CONCEPT OF SUBORDINATION …………251
2. 2. THE NEW QUALITY OF THE CHALLENGE …………………………………………………254
2. 3. RESPONSE BY AN ALTERNATIVE APPROACH …………………………………258
2. 4. THE LEGISLATIVE PROJECTS ……………261
3. EVALUATION …………………………………………263

Developing Competitiveness and Social Justice: The Interplay between Institutions and Social Partners　　　　　　　　　　　　Tiziano TREU

1. Premise. A global reflection. ……………………267
2. The end-of-the-century challenge: combining economic growth and employment. ………………270
3. A turning point for modernisation: the public

employment sector and small and small and medium enterprises. 277
4. The challenge of the quality of life and work. 281
5. Towards the globalisation of industrial relations? 285
6. Industrial relations and democracy : a new mission. 289
7. Towards the year 2000 : the role of social concertation. 292

The Implementation of the Amsterdam Treaty with regard to Employment : Co-ordination or Convergence?　　　　　Marco BIAGI

1. Introduction : A fundamental question 305
2. The new provisions of the Treaty : various inspirations in one Title 307
3. From Amsterdam to Luxembourg and beyond : the first semester of implementation 311
4. The preparation of the National Action Plans for Employment and the Cardiff European Council 316
5. From Cardiff to Vienna : monitoring or evaluating the national policies? 321
6. Eurowatching or convergence? 323

Towards a Revolutionised Working Life
　　　　　　　　　　　　Reinhold FAHLBECK

1. Introduction. Purpose 327

2. Points of departure ……………………………328
3. The role of capital versus the role of work ……………334
4. Whose Company? ……………………………336
5. The company and its members ……………342
6. A new actor's model ……………………344
7. Management ……………………………347
8. Labour unions ……………………………349
9. Product markets ……………………………355
10. Flexibility ……………………………356
11. A revolutionised working life? ……………………358

Labor Law Amendment to Reform the Korean Industrial Relations　　SOHN Chang-Hi

Introduction ……………………………363
I. Pursuit of Change and Reform ……………365
　(1) Wave of Democratization ……………367
　(2) Wave of Globalization ……………367
　(3) The Government Pledge ……………368
II. Passage of the Amendments ……………369
　1. From 'New Vision' to the First reform attempt　369
　　(1) Kim Young-sam's Vision for A New Industrial Relations ……………369
　　(2) Discussion at the Presidential Commission on Industrial Relations Reform (May 9・Nov. 12, 1996) ……………371
　　(3) The Amendment Proposal by the Government (Dec. 10, 1996) and its Abnormal Passage

　　　　in the National Assembly (Dec. 26, 1996)
　　　　..373
　　2. The Second Reform 375
　　　(1) Public Apology of the President Kim Young-
　　　　sam (Feb. 25, 1997) 375
　　　(2) Agreement of the political parties on the
　　　　Second Labor Law Reform (Mar. 8, 1997)
　　　　and its Passege in the National Assembly
　　　　(May. 10, 1997) 376
　　　(3) Things to be Kept in Memory through all
　　　　the Course of amendments 377
　　3. The Third Reform with New Acts Added
　　　(Feb. 14, 1998) 379
III. Significance and Content of the Newly
　　Amended Labor Law-referring mainly to
　　Mar. '97 Amendment 382
　　1. Significance 382
　　2. Content 383
　　　(1) Building up base for voluntary negotiations...383
　　　(2) Moderating restriction in the labor market
　　　　to foster more flexibilitiy 384
　　　(3) Eradication of unreasonable system and
　　　　practices 385
　　　(4) Rationalization of concerted action and
　　　　dispute adjustment 385
　　　(5) Reasonable Re-organizing the Labor

     Administration ···386
  (6) Base-building for the Participatory and
     Cooperative Industrial Relations ··················386
 IV. Evaluation and Prospect ···387
  1. Evaluation ···387
  2. Prospect ··389

Early Ideologies of French Unionism
Jacques ROJOT

 INTRDUCTION ···393
 GENERAL COMMENTS : ···396
 ELEMENTS OF "SPONTANEOUS" WORKER'S
  ORGANIZATIONS IDEOLOGIES. ·····························402
 THE COMMUNIST INFLUENCE. ·····································407
 OTHER SOCIALIST INFLUENCES. ·································414
 OTHER THEORETICIANS AND IDEOLOGUES. ·········419
 REVOLUTIONARY UNIONISM ··422
 CATHOLIC UNIONISM ··436
 CONCLUSION ··436

The Social Dumping Debate   Bob HEPPLE

 LIBERALISATION SEEN FROM NORTH
  AND SOUTH ···441
 SOCIAL CLAUSES IN TRADE AGREEMENTS ··········444
 AN ALTERNATIVE : THE 1998 ILO
  DECLARATION ··447
 SOCIAL PROVISIONS IN INVESTMENT
  AGREEMENTS ···451

目　次

TWO APPROACHES TO SECURING
　　MINIMUM LABOUR STANDARDS……………………457
THE TASK AHEAD …………………………………………462
年　　譜
著作目録

執筆者一覧

〈A　雇用平等及び労働環境法〉
　　　山川隆一　　　筑波大学社会科学系教授
　　　香川孝三　　　神戸大学大学院国際協力研究科教授
　　　山口浩一郎　　上智大学法学部法律学科教授
　　　渡辺　章　　　筑波大学社会科学系教授
　　　小畑史子　　　富山大学経済学部経営法学科助教授
　　　中嶋士元也　　上智大学法学部地球環境法学科教授

〈B　雇用政策と労働法の新潮流〉
　　　菅野和夫　　　東京大学大学院法学政治学研究科教授
　　　松田保彦　　　帝京大学法学部教授・横浜国立大学名誉教授
　　　荒木尚志　　　東京大学大学院法学政治学研究科教授
　　　Roger BLANPAIN　　　Leuvan University
　　　Manfred WEISS　　　The J. W. Goethe University
　　　Tiziano TREU　　　University of Milano
　　　Marco BIAGI　　　University of Modena
　　　Reinhold FAHLBECK　　　Lund University
　　　SOHN Chang-Hi　　　Hanyan University
　　　Jacques ROJOT　　　University of Paris I
　　　Bob HEPPLE　　　The University of Cambridge

A　雇用平等及び労働環境法

セクシュアル・ハラスメントと使用者の責任

山 川 隆 一

はじめに

　近年，職場におけるセクシュアル・ハラスメントをめぐる裁判例の増加が目立っている。そして，これらの裁判例においては，原告側の主張する加害行為が存在したか否かという事実認定の問題に加えて，セクシュアル・ハラスメントは被害者のいかなる権利・利益を侵害するものと位置づけられるのか，加害者の不法行為責任の有無をどのような基準で判断するのか，使用者はセクシュアル・ハラスメントについていかなる責任をどのような場合に負うのかなど，様々な法律問題が検討の対象となる。

　これらのうちで，最後の使用者責任の問題に関しては，近年いくつかの興味深い展開がみられる。すなわち，まず使用者責任の法的構成については，従来は民法715条に定める不法行為責任と解する立場が一般であったが，最近では債務不履行責任をも肯定する裁判例がみられる[1]。また，従来の裁判例では，セクシュアル・ハラスメントが民法715条1項の「事業ノ執行ニ付キ」という要件をみたすとするものが多かったが，最近ではこれを否定する事例も現れている[2]。さらに，1997年の改正により新設された男女雇用機会均等法21条により，使用者がセクシュアル・ハラスメントを防止するための配慮義務を負うに至ったことから，使用者がそうした配慮を行った場合には責任が否定されるかという問題も生じうる。

　本稿は，セクシュアル・ハラスメントに関する使用者責任をめぐる以上の

---

1) 後注12)・13)とその本文参照。
2) 後注9)とその本文参照。

ような法律問題のうち，民法715条等における使用者責任の判断基準を中心に検討を加えるものである（会社役員等が加害行為を行った場合には，民法44条により法人の責任が問われるが，同条の「職務ヲ行フニ付キ」という要件については，「事業ノ執行ニ付キ」と同様の解釈がなされることが多いと思われる）。検討にあたっては，まずわが国における問題処理の状況を整理したのち，セクシュアル・ハラスメントの法理が早くから発達したアメリカ合衆国における状況を紹介し，日本法との比較を行った上で，わが国における解釈論について検討を試みることとしたい。

1 わが国における問題処理の状況

(1) セクシュアル・ハラスメントの法的位置づけ

アメリカ合衆国では，職場におけるセクシュアル・ハラスメントに対しては，州の不法行為法等を根拠としても救済を求めうるが，人種・皮膚の色・宗教・性別・出身国に基づく雇用差別を禁止する1964年公民権法第7篇（以下第7篇ということがある）を根拠として使用者の責任が追及されることが多い。後述するように，第7篇は，「雇用条件」に関するあらゆる形態の差別を包括的に禁止しているため，性的要求を拒否したことなどを理由として雇用上不利益な決定を行う対価型ハラスメントのみならず，性的ないやがらせにより職場環境を悪化させる環境型ハラスメントも，雇用条件についての差別を構成する場合には，同法違反と評価されうるのである。

これに対してわが国においては，雇用機会均等法の1997年改正に至るまでは，セクシュアル・ハラスメントを直接的に規律した法令は存在しなかった。冒頭で述べたように，改正後の均等法21条は，使用者がセクシュアル・ハラスメントを防止するための配慮義務を負う旨を定めるに至ったが，同条については，行政上の規制を行っているに留まり，使用者の民事責任を直接に基礎づけるものではないとする理解が有力である[3]。また，雇用機会均等法は，

---

3) 菅野和夫・労働法（第5版）168頁（1999），奥山明良・職場のセクシュアル・ハラスメント160頁（1999），野間賢「セクシュアル・ハラスメントと使用者の職場環境配慮義務」日本労働法学会誌91号132頁（1998），石井妙子「企業のセクハラ防止義務と法的対応」季労186号54頁（1998）など。

配置や解雇など特定の行為類型を取り出して差別を禁止しているため、セクシュアル・ハラスメントがこれらの類型に該当する場合（対価型についてはこうした事案がありうる）には同法違反が成立しうるものの、そうした場合を除けば、被害者の民事上の救済は、民法などの一般法令によらざるをえないこととなる。

民法のもとでの救済を考える場合、まず、加害行為としてのセクシュアル・ハラスメント自体についてどのような法的位置づけを行うかを検討する必要があるが、加害行為者に対しては不法行為責任を追及するのが一般であるため、セクシュアル・ハラスメントが不法行為法上いかなる法的利益を侵害するのかという問題が生じる。この点につき、裁判例は、事案の内容に応じて、「性的自由」、「性的自己決定権」、名誉その他の人格権等の侵害があったと判断するものが多い[4]。しかし、リーディングケースである福岡セクハラ事件においては、裁判所は、被害者である女性の私生活に関わる噂を流すことなどによるハラスメントに関して、「働きやすい職場環境の中で働く利益」が侵害されたものと判示している[5]。

次に問題となるのは、セクシュアル・ハラスメントの不法行為法上の違法性をどのように判断するかである。この点は、環境型ハラスメントについて特に問題となるが、後述するように、アメリカ合衆国では、重大または執拗ないやがらせ行為であれば、雇用条件における差別と評価しうるほどの職場環境の悪化をもたらし、第7篇における違法性を備えると解されている。わが国でも、加害行為の重大性や反復性などを考慮しながら、違法性を肯定しうる範囲について一定の枠を設定する立場が多くみられる[6]。裁判例においても、男性上司が部下の女性に対して行ったその意に反する性的言動につき、それがすべて違法と評価されるものではないとしたうえで、その行為の態様、行為者である男性の職務上の地位、年齢、被害女性の年齢、婚姻歴の有無、

---

4) 裁判例の動向については、山川隆一「わが国におけるセクシャル・ハラスメントの私法的救済」ジュリスト1097号69頁（1996）、水谷英夫「日本におけるセクシュアル・ハラスメントの現状と判例の動向」法律のひろば1998年5月号8頁、奥山・前掲注3)書57頁以下など参照。

5) 福岡地判平成4・4・16労判607号21頁。

6) 山田省三「セクシャル・ハラスメントの法理」季労155号57頁（1990）、山川隆一「セクシュアル・ハラスメントと不法行為」ジュリスト1005号51頁（1992）など。

両者のそれまでの関係，当該言動の行われた場所，その言動の反復・継続性，被害女性の対応等を総合的にみて，それが社会的見地から不相当とされる程度のものである場合には，人格権を侵害するものとして違法性を認めることができるとの一般論を示したものがある[7]。

(2) 使用者責任をめぐる問題処理の状況
(a) 法的構成

セクシュアル・ハラスメントについての使用者責任に関しては，事案に応じて様々な法的構成がありうる。まず，対価型ハラスメントの場合，性的要求を拒否した被用者に対して解雇や配転などにより不利益を与える形をとるから，当該被用者は，そうした行為が法律行為であれば，その無効確認の訴えを起こすなどして使用者の責任を追及することが可能である。また，法律行為以外であっても，使用者の人事権の行使として行われた行為は，加害者が事業の執行につき行ったものとして，民法715条等により使用者の不法行為責任を追及することができるのが通常である。これに対して，環境型ハラスメントの場合には，加害者の職務とは直接には関わりがない行為であることが多いため，使用者責任の有無が大きな問題となる。

そこで，環境型ハラスメントについての使用者責任の法的構成をみると，以下述べるように，(1)加害者の行為につき民法715条または44条を適用するものが多いが，その外に，(2)加害者と被害者を監督する立場にある管理者が職場環境の調整を怠ったことについて民法715条等を適用するものもあり，さらに，(3)使用者自身が職場環境調整義務に違反したとして債務不履行責任を負うとするものも現れている。

(b) 不法行為責任(1)――加害者の責任を基礎とするもの

以上のうち，加害行為者につき民法715条等を適用した裁判例においては，使用者責任を肯定したものが多くみられる。その際に中心的な問題となるのは，加害行為が「事業ノ執行ニ付キ」なされたものといえるかであるが，これら裁判例は，加害行為と職務との関連性に着目し，加害行為の内容の他に，

---

[7] 金沢セクハラ事件・名古屋高金沢支判平成8・10・30労判707号48頁。また，横浜セクハラ事件・東京高判平成9・11・20労判728号23頁も参照。

行為がなされたのが職場またはその延長とみられる場所であったか，行為がなされた時間が労働時間中またはそれに準ずる時間中といえるか，発言によるセクハラの場合にはその内容が職務に関連しているか，さらには，加害行為者と被害者の関係，特に，加害者が上司としての地位を利用して行為におよんでいるかなどを考慮して，この要件への該当性を判断している。

たとえば，横浜セクハラ事件における東京高裁判決は，営業所長がその部下である女性に対して行った身体的接触ないし強制猥褻的な行為に関して，これらの行為は，営業所内において，所長によりその部下である女性に対し，勤務時間内に行われ，または開始された行為であり，上司としての地位を利用して行われたものであることを理由に，このような行為は，会社の事業の執行行為を契機とし，これと密接な関連を有するものであるとして，会社の使用者責任を肯定している[8]。

これに対して，三重セクハラ事件判決は，上司の加害行為は職務に関連するものではないとして，民法715条の使用者の責任を否定した。この事件は，看護婦と二人一組で病院の夜間勤務を行っていた男性上司が，休憩室で仮眠中の看護婦に対して身体的な接触を行うなどした事案であるが，判決は，こうした上司の行為は，仮眠中の看護婦を起こそうとして行われたものではなく，個人的な行為にとどまるとして，職務との関連性を否定している[9]。このような判断基準による場合，セクシュアル・ハラスメントはほとんどの場合に個人的な行為と評価されることになると思われ，従来の裁判例との対比からすれば異例であると評しうるが，いかなる場合に職務との関連性を肯定できるのかという問題を提起したことは確かである。

民法715条の適用をめぐっては，次に，同条1項但書にいう，使用者が加害行為をなした被用者の選任監督を尽くしたことに基づく免責が認められないかが問題となる。この免責規定は現在ほとんど適用されることがないため，セクシュアル・ハラスメントに関する裁判例も，免責を認めることに対しては消極的である。この免責規定の適用が主張された兵庫セクハラ事件におい

---

8) 東京高判平成9・11・20労判728号25頁。最近では，上司としての地位の利用という要素を重視するものが多い。水谷・前掲注4) 論文18頁以下の表参照。

9) 津地判平成9・11・5労判729号59頁。その他に，連合滋賀事件・大津地判平成8・10・14判時1623号129頁参照。

ては，病院の洗濯係である女性に対する洗濯長による性的な言動についての使用者責任が問題となったが，判決は，乾燥室での作業等男女職員が接近して作業をする状況があり，セクシュアル・ハラスメントの機会が少なくないと考えられること，職場で優越的地位にある洗濯長は従来から職場の女性の体型等について不適切な言動に出ることがあり，それが職場の女性間では相当認識されていたことなどから，病院として洗濯長の行為を予見することが不可能であったとはいえないとして，同人の選任・監督につき注意を尽くしたという主張を排斥している[10]。

(c) 不法行為責任(2)——管理者の責任を基礎とするもの

前記の福岡セクハラ事件判決は，加害者の不法行為について民法715条を適用したが，それに加えて，加害者と被害者を監督する立場にある管理者が個人として不法行為責任を負うとした上で，それについても民法715条を適用して使用者の責任を認めた[11]。同事件においては，出版社の編集長がその部下である原告に対していやがらせ行為を行ったために同女の職場環境が悪化したにも関わらず，両者を監督する立場にあった会社の経営幹部は，十分な調査や解決のための努力をすることなく，編集長には3日間の自宅謹慎を命ずるにとどめる一方，原告に対しては退職を勧告するという態度をとったが，判決は，上記経営幹部は職場環境を調整するように配慮する義務を怠ったとして，同人につき不法行為の成立を認め，その不法行為について使用者責任を肯定している。以上の構成は，「働きやすい職場環境の中で働く利益」が不法行為法上保護に値する利益であることを前提として，職場の管理者にはその職務を遂行するにあたり職場環境を調整する注意義務があるという理解に立つものである。

(d) 債務不履行責任

ところで，福岡セクハラ事件判決は，使用者は「働きやすい職場環境を保つように配慮する注意義務」を負うと判示していたが，それは被告会社の不法行為責任を肯定する行論の中でのものであり，判決のいう「義務」は，管

---

10) 神戸地判平成9・7・29労判726号111頁。
11) 労判607号23頁。職場環境調整義務違反による使用者の不法行為責任を認めた最近の例としては，沼津セクハラ（F鉄道工業）事件・静岡地沼津支判平成11・2・26労判760号38頁がある。

理者にとっての不法行為法上の注意義務を意味するものであった。しかし，三重セクハラ事件判決は，使用者は被用者に対し，労働契約上の付随義務として，信義則上，「職場環境配慮義務，すなわち被用者にとって働きやすい職場環境を保つように配慮すべき義務」を負っていると判示して，使用者は，労働契約上職場環境配慮義務を負うこと，それゆえ，この義務に違反した場合は債務不履行責任が生ずるとの理解を示した[12]。

また，京都セクハラ事件において，京都地裁は，被用者による更衣室内の隠し撮りにつき適切な措置をとらなかったことや，隠し撮りを行った被用者と原告が男女関係にあるような取締役の発言により原告が退職せざるを得なくなったことに関して，使用者は雇用契約上の付随義務として，原告のプライバシーが侵害されることのないように職場環境を整える義務，および同人が意に反して退職することのないように職場環境を整える義務があると判示している[13]。

このような債務不履行構成に対しては，セクシュアル・ハラスメントにより侵害される法的利益が人格的利益であることから，労働契約上の付随義務として一般に人格的利益の配慮義務を認めうるかについて疑問が示されているが[14]，他方で，債務不履行構成を支持する見解もかなりみられる[15]。また，セクシュアル・ハラスメントは一般に職務に関連する行為とはいいにくいとした上で，債務不履行構成によれば，使用者が配慮を尽くした場合，不法行為構成では認められにくい使用者の免責が認められる可能性があると述べるものがある[16]。

しかし，「職場環境配慮義務」を契約上の義務と解する場合でも，その内容は，管理者の負う不法行為法上の注意義務のそれと実質的には変わりがな

---

[12] 津地判平成9・11・5労判729号59頁。
[13] 京都地判平成9・4・17労判716号53-54頁。
[14] 奥山・前掲注3)書123頁（ただし，例外的に債務不履行責任を認める），山川・前掲注4)論文70頁など。
[15] 福島瑞穂「セクシュアル・ハラスメントと法」労旬1228号17頁（1989），松本克美「セクシュアル・ハラスメントに対する慰謝料請求」ジュリスト985号125頁（1991），山崎文夫「セクシュアル・ハラスメント防止の配慮義務と新指針」労働法律旬報1439号44頁（1998），野間・前掲注3)論文131頁など。
[16] 石井・前掲注3)論文60頁。

いと思われる（時効などの点では差が生じうるが）。たとえば，三重セクハラ事件において職場環境配慮義務違反が認められたのは，上司の性的な言動により夜間勤務の看護婦の職場環境が悪化していたことを知りながら，病院が迅速な対応をしなかったことを理由とするものである。これは，福岡セクハラ事件において，会社の経営幹部が編集長のいやがらせ行為に対して適切な対処をしなかったことにつき責任を認めたことと共通する判断といいうる。そうすると，むしろ，使用者がいかなる対応を行えばセクシュアル・ハラスメントに関する責任が否定されるかという問題がより重要となるのではないかと思われる。

(e) 使用者責任をめぐる課題

以上みてきたように，セクシュアル・ハラスメントに関する使用者責任をめぐっては，なお検討すべき問題が存在する。そして，それらのうち実際上特に重要となるのは，加害行為者の責任を基礎とした使用者責任に関して，「事業ノ執行ニ付キ」という要件をどのように考えるかであり，また，管理者ないし使用者がセクシュアル・ハラスメントを防止するための配慮を行った場合に免責されることがありうるかである。これらの問題については，アメリカ合衆国における裁判例の展開が参考になるので，以下ではアメリカ法の検討を行い，日本法にとっての示唆を探ることとする。

2 アメリカにおける使用者責任

(1) セクシュアル・ハラスメント法理の概観

先にみたように，アメリカ合衆国においては，職場におけるセクシュアル・ハラスメントにつき，人種・皮膚の色・宗教・性別・出身国による雇用差別を禁止する1964年公民権法第7篇を根拠として訴えが提起されることが多い。第7篇には，セクシュアル・ハラスメントを直接に規律した規定はないが，雇用条件（terms and conditions of employment）に関する差別を包括的に禁止しているため，セクシュアル・ハラスメントが雇用条件における差別を構成する場合には，第七篇違反として把握することが可能となる[17]。

この点は，人事権の行使という形を取らない環境型ハラスメントにおいて特に争われたが，合衆国最高裁は，1986年の Meritor 事件——Vinson 事件と

も呼ばれる——において，重大または執拗ないやがらせ行為により職場環境が悪化した場合には，雇用条件に関する差別がなされたものとして第7篇違反が成立する可能性を認めるに至った[18]。また，その後最高裁は，環境型ハラスメントにより雇用条件が不利益に変化したかの判断にあたっては，被害者に精神的な被害などの結果が生じたことは不可欠な要件ではないと判示し[19]，さらに，同性間の性的な言動によるハラスメントであっても，第7篇違反は成立しうるとの判断を下している[20]。

(2) 使用者責任をめぐる問題処理の状況

本稿で検討する使用者責任の問題については，監督者が部下に対して行ったセクシュアル・ハラスメントにつきいかなる場合に使用者が責任を負うかが中心的な問題となる（同僚や顧客の行為に対する責任については後述する）。この点に関し，合衆国最高裁は，Meritor事件において，使用者がセクシュアル・ハラスメントの事実を知っていた場合やそれと同視しうる場合に限り使用者責任が生じるとの主張を排斥する一方で，監督者の行為につき自動的に使用者責任が生じるわけでもないとして，いわば折衷的な立場を示唆したが，具体的な判断基準については，使用人の行為についての雇用主の責任を判断する際に用いられるコモンロー上の代理（agency）法理を参考に決すべきであると述べるにとどまった[21]。その結果，その後の下級審裁判例においては，

---

17) アメリカ法については，奥山明良「アメリカに見る労働環境と性差別」判タ523号18頁（1983），同「アメリカの働く女性と性的いやがらせ」成城法学23号1頁（1987），水谷英夫「雇用における『性的いやがらせ』」法学50巻6号91頁（1987），林弘子「職場におけるセクシュアル・ハラスメントの比較法的検討」桑原洋子先生還暦記念・家族・労働・福祉203頁（1991），上田純子「セクシュアル・ハラスメント（上・下）」ジュリスト1047号52頁，1048号90頁（1994），福島瑞穂他・セクシュアル・ハラスメント（新版）37-132頁［中下裕子］（1998），中窪裕也「アメリカにおけるセクシュアル・ハラスメント法理の新展開」ジュリスト1147号10頁（1998）など参照。また，日米両国のアプローチの違いについては，Ryuichi Yamakawa, *We've Only Just Begun : The Law of Sexual Harassment in Japan,* 22 HASTINGS INT'L & COMP. L. REV. __（1999刊行予定）参照。

18) Meritor Saving Bank, FSB v. Vinson, 477 U. S. 57 (1986).

19) Harris v. Folklift Sys., Inc., 510 U. S. 17 (1993).

20) Oncale v. Sundowner Offshore Serv., Inc., 118 S. Ct. 998 (1998).

使用者責任についてさまざまな立場が採用され[22]，最高裁による統一が待たれることとなった。また，下級審裁判例においては，使用者がセクシュアル・ハラスメントを禁止する方針を明確にして苦情処理の体制を整え，事件が起きた場合に迅速・適切な措置を取った場合には，使用者は責任を免れるとするものがみられるに至っていた[23]。

こうした裁判例における使用者責任の法的構成は，コモンロー上の代理法理に照らすと，おおむね次の四つに分けられる[24]。まず，①使用者が職場におけるセクシュアル・ハラスメントの事実を知っていた，あるいは知りうべきであったにもかかわらずそれに対して適切な措置を取らなかった場合には，使用者に過失（negligence）があったものとしてその責任を問われる。この責任は，加害行為者に代わって使用者が責任を負うというよりは，使用者自身の責任というべきものである。次に，被用者のセクシュアル・ハラスメントについて使用者がその過失の有無を問わず責任を負うとする構成があるが，これは，被用者の行為について使用者が代位責任（vicarious liability）を負うものとして位置づけられる。そしてこの構成は，さらに，②被用者が職務の範囲内で（within the scope of employment）行った不法行為については使用者が責任を負うという構成，③被用者が使用者から代理人（agent）としての権限を与えられているかのごとき外観（apparent authority）のもとで行った行為については使用者が責任を負うという構成，④被用者が「代理関係に助けられて（aided by agency relation）」行った行為——使用者との代理関係を利用した行為とも表現できよう——については使用者が責任を負うという構成の三つに分けることができる。

(3) 最近の合衆国最高裁判決

(a) Ellerth 事件と Faragher 事件

---

21) *Meritor,* 477 U.S. at 72.
22) *See* BARBARA LINDEMANN & DAVID D. KADUE, SEXUAL HARASSMENT IN EMPLOYMENT LAW 232 (1992).
23) *E.g.,* Gary v. Long, 59 F.3d 1391 (D.C. Cir. 1995).
24) *See* RESTATEMENT (SECOND) OF AGENCY § 219 (1957).
25) Burlington Indus., Inc. v. Ellerth, 118 S. Ct. 2257 (1998).

2 アメリカにおける使用者責任

　こうした中で，合衆国最高裁は1998年6月に，Ellerth事件[25]とFaragher事件[26]において，使用者責任に関する重要な判決を下した。両事件とも，女性被用者が男性上司から性的な言動を受け，ひいては辞職せざるを得なくなったとして，第7篇に基づき訴えを提起した事案であり，上司のセクシュアル・ハラスメントによる使用者責任が中心的な争点となった。ただし，Ellerth事件においては，上司が女性被用者に対して，性的要求を拒否すれば雇用上の不利益を与える旨の発言を行ったとの主張がなされたため，そのような行為が対価型ハラスメントと環境型のいずれに当たるか，ひいては両者の区別の意義いかんも問題となった。また，両事件のいずれにおいても，使用者はセクシュアル・ハラスメントの禁止や苦情処理の手続を定めた社内規定を有していたため，そうした使用者の対応がいかなる法的意味を持つかも問題となっている。

　両事件の中心的な争点である使用者責任の判断基準に関しては，合衆国最高裁は両判決を通じて同一の命題を提示した[27]。すなわち，①原告に対する監督権限を持つ上司が違法な環境型セクシュアル・ハラスメントを行った場合には，使用者は代位責任を負うが，②現実に不利益をもたらす雇用上の行為（tangible employment action）がなされていないのであれば，使用者はセクシュアル・ハラスメントへの対応措置に基づく積極的抗弁（affirmative defense）を提出しうる，というものである。そして，後者の抗弁は，(i)使用者がセクシュアル・ハラスメントの防止と迅速な是正のために合理的な配慮を尽くしたこと，及び，(ii)原告が合理的理由なくして使用者の用意したこれらの機会を利用せず，またはその他の被害回避のための手段をとらなかったこと，という二つの要件からなると述べられている。

　以上のうち，使用者責任の判断基準については，コモンロー上の代理法理を出発点とした考察がなされている。前述したように，同法理における使用者責任の法的構成には諸種のものがあるが，両判決においては，「職務の範

---

26) Faragher v. City of Boca Raton, 118 S. Ct. 2275 (1998). これら両判決については，中窪・前掲注17)論文が要を得た解説を行っている。また，Faragher事件については，山川隆一「監督者による環境型セクシュアル・ハラスメントと使用者の責任」労働法律旬報1457号49頁（1999）参照。

27) *Ellerth*, 118 S. Ct. at 2270 ; *Faragher*, 118 S. Ct. at 2292-93.

囲内」という構成，及び「代理関係の利用」という構成による使用者への帰責の是非が主な検討の対象となった（なお，代理人としての外観に基づく責任は，代理権限が実際に存在し，その濫用が問題となるセクシュアル・ハラスメントについては通常は妥当しないとされた）。なお，従来，対価型と環境型の区別が使用者責任の有無と結びつけられる傾向があったが，Ellerth事件判決は，両者の区別は使用者責任の判断にとって決定的なものではないと判示している[28]。

　これらの点に関する両判決の論理には若干のニュアンスがみられるが，おおむね共通する点を述べると，まず，「職務の範囲内」という構成は，被用者が部分的にせよ使用者の利益を図る目的で加害行為を行った場合を想定したものであり，もっぱら行為者本人の欲求をみたすために行われる環境型ハラスメントについては通常は妥当しないと判断された。他方，「代理関係の利用」という構成は，具体的に雇用上の決定がなされた場合に妥当するのは明らかであるが，そうした決定がなされていない場合であっても，被害者に対して人事上の権限をもつ上司のセクシュアル・ハラスメントは，被害者の抵抗を困難とするなどの点で代理関係を利用したものと評価しうると判断されている。

　かくして両判決は，「代理関係の利用」という法的構成を採用したが，使用者が監督者の環境型ハラスメントにつき自動的に責任を負うわけではないとしたMeritor事件判決，及び雇用差別の防止を重視する第7篇の法目的と代理法理との調和を図るために，使用者に対して，先に述べた，セクシュアル・ハラスメントの防止及び是正のための対応を行ったこと，及び，原告が合理的理由なくして被害を回避する措置をとらなかったことを内容とする積極的抗弁を認めた（ただし，この抗弁が認められるのは，具体的な雇用上の決定がなされていない場合に限られる）。そして，使用者がセクシュアル・ハラスメントを禁止する規定を設け，苦情処理手続とともにこれを被用者に周知させる

---

[28] *Ellerth*, 118 S. Ct. at 2265. 従来は，環境型ハラスメントについては，同僚の行為であると監督者の行為であるとを問わず，使用者自身の過失責任の問題として処理される傾向が強かったが，今回の合衆国最高裁判決は，監督者の環境型ハラスメントにつき（免責の途を残しつつ）代位責任を認めたものと位置づけられる。*See* Robert K. Robinson et al., *Vicarious Liability for Hostile Environment Sexual Harassment : Examining the Implications of the* Ellerth *and* Faragher *Decisions*, 1998 LAB. L. J. 1232, 1239.

ことは，前者の要件該当性の判断にとって重要な意味をもち，また，被害者がこうした手続を利用しなかった場合には，後者の要件がみたされたと判断される可能性が高くなると述べられている。

(b) 両判決の意義

以上のような両事件最高裁判決の意義は，第一に，上司による環境型ハラスメントについては，「代理関係の利用」という代理法理上の観念を基礎として，使用者は当該行為についての認識（の可能性）に関わりなく責任を負うという法的構成を明らかにしたことにあり，第二に，現実の雇用上の決定がなされていない限り，使用者は，セクシュアル・ハラスメントを禁止するとともに問題が生じた場合の苦情処理手続を整備することによって，その責任を免れることができる枠組みを示したことにある。特に後者については，差別の予防という政策的観点に基いて積極的抗弁を認めたことに特色がある。こうした合衆国最高裁の立場は，使用者に対してセクシュアル・ハラスメントへの対策を実施することを促すのみならず，被用者もそれにより被害を予め回避しうる環境を期待できる点で，両者にとって望ましい（win-win）枠組みであると評価する女性団体のコメントが伝えられている[29]。

他方，両判決とも，上司による部下に対するセクシュアル・ハラスメントが問題となった事案にかかわるものであるため，同僚によるハラスメントに関する使用者責任については直接には判断が示されていない。もっとも，Ellerth 事件においては，同僚によるハラスメントは一般に「代理関係の利用」という要件をみたさないという理解が示されており[30]，従来の裁判例も，同僚のハラスメントについては，当該行為を使用者が知り，または知りうべきであったのに何ら措置をとらなかった場合に使用者の責任が生じると解するものが一般である[31]。この場合の使用者責任は，自らの過失に基づく責任と位置づけられる。逆にいえば，両判決は，セクシュアル・ハラスメントに関する使用者責任の法的構成が多様なものであることをも示しているという

---

29) Linda Greenhouse, *High Court Clarifies Law on Workplace Sexual Harassment*, N. Y. TIMES, June 27, 1998 (citing the comment by Kathy Rodgers, executive director of the NOW Legal Defense Fund).

30) 118 S. Ct. at 2268.

31) *See id.*

ことができる。

(4) 日本法との比較
(a) 使用者責任の法的位置づけ

アメリカ合衆国においては，公民権法第7篇のもとでのセクシュアル・ハラスメントに関する使用者責任は，基本的にはコモンロー上の代理法理により判断される。この法理は，被用者の不法行為に対して使用者がいかなる場合に責任を負うかをめぐって発展してきたものであるので，民法715条を用いてセクシュアル・ハラスメントに関する使用者責任を判断する，わが国の手法との間に共通性を見出すことができる。もっとも，アメリカ法の代理法理が被用者の行為についての代位責任を問題としているのに対し，民法715条については，起草者は，使用者自身の被用者に対する選任監督の過失に基づく自己責任とする理解に立っていた[32]。しかし，その後の判例や学説の展開により，同条は，報償責任や危険責任に基づく代位責任に近づけて理解されるようになっているので[33]，現在においては，使用者責任一般の位置づけについても，日米間に相当の共通性があるということができる。

次に，アメリカ法においては，被用者の加害行為に基づく代位責任とは別に，使用者がセクシュアル・ハラスメントの事実を知り，または当然知りうべきであったのに適切な措置をとらなかった場合，使用者自身の過失による責任の成立が認められている。この過失責任は，わが国における，管理者の職場環境配慮義務違反に基づく不法行為責任や使用者自らの債務不履行責任と同様のものと位置づけられる。わが国では，これらの責任と加害行為者の不法行為責任に基づく使用者の責任との関係は必ずしも明確に意識されてこなかったが，アメリカ法においては，使用者自らの過失責任と代理法理に基づく代位責任は別次元の，すなわち両立可能なものとして位置づけられてい

---

[32] 梅謙次郎・民法要義（巻之三債権編）895頁（1912，復刻版，1983）。また，田上富信「使用者責任」民法講座6・事務管理・不当利得・不法行為460-471頁（1985）参照。

[33] 同論文473-480頁参照。ただし，同条1項但書により使用者の免責が認められている以上，純粋な代位責任というよりは中間的な責任としての位置づけも可能であり，最近では自己責任的要素を肯定する説も唱えられている。四宮和夫・不法行為682頁（1985）参照。

る。こうした位置づけは，日本法の解釈についても妥当するものといえよう。
　(b)　「職務の範囲内」と「代理関係の利用」
　以上の法的構成のうち，加害行為者の責任を通じた代位責任については，わが国の民法715条は「事業ノ執行ニ付キ」という要件を課しているが，アメリカの代理法理においても，「職務の範囲内」という，これと共通性のある表現が用いられている。しかし，アメリカ法においては，「職務の範囲内」の行為に該当するためには，部分的にせよ被用者が使用者の利益を図る目的でその行為を行ったことが要求されており，環境型ハラスメントはこうした要件を一般にはみたさないとされている。他方，民法715条のもとでは，判例上，被用者の主観は問題とされておらず[34]，セクシュアル・ハラスメントについても一般に同条を適用する判決が多い。そうすると，わが国における「事業ノ執行ニ付キ」という概念は，「職務の範囲内」という概念に比べて広く理解されているといいうる。

　もっとも，アメリカ法においては，「職務の範囲内」における行為に加えて，「代理関係の利用」による行為についても使用者責任が認められる。ひるがえって，わが国においてセクシュアル・ハラスメントにつき使用者責任を肯定した判決をみると，上司が加害行為を行うについてその地位を利用したことを，「事業ノ執行ニ付キ」という要件の該当性を肯定する根拠としてあげるものが増えている[35]。そうすると，わが国においては，民法715条における「事業ノ執行ニ付キ」という概念の中に，アメリカ法における「代理関係の利用」という要素が含まれているものと位置づけることができそうである。

　(c)　使用者の免責
　最後に，環境型セクシュアル・ハラスメントに関し，使用者の予防措置および事後の対応を理由とする抗弁については，合衆国最高裁は，代理法理とは別に，同法理と第7篇における差別の防止という政策の調和を図るものとして位置づけている（代理法理上は，代位責任の要件が厳格である反面，民法715条1項但書のような免責事由は認められていないようである）。他方でわが国にお

---

34)　大判大正10・6・7刑録27輯506頁など。
35)　前掲注8）とその本文参照。

いては，民法715条1項但書において，使用者が被用者の選任監督を尽くしたことに基づく免責が認められているので，こうした抗弁の根拠規定が存在するといいうる。しかし，実際上，この免責の主張はほとんど認められていないので，そのこと自体を再検討する必要が生じるとともに，「事業ノ執行ニ付キ」等の要件の解釈によりこれを実現しうるか否かを検討することも必要となる。

他方，使用者自身の過失または職場環境配慮義務違反による責任については，使用者がセクシュアル・ハラスメントに対して適切な措置をとった場合には，日米いずれにおいても，そもそも責任が成立しないこととなる。

なお，以上のような日米の法状況を対比すれば，おおむね図1のようなものとなろう。

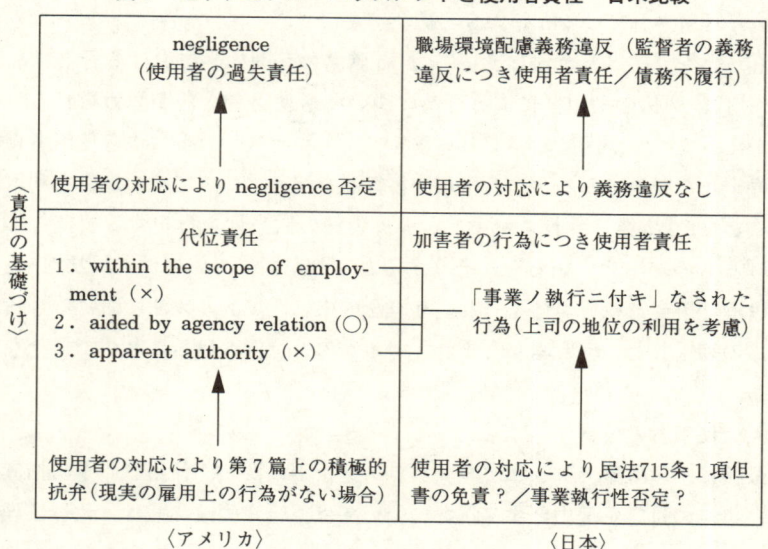

図1 セクシュアル・ハラスメントと使用者責任――日米比較

〈責任の基礎づけ〉

negligence （使用者の過失責任） ↑ 使用者の対応により negligence 否定	職場環境配慮義務違反（監督者の義務違反につき使用者責任／債務不履行） ↑ 使用者の対応により義務違反なし
代位責任 1. within the scope of employment（×） 2. aided by agency relation（○） 3. apparent authority（×） ↑ 使用者の対応により第7篇上の積極的抗弁（現実の雇用上の行為がない場合）	加害者の行為につき使用者責任 「事業ノ執行ニ付キ」なされた行為（上司の地位の利用を考慮） ↑ 使用者の対応により民法715条1項但書の免責？／事業執行性否定？
〈アメリカ〉	〈日本〉

3 日本法の検討

以上のようなアメリカ法の状況をふまえて，日本法のもとでのセクシュアル・ハラスメントに関する使用者責任について検討を加えることとする。検

討にあたっては，まず，民法715条に基づき使用者の責任を基礎づける場合に，どのような法的構成が考えられるのかについて，簡単な整理を行う。次に，加害行為者の責任を通じて使用者責任を基礎づけるにあたって，セクシュアル・ハラスメントが「事業ノ執行ニ付キ」行われたものといいうるのはいかなる場合かを検討する。そして最後に，使用者がセクシュアル・ハラスメントの予防措置や事後の対応措置を行った場合に，その責任が否定されることがあるかという問題について考察を加えることとしたい。

(1) 使用者責任の法的構成

職場におけるセクシュアル・ハラスメントについて使用者が負う損害賠償責任は，①加害行為者の不法行為責任により基礎づけられる場合（図2のA）と，②当該職場の管理者または使用者自身の職場環境配慮義務違反により基礎づけられる場合とに分けることができる。以上のうち②については，使用者自身が労働契約に基づき職場環境配慮義務を負うとの見解によれば，使用者はその義務に違反した場合に債務不履行責任を負うと解することとなるが（図2のB），そうした見解を採用しない場合でも，管理者の職場環境配慮義務（不法行為法上の注意義務）違反を基礎として，使用者は同人の不法行為責任を介して民法715条により責任を負うと解することができる（図2のC）。

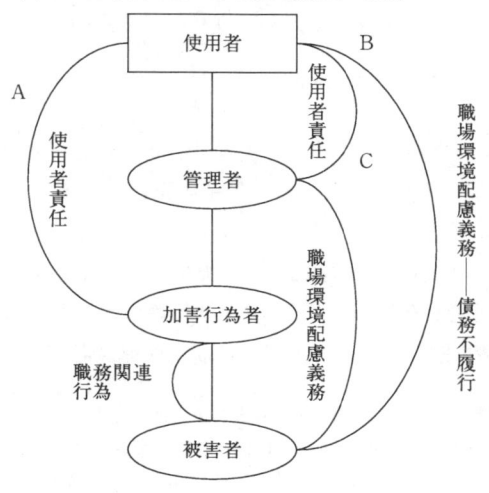

図2　日本法における使用者責任の構成

いずれにせよ，アメリカ法の検討が示すように，①と②の構成は排他的なものではなく，加害行為者の不法行為責任を通じて使用者責任を基礎づけることができない場合でも，職場環境配慮義務違反を基礎とする責任を問うことは不可能ではない（①の構成はアメリカにおける代位法理に基づく責任に，②の構成は使用者の過失責任にそれぞれ対応するものといえよう）。たとえば，問題となった加害行為が職場と関係なく行われたため，民法715条の「事業ノ執行ニ付キ」という要件をみたさない場合でも，当該加害行為により被害者の職場環境が悪化し，しかも管理者が何らそれを改善するための措置をとらなかったときには，なお使用者の責任が認められる余地がある。職場において出所不明の噂を立てられた事案のように，加害行為者を特定することができない場合や，顧客によるハラスメントのように加害行為者につき民法715条を適用することができない場合にも，同様のことがいいうる。

また，以上とは逆に，職場の管理者ないし使用者が，環境型セクシュアル・ハラスメントが発生したことを知ったのち，直ちに職場環境の悪化を防ぐための適切な措置をとった場合などは，職場環境配慮義務違反に基づく使用者の責任は追及できないことが多いであろうが[36]，かかるセクシュアル・ハラスメントが「事業ノ執行ニ付キ」なされたものであれば，なお使用者は責任を負わざるをえないことがありうる。このように，職場におけるセクシュアル・ハラスメントについての使用者責任は，二つの両立しうる法的構成により把握され，一方が他方を完全にカバーするものではないということができる。

(2) セクシュアル・ハラスメントと「事業ノ執行ニ付キ」

(a) 民法715条の解釈における「事業ノ執行ニ付キ」

環境型セクシュアル・ハラスメントについて使用者の不法行為責任を追及する場合，その法的根拠は民法715条であることが多いが，同条の適用にあたって最も問題となるのが，「事業ノ執行ニ付キ」という要件である。そこで，この要件の解釈をめぐる一般的な状況を確認しておくと，判例は，いわ

---

36) 加害行為者の不法行為法上の注意義務違反は，必ずしも使用者の職場環境配慮義務違反に直結するものではない。山口浩一郎他・座談会「セクシュアル・ハラスメントの法律問題」ジュリスト956号30頁（1990）［山口発言］参照。

ゆる「外形理論」を確立させてきた[37]。すなわち,「被用者ノ当該行為ガ外観上職務執行ト同一ナル外形ヲ有スルモノナルニ於テハ……事業ノ執行ニ付第三者ニ加ヘタル損害ナリトイフヲ妨ゲ[ズ]」[38]とし,また,「民法715条に所謂『事業ノ執行ニ付キ』とは,被用者の職務執行行為そのものには属しないが,その行為の外形から観察して,恰も被用者の職務の範囲内の行為に属するとみられる場合をも包含する」[39]との一般論を明らかにしてきたのである。

しかしながら,この「外形理論」に対しては,取引行為型の不法行為については妥当しても,外形に対する相手方の信頼が問題とならない事実的な不法行為には妥当しないとの批判や,この理論は抽象的にすぎ,判断基準としては実質的意味を有しないなどとの批判が有力に唱えられている[40]。もっとも,前者の批判に関しては,判例も外観理論を貫いてはおらず,被用者による職場での喧嘩・暴行行為が問題となった事案では,「事業の執行行為を契機とし,これと密接な関連を有すると認められる行為」であれば,行為の外形を問題とすることなく使用者の責任を認めていることが指摘できる[41]。

また,外形理論の実質的意味をめぐる後者の批判との関連では,この理論が現実に果たしている機能を探求する試みがなされ,その結果,判例はまず職務との密接な関連性を有無を問題とし,かかる関連性が認められない場合には,被用者の職務内容からみて加害行為を行うことが容易な状況にあったか否かを重視していると指摘されている[42]。外形理論を採用した判例においても,問題となった加害行為と職務との間に相当の関連性があり,被用者が

---

37) 神田孝夫・叢書民法総合判例研究・使用者責任(新版)55-85頁(1998)参照。
38) 大判昭和15・5・10判決全集7巻699頁(信用組合の従業員が権限なくして質権設定のための認証書を発行した事案)。
39) 最二小判昭和36・6・9民集15巻6号1546頁(協同組合の書記が手形を偽造した事案)。
40) 田上富信「使用者責任における『事業ノ執行ニ付キ』の意義」現代損害賠償法講座6・使用者責任26頁,58頁(1974)参照。
41) 最三小判昭和44・11・18民集23巻11号2079頁など。セクシュアル・ハラスメントに関わる事案でも,こうした定式を用いた裁判例がある。前掲注7)・横浜セクハラ事件など。
42) 神田・前掲注37)書94,99頁。加害行為の容易性を考慮したと見られる判決としては,最三小判昭和46・12・21判時658号32頁(自動車を自由に持ち出せる状況にしておいたために起きた事故につき使用者責任を肯定)などがある。

当該加害行為を行うことが客観的に容易である状況に置かれていた場合には，同理論を適用するのが妥当であると述べたものがある[43]。最近の学説は，こうした判例の実質的機能を直視して，それを「事業ノ執行ニ付キ」の解釈論に取り入れるものが多くなっており，「職務関連性」の他に「加害行為の近接性」を判断要素とする見解が有力である[44]。筆者も，こうした最近の学説の立場を支持すべきものと考える。

(b) セクシュアル・ハラスメントについての準則

以上の考察を前提として，環境型ハラスメントが民法715条にいう「事業ノ執行ニ付キ」という要件をみたすかどうかについての判断基準について検討を加えることとする。ただし，先にみたように，セクシュアル・ハラスメントにつき民法715条を適用するにあたっては，管理者の職場環境配慮義務違反を介する構成と，加害行為者の権利侵害行為を介する構成とがありうる。前者の構成においては，事案に応じて職場環境の悪化を防止ないし是正することは，管理者の職務に属することであるので，それを怠ることが「事業ノ執行ニ付キ」という要件に該当することには問題がないと思われる[45]。それゆえ，ここでの検討の中心は，後者の構成において，上司や同僚のセクシュアル・ハラスメントが「事業ノ執行ニ付キ」という要件をみたすか否かである（また，対価型ハラスメントは使用者の人事権の行使としてなされるのが通常であり，使用者責任を肯定するのに特に問題は生じないので，以下では環境型を主に念頭に置いて検討する）。

① 上司によるセクシュアル・ハラスメント

まず，上司が指揮監督下にある部下に対してセクシュアル・ハラスメントを行った場合，わが国の裁判例は，加害行為のなされた時間や場所，加害行

---

43) 最三小判昭和40・11・30民集19巻8号2049頁（権限のない被用者が代表者の机の中から印章を取り出して手形を偽造した事案）。

44) 平井宜雄・債権各論Ⅱ（不法行為）235頁（1992），國井和郎「事業の執行」新・現代損害賠償法講座第4巻・使用者責任ほか74頁（1997）など。「加害行為への近接性」の他，「使用者の支配領域内の行為」（内田貴・民法Ⅱ・債権各論455頁（1997））などの表現も用いられる。

45) こうした構成は，セクシュアル・ハラスメント以外の事案で従来から認められている（最三小判平成4・10・6判時1454号87頁（私立大学の応援団員の上級生の暴行による死亡につき，大学執行部等の監督義務違反を介して民法715条を適用した）など）。

為が発言による場合にはその内容と職務との関連性なども考慮して，加害行為と職務との関連性を判断しているが，先にみたように，上司としての地位を利用して加害行為に及んだことに言及する判決も増えている。合衆国最高裁も，代理法理の適用にあたり，代理関係を利用したことを理由として，上司の加害行為についての使用者責任を認めているところである。

　前述したとおり，民法715条における「事業ノ執行ニ付キ」判断にあたって実質的に考慮されているのは，加害行為と職務との密接な関連性のほかに，使用者が加害行為を容易にする状況を作り出したこと，すなわち加害行為への近接性という要素であった。そこで考えるに，職場の上司は，部下に対して職務遂行に関する一定の指揮監督権限を有し，また，部下の人事考課における第一次的評価権限や異動に関する意見の具申権限を有するのが通常である。こうした上司がセクシュアル・ハラスメントに及んだ場合には，部下の抵抗は，それ以外の者の行為に比べて困難になる可能性が高い。かくして，上司は，その地位を利用して部下に対するセクシュアル・ハラスメントを行うことが容易な状況に置かれているといえそうである。そうすると，上司がその地位を利用して部下に対するセクシュアル・ハラスメントに及んだ場合には，地位の利用という事実が，「事業ノ執行ニ付キ」という要件の該当性を基礎づける方向に働くと解すべきである[46]。

　もっとも，地位の利用という事実は，「事業ノ執行ニ付キ」の該当性判断における唯一の基準になるとまではいえないと思われる。前述したように，アメリカの代理法理における「職務の範囲内」という概念は，被用者が部分的にせよ使用者の利益を図った場合をいうと解されているため，使用者の代位責任を基礎づけるにあたっては，「代理関係の利用」が決定的な基準となるが，民法715条の「事業ノ執行ニ付キ」の該当性判断においては，被用者の意図は無関係であると理解されており，同僚によるセクシュアル・ハラスメントについて後述するように，「地位の利用」類型に当たらなくとも，「事業ノ執行ニ付キ」という要件をみたす場合がないとはいえないからである。また，わが国の人事管理においては，人事権が中央集権的に行使されること

---

[46]　神田・前掲注37)書139頁，石井妙子「セクシュアル・ハラスメントと企業の法的責任・防止義務」労判752号7頁（1999）など。水谷・前掲注4)論文16頁も同旨か。

が多いため，職場における上司の権限には曖昧な部分があり，「地位の利用」を唯一の決定的な基準とすることには無理があると思われる。そうすると，「地位の利用」という事実は，「事業ノ執行ニ付キ」の該当性判断における一つの重要な要素として位置づけるべきものであるが，後述する加害行為の時間や場所など他の要素を考慮する必要はなお残るといいうる。

なお，こうした立場によると，実務上，いかなる場合に上司がその地位を利用してセクシュアル・ハラスメントに及んだといえるかが問題となる。この点は各事件の事実関係に依存するものであり，常にこうした認定がなされうるわけではないが，性的要求を拒んだ場合の報復措置やこれを受け入れた場合の利益誘導に上司が言及することや，暗黙のうちにそうした措置をほのめかすことなどは，地位の利用の認定を容易にすると思われる。

② 同僚によるセクシュアル・ハラスメント

従業員が指揮監督関係のない同僚に対してセクシュアル・ハラスメントを行った場合には，「地位の利用」という要素を認めることは困難となる。また，被害者と同一の職場で働いていること自体から，加害行為への近接性を一般に認めることも困難であろう（そう解すると，従業員間のあらゆる不法行為が使用者責任を基礎づけるおそれがある）。そこで，同僚によるセクシュアル・ハラスメントに関しては，職務との密接な関連性が重要な判断要素とならざるをえない。アメリカ法においては，「職務の範囲内」が狭く理解されているため，「代理関係の利用」類型に当たらない同僚間のハラスメントについては，使用者自身の過失責任を問うほかはないのが通常であるが，わが国においては，「事業ノ執行ニ付キ」という要件は比較的広く解されているので，同僚間のハラスメントについてもなお使用者責任を認める余地がある。

こうした同僚間のハラスメントは，先にみた職場における喧嘩・暴行などとおおむねパラレルに考えることができる。そこで，それらの事例と同様に，セクシュアル・ハラスメントが事業の執行を契機として行われ，これと密接な関連を有する場合には，「事業ノ執行ニ付キ」という要件をみたすものと解しうると思われる。この点の判断も事案の内容に依存するものであるが，まず，加害行為のなされた時間や場所が考慮要素となることはいうまでもないであろう。しかし，職場内でかつ勤務時間中であっても，全くの私憤から突然に喧嘩がなされたような場合には，「事業ノ執行ニ付キ」なされた行為

とはいえないと思われるから，セクシュアル・ハラスメントについても，職務の遂行が加害行為の契機となったことや，加害者が職場の人間関係や取引関係に関連して加害行為に及んだことなど，それ以外に職務との関連性を基礎づける要素も原則として必要となると考えられる（他方で，時間的・場所的に職場との関連性が薄い行為でも，「事業ノ執行ニ付キ」なされた他の加害行為の延長として行われた場合には，なお使用者責任の対象となりえよう[47]）。

なお，このような理解により，同僚間のハラスメントが「事業ノ執行ニ付キ」なされた行為に該当しないとされる場合でも，それにより職場環境が悪化したときには，管理者の職場環境配慮義務違反を通じた使用者責任を追及する余地が残ることには留意する必要がある（アメリカ法においては，同僚によるハラスメントについてはこうした構成が一般に用いられており，わが国でも，顧客や取引先によるハラスメントについてはこれを用いる他はない）。

(c) 使用者の措置による免責の可否
① 民法715条1項但書

最後に，使用者がセクシュアル・ハラスメントに対して事前の防止措置ないし事後の是正措置等を行った場合に免責されるか否かという問題を検討する。ただし，ここでも，管理者の職場環境配慮義務違反を通じた使用者責任と加害行為者の不法行為を通じての使用者責任とでは，問題の次元が異なることに留意すべきである。すなわち，まず前者の構成によれば，管理者がセクシュアル・ハラスメントに対して迅速かつ適切な措置を行ったために職場環境配慮義務違反が成立しない場合には，同人の不法行為責任が認められない点で，使用者責任を追及することができなくなる（使用者自らが職場環境配慮義務を負うと解する立場でも，同様に債務不履行責任を追及できなくなる）。アメリカ法において使用者に過失が認められない場合と同様の状況である。

これに対して，加害行為を通じた使用者責任を追及する場合には，民法715条1項但書が，使用者が被用者の選任及び事業の監督について相当の注意をなした場合の免責を認めているので，セクシュアル・ハラスメントにつ

---

47) 山川・前掲注4)論文73頁。東京セクハラ（広告代理店）事件・東京地判平成8・12・25労判707号25頁では，上司が入院中の原告を見舞った際の行為につき，上司の勤務時間中であることや会社の業務に関する会話がなされていたことを理由に事業の執行性を認めるが，本文のような観点からも検討すべきであったと思われる。

いて使用者が予防措置をとったことにより免責を認めうるかが問題となる（職場環境配慮義務違反については，職場環境の悪化に対する管理者の事後の対応が主として問題になろうが，ここではむしろ，——問題が起きた場合の苦情処理手続の整備を含めて——被用者の監督にあたっての事前の予防措置のあり方に重点が置かれると思われる）。もっとも，民法715条1項但書は現在殆ど空文化しており，古い判決[48]を除けば，これを適用して免責を認めたものはみられないのが実状である。これは，起草者によれば被用者の選任・監督についての使用者の過失責任に基礎を置くと理解されていた民法715条が，その後の学説や判例において，報償責任や危険責任の原理に基礎を置く代位責任的な位置づけを与えられてきたことを反映するものといいうる[49]。

しかしながら，代位責任と自己責任とは必ずしも二者択一的なものではなく，使用者責任にどのような性格を与えるかは，立法政策により異なる結論がとられうる。そして，民法715条1項但書が置かれている以上，わが国の使用者責任は，被用者の選任監督に注意を尽くしたことを証明することによって使用者に免責を受ける機会が与えられた中間的な代位責任の制度がとられているということもできる[50]。実際，近年の民法理論においては，免責事由を柔軟に活用しようとする方向が提唱されているところである[51]。

また，セクシュアル・ハラスメントについては，加害行為がなされた後に裁判を通じて損害賠償による救済を図るよりも，使用者が企業内における禁止措置を整備することを通じて，被害の発生を未然に予防する方が適切だと考えられるので，それを促進する観点からも，上記のような方向で解釈論を構築することが望ましいと思われる[52]。アメリカ法においては，代理関係を

---

48) 大判昭和15・5・8法律新聞580号7頁など。
49) 神田・前掲注37)書210頁。
50) 前掲注33)参照。
51) 神田・前掲注37)書211頁など。
52) 木下潮音「セクシュアル・ハラスメントに対する使用者の責任」自由と正義1998年6月号115頁など。使用者に絶対的な責任を課すと，現実に生じた事案が隠蔽されるおそれがあるとの指摘もある。Robinson et al., *supra* note 28, at 1236. なお，ここで問題となる使用者の措置は，主にセクシュアル・ハラスメントの事前の防止策であり，職場環境の悪化への対処とは次元が異なるので，加害行為者の責任を通じた使用者責任と職場環境配慮義務違反に基づく使用者責任との区別はなお存在しうる。

利用したハラスメントについて，代理法理上は特段の免責事由がないにも関わらず，政策論的解釈により免責事由が創設されたが，わが国の民法には免責事由を定めた規定がある以上，それを利用するのはより自然であるといえよう。

② 「事業ノ執行ニ付キ」の解釈

もっとも，民法715条1項但書の免責事由を実質上空文化させている判例の立場は直ちには変更されないと予想されるので，実務的な観点からは，より受け入れられやすい解釈論についても検討する必要がある。そして，前述したように，「事業ノ執行ニ付キ」の判断にあたり「加害行為への近接性」を要素に含める立場においては，使用者が被用者に対して加害行為を困難にする監督上の措置をとっていたかどうかが，「事業ノ執行ニ付キ」という要件該当性の判断に影響を与えうると思われる。実際，判例においては，使用者がそうした措置をとらなかったことが，責任を基礎づける判断要素とされることがある[53]。会社代表者による印章の管理が不十分であったため，権限のない被用者が手形を偽造した事案[54]や，オートバイの鍵の管理が不十分であったために，運転業務と関係のない被用者がこれを私用のために運転して事故を起こした事案[55]などがその例である。また，他方では，使用者が当該行為を防止する措置を講じていたことを考慮して責任を否定したものもみられる。例えば，使用者が出張のために自家用車を用いることを禁止していたにも関わらず，被用者が自家用車で出張して事故を起こした事案において，最高裁は「事業ノ執行ニ付キ」という要件の該当性を否定している[56]。

そうすると，免責事由に関する判例の現状を前提としても，セクシュアル・ハラスメントについては，使用者がこれを明確に禁止するとともに，事件が発生した場合の対応を明示した措置を設け，そのことを被用者に周知させた場合には，「事業ノ執行ニ付キ」という要件への該当性が否定されうると解するのが妥当ではないかと思われる[57]。このような制度が設けられた場合

---

53) 神田・前掲注37)書211頁，田上・前掲注40)論文49頁など参照。ここでは，民法715条1項但書による免責の問題とすべき事柄が，「事業ノ執行ニ付キ」という要件該当性の問題として扱われているといいうる。
54) 最三小判昭和40・11・30民集19巻8号2049頁。
55) 最一小判昭和46・9・16判時645号74頁。

には，使用者は加害行為防止のために相当な措置をとったものといえるので，加害行為への近接性という要素を否定することができるからである（このような場合でも，同一の職場にある以上は，セクシュアル・ハラスメントを行う機会が存在することに変わりはないが，先にみたように，被害者と加害者が同一の職場で就労していることのみでは，加害行為への近接性を基礎づけることは困難であるので，以上の解釈には影響を与えないと思われる）。

　もちろん，加害行為への近接性という要素は，「事業ノ執行ニ付キ」の唯一の判断基準ではないので，事案の内容によっては，上記のような措置がとられている場合であっても，なお使用者責任が認められることがありうる。特に，対価型のセクシュアル・ハラスメントは，人事権の行使という形を取ることが多く，加害行為それ自体が職務の遂行としての性格をもち，あるいは職務と強度の関連性をもつといいうるから，使用者責任を否定することは一般に困難だと思われる。

　最後に，このような見解に立つ場合，具体的にいかなる措置をとれば「事業ノ執行ニ付キ」への該当性が否定されるかが問題となる。この点に関しては，改正雇用機会均等法21条に基づき，セクシュアル・ハラスメント防止のための使用者の配慮措置に関する指針が発表されており，そこでは，配慮措置の内容として，(i)セクシュアル・ハラスメントに関する方針の明確化・周知，(ii)相談及び苦情への対応体制の整備，(iii)被害が生じた後の迅速かつ適切な対応があげられている[58]。雇用機会均等法21条は私法上の権利義務関係に直ちに影響を与えるものとはいえないが，上にあげた指針の内容は，従来の

---

56)　最一小判昭和52・9・22民集31巻5号767頁。ただし，自動車の運転助手に対して内部的に単独での運転を禁止しつつ，一定の例外も黙認していた事案で，同人の単独運転による事故につき使用者責任を認めた例がある（最一小判昭和34・4・23民集13巻4号532頁）。また，上司がいわゆる飲み会を催した際に部下に対して行ったセクシュアル・ハラスメントについても，会社がそのような会合をしないように口頭で通知していただけでは業務執行性は否定されないとされた例がある（大阪セクハラ（S運送会社）事件・大阪地判平成10・12・21労判756号26頁）。このように，単に一定の行為を禁じたのみでは加害行為への近接性は失われるとはいえないが，より実効性のある当該行為の防止措置をとれば，責任を否定する余地はあるといえよう。

57)　山川・前掲注4)論文73頁参照。

58)　平成10・3・13労働省告示20号。

合衆国の裁判例があげてきた使用者の免責事由とほぼ一致するものである。

先にみたように，使用者がセクシュアル・ハラスメントを明確に禁止し，被害が生じた場合の是正手続を設けて，これを被用者に周知させれば，「事業ノ執行ニ付キ」の基礎をなす加害行為との近接性が切断されると解することができる。また，そうした措置がとられていても，加害行為が現実に行われた場合，それを放置しておくと，職場環境配慮義務違反を通じた使用者責任が発生するおそれがあるが，管理者が迅速に適切な措置をとれば，私法上の配慮義務を尽くしたものと評価されうると思われる。これらの措置の具体的な内容と使用者責任の成否との関係は各事案により変わりうるものであるが，上記の指針があげる使用者の配慮義務の内容は，これらの措置とおおむね重なるものであるので，指針に従って適切な措置がとられた場合には，実際上，使用者の責任は否定されることが多くなるものと予想される[59]。

おわりに

本稿は，セクシュアル・ハラスメントに関する使用者の責任につき，民法715条の解釈を中心に，日米比較をふまえた検討を行ったものである。そして，検討の結果，民法715条の使用者責任においては，①加害行為者の個人責任を通じた構成と，②管理者の職場環境配慮義務違反を通じた構成とが併存しうること，同条における「事業ノ執行ニ付キ」の解釈にあたっては，上司がその地位を利用したか否かが重要な要素となること，及び，使用者がセクシュアル・ハラスメントの防止措置と事後の対応措置をとれば，上記①および②の使用者責任が否定されうることなどを示した。いかなる場合に上司としての地位を利用したといいうるかなど，なお課題も多く残されているので，今後さらに検討を行う必要があると考えている。

---

59) 結論同旨，菅野・前掲注3)書168頁，奥山・前掲注3)書149頁。指針と私法上の配慮義務・注意義務の差異を指摘するものとしては，浅倉むつ子・均等法の新世界108頁 (1999) などがある。

＊ 校正段階において，日本労働法学会誌94号（1999）所収の，林弘子教授・水谷英夫弁護士の各論稿，ならびに山田省三教授・高木紘一教授のコメントおよび総括に接した。

日本との比較で見る東・東南アジアの女子労働の現状と法制度

香 川 孝 三

はじめに

　日本の男女雇用機会均等法案を作成する段階で，アメリカ，イギリス，ドイツ，フランス，スウェーデン等の先進国の男女雇用平等に関する法律が参照されている。これらの国々は経済的に発展しているという点で，日本と共通性がある。しかしこれには次の問題を含んでいる。経済的な発展が雇用平等をもたらすという考えを前提とすれば，欧米を日本の未来像のように考えることができるが，はたしてそうなのか。OECD加盟国23ヵ国の中で「女性の働きやすさ」の指標が日本は19位で低いことが発表されている[1]。経済発展は雇用の在り方に重要な影響を与えているが，それだけでは十分ではないことを示している。別の言い方をすれば，雇用平等を考える場合には経済的側面だけではなく，社会的文化的背景や社会規範もかかわっていることを無視できない。社会的文化的背景や社会規範を考慮するとすれば，日本はアジアに位置していることから，アジアとのかかわりの中で雇用平等問題を見る必要性がある。

　これまで労働法研究者でアジア諸国の労働法を研究する者が少ないこと，アジア諸国の女性労働に関する資料が少なく，しかも入手しがたいこと，統計資料も信頼性に欠けていることもあって，このような視点から日本の女子労働法制や男女雇用平等法制が考察されることはあまりなかったように思われる。そこで，本稿では，資料面での制約があるが，アジアの内，東アジアと東南アジアを中心に限定し（もと社会主義国は除く），日本の女子労働法制

---

[1]　朝日新聞1998年5月31日朝刊。

との比較を念頭におきつつ，東・東南アジアの諸国の女子労働の現状とその法制を分析したいと思っている。

1　東・東南アジア諸国の女子労働に関する実態

(1)　女性の労働力率の増加

韓国では女性の労働力率は1965年30.9%から1992年44.4%に増加している。台湾でも1978年39.13%から1996年45.76%に増加している。マレーシアの女性の労働力率は1970年36%から1995年48%であり，特に製造業就業者の内女性が占める割合は1970年29%から1995年43%に増加している。シンガポールでは1982年45.2%，1986年45.6%，1996年51.5%となっている。タイの都市部では1971年39%から1989年58.1%に増加し，東南アジアではもっとも高い数字になっている。農村部では1971年71.1%から1989年73%で増減はあまりない。インドネシアでは労働統計には統計毎に定義を変更するという問題点があるが，都市では1971年23.2%から1995年36.3%，農村では1971年35.3%から1995年43.7%に増加している[2]。どの国も女子の労働力率を増加させ，現在は50%前後になっている。日本では1969年に50.1%であり，経済発展が早かったために他のアジア諸国より早く50%を越えているが，その後はあまり増えていない。1993年には50.3%であり，他のアジア諸国が急速に日本に近付いている。タイは日本を上回る率になっている。

ここでいう労働力率には被雇用者だけでなく農業や自営業者，家族従事者も含まれる。雇用平等は主として被雇用者で問題となるので，雇用率を取り上げるべきであろうが，国際比較をする時労働力率しか利用できなかった。日本，シンガポール，香港では農業に従事する者の割合が低いし，韓国，台湾では低下しつつあるが，それ以外の国ではまだ高いこと，さらに被雇用者

---

[2]　韓国，マレーシア，フィリピン，タイの女子労働力率の数字はSusan Horton ed., Women and Industrialization in Asia, Routledge, 1996, pp. 169, 210, 248, 276。インドネシアについては山本郁郎「インドネシアにおける規制緩和政策と労働市場の変化」社会政策学会年報42集31頁，台湾については呉慎宜「台湾の男女工作平等」1998年第四回ソーシアル・アジア・フォーラム提出論文，シンガポールについてはYearbook of Statistics Singapore 1996, p. 40.

や自営業者・家族従事者の中にはインフォーマル・セクターに従事する者を含んでいることを考慮しておかなければならない。

　アジア諸国の多くは植民地であったが，植民地時代には農業・鉱業を中心とし，それもプランテーションを中心としてモノカルチャーな一次産品を生産し，それで旧宗主国の工業製品を購入するという経済政策が採用されていた。旧宗主国が自国の必要とする食料や原料を供給させるために，農業に従事する者が当然多かった。そこでは女性は無給の家族従事者として分類された。

　独立後，アジア諸国は農業より生産性が高いことを期待できる工業化政策による経済発展政策が採用され，それが女性の労働力率に大きな影響を与えている。1960年代の輸入代替型から1970年代以降輸出志向型の工業化に重点が置かれるようになって，外国資本と先進国の技術が導入され，人件費の安い労働力を使う労働集約型の製造業（繊維，アパレル産業や電機・電子産業等）に農村出身の若年女性が雇用されるようになった[3]。産業別就業者数を見ると，日本，シンガポール，香港を除いて，まだ農業に従事する割合が高いが，製造業とサービス業，小売業が伸びているのが分かる[4]。サービス業と小売業に従事する女性が増えているが，これは都市の雑業に従事する女性が増えていることを示している。つまりインフォーマル・セクターに従事する者が増えている。その者は独立自営業者として分類される。一方教育が普及するにつれて高学歴の女性がフォーマル・セクターに入って男性と対等に仕事をするようになった。その結果女性労働の2極分化がはっきり見られるようになったと言える。インフォーマル・セクターに従事する女性は家族総出で働かざるをえず，生計維持のために働く必要性が高いし，高学歴の女性は生活のためだけでなく自己実現のために働き，労働力率を高めている。最近になって経済発展によって中産階層が生まれており，これが女性の労働力率にどのような影響を与えるか注目される。専業主婦を増やすのかキャリアウーマンを増やすのか。これは労働力率のカーブに変化をもたらす可能性があるからである。この点についてはまだ明確な答は出ていない。

---

[3] 藤井光男編著『東アジアの国際分業と女性労働』ミネルヴァ書房，1997年2月参照。
[4] Susan Horton ed., op. cit., p. 18.

(2) 女性の年齢別の労働力率

男性の年齢別労働力率はすべての国で台形型である。若い年齢で急速に上昇し，25～30歳でおよそ97％に達し，50歳までは安定しており，引退年齢になると急速に低下するからである。

女性の年齢別の労働力参加率を見ると，M型，台形型（逆U型・高原型），初期年齢ピーク型（逆V型）の三つの類型がある[5]。M型は日本，韓国，台形型はタイ，台湾，インドネシア，フィリピン，マレーシアである。シンガポールと香港が初期年齢ピーク（逆V型）であるが，しだいに台形型に近付きつつある。そこで，おおまかに言って父系社会の日本，韓国はM型，双系社会[6]の東南アジアは台形型であると言えるのではないかと考えている（図1～図4を参照）。

(a) M型の国

日本と韓国の女性の年齢別労働力率はM型になっているのはなぜか。M型は結婚，子育ての時期に労働市場から引退し，それが終わってから再び労働市場に参入することを意味する。これは妻・母親としての役割が強調されており，男は外で稼ぎ，女は内で家事や育児を担当するという役割分業から子育ての時期には労働市場から引退する。しかし，育児が終われば働く女性が増えるが，家事との両立を図ることが求められ，多くがパートタイマーとし

---

[5] 年齢別女性労働力率を類型化したものとしてJ. D. Dulland, The Labour Force in Economic Development : A Comparison of International Census Data 1940-1966, Princeton University Press, 1975。アジア諸国を対象に比較したものとしてLin Lean Lim, "The Feminization of Labour in the Asia-Pacific Rim Countries : From Contributing to Economic Dynamism to Bearing the Brunt of Structural Adjustments", in Naohiro Ogawa, Gavin W, Jones and Jeffrey G. Williamson ed., Human Resources in Development along the Asia-Pacific Rim, Oxford University Press, 1993, pp. 175-209 および Susan Horton ed., op. cit., pp. 7-16 参照。

[6] 東南アジアの伝統的な親族組織の特徴は父系でも母系でもない「双系制」にあるとされている。双系制は父系と母系の双方を同時に重視し，父系と母系の双方の祖先を中心とした子孫につながる親族の関係を意味している。双系制のもとでは男女の均等相続が原則であり，夫婦の財産は個々に所有され共同財産にはならないこと等で女性の地位が父系制に比べて高くなる。北原淳編・東南アジアの社会学，世界思想社，1989年，15頁以下。

て働いている。正規の従業員として働けば男性と同様に厳しい労働に従事しなければならず，そうなると家事労働を果たせないからである。日本でM型が見られるのは1920～30年代ごろからである。1900年代には台形型であり，工業化が進んでいない段階の場合には農業部門の家族従事者や自営業者やその家族従事者として就労する機会が多く，子育て期であっても就労を継続しやすいためである。工業化がM字型の就労を生み出している。1980年代以降から，底の落ち込みの年齢が晩婚化によって25～29歳層から30歳台前半に移動し，さらに底が上方に上がっているが，これは育児期にもやめないで継続勤務する女性が増えていることを示している。

韓国では，李氏朝鮮において父系始祖を根元とする父子血統が重視され，女性は宗親会の系譜から排除され，血統継承の手段的存在とされていた[7]。父子血統に基づく祭祀相続や長子の財産相続制度が取られ，男尊女卑と役割分担の意識が強固で，儒教の伝統が日本や台湾より強い。日本と韓国は父性社会とされているが，韓国が父性社会としての特徴を強く維持している。韓国では工業化実現のために若年女子の労働力を活用しているが，結婚とともに退職するケースが多く，雇用率だけを見ると初期労働ピーク型である[8]。家事育児のために引退し，育児期が終わっても雇用者として再登場する女性が多くない。韓国では家族従事者・自営業者が多いために，それらを含めた労働力率ではM型であるが，被雇用者だけを見ると初期労働ピーク型になっているということである。韓国では両班層の労働を嫌う意識があって，女性の戸外労働は階層の低さを示すものとされ，高学歴の女性の労働力率があがらない傾向にあり[9]，この点は同じ父性社会とされている日本と異なっている。

(b) 台形型の国

台形型になる理由はなにか。一つの理由として，統計には農業従事者や家族従事者，インフォーマル・セクターに従事する者も含んでいるので，子育て期かどうかに関係なく生活維持のために働き続けるケースが多いことが考

---

7) 李効理（梁澄子訳）「韓国の家父長制と女性」林玲子・柳田節子監修『アジア女性史』明石書房，1997年6月，343頁。
8) 田中かず子「M字型カーブ」日本労働研究雑誌408号5頁。
9) 瀬地山角『東アジアの家父長制』勁草書房，1996年11月，226頁。

えられる。次に雇用されている者でも子育ての時期にやめないで勤められる状況にあることが考えられる。公的な託児所は限られているが，家族・親戚の中で面倒を見てくれる人がいるので働き続けられる。さらに家事労働の負担が重くない場合がありうる。特に東南アジアの都市に住む中国系の人々は屋台で外食をする場合が多く，三食とも外食で家庭には包丁のないところさえある。さらに働き方にもよるのではないか。長時間で不規則な労働であれば働きにくいが，残業や休日労働が少なく，規則的に働くことができればやめなくてもよい場合がありうる。

　台湾では中国南部の社会規範の影響があり，女性が外で働くことを嫌う傾向が小さい[10]。小さな子供がいてもやめないで働く傾向が強い。保育所より親族や祖父母が子の面倒をみる。それは子供は一族の宝という伝統意識があるからとされている。たとえ子育て期にやめても転職が容易なため別の会社に再就職しやすい。日本の大企業では年功序列や長期雇用の慣行のためにキャリアの空白があることが女性を不利にしているが，台湾ではその傾向が少ない。このことが高学歴女性の労働力率を非常に高くしている。

　フィリピンでは重層的な女性の労働市場になっており[11]，官庁・大学・一流企業で働く高学歴の専門職や管理職につくエリート・キャリアウーマン（1割にも満たない層）と貧しい農村から排出される工場労働者やインフォーマル・セクターで働く女性とが存在する。前者の場合，富裕層（寡頭的支配層オリガーキーや大地主制アシエンダ）や一部中間層出身の女性の社会進出が活発であり，それを支えたのが均等相続制によって男女平等を保障する伝統的な双系制を特色とする社会構造が，今も生きていることにある。エリート層は男女の差別はない。家事使用人を雇えるので家事労働から解放され，結婚・出産で退職しなくてすむ。これは貧しい女性の犠牲の上でエリート層の雇用平等が実現していると言えよう。低所得層の女性は多国籍企業，地場産業，インフォーマル・セクター，海外等あらゆる場で，生活維持のために家族総出で働かざるをえない状況にある。経済発展につれて高等教育を受けて

---

10) 瀬地山角・前掲書，260頁，陳珍珍「台湾における女性の就業パターン」日本労務学会年報26回全国大会，1996年12月，44-48頁。

11) 永野善子「重層的な女性労働市場」アジア経済研究所編『第三世界の働く女性』明石書房，1996年3月，73頁。

専門職として勤務する中産階層が生まれているが，家事分担者がおれば雇用を継続できる状況にある。

　タイの諺に「男は象の前足，女は後ろ足」というのがある[12]。上座部仏教であるために男性だけが出家でき，それで父母に対して功徳をもたらすが，一方娘に対しては孝行を別の形，つまり家の仕事，労働者あるいは売春婦をしても収入を得ることが期待されている。タイ女性が忍耐強く働く背景には，父母への孝行をしたいという意識がある。女性は男性より物質的な人間であり，そのために女性は生産活動に従事すべきであるという考えがある。このように上座部仏教が男性優位のイデオロギーを提供している。しかし，ここでも女子労働の多重構造があり，上層部門の女性は20世紀初頭から職を持ち，高等教育機関を経て就業している。家事使用人がいて家事労働を一人で背負い込んでいない。そのことによって子育て期にも継続して働くことが可能になる。これに対して貧困から教育を十分受けていない女性は生活維持のためにどこででも働き続けなければならない。さらにタイでも経済発展によって中産階層が生まれ，専門職や公務員，ホワイトカラーとして働き続ける女性が出てきている。

　マレーシアでは，人種を問わず「男は仕事，女は家庭」という性別役割分業の意識が濃く，良妻賢母主義の伝統的価値感が支配している。しかし家庭における既婚女性の地位は比較的高い。マレー社会ではヌグリスンビランやマラッカの一部にある母系制を除いて双系制であり，双系制の相続によって既婚女性の土地所有が多く見られる。イスラム法では女性は男性の2分の1，慣習法では均等に財産が分けられるからである[13]。イスラムの教えで未婚女性は隔離すべしという慣習（パルダ）がある。家事や育児の大半は十代の少女が担当していた。女の子供は目上の人や両親に従順で，礼儀ただしく恥の意識を持ち，伝統的価値を尊重するよう育てられる。長女は母の代わりに家事をし，兄弟のめんどうを見るよう義務づけられている。それが工業化政策によって農村（カンポン）から都会に出ていく。未婚女性のこの移動は，結婚する

12）　宮本マラシー「諺にみるタイの女性と現状」大阪外国語大学女性研究者ネットワーク編『地球のおんなたち』嵯峨野書院，1996年5月，46頁。

13）　遠野はるひ「マレーシア」森健・水野順子『開発政策と女性労働』アジア経済研究所，1985年3月，132頁。

までは両親の保護と監視のもとにあるべきであるとする伝統的価値感と対立する。素直で従順で，手先が器用だということで若年の女子（ブミプトラ政策のためにマレー系が多い）が電機・電子産業に雇用されるが，結婚と同時に退職する場合が多い[14]。インド系の女性の多くは，プランテーションで働いているが家計補助のために継続して働いている。インド系の女性はヒンズー教の教えから女性は男性の従属物であるという意識を持っており，低階層の女性ほど雇用平等からは縁遠い。これに対して経済力を持つ中国系は血のつながりを重視し家族の相互扶助の考えが強いために子供の面倒を両親・親戚に頼めるし，外食が多いので家事労働のウエイトが小さいので継続して働ける。

インドネシアは多様な社会構造を持っており，バリ島やスマトラのバッタ族は父性社会，スマトラのミナンカバブは母系社会であるが，それ以外の多くの民族は双系社会を形成している[15]。人口の約9割を占めるイスラム教徒にとっては，成人男女に結婚を義務づけ，健全なる家庭を営み，次の世代の良きムスリムを養育すべきであると言うイスラム教の教えが生きている。夫は生計を維持し，妻は家庭を維持し，子供を立派なムスリムとして育てるという役割分業の考えが強い。しかし，妻はその責任を果たした上で社会で働くのは構わないとされている。この点がアラブのイスラム教徒とは異なる。というのはアラブの女性と比較して，同じイスラムであるが女性の社会的地位は高い。生産活動に従事するだけでなく，家庭においても夫と対等の発言権を持っている。「ゴノ・ギニ（gana-gini）」と呼ばれる慣習（結婚後夫婦が獲得した財産は共有財産になり，等分の持分権を有する）がある。これはジャワだけでなく，インドネシアの各地で見られる。夫だけの収入によって生活できる中および上の階層では，高学歴の妻は家事・育児は家事使用人にまかせ，企業，学校や官庁で活躍している。下の階層の女性は生活維持のために結婚，出産があっても雇用を継続せざるをえない。同じ企業にそのまま続けるというより転職を繰り返しながらも働き続けざるをえない。これが台形型の労働力率を形づくっている。

(c) 初期年齢ピーク型の国

---

14) 吉村真子「1990年代のマレーシアの労働力構造」大原社会問題研究所雑誌464号5頁。
15) 黒柳春夫「インドネシアの家族・親族」北原淳編・前掲書，143頁。

この型はシンガポールと香港で見られる。シンガポールと香港は経済的には先進国並みに発展し，農業部門がきわめて小さいので，労働力のほとんどは被雇用者や自営業者やその家族従事者である。シンガポールは中国系が4分の3を占め，マレー系1割5分，インド系1割という構成であるが，マレーシアのように特定の人種優先政策を取っていないが，三つの人種のバランスを維持しようとしている。人口から言って中国系社会が中心であり中国南部からの移住者が多く住んでおり，香港とともに中国南部の社会構造をベースとしているので，女性が外で就労することへの抵抗は少ない。しかし25～29歳の女性の労働力率がピークで30歳以降下がるのは結婚・出産のためである。しかし，その下がり方はしだいになだらかになっており，45～49歳の女性のそれは53．9％にもなっており，台形型に近付きつつある。香港も同様でシンガポール以上に各年齢別の労働力率が上がっており，台形型に近づいていると言えよう[16]。シンガポール，香港とも中流以上の家庭で，専門職や管理職の女性はフィリッピン等からの家政婦を雇用するケースが多いとされていること[17]，フレックス・タイム制の導入が浸透しはじめ家庭責任や育児におわれる女性も勤務時間を選択できるようになっていること[18]，パートとして働く女性が増えていること，保育所の増設や保育に対する補助金の支給[19]が，労働力率の上昇に寄与している。

先進国ではM字型から台形型（逆U型）に移行しているか，移行しつつある。イギリスでは資本主義初期の時代には児童も女性も労働力として参加させられてきたが，工場法によって女性の労働を制限し，男性の稼ぎによって家族が生活できるシステムが出来て，女性が家事労働に専念し始めた。その結果男と女の役割分業が生じたために19世紀後半頃にM型になり，最近になるまでM型であり，しだいに底が浅くなるM型に変化しつつある。アメリカの労働力率は1940年代まで初期年齢ピーク型であったが，1940年代から1970

---

[16] Naohiro Ogawa, Gavin W. Jones, Jeffrey G. Williamson ed., op. cit., p. 197.
[17] 働く女性のための税金優遇制度によって，メイドを雇用しなければならない女性には「外国人メイド課税」の2倍の額の控除を認めている。
[18] シンガポール188号84頁（日本シンガポール協会発行）。
[19] 半日保育の場合子供一人当たり月75ドル，全日子供一人当たり月150ドルが支給されている。IMFJC，252号，9頁。

年頃までM型を形成した。1960年代からM型の底が浅くなり，1980年には台形型に移行している。スウェーデンでは1980年にはM型から台形型に移行している。日本も1920～30年代にすでにM型になり[20]，高度経済成長期以降M字型の底があがることによって台形型に移行することを目指している[21]。これに対して台形型を描く国が東南アジアに存在することは何を意味するのであろうか。東南アジアでは農業部門，インフォーマル・セクターに従事する者は多いために自営業者や家族従事者として働く者の割合が高いために，女性の労働力率が雇用率を示すことにはならない。そこで経済発展がさらに進めば，フォーマル・セクターに従事する者が増加し，雇用率も上昇し台形型を維持するのであろうか。それとも経済発展によって専業主婦が増えてM型に転化するのであろうか。日本がこれから台形型を目指すのであれば，東南アジアはすでに先取りしていると見ることも可能であろうが，労働力率の中身が違うので，それは無理であろう。

(3) 男女間の賃金格差・管理職に占める女性の割合

国連開発計画の1995年版報告書『ジェンダーと人間開発』（発行：国際協力出版会）42頁にある「非農業における男性賃金に対する女性賃金の割合」の表の中で，男性賃金を100とした時の女性賃金の数字がのっている。アジアだけを拾い上げると，高い順からベトナム91.5，スリランカ89.8，シンガポール71.1，香港69.5，タイ68.2，フィリピン60.8，中国59.4，韓国53.5，バングラデシュ42となっている[22]。台湾はこの統計に含まれていないが，別の統計では71.6になっている[23]。さらに日本も入っていないが，この統計年

---

[20] 千本暁子「20世紀初頭における女性の有業率とM字型就労」阪南論集・社会科学編32巻2号。1996年9月，1-15頁。

[21] 日本の都道府県によっては台形型に近い型を取っているところがすでにある。岩手県，山形県，青森県，秋田県，福島県，新潟県，富山県，石川県，福井県，鳥取県，島根県，徳島県，高知県，佐賀県，熊本県，宮崎県がそれである。陳珍珍「日本における地域別の女性の就業パターン」日本労務学会第28回全国大会研究報告論集181頁。

[22] 出典は United Nations, "Women's Indicators ans Statistics Data-base", Version 3. CD-DOM, Statistical Division, New York, 1994.

[23] Department of Budget, Accounts and Statistics (Republic of China), A Survey Report on Application of Manpower (1997), p. 15.

が国によって異なるが1990年前後なので，日本の1992年の数字を見ると，パートタイマーを含むと50.9，それを除くと61.5となっている。パートタイマーを含むと韓国より低い数字になっている。それを除いてもフィリピンと変わらない。

行政および管理職に占める女性の割合[24]であるが，先と同じ資料の67頁には，男性を100とした時の女性の数字がのっている。フィリピン38，タイ29，シンガポール19，香港19，中国13，日本9，インドネシア7，バングラデシュ5，韓国4，パキスタン3となっている。

本稿で取り上げた国すべての数字が出ていないが，日本は韓国とともに東南アジアのいくつかの国より男女の格差が大きいと言えそうである。その原因であるが，男女を問わず学歴資格によって賃金や処遇を決めるシステムが東南アジアに存在することが考えられる。さらに高学歴の女性が活躍できる背景に，家庭責任を軽くしてくれる家事労働者が存在することも日本とは異なっている。後で述べるように男女雇用平等を目指す法律が制定されている国があるが，それらがきちんと実施されていなくても，東南アジアでは男女格差が日本と韓国より小さい。これは経済発展によって男女の格差が解消するとは言えないことを示している。日本は賃金額自体が高いので男女の格差が大きくても，女子の賃金額が東南アジアの女性の賃金より高くなるにすぎない。ここで依拠する資料を前提とするかぎり東南アジアのいくつかの国より日本の方が男女格差が大きいことを自覚すべきである。もちろん東・東南アジアで男女格差が消えていないのは言うまでもない。

2　東・東南アジア諸国の女子労働法制

先に述べたように東・東南アジア諸国では，まだ雇用上の男女差別が存在するので，それを解決する一の方法として法的手段が用いられている。女子労働の法的規制は母性保護規定，弱い性であることから設けられる女子保護規定，男女雇用平等規定の3つに分けられる。前二つはここで考察の対象にするすべての国にもうけられているが，男女雇用平等にかかわる規定のない

---

24)　出典はILO, Yearbook of Labour Statistics, 1994, 53d issue, Geneva.

国がある。日本，韓国，フィリピン，香港には男女雇用平等に関する規定がある。インドネシアには一般的な機会均等と差別取扱の禁止規定が1997年の労働法によって定められている。タイでは1995年憲法に男女平等規定が復活し，賃金差別禁止規定を設けているが，1998年修正の労働保護法でも規定が設けられた。台湾が法案（男女工作平等法案）を作って審議中である。しかし，雇用差別に関するILO条約の批准状況は芳しくなく[25]，まだ国際的レベルに達していないことが分かる。しかし女性差別撤廃条約の批准をきっかけに，以前に比べれば，男女雇用差別に関する法制度が進展しつつあると言えよう。

(1) 包括的な男女雇用平等にかかわる法律が制定されている国

この範疇に入る国は包括的な男女雇用平等に関する法律を持っている日本，韓国，フィリピン，香港である。

日本では均等法で募集・採用，配置・昇進，教育訓練，福利厚生，定年・退職・解雇に関して差別的取扱を禁止しているが，罰則はない。その代わり企業名公表制度や調停制度の改善で強化を図っている。企業が積極的に取り組む措置の設定，育児介護休業制度による職業生活と家庭生活との両立，母性保護の強化をおこない，一方女子保護は労働時間規制を男女同じにして，均等扱いとし女性の職域拡大を図っていくことになっている。セクハラ防止

---

[25] 雇用平等に関するILO条約・差別撤廃条約の批准状況（○印が批准したところ）

	100号	111号	156号	差別撤廃条約（発効日）
カンボジア				○（92年11月14日）
中国	○			○（81年9月3日）
インドネシア	○	○		○（84年10月13日）
韓国				○（85年1月26日）
ラオス				○（81年9月13日）
マレーシア				○（95年8月4日）
ミャンマー				○（97年8月21日）
フィリピン	○	○		○（81年9月4日）
シンガポール				○（95年11月5日）
タイ				○（85年9月8日）
ベトナム		○		○（82年3月19日）
日本	○		○	○（85年7月25日）

の配慮義務も定められている。

　韓国では勤労基準法5条で男女の差別的待遇を禁止し，違反した者は500万ウォン以下の罰金に処せられる規定があったが，1984年12月女子差別撤廃条約批准を契機に国内法の整備に乗り出した。まず1987年10月29日制定の第六共和国憲法32条4項で「雇用および勤労条件において性差別を受けない権利」が明文化され，さらに1987年11月28日男女雇用平等法が制定され，1988年4月1日から施行された。これは与党であった民正党議員44人の共同提案で10月5日国会に提出され，11月28日に制定された。2ヵ月という短期間で成立した。1987年末の大統領選挙で女性の支持を得るためであったとされている[26]。その内容は日本の男女雇用機会均等法によく似ており，募集・採用で男女に平等な機会の提供，教育・配置・昇進で差別待遇の禁止が定められ，罰則はなかった。しかし，1989年3月8日改正され，罰則規定をもうけ，日本より強力な規定を設けた。「事業主が賃金，定年・退職および解雇などで違反した場合は，2年以下または500万ウォン以下の罰金に処す。募集と採用，教育，配置，昇進などにおける性差別と，育児休職条項に違反した場合は250万ウォン以下の罰金に処す」（22条）と規定された。さらに同一価値労働同一賃金の規定を設けた（6条の2）。1991年「雇用における性差別撤廃のためのガイドライン」を制定し，行政指導による改善がなされるが，罰則の適用を受ける事例も出てきている[27]。1995年改正して，募集，採用における職務遂行に不必要な身体条件等の提示を禁止したり（6条2項），福利厚生での差別を禁止した。男女雇用平等法制を促進する一方，勤労基準法上の女子保護規定は存続している。深夜労働と休日労働の禁止（女子の同意と労働大臣の許可があれば別），時間外労働時間数の規制，坑内労働の禁止が定められている。今後廃止論議が出てくるものと思われる。母性保護として生理休暇，産前産後休暇，育児時間の規定がある。1995年12月（1996年施行）女性発展基本法を制定して，1998年～2002年の第一次女性政策基本計画を策定してい

---

26)　水野順子「効力を発揮した『男女雇用平等法』」アジア経済研究所編・前掲書，38頁，広木道子「韓国」柴山恵美子編『新・世界の女たちはいま』学陽書房，1993年7月，223頁。

27)　孫昌熹『韓国の労使関係——労働運動と労働法の新展開』日本労働研究機構，1995年11月，323頁。

る。男女雇用平等政策は日本とよく似た動きをしているが，罰則によって強力な立法を制定していることに特色がある[28]。しかし，OECD加盟国の中で日本より女性が働きにくい国とされている。日本以上に男女の格差が大きいことが罰則付きの法律を生み出しているといえよう。

フィリピンでは，1974年制定の労働法典が女子労働法制の基本法である[29]。これは男女雇用平等規定を拡大する一方，母性保護や女性保護の規定を廃止または緩和する方向を示している。母性保護として4人目の子供までの出産休暇[30]，女性用の便所・洗面所等の施設，託児所の設置，家族計画の規定があるが，1952年「女性および児童労働法」によって認められた育児時間は廃止している。女性保護として深夜労働の禁止は継続して存在しているが，その例外を認めるケースを拡大している。さらに深夜時間の終了を1時間早めて午前6時としている。18歳以下の女子の雇用制限の廃止，重量物の運搬および立ち仕事禁止の廃止，休憩付与の廃止がなされ，女子保護の範囲が縮小されている。

これに対して差別禁止規定は拡大されている。まず女性であることを理由とする労働条件の差別が禁止されている。これは同等価値労働には同一賃金を支給すること，昇進・訓練・研究・奨励金に関して男子を優遇することの禁止を意味している。さらに結婚・妊娠・出産を理由とする解雇禁止，福利厚生を受けていることを理由とする解雇禁止を定めている。これらの規定違反には1000ペソ以上1万ペソ以下の罰金，3ヵ月以上3年未満の禁固刑，ま

---

28) 海外労働時報224号17頁以下に女性労働力の積極的活用のための政策提言がなされているが，経済状況の悪化のために構造調整を余儀なくされており，その実施は困難であろう。

29) 歴史的経緯については神尾真知子「フィリピンにおける女性労働者の保護と平等」家族・労働・福祉刊行委員会編『家族・労働・福祉』永田文昌堂，1991年10月，283-308頁，労働法典の翻訳は日本労働研究機構編『フィリピンの労働事情』日本労働研究機構，1994年3月，239-358頁参照。

30) 法律上の配偶者の出産（第1子から第4子までに限定）の際に男性も7日間の有給出産休暇をとることができる Paternity Leave Act of 1996 がある。海外労働時報246号9頁。

31) フィリピンの雇用平等と女性保護について，ホセ・モヤ「フィリピンにおける女性保護立法の是非」海外労働時報156号69-72頁，ILO., Labour Law Documents, 1989-PHl 3, p. 100.

たは両方が課せられる。この労働法典の規定を強化するために，アキノ政権は1989年職場における女性差別禁止法を成立させた[31]。これは同等価値労働同一賃金に反する使用者に罰則を課すことと昇進，訓練に際し男子を有利に扱うことを禁止し，それに違反する使用者に罰則を課す規定を設けている。さらに1995年2月反セクシュアル・ハラスメント法が制定されている[32]。アジアでは最初のセクハラに関する法律である。ここでは雇用の場だけでなく教育・訓練の場も含まれ，対価型と環境型のセクハラが対象とされている。違反者には1ヵ月以上6ヵ月以下の禁固，1万ペソ以上2万ペソ以下の罰金，または両方が課せられる。さらに使用者が被害者からセクハラの連絡を受け，なんらの措置も講じない場合，セクハラから生じる損害賠償の責任を負うことを明記している。企業内でセクハラの調査委員会を設置して調査し，セクハラの存在が認定されると処分をおこなう権限が付与されている。フィリピンでは女性保護を縮小しつつあるが，完全になくなっていないので，それと雇用平等との関係をどうするかが議論されている。両立できるのかどうか，それが女性の雇用の機会を拡大できるのかが問題となっている。

フィリピンの法制度だけを見れば，日本以上に整備され罰則付きの雇用平等法制を見ることができる。雇用平等実現のために女性保護を少なくしていく方向も示されている[33]。

香港では1991年制定の人権条例の中で公共部門での女性差別を禁止しているが，民間部門にまで適用されていないので，性差別に対する今後の法政策を検討する作業委員会が政庁内に設置された。その報告書では経済に悪影響があり，実施が困難であることから性差別禁止法の導入を勧告しなかった[34]。しかし，政庁は女性差別禁止条約の批准のために性差別禁止に関する条例を

---

32) ILO., Labour Law Documents, 1995-PHL 1, p. 68-69，翻訳は神尾真知子「フィリッピンの反セクシュアル・ハラスメント法およびフィリッピン労働雇用省における反セクシュアル・ハラスメント法施行規則」帝京平成大学紀要8巻2号53-60頁。

33) 女性の国作りに果たす役割を認めて男子と平等な取扱を保障することを宣言し，成年女子に成年男子と同様な行為能力を認め，クラブ組織への入会権の平等取扱，軍の学校への入学への平等の機会の提供を定める Women in Development and Nation Building Act, 1992 が制定されている。ILO., Labour Law Documents, 1992-PHL 2, pp. 88-90.

34) ン・セク・ホン「香港における職場での性差別」海外労働時報201号62頁。

制定することに政策を転換した。イギリスの1975年性差別禁止法やオーストラリアの連邦法である1984年性差別禁止法の影響を強く受けて、1995年6月に性差別禁止条例[35]が制定された。これは直接差別だけでなく間接差別も禁止の対象としていること、雇用における差別だけでなく、職業紹介所、労働組合・使用者団体、教育訓練機関等での差別も規制の対象としている点に特色がある。雇用差別禁止については性、婚姻関係の有無、妊娠を理由とする募集、昇進、配転、訓練、賃金や付加給付に関して差別的扱いをすれば不法行為として15万香港ドル以下の損害賠償の支払いを裁判所が命じる。対価型と環境型のセクハラに対する賠償責任も同様である。機会均等委員会は公式調査をおこない違反が認められる場合には差別停止の通告をおこなうことができる。

(2) 包括的な男女雇用平等にかかわる法律が制定されようとしている国
この範疇には台湾が入る。

台湾では、憲法7条に男女間の平等の規定を定め、労働基準法25条では、使用者は性別により差別待遇してはならないこと、労働の効率が同じ者に対し、同等な賃金を支払うべきことが規定されている。就業服務法5条では、使用者は求職者または従業員に対し、性別をもって差別してはならないとしている。就職差別の認定のために公労使代表による「就業差別評議委員会」が組織されているが、差別であると認定された事例はでていない。託児所設置のための補助金制度や再就職のための訓練費用の補助制度が設けられている。これらの法律では、その適用対象が異なったり、規定も不十分なことから、行政院労工委員会は男女工作平等法案を作成し、行政院で審議中である[36]。

その内容であるが、まず募集、選考、採用で性別による差別待遇が禁止されている。ただし仕事の性質のために特別な者は除外される。次に、同一労

---

[35] ILO., Labour Law Documents, 1995-GBD 1, pp. 70-110, および海外労働時報212号23頁、213号26頁、215号27頁、233号23頁、244号25頁参照。

[36] Liou Chih-Poung, "Latest Developments in the Taiwan Individual Labour Relations Laws", Papers presented to International Workshop at Aoyama Gakuin University, Faculty of Law, 12-14 March, 1998.

働同一賃金の原則，教育・訓練，福利厚生に関して性別による差別待遇を禁止している。さらに定年，退職，解雇に対して性別による差別待遇を禁止している。結婚・妊娠・出産，育児による解雇が禁止され，その解雇は無効とされている。出産休暇，育児時間，介護休暇，再就職の機会の援助，対価型のセクハラ禁止と防止措置，差別待遇の救済として労働監督機関に通報することができる。差別禁止のために広範囲な雇用上の差別を禁止しているが，罰則の規定はみられない。ここに日本の男女雇用機会均等法の影響をみることができる。

(3) 包括的な男女雇用平等法はないが，それを目指している国

この範疇に入る国はタイとインドネシアである。

タイでは1972年労働者保護に関する内務省令[37]で女子労働保護規定として深夜労働禁止（連続操業，交替制勤務等の場合には除く），鉱業・建設・爆発物可燃物製造，重量物の運搬等の危険有害業務の禁止，18歳未満の女性を風俗営業に雇用することの禁止が定められ，母性保護として90日の出産休暇（45日分は賃金支給），不妊手術のための休暇，妊娠中の女子の一時的配転，妊娠を理由とする解雇の禁止が定められている。その後国会の審議を経ない省令で定められていることへの疑問があり，法律によって労働条件を定めることになった。その結果新しい労働者保護法が1998年1月7日可決され，8月19日施行された。それには先の規定に追加して，男女同じ権利を保障すること，妊娠中の女子の時間外労働禁止と休日労働禁止，使用者や監督者による女性従業員への性的虐待の禁止，危険業務の範囲を拡大しトンネルでの業務が禁止されている[38]。セクハラについての禁止規定とそれに違反する使用者の責任を定めた点に大きな特徴がある。

タイの1974年施行の憲法に，男性と女性が平等の権利を有することを明記したが，1976年軍事政権下で女性の権利に関する条項が削除された。1995年憲法で男女平等規定が復活したことがきっかけで，女性差別禁止法の草案作

---

37) 村嶋英治訳『労働者保護法解説』バンコク日本人商工会議所，1985年11月。

38) この新しい労働保護法は1998年8月19日から施行される。その内容については海外労働時報249号5頁，268号28頁および小暮康二「新労働者保護法（1998年）の概要」バンコク日本人商工会議所所報433号37頁。

成の動きが出てきた[39]。しかしその草案がどのような内容なのか不明である。男女平等の取扱やセクハラの規定が労働保護法に設けられたことは，これから包括的な雇用平等法を作っていく一段階とされている。現在は雇用平等法制を研究している段階にある[40]。その一部は先に述べた1998年施行予定であった労働者保護法に反映されている。

インドネシアでは1925年の「児童労働および女子の深夜労働に関する条例」で午後10時から午前5時までの労働が禁止されているが，1989年の労働力大臣令によって深夜労働の強い必要性と女子の安全，健康，道徳の保護を条件のもとで労働力省地方事務所の許可があれば深夜での労働が可能になっている。1948年法律1号で坑内労働禁止，危険有害労働禁止（未施行），2日間の生理休暇[41]，6週間の有給の産前休暇と6週間の有給の産後休暇（医師の診断書で3ヵ月まで延長可能），授乳時間が定められている。1969年労働基本法2条には「差別があってはならない」という一般的規定があるだけである。1989年の労働大臣決定では結婚・妊娠・出産を理由とする解雇を禁止し，違

---

39) 海外労働時報230号5頁。

40) 在タイ日本国大使館の木暮康二氏からの筆者あての1998年9月10日到着の返信による示唆である。この件について木暮氏に感謝申し上げる。

41) 生理休暇の規定は日本，韓国とインドネシアで定められている。韓国は日本を参考に規定を設けたが，インドネシアはどうか。旧宗主国であったオランダには生理休暇を法律で規定したことはない。日本で生理休暇制度が最初に定められたのは昭和6年12月千寿食品研究所で認められた5日間の有給生理休暇であったとされており，戦前から生理休暇を組合が要求していた。戦時下に国力増強のために女子の労働力を活用したが，生理中の勤務で健康を害する調査事例があった。そこで1943年7月女子勤労動員要綱で「月経時の保護」として「初潮時における適切なる指導の徹底，女子の労務係員をして各自の予定日を知り置く施設設置，重労働の禁止抑制，脱脂綿の配置」を決めている。1994年6月の女子挺身隊受入側措置要綱でも生理中の女子を就労させる場合の特別の考慮を払うべきことを決定している。産めよ増やせよの時代であり，出産にかかわる生理中の勤務が負担になって出産が減少することをおそれて生理休暇が取り入れられたのであろう。それが日本軍が軍政を敷いたインドネシアに入ったのでないかという仮説を持っている。今のところ仮説の段階にすぎない。浅倉むつ子「生理休暇の生成過程と権利構造」労働法律旬報921号23頁，拙稿「インドネシアの労働事情調査」国際産研14号25頁。

42) 水野広祐「インドネシアにおける農村出身女子労働者保護問題」アジア経済33巻6号26頁。

反する使用者には罰則を課している[42]。しかし，規定はあってもまだ施行されていなかったり，規定通り実施されているかどうか疑問視されている。

インドネシアの労働法規は錯綜しているために，それらを整理し体系的な法律とするために1997年9月11日新しく労働法が成立し[43]，1998年10月1日より実施されることになっていたが，延期されている。その中で使用者にすべての者に対する差別の禁止と均等な就労機会を与えることを義務づけ，さらにすべての従業員の差別禁止と平等な扱いを義務づけている。この違反には4年以下の禁固刑または4億ルピア以下の罰金またはその両方がかせられている。どのような理由による差別を禁止するかは何も規定していないが，女性であることを理由とする差別も含まれると思われる。母性保護として妊娠中，および授乳中の女性の一定時間帯の就労禁止，2日間の生理日の勤務の強制禁止，授乳時間の付与，産前1ヵ月（医師の診断書により3ヵ月まで延長可能）と産後2ヵ月の休暇（流産の場合は1ヵ月半の休暇）付与し，しかもその間の賃金カットはできないし，違反すれば罰則が課せられる。母性保護がより手厚くなっているのに対し，女性保護として坑内労働禁止（許可を得た場合等には例外として認められる）だけが規定されている。残業や深夜労働は男子と同様に認められており，女性保護規定が非常に少なくなっている。

(4) 男女雇用平等に関する法律も法案も存在しない国

この範疇にはマレーシア，シンガポールが入る。シンガポールはアジアNIESとして，マレーシアもそれにつぐ経済発展を遂げているのに，男女雇用平等に関する法律を作成する予定もない。それには以下の特殊事情が存在する。

マレーシアでは1955年雇用法で深夜労働禁止（交代制の場合労働大臣の許可によって深夜労働が可能なため軽工業部門には女子が深夜交代勤務に就いている事例が多い），坑内労働の禁止，60日の出産休暇（一定条件で出産手当がつく），不妊手術を受けるための休暇制度が定められている。深夜労働以外の時間規制は男女とも同じであるが，月収1500リンギ以上の女性事務職労働者には雇用

---

[43] 日本インドネシア協会編・インドネシア経済法令時報1997年12月号および1998年1月号に翻訳が掲載されている。この法律は1998年スハルト元大統領の退陣となった政変のために，2000年10月1日まで施行が延期されている。

法が適用されないので深夜労働は禁止されない（女性ブルーカラー労働者には月収額に関係なく適用になる）。したがってエリート層の女性には女子労働保護の範囲が狭くなるという特色を持つ。1997年末にはパートタイマーの年休，フレックス時間制，休憩時間に関する規定が導入され，パート就労の拡大を目指している。

マレーシアには雇用平等に関する法律，男女の賃金平等に関する規定もないが，これはブミプトラ政策によってマレー系優遇政策を採用しているためである。マレーシアは主としてマレー系，中国系，インド系の三つの人種から構成されており，その中でマレー系の経済的地位向上のためにマレー系の男女を優遇する政策が採られていることから，国民一般に適用する雇用平等や賃金平等政策を採用しにくい状況にある。そのために女性差別撤廃条約を批准したのが1995年で遅かった。

シンガポールでは憲法12条で宗教，人種，血統，出生地による差別を禁止しているが，性差別を禁止する規定はない。1968年雇用法でも宗教，人種，家系または出生地を理由とする差別の禁止しか定めていない。雇用法では女子ブルーカラー労働者の深夜労働禁止，すべての女子労働者の坑内労働の禁止，産前産後4週間の休暇（一定の条件で有給）制度がある。しかし，深夜労働以外の時間規制（時間外労働，休憩時間，変形労働時間）は男女とも同じであるが，月収1500シンガポール・ドル以上の労働者には労働時間規制の適用がなく，収入の多いエリート層の女性には労働時間規制がないことになる。女子労働保護の範囲が狭いのはマレーシアと同じである。さらに女性差別撤廃条約を批准したのがマレーシアより遅い。日本と比べれば女子の活躍の場の広いシンガポールであるが，雇用平等に関する法律を制定しないのはなぜか不思議である[44]。人種間のバランスを優先した結果だろうか。

以上のとおり，マレーシア，シンガポールを除き，男女雇用平等を目指す法律を作成したり，作成しつつある。特に女性差別撤廃条約の批准をきっかけに，その方向が明確になっている。その際，日本のような行政指導によっ

---

44) Yee Shoon Foo, "The Provision of Women in Labour Law and Social Security in Singapore", Flerida Ruth P. Romero ed., First Asian Congress of Labour Law and Social Security, University of the Philippines Law Center, 1982, p. 518.

て雇用平等を促進するという柔軟な手段ではなく，罰則によって強制する方法が採用されている。なぜ違いが生じるのか。行政に対する認識に違いがあるためなのか。さらに雇用平等規定と女性保護規定とのかかわりが今後重要な問題となってくるように思われる。方向としては女性保護規定をなくすことが示されているが，東・東南アジアではまだ，そこまでの詰めが十分になされていない状況にある。

おわりに

　これまでほとんど無視されてきた東・東南アジアの女子労働の実態とその法制について，若干の分析をおこなってきた。日本は先進国ばかりに目を向けて，OECD23ヵ国の中で，「女性の働きやすさ」指標が19位で遅れていることを気にしているが，本稿で考察した東南アジアのいくつかの国々にも遅れをとっている。女子労働法制でも罰則を設けている国があり，日本より強力な措置をとっている国が存在している。それには実態を無視して法制度だけ立派なのではないかと言う批判があろうが，それなら日本は男女雇用機会均等法を作りながら，なぜ男女格差が東南アジアのいくつかの国より大きいままなのかが問われるべきであろう。東南アジアの国々は重層構造になっており，下層の女性の悲惨な労働実態がみられる一方，上層階層の男性以上に活躍する女性もいる。どちらに注目するかによって見方が変わってくるが，今回は統計資料と法制度に基づいてまとめた。この論文では南アジアは考察の対象からはずしているが，それを含めて今後各国毎に法制度と実態の関係の検討を深めていきたいと思っている。

日本との比較で見る東・東南アジアの女子労働の現状と法制度

図1　韓国・台湾の女子労働力率

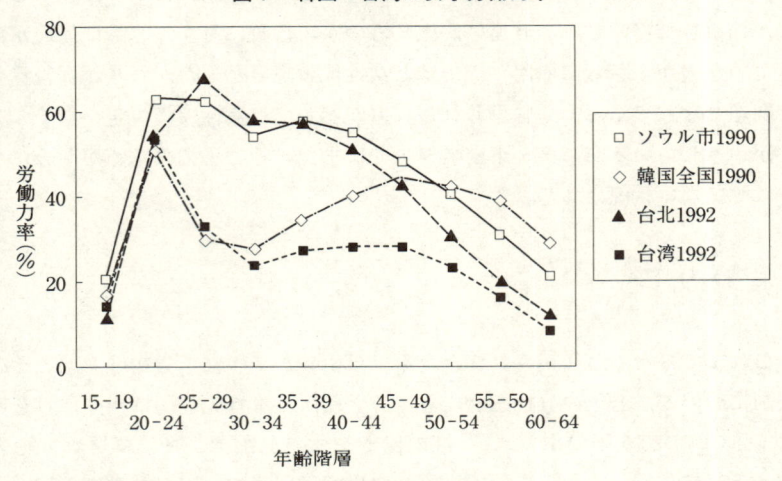

凡例：
- □ ソウル市1990
- ◇ 韓国全国1990
- ▲ 台北1992
- ■ 台湾1992

縦軸：労働力率(％)
横軸：年齢階層（15-19, 20-24, 25-29, 30-34, 35-39, 40-44, 45-49, 50-54, 55-59, 60-64）

（出典）　瀬地山角・東アジアの家父長制261頁

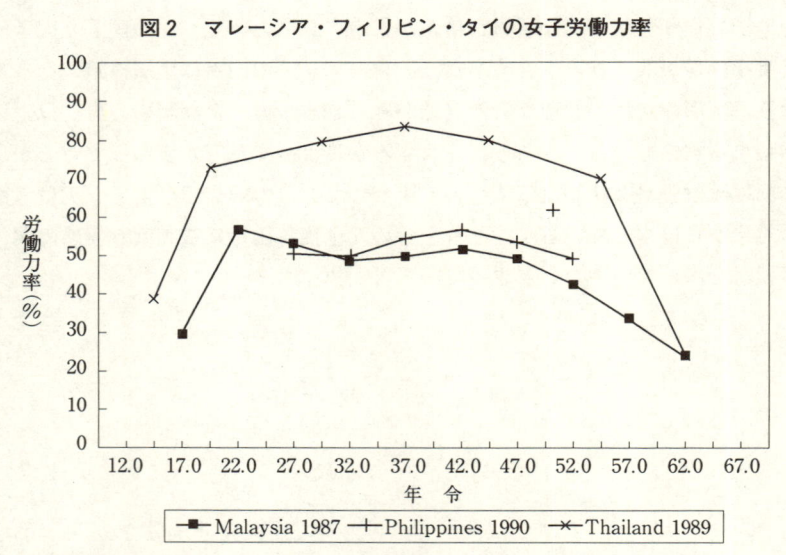

図2　マレーシア・フィリピン・タイの女子労働力率

縦軸：労働力率(％)
横軸：年令

凡例：
- ■ Malaysia 1987
- + Philippines 1990
- × Thailand 1989

（出典）　Susan Horton ed., Women and Industrialization in Asia, 11p

おわりに

図3　インドネシアの女子労働力率

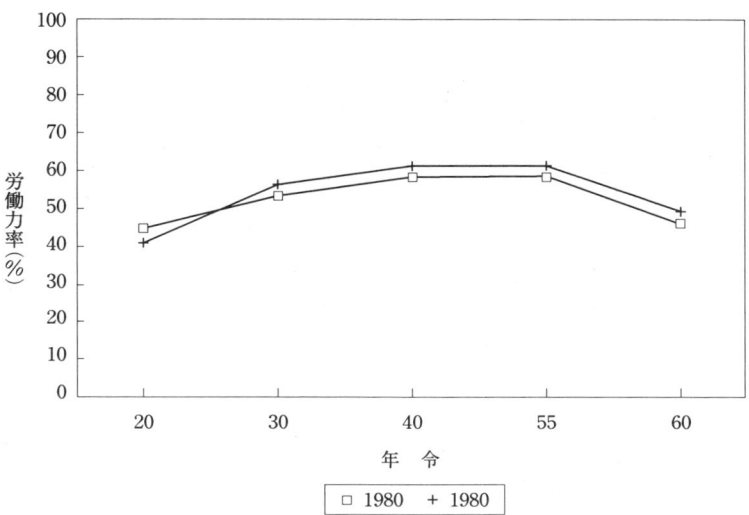

（出典）　Susan Horton ed., Women and Industrialization in Asia, 13p

図4　シンガポール・ホンコンの女子労働力率

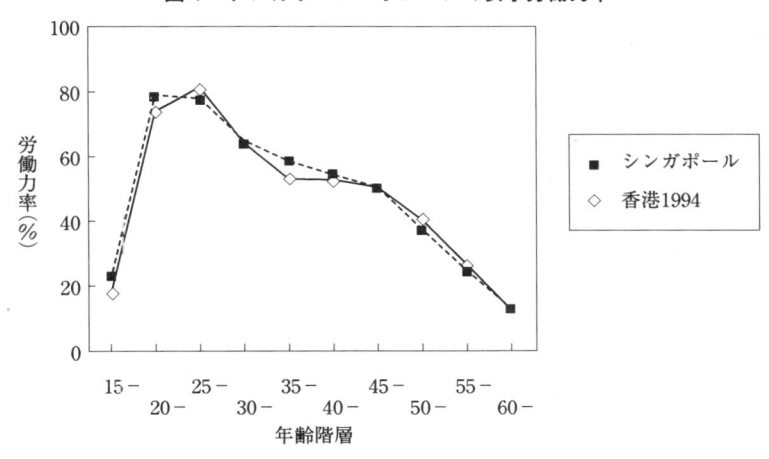

（出典）　瀬地山角・東アジアの家父長制265頁

イタリアにおける雇用平等の展開と現状

山口浩一郎

1 保護から平等へ

　他の国がそうであったように，イタリアでも元来女性労働は保護の対象であった。憲法に，「女性労働者は男性労働者と同じ権利を有し，労働の同一性にもとづき同じ報酬を受けるものとする」として平等原則を宣明してはいたが，つづけて，「労働条件は，女性労働者に不可欠の家庭責任の遂行を許すものでなければならず，かつ，母親と幼児にたいし適切な特別の保護を保障するものでなければならない」と定めて保護政策を表明していたので（37条1項），第二次大戦後も戦前の保護立法が維持されてきた[1]。

　戦後は，この方向にそって保護政策が進められてきた。1963年には，女性労働者に対する結婚を理由とする解雇を禁止する法律（1963年1月9日法7号）とすべての公職への就任権を保障する法律（1963年2月9日法66号）が制定され，1971年には，母親労働者の保護に関する法律（1971年12月30日法1204号。いわゆる母性保護法）が制定された。1971年法は，産前産後の休暇（産前2ヵ月，産後3ヵ月。有給，期間中の解雇禁止）や育児休業（最高3年，30%の賃金保障）などを定めており，当時の母性保護法としては最も進んだものであった。

　このような伝統的な保護政策のなかで，1970年代から，国際的な潮流にのって平等の要求が姿をあらわした。この動きが立法となって結実したのが，1977年の労働の分野における男女間の待遇の平等に関する法律（1977年12月9日法903号。いわゆる雇用平等法）である。この法律は賃金および待遇面

---

[1]　その代表は，1934年4月26日の女子および年少労働者の保護に関する法律（第653号）である。この法律は，女子と年少者にたいし，危険有害業務，重量物取扱業務，深夜業の3つを禁止していた。

表1　女性労働にたいする法政策

時　期	原　則	内　容
憲法制定(1948年)から1960年代	憲法(37条1項)での平等原則 法律での保護政策	1934年法(653号) ・危険有害業務の禁止 ・重量物取扱の禁止 ・深夜業の禁止
1970年代と1980年代	女性労働者にたいする形式的平等(憲法37条1項,労働者憲章法15条)	1977年法(903号) ・重労働の禁止の廃止 ・深夜業の禁止の維持 ・賃金・待遇等の平等規定の導入 ・差別行為の無効 ・休業権の男性労働者への拡大
	母親労働者にたいする特別の保護(憲法37条1項)	1971年法(1204号) ・義務的休業 ・任意的休業 ・休業の権利
1990年代	実質的平等(憲法3条2項)と平等機会の推進	1991年法(125号) ・直接および間接差別 ・アファーマティブ・アクション ・立証責任の転換 ・平等委員会と平等アドバイザー 1992年法(215号) ・女性起業の促進 1993年法律命令 ・行政組織における平等機会の推進

出所：F. Carinci ed altri, Diritto del lavoro 2, Torino, 1998, p. 203

での平等を宣言し，差別行為を無効とするなど平等政策を前面にだしたものであったため，国際的にも雇用平等立法として認知された。しかし，他方では，深夜業の禁止を維持するなど伝統的な保護政策と妥協した点があり，母性保護法もそのまま残されたので，1990年代に入ってから，雇用平等のさらなる展開をはかる立法がおこなわれた。

　そのうち最も重要なのは，1991年の労働における男女の平等を実現するための積極的行動に関する法律（1991年4月10日法125号。いわゆる積極的行動法）である。これは平等実現のためのアファーマティブ・アクションを定めたものであるが，同時に間接差別も差別とすること，訴訟における立証責任の転換，平等委員会と平等アドバイザーの役割などについても定めている。この

後，1992年には女性企業家のための積極的行動に関する法律（1992年2月25日法215号。いわゆる女性起業援助法），1993年には公務における平等関係 EU 法規の遵守義務を定めた法律命令（1993年2月3日法律命令29号）がだされた。

こうして，イタリアでは，雇用平等は新しく実質的平等を追求する段階に入っているが，女性労働の特殊性と調和させつつこれをどう実現していくかが大きな課題となっている（表1参照)[2]。

2 賃金の平等——同一労働同一賃金の原則

賃金の平等は雇用平等法（1977年）の制定以前から問題となってきた。憲法は，「女性労働者は男性労働者と同じ権利を有し，労働の同一性にもとづき同じ報酬を受ける」と定めているので（37条1項），このもとで，同一労働同一賃金が法原則として肯定されるか否か（とくに請求権を根拠づけるような法原則かどうか）が議論されてきたのである。この間学説・判例とも紆余曲折があったが[3]，判例は現在でも同一労働同一賃金の原則それじたいを実定法の法原則としてはみとめず[4]，ただ，賃金格差に合理的理由がなく客観的な正当性がなければ，信義則（民法1175条，1375条）違反として損害賠償の対象となるとしている[5]。つまり，信義則の一内容（あるいは一場面）として，

2） 1977年の雇用平等法までの，女性労働に対する法政策をあとづけたものとして，M. V. Ballestrero, Dalla tutela alla parità, Bologna, 1979 がある。

3） R. Pessi, Il problema della discriminazione femminile, Relazione al XI congresso nazionale dell' AIDLASS, pp. 16-18 参照。

4） 例えば，Cassazione, 5 marzo 1986, n. 1444, RIDL, 1986, II, 717. 憲法37条の趣旨は平等待遇でなく，女子・年少者（いわゆる弱者）の保護（すなわち特別待遇）にある，というのが大きな理由である。

5） 1989年の憲法裁判所の判決（9 marzo 1989, n. 103, RIDL, 1989, II, 389）を契機として，このような立場がとられるようになった。最近の例として，Cassazione, 8 luglio 1994, n. 6448, RIDL, 1995, II, 304；Cassazione, 17 maggio 1996, n. 4570, RIDL, 1996, II, 765.

なお，雇用平等法は，「女性労働者は，要求される給付が同じかもしくは同じ価値のものであるかぎり，男性労働者と同じ報酬を受ける権利を有する」と定めたが（2条1項)，この趣旨は差別行為の禁止にあり，違反の法的効果は差別行為の無効であって（労働者憲章法15条参照)，差額請求権の附与ではない。このため，雇用平等法の制定によっても，同一労働同一賃金の原則をめぐる議論は基本的には変わらなかった。

同一労働同一賃金が肯定されているのである。

　同一労働同一賃金の原則をめぐって議論された問題の一つは,「同一労働」となにかということであった。これには対立する二つの考え方が提起され，一つは同一労働とは職務の同一性（parità di mansioni）を意味するとするもので，もう一つは能率の同一性（parità di rendimento）を意味するとするものである。第一の考え方では，男女の労働者が同じ資格を有し同じ職務についているときには，経済的待遇が同じでないことは違法になる。第二の考え方では，職務が同じでも，能率（あるいは業務遂行力）が違えば待遇の違いは正当化される。憲法の規定だけの時期には，労働契約の有償性から能率同一説が有力であったが，雇用平等法制定後は職務同一説で落着している[6]。というのは，雇用平等法は「報酬を決定するための職務分類のしくみは，男女に共通の基準を用いなければならない」（2条2項）としたので，これが同一職務同一賃金説の根拠とされているのである。現に，労働協約の賃率表では，性別を問わず，同一職務には同じ賃金が支払われるようになっている[7]。

　現在議論されているのは，同一労働同一賃金の「双方向性」（bidirezionalità）という問題である。従来，判例は同一労働同一賃金の原則は女性労働者のためにしか存在しないとの立場をとってきたが[8]，この妥当性が問題とされている。歴史的，沿革的には判例の立場は妥当であるとしても，雇用平等法の後に積極的行動法が制定され，性差別を広く「性を理由に差別すること」（4条1項）と定義している以上，もはやこの立場の妥当性は疑わしく，同一労働同一賃金の原則は男性労働者にも適用される（つまり，この原則は双方向性がある）といわれている[9]。

---

6) F. Carinci ed altri, Diritto del lavoro 2, Torino, 1998, p. 182 ; G. Pera, Diritto del lavoro, Padova, 1996, p. 361.

7) 1960年代前半までは，労働協約上も男女別々の賃率表が定められていた。

8) 前掲 Cassazione, 5 marzo 1986, n. 1444. この事件では，男性労働者が女性労働者より低い賃金を支払われていた。

9) F. Carinci ed altri, op. cit., p. 183. 雇用平等法は育児休業の取得権を男性労働者に拡大しているから（7条），同法の精神は「双方向性」にあるといえる。

3 待遇の平等――差別の禁止

雇用平等法は，労働関係の成立から消滅までの全局面で男女間の差別を禁止し，待遇の平等を実現しようとしている。具体的にいえば，採用での差別（1条），賃金での差別（2条），配置・昇進での差別（3条），解雇その他での差別（13条）等を禁止している。

採用では，結婚，家族，妊娠の有無を問題にすることと，募集広告や事前選考で性別を指示することが明示的に禁止されているが（1条2項），それだけでなく採用後の研修や訓練での差別も禁止されている（同3項）。他の国でいう真正職業適格（bona fide occupational qualitication――性別による採用が許される職種）にあたるものとして，モード，芸術，演劇関係で一方の性にしかできない労働があげられている（5項）。労働協約でとくに過重な労働として掲記された職務は，男性のみの採用が許される（4項）[10]。

配置・昇進についても差別が禁止されている（3条1項）。昇進について労働協約が特別の要件を定めている場合は別として，母性保護法による産前産後の休暇期間は出勤したものとして扱わなければならない（同2項）。例えば，勤続3年で昇進という場合，3年間には産前産後の休暇による欠勤期間を算入しなければならない。

雇用平等法が制定されたときは，老齢年金の受給資格が異なっていたので，待遇の平等のため，女性労働者は年金の受給資格年齢（当時は55才）に達しても，男性労働者（受給資格年齢は60才）と同じ年齢まで働くことができる旨の規定がおかれた（4条）。しかし，この規定は逆差別で違憲であると判断された[11]。

女性労働者にたいする深夜業の禁止は，雇用平等法でも維持された（5

---

[10] したがって，交替制労働があるとか深夜業があるというだけでは，女性を採用しなくてよい理由にはならない（Pretura Milano, 14 luglio 1979, RGL, 1980, II, 444; Pretura Taranto, 23 luglio 1981, FI, 1982, I, 1）。また，労働協約で掲記された場合でないと例外にならない。雇用平等の促進のため，職業紹介では従来の家事労働という職種区分がなくなり，多くの女性が一般リストに登録し重労働に従事する事態が出現して，一時問題になったことがある。

条)。ただ，禁止は管理職と医療業務従事者を除外し，対象を製造業に限定した（1項）。そして，労働協約で定めるときは，深夜業の禁止じたいが解除されることとした（2項)[12]。しかし，深夜業の禁止は EU レベルで問題となり，イタリアのこの規定も，若干の曲接の結果平等原則に反すると判断された[13]。

解雇，配転，懲戒処分での差別も禁止される（13条，労働者憲章法15条2項）。差別にあたる行為は法的に無効とされる（憲章法15条1項）。

これ以外にも，雇用平等法は，社会保険の領域で，家族手当を女性労働者にも支給されるようにし（9条），遺族給付の受給を寡夫にも可能なようにしている（11条）。

上にみてきたように，雇用平等法の基本的な考え方は，男女の形式的な平等を前提とし，そうでないものを差別として禁止するということであった。しかし，社会保険の領域のように平等取扱いの規定によって自動的に効果が生じるところや，同一職務における男女の格差賃金のように誰れの目にも截然とした差別が存在したところ以外では，この法律は思ったほどの役割をはたすことができなかった。その意味では，雇用平等法の機能は不十分なものであったのである[14]。

---

[11] Corte Costituzionale, 21 aprile 1988, n. 498, FI, 1988, I, 1769. この規定が有効なら，男性はそうでないのに，女性は老齢年金をもらいながら労働をつづけることができるようになるというのがその理由である。なお，年金受給資格年齢の違いは合憲であると判断されていた（Corte Costituzionale, 15 luglio 1969, n. 137, FI, 1969, I, 2010）。

[12] この結果，労働協力で労働時間を再編成して，女性労働者の深夜業を可能にすることが試みられた。例えば，繊維産業では，日曜を休日とし，月曜〜土曜の6日を1シフト6時間の4交替で勤務する方式が採用された。

[13] Corte di giustizia europea, 5 dicembre 1997, Il Sole-24 Ore, 5 dicembre 1997. イタリアの憲法裁判所は，深夜業の禁止を必ずしも憲法違反とは考えていなかった。とくに，Corte costituzionale, 6 luglio 1987, n. 246, FI, 1987, I, 2605.

[14] この点は，多くの文献が一致して指摘するところである。なお，バッレストレーロ「女性労働と差別——イタリアの男女均等待遇法」日本労働協会雑誌311号31頁以下も参照。

4 セクシュアル・ハラスメント

EC委員会は，1991年11月27日に「職場における女性と男性の尊厳の保護に関する勧告」と「行動規範」を採択したので，各国とも国内法や労使交渉での対応が求められている[15]。イタリアでは，これをうけて，1994年の化学産業労働協約は労働協約として初めて次のような規定をおいた。「事業所の組織における種々の責任レベルでの労働者間の関係は，相互の廉潔を尊ぶべきものとする。とりわけ，以下のことをしてはならない。①性的意味あいのある攻撃的言動……」[16]。他の産業でも，これにならう例がでてきている[17]。

現在のところ，セクシュアル・ハラスメントについて特別の法規定は作られていないが，イタリアの国内法では，被害者は即時退職（予告なしの辞職）が可能であり，精神的・身体的な損傷があれば，損害賠償の請求も可能だとされている[18]。身体的損傷のなかには，反応性うつ病のような精神障害も含まれる。損害賠償責任は，行為者である同僚労働者だけでなく，直接使用者も負う点に特徴がある。使用者のこの責任は，保護義務（民法2084条）に由来する契約責任である[19]。

刑事責任の面では，1996年の性的暴力にたいする法律（1996年2月15日法66号）がある。この法律は，暴力および威迫とならんで，「権威の濫用」（abuso di autorità）により性的行為をおこなうこと，あるいはおこなわしめることを性的暴力と定義し，セクシュアル・ハラスメントもこれに該当しう

---

15) 浜口桂一郎『EU労働法の形成』日本労働研究機構・平成10年・201頁以下参照。
16) 1994年3月19日の全国化学産業協約48条1項の規定。
17) 1994年7月1日の全国金属産業協約（私企業部門）は，次のように定めている。
「労働者間の関係は，事業所組織のすべての責任レベルにおいて，相互の廉潔とたしなみを尊ぶべきものとする。
　労働者の尊厳にあわせ，上司は，部下と協力的で丁重な関係を作るものとする。
　……故意に性的状態にふれる不適切な，攻撃的でしつような言動はしてはならない。
　右の言動を予防するため，会社は，……全国平等機会委員会がおこなった提案を採用するものとする」（一般規定第3部18条2項〜5項）。
18) Pretura Milano, 14 agosto 1991, Rep. Giur. Lav., 1992/93, 226.
19) Cassazione, 17 luglio 1995, n. 7768, NGL, 1995, 740.

るようになっている。

5　間接差別の問題

　雇用平等法の影響は思いのほか小さく，不満足な成果しかえられないことが年々明らかになった。そこで，何年にもわたる議論の後，法政策は差別の禁止（形式的平等）から平等の積極的推進（実質的平等）に向うことになった。このために制定されたのが積極的行動法（1991年）である[20]。

　積極的行動法は，雇用平等法と違い，間接差別を正面から救済の対象とすることを表明した。すなわち，「間接的であれ，性別を理由に労働者を区別し不利益な結果をもたらすいかなる行為もしくは行動も，1977年12月9日の法律（903号）にいう差別にあたるものとする」とし（4条1項），さらに，「比例的にみて他方の性の大多数の労働者に不利益をもたらすもので，かつ，労働活動の遂行に不可欠でない条件に関する基準を採用した結果である不利益な待遇は，すべて間接差別にあたるものとする」（同2項）と定めた。前者（1項）は差別行為の態様を広くとらえ直接差別を再定義したものであるが，後者（2項）は間接差別を正面から定義したもので，労働活動の遂行に不可欠な基準でなく，かつ，一方の性に不釣合に不利益な結果を生ぜしめているものは，形式的には中立あるいは平等の基準あるいは要件（例えば，勤続年数とか身体的条件）の適用であっても，差別になることを明らかにしたものである。

　間接差別の判断にあっては，いくつかの注意すべき論点がある[21]。第一は，男女を比較する際の単位あるいは範囲をどうとるかという問題で，差別行為の主体が通常は使用者であることから，事業所単位で比較すべきだとされている。第二は，比例的にみて他方の性に不釣合に不利益な結果という場合の，「比例的」（proporzionalmente）とはどの程度のものをいうのかという問題である。これは数字では示すことができず，「男性に比べ女性の数が極めて少

---

20)　簡単な紹介として，トレウ「労働における女性の機会均等に関するイタリアの新法」日本労働研究雑誌385号71頁以下がある。

21)　F. Carinci ed altri, Diritto del lavoro 2, Torino, 1998, p. 187 e seg. ; G. Pera, Diritto del lavono, Padova, 1996, p. 368 参照。

ない」状況をさすものとされている。第三は，労働活動に不可欠の基準とか要件とはなにかという問題である[22]。一般的な考え方としては，解雇制限の場合の「正当な動機」(guiustificato motivo) を類推して[23]，労働にとっての具体的な必要性と結果の回避可能性（他に代替的な手段があったかどうか）を考慮して判断すべきだといわれている。このような考え方によれば，一定レベルの学歴の要求は，当該職務の遂行に必要であるかぎり，女性労働者に不利な結果をもたらしても正当な基準ということになり，勤続年数とか柔軟性（時間外労働や配転への適応性）も，当該職務の遂行にとって重要であれば正当な基準となる。

　これにたいし，労働の質とか能率といった基準（日常用語では「やる気」とか「有能」と表現される基準）は，それじたいは正当な要求であっても具体性がなく，労働に不可欠の条件とはいえないので，この基準にもとづいて女性労働者に不利な採用，昇格，加給等がなされていれば，間接差別にあたることになる。

　間接差別にあたるか否かが実際に争われた例としては，警察官の採用における身長要件がある。市町村が採用する交通巡査 (vigili urbani) の場合は，身長は不可欠の要件でなく間接差別だとされ，逆に国が採用する治安警察官 (polizia) の場合には不可欠の要件とされ，判例の態度も一定していない[24]。統計でみると，賃金について男女間には顕著な格差があるから，職務分類や格づけのしかた等には間接差別として問題になる点がありそうであるが（例えば，伝統的な女性の職種を低く格づけるなど），これらが争われた例はない。

　イタリアでは，他の国のように間接差別が訴訟で争われることはあまりない。

---

[22]　実際にはこれが一番議論の多い問題である。この基準に該当すれば差別にあたらないということになるので，採用，格づけ，賃金，昇進等について，女性に不利な人事管理が許されることになるからである。

[23]　解雇制限法（1966年7月15日法604号）は，解雇に正当な理由または正当な動機を要求している。

[24]　F. Carinci ed altri, op. cit., p. 186 参照。

6 アファーマティブ・アクション

雇用平等法は差別行為を禁止したが、それだけで差別は解消されなかった。差別という状態は特定の行為や行動の結果ではなく、永い間くりかえされ容認されてきた行為や行動の累積であることが多く、それらは、学校教育、職場慣行、家庭生活、さらには社会文化などによって歴史的に形成されてきた側面があるので、禁止行為を拡大していけば解決するという問題ではない。これが、積極的行動法が、間接差別の禁止のほかにアファーマティブ・アクションを定めた理由である[25]。

もっとも、イタリアでは、1984年のEC勧告をうけて[26]、積極的行動法の制定以前にも、労使間の団体交渉でアファーマティブ・アクションがおこなわれていた。それらのなかで注目されるのは、多くの産業で労働協約により設置された全国あるいは地方レベルでの労使合同委員会（commissione paritetica）である。これは、労使が共同で女性労働者の状態を研究し、雇用平等を推進することを目的としていた[27]。

このような状況を背景として制定された積極的行動法は、「女性の雇用促進および労働における男女の実質的な平等の実現」を目的とすると定め（1条1項）、さらに詳細に、(1)教育、訓練、就職、昇進等における事実上の不

---

[25] アファーマティブ・アクションを中心とした雇用平等立法の実施状況については、『諸外国のアファーマティブ・アクション法制』東京女性財団・平成8年の「第7章・イタリア」（松浦千誉教授執筆）、亀田利光「イタリアにおける男女平等のためのポジティブ・アクション（上）、（中）、（下）」大原社研雑誌453号1頁、454号23頁、455号21頁以下を参照。

[26] 「女性にたいするポジティブ・アクションの促進に関する理事会勧告」（84/635/EEC）

[27] 実例は、F. Sabbatucci, Contratti a confronto, Roma, 1988, pp. 231-236. 例えば、繊維産業の労働協約は次のように定めている。「協約当事者は、1984年12月13日のEEC勧告（635号）と男女の平等に関する立法を実施し、女性従業員のために積極的行動を推進することを目的として、研究と調査活動をおこなうことに合意する。

右に定めたところにより、当事者は、1987年内に作業グループを設置するものとする。作業グループは、実行可能性を確認し、女性従業員のための積極的行動案の大綱を定めることができる」。

平等の撤廃, (2)職業選択の多様化の促進, (3)性別により異なる結果をもたらす労働条件の廃止, (4)女性の少ない分野での参入推進を, 積極的行動の目的として掲げた（同2項）。しかし, この目的のためにどのような行為がなされるべきか, すなわち, アファーマティブ・アクションの内容については, とくに規定はおかれなかった。

立法の途中で, 形式的平等と実質的平等の関係, 差別と区別の違い, あるいは平等普遍と特殊性の関係など十分つめた論議がなされなかったこともあって, 積極的行動は, その実施にあたって, 実質的平等の意味だけでなく性差による違いの評価という難しい問題に直面することになった[28]。アファーマティブ・アクションは, 女性労働を男性労働に同化させることが目的なのではなく, 女性労働をそれとしてみとめ男性労働と同じ評価をすることが, その目的であると考えられていたからである。

1992年には女性企業家のためのアファーマティブ・アクション法が制定され, 女性企業（「女性が支配的に資本参加し運営している企業」で, 株式会社だと, 株式の3分の2以上が女性によって保育され, かつ, 取締役会の3分の2以上が女性で構成されている場合）にたいし, 特別の融資とか免税措置がとられることになった。

積極的行動法が予定するアファーマティブ・アクションの推進主体は種々で, 特別機関（平等委員会, 平等アドバイザー）, 企業（私的部門, 公的部門）, 労働組合, 職業訓練センターがあげられている（1条3項）。ここであげられている主体の列記は例示的なもので, アファーマティブ・アクションへの財政的援助を求めうる資格を示したものとして意味があるにとどまり, 行動主体を限定したものではない[29]。

実際には企業のおこなうアファーマティブ・アクションが重要であるので, 企業と最も代表的な労働組合が合意にもとづいておこなうものは, 助成措置をうける上で優先権がみとめられている（2条4項。実例は表2参照）[30]。労使

---

[28] このため, 伝統的に男性労働者のものとされてきた職種に女性労働者の参入を可能にするため, 女性労働者のために開かれた州の職業訓練コースが, 裁判所により差別で違法とされる等の事態が生じた（例えば, Pretura Genova, 4 giugno 1984）。

[29] 例えば, 1条3項で列記されていない, 経営内組合代表とか州雇用委員会がアファーマティブ・アクションをおこなっても, それは違法ではない。

イタリアにおける雇用平等の展開と現状

表2　1991年度に助成金を受けた企業

申請主体	アファーマティブ・アクション	交付金額(リラ)
ザヌッシ社―関連産業 (ポルデノーネ)	女性従業員のアウトプレイスメントを助成する提案	140,000,000
ザヌッシ社―関連産業 (ポルデノーネ)	女性従業員の職業上の地位を強化する提案	84,000,000
ザヌッシ社―本社と工場 (コネリアーノ・ベネト)	女性従業員の職業上の地位を強化する提案	40,000,000
ゼルトロン社 (カンポフォルミード)	女性従業員の職業上の地位の強化およびキャリアの発展のための提案	50,000,000
ロンバルディア銀行 (ベルガモ)	事業所内の平等委員会の構成員の企画能力の発展のための提案	35,000,000
イタルテル社 (ミラノ) [他に35社]	イタルテル社の公共事業実施地（ミラノ，ラクイラ他）における機会平等監督官設置の提案	550,000,000

出所：Comitato nazionale pari oppurtunità, Le opportunità crescono, Roma, 1993, p. 128 e seg.

の合意は種々のレベル（全国，地方，企業，事業所）でなされているが，ガイドラインやパイロット計画を定めているものが多い（表3参照）。イタリアでは，採用・昇進における「割当制」とか女性の優先雇用は反対意見が強い[31]。

公務部門ではもっと進んで，積極的行動法施行1年以内に，アファーマティブ・アクション計画を作らなければならない（同6項）。私的部門と違い，公務部門では労使の団体交渉によるアファーマティブ・アクションが期待さ

---

30) M. L. DeCristofaro (a cura di), Lavoro femminile e pari opportunità, Bari, 1989, p. 239 e seg. にも，イタルテル，エネルなどの企業における当時のアファーマティブ・アクションの例が紹介されている。

31) F. Carinci ed altri, Diritto del lavoro 2, Padova, 1998, p. 199.

32) 公務部門では，その後1993年2月3日に，行政組織の合理化と公務における規律の改正に関する法律命令（29号）がだされた。そこでは，人的資源管理のため，「公行政は，就職と待遇について男女の平等と平等な機会を保障する」と定め（7条1項），平等な機会を保障するため，「公行政は，……理由があって不可能な場合を除き，採用委員会の少なくとも3分の1は女性を委員に充てる」と定めた（61条1項）。

表3 労働協約に定めるアファーマティブ・アクションの例

協約	実施機関	内容
食品産業	全国労使合同委員会	① 食品産業における女性雇用の点検 ② 立法の展開の監視 ③ 伝統的でない職種への女性の参入の検討 ④ 出産後の復職支援 ⑤ セクハラの防止 ⑥ アファーマティブ・アクションの推進
繊維産業	平等機会作業グループ	積極的行動案の大綱提案
旅行・観光産業	平等機会労使合同グループ	① 旅行・観光産業における女性雇用の点検 ② 雇用平等における立法と実態の展開の監視 ③ アファーマティブ・アクション案の決定
金属産業	平等機会全国労使合同委員会	① 女性雇用状況の点検と職業訓練の提案 ② 出産後の復職支援 ③ 地域労使合同委員会へのアファーマティブ・アクションの指示 ④ 平等機会推進のための提案 ⑤ セクハラの防止 ⑥ 地域労使合同委員会の支援
	平等機会地域労使合同委員会	① 女性雇用の点検 ② 州と協力した職業訓練 ③ 出産後の復職支援 ④ アファーマティブ・アクションの提案 ⑤ セクハラの防止

出所：Memento pratico IPSOA, Lavoro, 1997, pp. 788-789

れず，実質的な雇用平等も思ったほど進んでいないため，とくにこのような義務が当局に課されたのだといわれている[32)33)]。

7 平等委員会と平等アドバイザー

雇用平等法の欠陥は，平等実現の制度的な担保が十分でなかったことであった。この点についての反省から，積極的行動法は，行政および司法の両

---

33) 1999年3月初旬，イタリア政府は，議員など公職における男女平等を促進する憲法改正案を提出することを閣議で了承した。国会が承認すれば，女性議員の数や割合を規定することが可能になる。

表4 平等推進機関の権限

機関	権限	1991年法との関係
平等アドバイザー 1）一般	a）積極的行動の推進	1条3項
	b）裁判所への報告義務	8条6項
	c）公共団体の積極的行動案にたいする所見	2条6項
	d）調停の仲介	4条4項
	e）職業紹介についての権限	8条6項
	f）労働監督署への情報請求	8条7項
	g）雇用平等の実現に有益な事柄の提案	8条7項
2）州	a）訴えの提起	4条6項
	b）企業の隔年報告の提出先	9条2項
	c）報告不提出の際の労働監督署への通知	9条4項
3）州および県	a）女性労働者の訴えへの関与	8条8項
	b）女性労働者の委任による訴えの提起	8条8項
	c）地方公共団体の平等機関の構成員となること	8条6項
平等委員会	a）積極的行動の採択と推進	1条3項と6条1項c号
	b）雇用平等立法の適用状況の確認	6条1項f号
	c）集団紛争の解決案の提示	6条1項g号
	d）所見の編さん	2条6項および6条1項d号
	e）行動規範の作成	6条1項e号
	f）平等機会の目標達成の確認	3条2項
	g）社会への情報提供活動	6条1項b号

出所：Memento pratico IPSOA, Lavoro, 1997, p. 788

面で特別の配慮をした。

行政面でのそれは，全国平等委員会と平等アドバイザーという雇用平等推進のための特別機関の権限を拡充したことである（表4参照）[34]。全国平等委員会（Comitato nazionale della parità）は1983年に設置されたものであるが，従来法律等の提案権，情報請求権，ガイドラインの作成権などがみとめられていただけであったのにたいし，積極的行動法は，新しくアファーマティブ・アクションの提案権，財政的支援（助成）の勧告権，実施状況の監督権を

34）司法面については次節参照。
35）従来の権限で縮小されたものもあった。女性労働者への助言権は平等アドバイザーの権限に移され，差別行為についての調査権は，労働監督署への情報請求権に変わった。

権限に付加した（6条)[35]。この委員会はもともとアメリカやイギリスの雇用平等委員会（Equal employment opportunity commission）を参考に作られたものであるが，イタリアの場合，その役割は提案，諮問的なものが中心で，それほど強い権限はもっていない。

これにたいし，平等アドバイザー（Consigliere di parità）は1984年にできた制度であるが，その権限が強化された。積極的行動法は，平等アドバイザーに州雇用委員会の正式の委員としての地位を与えるとともに，集団的な差別行為についての固有の提訴権（4条6項）と女性労働者の委任にもとづく提訴権（8条8項）をみとめた。この提訴権を全国平等委員会でなく平等アドバイザーにみとめたことについては批判もあるが[36]，差別行為についての提訴権を女性労働者個人にしかみとめなかった雇用平等法と比較すると，大きな改善である。

8　訴訟と立証責任

雇用平等法は差別行為を無効とし，これについての提訴権を被差別労働者（個人）にみとめた（同13条，労働者憲章法15条，16条）。それだけでなく，差別行為にたいする差止請求や原状回復の途もひらかれた（雇用平等法15条1項）。この結果，例えば，採用で差別がなされると，裁判所はその採用行為の無効を宣言することもできるし，被差別労働者の採用を命じることもできるよう

---

36) 委員会の方が公平性や処理能力が大きいという批判である。しかし，そうであるかどうかは保障がなく，委員会が全国で一つなのにたいし，平等アドバイザーは各県におかれているところからみると，積極的行動法の選択は正しいとする意見も多い。平等アドバイザーの問題点は，その行動がばらばらで，平等委員会との結びつきが弱く，行動の調整のしくみがないことである。

37) とはいっても，これは，採用差別がおこなわれ，誰れも採用されなかったという事案についてのことである。採用差別がおこなわれ，Aグループは採用されたがBグループは採用されなかったという場合，採用の無効確認は可能だが，Bグループの採用命令がだせるか否かは争われている。多数説は，これを肯定すると，裁判官に労働者の採用権を与えるのと同じになるとして，消極に解している。この点につき，M. V. Ballestrero, Dalla tutela alla parità, Bologna, 1979, p. 175。立法論としては，この場合も集団差別訴訟にならない，裁判所が時間をかぎって段階的に差別状態を改善する是正命令をだせるようにすべきだ，といわれている。

になった[37]。しかし，このような救済はあくまでも労働者個人の提訴を前提とし，範囲も就職での差別と深夜業での差別に限定されているので[38]，その影響はかぎられたものであった。

　積極的行動法は，この点で三つの改革をしている。その一は，訴えの提起について機関訴訟（azione istituzionale）をみとめ，集団的差別について，平等アドバイザーに提訴権を与えたことである（4条6項）。これは，平等アドバイザー固有の提訴権である[39]。イタリアでは，女性の社会運動団体で決定的に代表的なものはないので，他の国々にみられる集団代表訴訟でなく，このような方式が選択された。

　その二は，上記の訴訟において，裁判所が期限をかぎって是正計画（un piano di rimozione delle discriminazioni——集団的差別の効果を除去する計画）を作ることを命じられるようにしたことである（4条7項）。是正計画はアファーマティブ・アクションと似ているが，アファーマティブ・アクションの目的は実質的な雇用平等の実現を妨げている障害をとりのぞくことで，対象となるのはなにも使用者の違法な行為にかぎられない。是正計画の作成は，あくまで使用者の集団的差別にたいするものである。しかし，他方，是正計画の作成は，一定期間内に差別を解消するために必要な措置をとることを義務づけられる点で，たんなる無効確認判決とも異なっている。例えば，特定職種で採用もしくは昇進について集団差別があったとすると，差別と認定された男女の不釣合いがなくなるまで，使用者は計画的にこれをなくする是正行為を継続していかなければならない。この点では，是正計画はアファーマティブ・アクションに似ているといえる。

　その三は立証責任で，原告が差別を推定させる事実を提出すれば，差別の不存在について被告が立証責任を負うとされたことである（4条5項）。いわゆる立証責任の転換である。統計等によって採用，配置・昇進，賃金，配転，解雇等について男女間の不均衡が明らかにされれば，差別の推定が働くので，被差別労働者（原告）の立証の負担はかなり軽減されるであろう。

---

38) 雇用平等法15条1項は，差止命令と原状回復の対象を1条（就職）と5条（深夜業の禁止）に限定している。

39) 個別的差別の場合，被差別労働者の委任にもとづいて平等アドバイザーは提訴権をもつことになる。

9　現状と課題

　積極的行動法は，雇用平等法の欠陥をおぎない実質的平等を推進させるために制定されたものであったから，その実施には多くの期待がよせられていた。議会もこの法律の実施には特別の関心をもち，1995年春に，上院の第11常任委員会（労働・社会保障所管）が調査をおこなった[40]。この調査報告でみるかぎり，およそ実情は次のようである——，

　(1)　積極的行動　　イタルテル，ザヌッシ，エネル等熱心な企業もないではないが，一般的にいって最初の熱情はうすれてきている。提出される案，承認される案とも件数がへってきているし，内容も研修とか教育訓練が中心で，資格，格づけ等労働組織を再編成するものは少ない。案の提出から承認までに1年半以上もかかっている。実際の助成金の交付にはさらに時間がかかっている。

　(2)　平等推進機関　　平等委員会は，①提案権（積極的行動法1条3項，6条1項a，c，e，g号），②諮問権（2条2項，5項，6項），③監督権（6条1項d，f，h号），④広報権（6条1項b号）と広い権限をもっているが，他の機関と権限が重複あるいは対立している点の調整がはかられておらず，実際の活動の障害になっている。平等委員会がこれまで主としておこなってきたのは，調査研究（とくに法律の解釈的研究と普及）である。独自の執行機関をもっていないので，監督権についてはなにもできていない。

　平等アドバイザーの方はもっと問題が大きい。平等アドバイザーは，司法警察権とか提訴権とか平等委員会より強い権限を与えられているのに，行政の無理解・無関心のため任命が遅れている。アブルッツォ，エミーリア・ロマーニア，ラツィオ，ウンブリア，カンパーニア，カラーブリア，サルデー

---

[40] 「労働における男女の平等を実現するための積極的行動に関する1991年4月10日法（125号）の（未）実施状況について」という調査（RIDL, 1996, III, 115）で，報告は9月26日の会議で承認された。データは全国的に集められ，ミラノ（3月1日），フィレンツェ（5月15日），ナポリ（5月22日）ではヒアリングがなされている。なお，平等委員会も，1993年6月に会議を開いて報告書を公けにしている（Comitato nazionale pari opportunità, Le opportunità crescono, Roma, 1993）。しかし，これは制定後間もない時期のものであるため，実施状況を判断するのには適切でない。

ニアでは、州の平等アドバイザーが任命されていない。県の平等アドバイザーは、上記の七州のほか、プーリアとマルケでも任命されていない。さらにもっと悲劇なのは、活動に必要な基盤整備がなにもできていないことである。与えられるのは一切合財で2万6000リラ〔＝1500円位〕の謝金だけで、活動費はおろか交通費もでず、部屋、机、電話、補助者も提供されない。こういう状態では活動などとても不可能だし、労働者が平等アドバイザーに相談にいこうとしても、誰れがアドバイザーでどこにいるのかわからない。

平等推進機関の現状は、積極的行動法にたいする事実上の反逆である。

(3) 訴訟　もともと雇用平等法でも訴訟（同15条）は少なかったが、積極的行動法による訴訟（同4条。平等アドバイザーの関与）はもっと少ない。直接裁判所に照会したところでは、フィレンツェ、ナポリが0件、ミラノが10件以下という回答であった。また、平等アドバイザーは訴訟に関与する権限と義務があるのに、訟務局の利用が許されていない（たてまえとしては許可があれば利用可能だが、公共部門で訴訟がおきる可能性があるので、実際には政府は許可していない）。訴訟という点では、積極的行動法の現状は極度に失望的である。

(4) 雇用状況報告　100人以上の従業員を雇用する事業所では、使用者は、2年に一度従業員の雇用状況を報告しなければならないが（9条）、これも一度も実施されていない。というのは、イタリア工業使用者連盟（Confindustria）と銀行協会（Assicrediti）傘下の事業主が、報告書の様式について異議を申立て行政訴訟を提起した（現在も係属中）ので、労働省は1992-93年度の報告期限を無期延期したからである。これでは、女性の雇用の促進といってもなんの手がかりもない。

(5) 財政　積極的行動法の実施のための予算は年100億リラで、10億リラが平等推進機関の行政経費、90億リラがアファーマティブ・アクションの助成費用となっている（11条）。しかし、10億リラはあまりに少ないし（公共部門の争議権の行使に関与する「保証委員会」の予算は2倍以上である）、平等アドバイザーへの割当分が明記されていない点も問題である。

(6) 起業援助法　積極的行動法の目標達成を支援するため、1992年に女性起業援助法が制定されたが、この法律も機能していない。予算措置がなされたのは漸く1995年になってからであり、施行細則なども厳格になりすぎて

いる。

　このような結果，いぜんとして女性の雇用はかぎられた職種に集中しており，相対的に低い格づけがなされ，賃金が低い（男性労働者より20～30％低い）という状況はあまり変わっていない。したがって，積極的行動法の役割は以前にもまして重要であるというのが，調査報告の強調するところである。

　そこで，今後の雇用平等の推進のため，調査報告は，以下の点を緊急提言としてまとめている——，

(1) 雇用状況報告　　様式を簡略化し，従業員規模40人あるいは50人以上のところを対象として，早急に実施すべきである。労働省は当事者間の対立を調整せよ。

(2) アドバイザー・ネットの完成　　年内に，すべての州および県のすべてのレベルで平等アドバイザーを任命すること。実行されないときは，政府が代って任命できるようにせよ。

(3) 平等アドバイザーの支援　　職務遂行に必要な施設，手段，用具を提供すべきである。ことに，州平等アドバイザーには予算に左右されないで使える事務所，机，電話，秘書等を供与し，「駆けこみ寺」の役割をはたさせるべきである。

(4) 訴訟にたいする法律扶助　　雇用平等のための訴訟はあまりに少ない。委任によるか職権によるかを問わず，平等アドバイザーが関与する訴訟には法律扶助を与えるべきである。必要であれば，そのために特別の基金を作るようにせよ。

(5) アファーマティブ・アクションの完全実施　　初期の熱情がうすれ，各種の助成金が有効に使われていない。アファーマティブ・アクションの助成金を完全消化せよ。利用の状態だけでなく不利用の理由も調査し，完全実施ができないときは，政府だけでなく州の責任も明確にすべきである。

(6) 機関と権限の再編成　　平等委員会の監督権限の十分な行使を可能にするため，専門事務局と審査会を強化すること。さらに，雇用状況，法の実施，不平等の除去のための「観視所」（Osservatorio）を全国と州レベルで設置すること。この機関は訴訟や紛争のフォローや分析もおこなう。

(7) 平等委員会の機能強化　　平等委員会は平等推進機関の地域ネットの核になるようにせよ。これが地域の中心となって，平等アドバイザーの定期

的な会合，経験交流，活動の共通目標の設定などをおこなう。
　(8)　権限調整　　労働省と重複または対立する他の公共機関の権限を廃止し，雇用平等関係のすべての所策を労働省に一元化せよ。

　以上に指摘された問題がどう動いていき，現状がどうなっているのかを知る資料はないが，問題の完全決着までにはまだかなりの時間が必要であろう。これまでみてきたイタリアの例は，少なくとも雇用平等は差別禁止の実体法規だけでは不十分で，訴訟のための手続規定，行政のための機構と手続，当事者の努力の支援措置など幅広い政策が必要であり，ある程度政策手段が整っても，実質的な雇用平等の進捗には多大の努力と時間を要することを教えている。

健康配慮義務に関する一考察

渡 辺 　 章

はじめに

　今日までのところ，労働者の健康保障法理は，事業者等に対する，労働安全衛生法規による労働者の生命，健康への危害防止の義務づけ，および労働契約上の信義則に基づく安全配慮義務または不法行為法上の注意義務等により形成されてきており，労働者の事業者（使用者）に対する「健康への権利の保障」の法理，あるいは「健康障害と労務提供義務との調整」の法理の形成という観点からの積極的な法理論構成はなされていない（この点に関する先駆的な考察として片岡昇「労働者の健康権」季刊労働法124号12頁以下，1982がある）。本稿もまた，事業主の労働災害防止義務・安全配慮義務および使用者の健康障害防止義務・健康配慮義務の側面から労働契約における労働者の健康にかかわる若干の問題を考察するものである。

1　安全配慮義務の意義および基本的性質について

　(1)　最高裁判決（川義事件）は，労働契約においては「通常の場合，労働者は，使用者の指定した場所に配置され，使用者の供給する設備，器具等を用いて労務の提供を行うものである」とのべて，使用者は，報酬支払義務にとどまらず，「労働者が労務提供のため設置する場所，設備もしくは器具等を使用し又は使用者の指示のもとに労務を提供する過程において，労働者の生命及び身体等を危険から保護するよう配慮すべき義務（以下「安全配慮医務」という）を負っている」と判示した[1]。最高裁判所が国家公務員（自衛隊員）の公務上の死亡災害に係る事件において安全配慮義務の法理を最初に明

らかにした判決（自衛隊八戸車両整備工場事件）では，「国は，公務員に対し，国が公務遂行のために設置すべき場所，施設もしくは器具等の設置管理又は公務員が国もしくは上司の指示のもとに遂行する公務の管理にあたって，公務員の生命及び健康等を危険から保護するよう配慮すべき義務（以下「安全配慮義務」という。）を負っている」とのべている[2]。

　安全配慮義務は労働契約上の信義則を法的根拠にしているが，その実質的根拠は，右に見たように使用者による労働場所の「指定」，設備・器具の「供給」，労務提供過程での「指示・管理」にある。したがって使用者に安全配慮義務違反があるといいうるためには，右のような「指定」，「供給」または「指示・管理」のいずれかの面（不作為も含めて）に，労働者の生命，健康に対する危険が内在し，それが顕在化したものといえなければならないであろう[3]。本稿では，このような危険が現実のものとなって労働者の生命，健康に具体的危険（被害）を及ぼすことを「業務要因性」ということにする。

---

1)　最三小判昭和59・4・10民集38巻6号557頁。本件は，宿直勤務中夜間の侵入者（盗賊）により刺殺された労働者の父母による損害賠償請求事件。判旨は，安全配慮義務の具体的内容として①宿直設備・施設の整備，②それが困難であるときは宿直員を増員するとか，③安全教育を十分に行うなどし，「物的施設と相まって労働者……の生命，身体に危険の及ばないように配慮する義務があった」と指摘している。

2)　最三小判昭和50・2・25民集29巻2号143頁。本件は，車両整備工場で就業中後進する大型自動車に轢かれて死亡した自衛隊員の父母による国に対する損害賠償請求事件。判決は，原審の破棄差し戻し判決のため当該状況における安全配慮義務の具体的内容について指摘はない。安全配慮義務は下請社外工労働者と元請負会社との関係においても認められている（鹿島建設・大石塗装事件・最一小判昭和55・12・18民集34巻7号888頁，三菱重工業事件・最一小判平成3・64・11労判590号14頁）。

　　なお，前記川義事件の「労働者が……使用者の指示のもとに労務を提供する過程において……」の判示部分は，本件（陸上自衛隊八戸車両整備工場事件）では「公務員が国もしくは上司の指示のもとに遂行する公務の管理にあたって……」とされている。安全配慮義務の「具体的内容」も同じであり，川義事件判旨は「労働者の職種，労務内容，労務提供場所等安全配慮義務が問題になる当該具体的状況等によって異なるべきもの」といい，本件（自衛隊八戸車両整備工場事件）は，「公務員の職種，地位及び安全配慮義務が問題となる当該具体的状況等によって異なる」といい，ことばの上の違いに過ぎない。

3)　川義事件において安全配慮義務の具体的内容として指摘されている宿直員の増員，十分な安全教育の実施（前注参照）は，本文にいう使用者の労務提供過程における「指示・管理」の問題である。

これは，労働災害補償給付に関する負傷・疾病等の業務上外の因果律の判定に係る「業務起因性」と敢えて区別する趣旨である[4]。

(2) 以上のべた安全配慮義務に対し，労働安全衛生法等の法令に基づいて事業者に義務づけられている労働者の生命，健康に対する危害防止義務を「労働災害防止義務」ということができよう。そして，労働災害防止義務を安全配慮義務の最低限度の内容をなすものと解することが可能であり，かつ妥当と解する。

(3) ところで，前記自衛隊八戸車両整備工場事件判決は，安全配慮義務の性質，内容および法的根拠に関する判示部分に続けて，「国が，不法行為規範のもとにおいて私人に対しその生命，健康等を保護すべき義務を負っているほかは，いかなる場合においても公務員に対し安全配慮義務を負うものではないと解すべきではない。」とのべて，使用者（国）は労働者（公務員）の生命，健康を保護すべき義務を不法行為規範および労働契約規範の双方により負うものであることを示唆している。

前言したように，使用者に安全配慮義務違反の債務不履行があるといえるためには，労働場所の「指定」，設備・器具の「供給」または労務提供過程における「指示・管理」のいずれかに，労働者の生命，健康への危険が内在し，それが顕在化したものと認められる必要があり，それが肯定される場合に，労働者の受けた生命，健康への被害は業務要因性に基づくものとして，労働契約上の信義則を根拠に，使用者に損害賠償責任を負担せしめうるものである。

これに対して，本稿で検討する健康配慮義務は，安全配慮義務と異なり，健康配慮義務とされているものの具体的内容または右の義務違反が問題になる具体的状況により，労働契約規範または不法行為規範のいずれかの性質を

---

[4]　「業務要因性」の用語をあてたのは，労災補償給付における業務起因性判断の「間接事実による推定の可否」に関して，「業務の加重性のアプローチ」のほかに，「使用者の義務違反からのアプローチ」（労基法違反，適正労働条件措置義務，健康管理義務，適正労働配置，看護・治療義務違反の存在）にまで拡大すべきであるとの見解があるが，そのような主張は事実的因果関係の論題に労働災害民事訴訟の手法（主観的義務違反に対する問責）を無限定に取り込むものだとの批判があることを考慮したためである（中嶋士元也「職業性循環器系疾患死の因果関係論」上智法学論集42巻3・4号合併号65-68頁，1999）。

有する義務と解される。

2 健康配慮義務の意義および基本的性質について

(1) 労働安全衛生法は，周知のように，労働災害防止義務のほかに労働者の生命，健康にかかわる規定として「健康の保持増進のための措置」（第7章65条～71条），「快適な職場環境の形成のための措置」（第8章71条の2～71条の4）の2章をおいている。後者（第8章）は暫く措き，健康の保持増進措置に関する諸規定により事業者に課せられている義務を「健康障害防止義務」ということができる。健康障害防止義務は，このように法令に基づく事業者の義務である。他方事業者は，私法上，労働者に対し健康の保持増進義務を負うと考えられるが，この義務を「健康配慮義務」ということができる。そして，労働災害防止義務と安全配慮義務との関係と同様に，法令で定める健康障害防止義務は健康配慮義務の最低限度の内容をなすものと解することが可能であり，かつ妥当と解する。

そこで，健康配慮義務の具体的内容を，さしあたって労働安全衛生法（第7章）所定の健康障害防止義務を手がかりに検討してみると，具体的措置義務の内容により，①業務要因性のある危険からの労働者の保護と，②直接業務要因性のない・労働者の肉体的，精神的素因ないし基礎疾病の発症，増悪の防止を含む健康自体の保護との，二つの性質の異なる保護目的が併存しているといえる。健康配慮義務の具体的内容が①の業務要因性のある危険からの保護を目的にしている場合は，右義務は第1節にのべた安全配慮義務と同様の意義，性質および効力の義務であり，健康配慮義務も安全配慮義務もことばの違いにすぎない。

健康配慮義務を安全配慮義務と法概念上区別する意義があるのは，②のように業務上の要因に直接かかわりのない，労働者の健康自体の保護のために事業者に課せられる措置義務ないし配慮義務をいう場合である。すなわち，安全配慮義務と健康配慮義務とはそれぞれ保護領域の差異に着目した区別が可能であり，そうした区別をすべきものであろう[5]。

(2) (a) そこで，労働安全衛生法に定められている事業者の健康の保持増進措置（労働者の健康障害防止措置）を，保護領域の違いに応じて安全配慮義

務および健康配慮義務に区別してみるとつぎのようになろう（行政官庁の措置規定および事業者の努力義務規定を除く）。

　㋐　安全配慮義務の内容になるべき健康障害防止措置

　　作業環境の測定・記録・結果の評価に基づく適切な措置（65条，65条の2）

　　健康障害のおそれのある一定の有害業務の作業時間の制限（65条の4）

　　一定の有害業務従事者に対する健康診断の実施（66条2項）

　　一定の有害業務従事者に対する歯科医師の健康診断の実施（66条3項）

　　都道府県労働基準局長の指示に基づく臨時健康診断の実施（66条4項）

　㋑　安全配慮義務または健康配慮義務のいずれかの内容になる健康障害防止措置

---

5)　本節(1)に掲げた片岡教授の論文では，「安衛法は結果的に労働者の健康診断を受診する権利を承認したことになるわけであるが，厳密にいえばそれは労働契約上の安全（健康）配慮義務を媒介して得られる結論であって，安衛法自体がそうした労働者の権利を直接承認しているわけではない。」とのべて両義務を同質のものとされておられる（15頁）。安西愈「企業の健康配慮義務と労働者の自己保健義務」（季刊労働法124号，1982）は，健康配慮義務の概念を，「『安全配慮義務』について健康管理面に限っていえば『健康配慮義務』ともいえるもの」とされ，同趣旨の裁判例をいくつかあげておられる（19頁，24頁）。同弁護士は，このような健康配慮義務が「労働契約の付随義務として問題とされるようになってきた。」とされ，その内容を，「性質上使用者の支配従属下において業務に従事中における，(1)当該職場の有害環境・有害要因・有害作業等，(2)使用者の指揮命令に基づく具体的な業務の遂行等，(3)企業内の組織的集団的共同生活関係，に起因して発生する労働者の健康障害」を問題とするものとされる。その法的根拠は，「人的な支配管理権限に内在する信義則」にあるとされている。要するに，基本的実質は安全配慮義務と異なるものでなく，具体的内容に多少の違いが認められるものである。諏訪康雄「職業病の総合精密検診は業務命令で強制することができるか――帯広電報電話局控訴事件」（判例時報1123号，1984）は，健康配慮義務は「安全配慮義務の下位概念」とし，「業務に起因する疾病を防止し，または，それが生じた場合にその増悪・拡大を防止するために，適切かつ具体的な措置をとることによって，労働者の健康が業務上の危険から保護されるよう配慮すべき義務」とされている（217頁）。この見解によれば健康配慮義務は，「業務に起因する疾病」からの労働者の保護を意味しているようである。岩出誠「従業員の健康管理をめぐる法的諸問題」（日本労働研究雑誌441号，1997）は，安全配慮義務と健康配慮義務との「具体的義務内容の重複性に照らし，両者の内容の総体を一括して，健康配慮義務と総称しておく。」とされ，健康配慮義務に固有の概念は問題にしておられない（13頁）。

労働者の健康に配慮した作業の適切な管理（65条の3）
海外勤務従事者に対する特別健康診断の実施（労安衛則45条の2）
事業者の健康診断の記録保存（66条6項）
健康診断の結果についての医師等からの意見聴取（66条の2）
健康診断実施後の労働者の実情を考慮した就業場所の転換その他の措置（66条の3）

(ｳ)　健康配慮義務の内容になる健康障害防止措置

雇入時および定期の一般健康診断の実施（66条1項）
結核の発病のおそれがあると診断された労働者に対する健康診断の実施（労安衛則46条）
給食の業務に従事する労働者に対する検便（労安衛則47条）
一般健康診断の労働者への通知（66条の4）
一般健康診断の結果に基づく保健指導（66条の5）
特定の疾病罹患者に対する就業禁止（68条）

(b)　筆者がこのように健康配慮義務を保護目的の性質により安全配慮義務と区別することが可能であり，かつ妥当と考えるのは，人は他人と接触するどのような場においても（私的生活の場か公的生活の場かを問わない），一定の，その場にふさわしい注意義務を負うべきものとの平凡な法常識を前提にしている。労働者は労務提供義務を履行するのであり，労務提供者にふさわしい健康を保持することは，労務提供義務をその債務の本旨にしたがって履行するための私的生活関係における自身の注意事項と考えられる。この場合，労働者自身の素因や基礎疾病が，①業務の客観的に危険な属性（使用者による労務提供場所の「指定」，施設等の「供給」，労務提供過程における「指示・管理」）のほか，②業務の量的，質的な「過重性の介在」によってその自然の経過を超えて発症・増悪したと認められる場合は，まさしく労働災害防止義務ないし安全配慮義務の違反の有無の問題である。(ｱ)に掲げる健康障害防止措置はこうした業務要因性に対応している。

(ｲ)に掲げる健康障害防止措置は，労務を現実に提供している労働者の既存の健康障害の状態には業務要因性のある負傷・疾病の場合と，本人の素因ないし基礎疾病による場合（敢えて表現するとすれば自己要因性の負傷・疾病）とがあり，当該健康障害防止措置は前者については安全配慮義務の問題となり，

2 健康配慮義務の意義および基本的性質について

後者については健康配慮義務の問題になると考えられるものである。

しかし，(ウ)に掲げられるような事業者の健康障害防止措置はそれ自体としては，労働者自身の健康に対する注意ないし自己管理に事業者が積極的に協力するよう義務づけられたものと解することができるのであり，その違反は・労・働・関・係・の・場・に・ふ・さ・わ・し・い・内・容・の不法行為法上の注意義務違反の問題として検討されるべき性質のものと解する。

(c) 安全配慮義務と健康配慮義務との法的根拠を，以上のように，前者は労働契約上の信義則に求め，後者は不法行為法上の注意義務に求めて区別するとしても，義務違反の内容の特定と義務違反に該当する事実の主張・立証は，原告の側にあることに変わりない（参照航空自衛隊芦屋分遣隊事件・最二小判昭和56・2・16民集35巻1号56頁）。しかし，両構成には時効，遺族固有の慰謝料，遅延損害金の起算点等の点で重要な違いは残されており[6]，両義務の法的性質を区別しておくことは依然有意味であると考える[7]。

---

6) 菅野和夫『労働法・第五版』374～375頁，1999。
7) 事業者が労働者の健康の保持増進に必要な注意義務を尽くす上で不可欠の要請は，事業者が労働者の健康に関し的確な情報を得ることである。そこで，事業者による労働者の健康情報の把握，管理，本人への通知および対応措置に関連するいくつかの裁判例から健康配慮義務の法的構成をみておく。

  (a) 健康診断実施義務違反

  (ア) 健康診断を実施せず，健康診断個人票も作成されていない状態で重篤な高血圧症の教職員（亡Ａ）が責任の重い数々の業務を同時期に行い，業務中脳内出血死した事例（真美学園事件・岡山地判平成6・12・20労働判例672号42頁）。判旨は，使用者は「雇用契約関係の付帯義務として，信義則上，健康診断やその結果に基づく事後措置等により，その健康状態を把握し，その健康保持のために適切な措置をとるなどして，その健康管理に関する安全配慮義務を負う」として損害賠償請求を一部認容した。他方，「本来他人には即座に計り知れ難い領域を含む健康管理は第一義的には労働者本人においてなすべき筋合いのもの」と判示し，亡Ａの過失を4分の3として過失相殺をした。

  (イ) 雇入前に実施した健康診断により労働者が肺結核に罹患していることを知りながら本人に通知せず，タクシー運転に約八カ月間就労させて病状を著しく増悪させ長期療養のやむなきに至らせた事例（京和タクシー事件・京都地判昭和57・10・7労判404号72頁）。判旨は，「被告会社は，原告を雇用したことに伴って労働者である同人の健康を保持し健康に異常の疑いがある場合には早期にその状態を確認して就労可能性の有無，程度を見極め異状が発見されたときは医師の指示に従って就労を禁止するか適当な軽作業に就かせもって健康状態が悪化しないように注意すべき義務があった」

としたが，慰謝料請求を大幅に縮減して一部認容するに際し「健康管理の最大の責任者は原告自身であって，……すべてを使用者に負わせるのは相当でない」としている。

(ｱ)事件は「安全配慮義務」違反と明言し，(ｲ)事件はそのような明言は避けている。両事件とも，前言したように，健康配慮義務違反の事例であり，不法行為法上の注意義務の問題として取り扱われるべき事案であったということができる。

(b) 業務上の傷病による療養休業の後復職した労働者の健康管理

(ｱ) 労働災害により重い傷害を負って約1ヵ月半の療養後，原職に復職し，宿直勤務中急性心不全により死亡した事例（石川島興業事件・神戸地姫路支判平成7・7・31労判688号59頁）。判旨は，亡Aが復職後に従事した業務は作業量，作業内容，作業時間（時間外労働，休日労働，深夜労働，宿日直労働を含む）の点において療養休業後の亡Aの健康状態にそぐわないものであったとし，使用者は雇用契約に付随する安全配慮義務に基づき「労働者が現に健康を害し，そのため当該業務にそのまま従事するときには，健康を保持する上で問題があり，もしくは健康を悪化させるおそれがあると認められるときは，速やかに労働者を当該業務から離脱させて休養させるか，他の業務に配転させるなどの措置を執る契約上の義務を負うものというべきであり，それは労働者からの申し出の有無に関係なく，使用者に課せられる性質のもの」として，損害賠償請求を認容した（過失相殺なし）。

(ｲ) 自閉症児の生活相談員（女性）が腰痛により約2ヵ月半の欠勤（第一次長期欠勤）の後原職に復帰し，さらに腰痛を悪化させ約10ヵ月余第二次長期欠勤を余儀なくされたとして損害賠償を請求した事例（大阪府立中宮病院松心園事件・大阪地判昭和55・2・18労判338号57頁）。判旨は，被告は「腰痛症などその業務から発生し易い疾病にかからぬよう適切な人員の配置，充分な休憩時間の設定・労働時間の短縮など労働条件の整備，疲労防止のための施設の整備などの職場環境の改善，準備体操・スポーツ・姿勢指導など職業病予防のための教育，定期健康診断，特殊検診などの健康管理を行い，職業病の予防・早期発見に努めるとともに，申告，診断などによりこれを発見したときは，就業制限，早期治療を行って病状の悪化を防ぎ，その健康回復に必要な措置を講ずる義務（安全配慮義務）を負っている」とし，原告が第一次欠勤後原職に復帰したのは被告の園長が原告の希望を受け入れ，業務内容について格別の指示を与えなかったことから，原告が第一次欠勤の原因となった患児の療養業務に就いた以上，「再発しないように適宜の措置をとるべき義務」を有しているところ，被告は右義務を尽くさなかったとして請求を認容した（原告が第二次欠勤の原因となった腰痛症，頸肩腕症候群に関し専門医の診察を受けていないことを主な理由に過失相殺を5割とした）。

(ｳ) 本態性高血圧症，心拡張症状の基礎疾病のある労働者が銀行オンラインシステムのプロジェクトリーダーとして稼働していたところ自宅で脳幹部出血死した事例（システム・コンサルタント事件・東京地判平成10・3・19判時1641号54頁）。判旨は，使用者は安全配慮義務を負い，その具体的内容として「労働時間，休憩時間，休日，休憩場所等について適正な労働条件を確保し，さらに，健康診断を実施した上，労働者の年齢，健康状態に応じて従事する作業時間及び内容の軽減，就労場所の変更等適

切な措置を採るべき義務」を負う，とした。亡Aは入社以来恒常的に相当程度過大な長時間労働に従事し，特に死亡前3ヵ月は月間300時間程度労働し「著しく過大」であり，被告は定期健康診断の結果により亡Aの高血圧症が相当増悪していたことを認識していたにもかかわらず，業務軽減措置等をとらなかったものであるとして請求を認容した。

(ア)事件は，特に，使用者は労働者の健康情報（健康状態）の把握と適正に処遇する義務を「本人の申し出の有無に関係なく」負うとしている点が注目され，(イ)事件は健康障害防止措置を含む義務内容の範囲の広さが注目される。しかし，これらの義務は，一般的健康障害防止義務を安全配慮義務に取り込んで判示したものと解すべきではなく，いずれも業務上の傷病・疾病に罹患した後の就労という特殊事情によって安全配慮義務の具体的内容とされたものと解される。(ウ)事件は，本人に素因ないし基礎疾病がある場合であり，したがって健康診断の実施およびその結果の評価に基づく適正な措置義務は，本来的には，健康配慮義務の問題であるというべきであるが，特に，「業務の過重性」の介在により，安全配慮義務の具体的内容に取り込まれたものと解される。

(c) 危険な体質・素因をもつ労働者と使用者の健康配慮義務

冠動脈硬化症ひいては急性心筋梗塞にかかる素因を有していた労働者が自宅で急性心筋梗塞で死亡した事例（住友林業事件・名古屋地判昭和56・9・30労働判例378号64頁）。判旨は，その死亡は過重な業務（安全配慮義務違反）によるものであるとの理由で亡Aの妻（原告）が会社に対してした損害賠償請求に関し，亡Aの死亡前約6ヵ月以前の勤務状況は「健康な者に対するものであれば特に苛酷，過重なものとはいいがたいが，右の如き危険な体質，要因を持つ者（亡A・引用者）に対する労務指揮としては過重な負担を課するもの」であり，「被告の右労務指揮は，亡Aの生命及び健康を確保するにつき配慮義務を十分に履行しなかった不完全履行に当たる」とした。判旨は，しかし，亡Aの死の結果を予見することは不可能であったとの被告の免責の抗弁を容れ，①亡Aは肉体的，精神的疲労故に休暇を上司に申し出ていなかったこと，②原告の妻も異常を知らず治療を強くすすめていなかったこと，③死亡した年の6年前から会社の実施した健康診断を受診していなかったこと，④会社は当初の健康診断の指定日以外でも受診できるように代替日を指定することにより便宜をはかったが強制する方法はとっていなかったこと，⑤強制的に亡Aに健康診断を受けさせる義務があったと認めることはできないこと，等の事情を指摘し原告の請求を棄却した。判旨は，労働者は「本来自己の体調や異常や健康障害の兆は，特段の事情がない限り，自己が気付くものであり，これに基づいて本人自らが健康管理の配慮をするもの」との見地を基礎にしている。

本件は，一応業務の過重性が認められたものの，主観的程度（危険な体質，要因を持つ者に対する労務指揮としては過重な負担を課するもの）にとどまるものとされたため，判旨は有責性の判断にあたり，会社は通常の健康状態の労働者に対する健康配慮義務の履行により損害賠償責任を免れるものとしたと解される。

3　健康診断をめぐる問題

(1)　事業者が労働安全衛生法の定めにしたがい行う健康診断（66条～66条の4）は，事業者が労働者の健康情報を得る手段として，また労働者に就業上の指示・管理を的確に行うための基本資料を得る手段として重要な意義を有する。

事業者が被用者に対し行う健康診断に関しては，つぎのような最高裁判決がある（津山税務職員事件・最一小判昭和57・4・1民集36巻4号519頁。原審破棄差戻）。事案は，国家公務員法73条1項2号（旧人事院規則10-1「職員の健康診断」，同10-1-1「職員の健康診断に関する細則」）に基づき，津山税務署長が岡山県の林野保健所に委嘱して税務職員の定期健康診断を実施し，被上告人は同税務署長から診断結果に関し要精密検査その他肺結核罹患の疑いに関し格別の通知を受けなかったことから勤務を続けていたところ，翌年の定期健康診断で重い肺結核に罹っていたことが判明し，治療のため6年2ヵ月の休職を含め10数年の療養生活を余儀なくされたというものである。被上告人は，定期健康診断をした医師のフィルム読影の過誤か税務署長への報告懈怠，または同医師の診断結果報告を通知された税務署長の被上告人に対する措置上の過誤のいずれかによって損害を受けたとして，国家賠償法1条（予備的に民法715条）に基づき国に対し損害賠償を請求した。原審（広島高岡山支判昭和51・9・13民集36巻4号587頁）は被控訴人の請求を一部認容。上告理由は，レントゲン写真による医師の検診等の行為の性質について公権力の行使に当たるとした原審判断の当否を争っている。以下，これに直接関連する部分のみに触れる。

（判旨）㈠　レントゲン写真による検診等の行為の公権力の行使該当性。レントゲン写真による検診と結果の報告は，「医師が専らその専門的技術及び知識経験を用いて行う行為であって，医師の一般的診断行為と異なるところはないから，特段の事由がない限り，それ自体としては公権力の行使たる性質を有するものではない，……本件における右検診等の行為は，本件健康診断の過程においてなされたものとはいえ，右健康診断におけるその余の行為と切り離してその性質を考察，決定することができるものであるから，右

3 健康診断をめぐる問題

特段の事由にあたるものということができ」ない。

　㈡　使用者責任の成否。(a)「本件における検診等の行為が上告人の職員である医師によって行われたものであれば，……上告人に対して民法715条の損害賠償責任を問擬すべき余地があり，……ひいて先に述べた一般的法理に基づいて上告人の賠償責任を肯定しうる可能性もないではない」。(b)しかし，「右検診等の行為が税務署長の保健所への嘱託に基づき訴外岡山県の職員である同保健所勤務の医師によって行われたのであるとすれば，右医師の検診等の行為は右保健所の業務としてなされたものというべきであって，たとえそれが林野税務署長の嘱託に基づいてなされたものであるとしても，そのために右検診等の行為が上告人国の事務の処理となり，右医師があたかも上告人国の機関ないしその補助者として検診等の行為をしたものと解さなければならない理由はないから，右医師の検診等の行為に不法行為を成立せしめるような違法があっても，そのために上告人が民法の前記法条による損害賠償責任を負わなければならない理由はない」。

　㈢　読影過誤の不法行為性。右判旨㈡(a)の部分において傍論としてつぎのように判示されている。「(多数者に対して集団的に行われるレントゲン検診における若干の過誤をもって直ちに対象者に対する医師の不法行為を認めるべきかどうかには問題があるが，この点は暫く措く。)」。

　(2)　最高裁判決の右㈠の判示が，定期健康診断のうち，担当医師の検診（本件では胸部レントゲン間接撮影と写真の読影）を公権力の行使に当たらないとした判断は，労働者に対し労働安全衛生法により健康診断を義務づけられている民間事業の場合も事業者の行為に当たらないとの判断を示唆するものであろう。その理由は，検診は医師がもっぱら専門的技術および知識経験を用いて行う行為であって，医師の一般的診断行為と異ならず，性質上，健康診断の過程におけるその余の行為と切り離して考察，決定することができるものだという点にある[8]。差戻審（広島高岡山支判昭和59・10・30労判444号40頁，控訴人の請求棄却）も同様に検診の公権力の行使性を否定し，医師の検診は，

---

[8]　ちなみに健康診断における検診（医療行為）以外の「その余の行為」には，実施の計画ないし委託，周知，実施運営上の指示，結果の記録，結果に関する医師等の意見聴取，一般健康診断の結果の労働者への通知等がある（労安衛法66条，66条の2，66条の4参照）。

実施義務者が健康診断実施の「職責を行使する前提となる疾病の有無，その疑いを純医学的に験知する行為」である，とその根拠をのべている[9]。

以上の判旨㈠の見解は，検診担当医師が健康診断の実施義務を負う国（または事業者）の職員ではなく，その委嘱を受けた第三者医療機関の勤務医である場合に関する判旨㈡の判断と相通ずるところがある。同判旨は，医師の検診等の行為は，委嘱を受けた保健所の業務としてなされたものというべきであって，実施義務者の機関ないし補助者として行為をしたものと解さなければならない理由はないとのべており，差戻審（前出）も検診は「純然たる医療行為とみるべきものであることからすると，本件検診に対し同税務署長（健康診断の実施義務者・引用者）が実質上も指揮監督を及ぼし得るものと解し

---

9) 判旨のこの部分に関する諸家の賛否の見解については，西村健一郎「国家公務員の定期健康診断における疾病の見過ごしと国家賠償の成否」（差戻審の判例研究）労判447号9-10頁（1985）に詳細にまとめられているので此処に繰り返えすことを避ける。その後，山田卓生教授は，判旨に疑問を呈され，「この考え方をとると，定期検診を，いわゆる下請（業務委託）という形で実施し，受託（下請）機関が民間である場合には（かなり多いという），公権力の行使にはあたらないことになってしまう。そして，検診結果を信頼して損害を受けた者は，責任を問えないことになるが，はたしてこれが妥当といえるか問題である。」とのべておられる（「定期検診における結核看過事件」ジュリスト医療過誤判例百選75頁，1985。なお，加藤新太郎「定期検診における結核過誤」同百選Ⅱ版，189頁，1996は定期検診の医師の過失の判定に関する考慮要素をあげておられることにつき後記注14参照）。

10) 東京海上火災事件（東京高判平成10・2・28労判732号14頁）。同事件判旨は，実施義務者に法的責任を負担させようとする考え方は，実施義務者（東京海上火災）に対し，「定期健康診断を実施する医師ないし医療機関の具体的な個々の医療行為につき指揮監督すべき責任を負わせることに帰着し，採用できない」とのべている。実施義務者に法的責任を負わせる考え方が委嘱先の医師の「個々の医療行為」につき指揮監督すべき責任をおわせることになるとの判示部分に賛同できない理由は後にのべる（後記(3)参照）。なお，右の見解は，事業者は「信義則上，一般医療水準に照らし相当と認められる程度の健康診断を実施し，あるいはこれを行い得る医療機関に委嘱すれば足りるのであって，右診断が明白に右水準を下回り，かつ，企業側がそれを知り又は知り得たというような事情がない限り，安全配慮義務の違反は認められない」との一審判決（東京地判平成7・11・30労判687号27頁）の判旨を引用し，これを受けて判示されているものである。この点についても，委嘱先の医療水準が，健康診断の実施義務者との間で結ばれる委嘱契約の内容とあたかも無関係であるかのように考えものであって賛同できないことも，後にのべるとおりである（後述(3)参照）。

難い。」，という点をその理由に加えている。近年の裁判例のなかにも，同様の理由で，被用者の定期健康診断を委嘱した医療機関の医師のレントゲン写真読影過誤に関し，健康診断実施義務者である事業者の法的責任を否定しているものがある[10]。

(3) 私見によれば，医師の検診を，健康診断実施上の「その余の行為」と切り離し，専門的独自性をもつものとして考察，決定することができるとの見解には疑問を呈さざるを得ない。以下，その理由をのべる。

健康診断の実施義務者は，実施に際し必要な事項を定め，被験者である労働者（担当する医師が被用者の場合は同時にその医師も含めて）に所要の指示を発するであろう。実施義務者の指示・管理事項には対象受検者の範囲・人数，回数を分けて行う場合は実施の時期と一機会当たりの対象受検者の範囲・人数，実施の期間・場所（実施医療機関），検診内容（検診項目），検診票の記載

---

11) (ア) 神戸市（垂水保健所）事件・神戸地判昭和59・5・28判時1139号92頁の「胃の集団検診」では，医師3名が胃の集団検査を受診した31人分の胸部エックス線間接撮影フィルム（1名につき6枚）を約18分で読影する体制（他の被検者を含めると合計208人分で全所要時間2時間）であった（市の保健所が実施したもので被検者は胃癌（ボルマン）型）を看過され，検診から約5ヵ月後に死亡し，相続人が市に対し損害賠償を請求した事案・請求棄却）。

(イ) 結核予防会宮城県支部事件（仙台地判平成8・12・16判時1603号94頁）では，エックス線検査による「肺癌の集団検診」のフィルムを1人の医師が400人分がひとまとまりになったロールフィルム1巻を1時間かけて読影する体制（1人あたり9秒）であった（老人保健法24条に基づき自治体から委嘱を受けた医療機関が住民を対象に行ったもので，フィルムの読影担当医師が陰影を異常と判断しなかったことにより治療機会を失したこと等を理由に受託医療機関に損害賠償を請求した事案・請求棄却）。

(ウ) 魚津郵便局職員事件（富山地判平成6・6・1判時1539号118頁）では，定期健康診断として実施した胸部エックス線間接撮影の読影医師は1人であるが，受検者数，医師が読影に割いた定期健康診断の被検者1人あたり，または被検者全体のために割いた時間は明らかにされていない（魚津郵便局勤務の郵政職員に対し，富山通信病院の管理する胃検診車内で行った定期健康診断のエックス線フィルム読影の過誤を理由に延命利益が侵害されたとして損害賠償を請求した事案・請求一部認容）。

(エ) 東京海上火災事件（東京高判平成10・2・26労判732号14頁）では，前記事件と同様に，定期健康診断の胸部レントゲン間接撮影フィルムの読影医師は1人であり，受検者数，医師が読影に割いた時間等は明らかにされていない（肺癌陰影の読影過誤を理由に会社，会社嘱託医師，会社の委託診療機関およびその勤務医に対し損害賠償を請求した事案・請求（控訴）棄却。一審は東京地判平成7・11・30労判687号27頁）。

欄への必要事項・調査事項（後述(4)参照）の記入，実施時間帯（就業時間内か，時間外か），検診結果の労働者への通知の時期・方法等があろう。検診を第三者医療機関に委託する場合は，検診結果の報告納期を含めて右のような事項のうちから必要な事項が「検診委託契約」に検診委託料金等とともに定められるであろう。

担当医師の行う検診もまた，こうした健康診断の全体的実施体制の枠内において行われるのであり，実施体制の諸条件と切り離し，かつそれら諸条件に左右されることなく，一般医療行為として独自の専門的技術ないし知識経験を用いて行う行為（純医学的行為）ということができるであろうか。

検診委託契約の内容を精査してみるとき，医師は，対象受検者数の多さによる「技術的制約」，担当医師が検診に割くことができる「時間的制約」[11]，担当を割り当てられる医師の数により採り得る検診の「方法的制約」（二重チェック方式が可能か否かといった面での制約），読影により要再検または要精密検査とした場合の手間ないし「手続的負担の制約」[12]，検診委託契約により健康診断実施義務者が支払うことを約している検診委託料との関係において検診にかけることができる費用面での「経営的制約」等の事情にかかわらず，独自に一般的臨床医の医療水準で医療行為を行うことが可能であろうか。これら医療行為の外部的要因のなかには，医師が健康診断において行う胸部レントゲン写真の撮影・読影等の医療行為の質的水準を相当な程度において低下させる誘因となるものの存在が認められる場合がないといいきれるであろうか。くりかえして言えば，医師はこのような社会的制約（検診委託契約の所与の諸条件の制約）の下でも，それらから自由に，独自に，「一般の医療行為」と異なることのない医療行為をなしうるものであろうか。そうとは思われない。

たしかに，事業者がその雇用する医師または他の医療機関に委託して行う

---

12) 読影により要再検または要精密検査とした場合の手間ないし「手続的負担の制約」とは，つぎのようなことをいう。読影医師が要再検と認めた場合はフィルムコマの受診者の過去何年かのフィルムを抽出してカットフィルムを作り，それを1枚のファイルに収納し，各フィルムを再読影（これを「比較読影」という）して最終的に要再検のものを決定する，というような手続である。結核予防会宮城県支部事件（前出注11(イ)）の認定によれば，再検査に先立つ右の比較読影の段階でも，これを行うには多大の時間と労力を必要とするとされている。

3 健康診断をめぐる問題

集団検診たる健康診断に要求される医療水準をどのように考えるかはもうひとつの重要問題である（後述(4)）。しかし，この種の問題は，健康診断の実施義務者が被用者たる医師に課す実施上の諸制約または第三者医療機関との間に結ぶ検診委託契約の内容自体に，医師の医療行為の質的水準を相当程度低下させる誘因が内在していると認められる場合も考えた上で検討される必要があるのではないか。そうすると，検診における医師の過誤に関し，医療行為の技術および経験知識の専門性を抽象的に説くことによって，常に実施義務者に法的責任がないといえるであろうか。疑問である。また，差戻審のいうように検診委託者（実施義務者）が検診を担当する医師に「実質上も指揮監督を及ぼし得るものと解し難い」といえるであろうか。これまた疑問である[13]。

したがって，実施義務者が担当の医師に対し検診・体制に関する指示・管理をし，または委託契約上の諸条件の支配をとおして，実施義務者たる事業者が医師の医療行為の技術および経験知識の専門性の質的水準に実質的影響を与えることは十分にあり得ると考えなければならない。しかして，実施義務者が医療機関の検診過誤に対し使用者責任（民法715条）を負う場合のあることが肯定されるべきである。

(4) 定期健康診断の検診を担当する医師の注意義務の程度に関し，前出津

---

13) 西村教授は，健康診断の検診にあたった医師の過誤に関し実施義務者には法的責任を認められないとの差戻審の結論を支持しつぎのようにのべておられる。(ｱ)通常の場合，履行補助者の故意過失については債務者が責任を負うのであるが，健康診断を実施するために履行補助者を使用することが積極的に許されて（要請されて）いること，(ｲ)医師の行為は実施義務者（管理者）が必要な措置をとるための前提事実（病気の有無，疑いの存否）を験知するための純医学的な行為であること，(ｳ)医師は実施義務者との関係で独立性が強いこと。以上から，実施義務者は履行代行者（検査の委嘱を受けた医療機関）の選任・監督に過失があった場合にだけ責任を負わなければならないであろう。(ｴ)事業者に過失責任を問うことは特に小規模の事業者に過大な負担を負わしめることになる。結局，医師の検診に過誤がある場合は当該医師または医師を雇用する医療機関に対し損害賠償を請求するほかない，と（前出判例研究10〜11頁）。右の理由のうち，(ｱ)は私見も格別の異議はない。(ｲ), (ｳ)に関しては本文においてのべたような側面にほとんど考慮を払われていない点で賛同しがたい。(ｴ)については誠にもっともな指摘ではあるが，実施義務者が委嘱先の医療機関に求償する法的手段はあるのであり，実施義務者にも過失のあり得ることを否定する理由にはならないと思われる。

山税務職員事件最高裁判決（85頁）は傍論において「多数者に対して集団的に行われるレントゲン検診における若干の過誤をもって直ちに対象に対する医師の不法行為を認めるべきかどうかには問題がある」とのべている（前出(1)）。これまでもこの問題に関しては同様の関心からそれぞれに指摘されている。曰く、(ｱ)定期検診実施者に不法行為があったとして「賠償を請求しうる程度まで強度にその利益を保障していると考えうるであろうか。……それほど重い責任を負わせた制度とは解すべきではなかろう。」、(ｲ)集団検診の場合は、受診者も検診の結果に十分な確実性がないことを予期すべきであるから、罹患を看過された場合でも、そのために病院の発見が遅れたとして直ちに損害賠償を請求できるかどうかはかなり問題である、(ｳ)定期健康診断の「医師のミスは、それを信頼した者への損害賠償責任を生ぜしめるほどのものなのか」、「自分の病気は、諸種の症状、異常から自ら気がつくべきで、定期健康診断だけを頼りにすべきではない」14)、と。

　裁判例のなかにも、レントゲン写真の読影の際、異常所見を見落とし、「異常なし」との判定結果を被検者へ通知したことに関して、胃の集団検診（本件では「胃集検」と略称されている）の方法に過失がないことのほか、「現在の胃集検の制度においては、一般に異常所見の見落としの可能性は否定できないことが明らか」といい、また「受診者の間においても、その精度に絶対的な信頼を置きうるものでないことの認識がむしろ広くおこなわれている」（傍点は引用者）といい、さらに被検者への通知に際して保健所長の「いま異常がないからといって将来も大丈夫とはいえません…という注意書が付記されていた」、等の点をあげて検査結果の通知内容に過失はなかったと判示しているものがある（前出注11神戸市（垂水保健所）事件。その対象者数等につき同注を参照)15)。

---

14)　(ｱ)村上義弘・津山税務職員事件一審判決判例研究、判例時報768号160頁（1975）、(ｲ)加茂紀久男・最高裁判所判例解説民事編昭和57年度(20)事件337頁（1987）、(ｳ)山田卓生・前出注975頁。加藤新太郎・前出注9頁は、定期検診における医師の過失の判定については、「①過誤の内容、②定期検診の性質——集団検診か人間ドックのようなものか、③その検診において期待されているレベル——勤務先の健康管理上実施されるものか本人の自覚に基づいて受診するものか、④その検診の効果として受診者に表示されているもの、⑤同じレベルの検診における医療水準、⑥当該罹患発見の難易」などを考慮要素にあげておられる。

3 健康診断をめぐる問題

　また，定期健康診断（胸部レントゲン撮影および読影）における肺がんの陰影見落としが注意義務違反に当たるかが問題になった事例では，「集団検診において数百枚のフィルムを読影するなどの読影条件などを考慮すると，本件レントゲン写真については，間接フィルム読影に熟練したものでも『異常なし』とする可能性があり，本件レントゲン写真が，定期健康診断において読影された他の数百枚のレントゲン写真と同一の機会に，当該被検者に関する何らの予備知識なく読影された場合，当時の一般臨床医の医療水準を前提にすれば，右異常を発見できない可能性の方が高いことが認められる。」とするものがある（前出注10東京海上火災事件）。

　さらに，「大量のフィルムを読影するという状況」での医師に要求される注意義務の水準と，そのなかから取り出した特定のフィルムを読影する際に医師の要求される水準とを区別し，後者の場合には「認識した個別の検査結果の異常の存在を前提に一般的に医師に要求される注意を払って判断しなければならない」とする裁判例も見られる（魚津郵政事務官事件・富山地判平成6・6・1判時1539号118頁）。

　このように，定期健康診断の医師の注意義務の基準に関し特別の考慮を要

15）　本件胃の集団検診は老人保健法（昭和57年法律80号）24条により市町村において40歳以上の住民に対し行うこととされている「医療等以外の保健事業」として行われたものと考えられる。その実施基準は厚生省告示（「医療等以外の保健事業の実施の基準」昭和57年厚告185号）に具体化されている。それによれば，健康診査は年1回行うこととされ，「基本健康診査」，「がん検診」，「総合健康診査」の3種類があげられ，胃がんに関しては「問診及び胃部エックス線検査」を行うこととしている。レントゲン写真の読影は右の「問診」の記録とあわせて読影されるはずのものであるが，本件ではこの点に関して触れるところはない。しかし，判旨のあげるような「可能性」や「認識」や「注意書」を医療行為の過失の有無の判断基準と考えるべきものなのであろうか。普通の被検者は，検診の結果「異常なし」という通知を受けたときは，ひとまず「よかった」と安心するであろう。そしてその「安心」が〈過度の信頼〉とまではいえない場合は，その信頼は法的に保護されるべきである。そうした〈合理的な信頼〉がかえって治療機会を逸する原因になり，実際にそのような結果になった場合にも検診に過失は認められないというのでは，老人保健法の創設した保健事業自体に対する被検者の信頼を著しく損なうのであり，「疾病の予防……等の保健事業を総合的に実施し，もって国民保健の向上…を図る」同法の目的（1条）からみても妥当性を欠くというほかない（ちなみに，本事件の被検者は当該通知の約2ヵ月余の後に「胃がん（ボルマン」型）」と診断され開腹手術をし，約5ヵ月後に死亡している）。

する要因としてあげられる第一は被検者の集団性（対象者数が多いこと）である。

筆者は今のところ，この点に関しては，前出結核予防会宮城県支部事件（注11参照）において言及されているところの，集団検診における「特異性と感受性の妥協点」という視点から検証し判断する方法に一定の有効性を見出し得るように思われる。「特異性」とは治療を要する病変のみを発見することをいい，「感受性」は治療を要する病変を見落とさないことをいう。感受性を上げるためにはレントゲンの読影にあたり病変の疑われる陰影までもすべて要再検とする必要があるが，その結果特異性が下がり無用に再検査を受ける必要のある人を増やすことになり，再検査受診者には多大の精神的，時間的負担等をかける一方，再検査の結果異常でない者の割合が増加し，集団検診の信頼性を損ない，受検者の低下を招くとされている（労働者に対して行われる定期健康診断については受検者の低下といった事態は生じないが，要再検とされた者に多大の精神的，時間的負担がおよぶことは変わりない）。逆に，特異性を上げるために明らかに異常と思われる者だけを要再検とすると，感受性が下がり，再検査と治療を必要とする人を見落とす可能性が大きくなる。右事件の判旨によれば，特異性と感受性との妥協点は，要再検とされる者の比率を2〜4％とするのが普通で，5％を超えると読影方法になんらかの問題があるというのである（医師の証言）。

また，別の事件では，読影過誤が問題になった写真を含めた合計283枚のフィルムを医師10人に被検者に関する一切の情報を与えることなく読影させた結果，要請密検査とされた写真の枚数は平均3.6％であったとの事実（意見書を提出した医師の実験結果）を示している（前出東京海上火災事件）。このようにみると，医師が読影する写真の数の多さによってなお変動する可能性は否定できないとはいえ，「一般臨床医の医療水準」を前提とした場合，要再検（要精検とされるものを含めて）とされる者の合理的割合の上限をおおむね被検者の3〜4％程度と設定することができるならば，検診がはたしてこのような特異性・感受性の妥協点の枠内で行われたかどうかが問われることになろう。右の枠内で行われた場合には，特段の事情がないかぎり，健康診断が一般臨床医の医療水準の質的低下をきたさない範囲内で行われたとの推定が成立すると考えてよいであろう。そしてこのことは，健康診断の実施管理

にあたった実施義務者または担当医療機関（ないし医師）において主張立証すべきである。もちろん，右の感受性と特異性との妥協点は今後さらに研究の積み重ねられるべき問題であるが，現状においてはこのような基準によって，健康診断における実施体制の適切性（実施義務者の注意義務違反の有無）および担当医師の注意義務違反の有無（一般的臨床医の医療水準で検診を行ったか否か）を判断することが合理的であるように思われる。

次に，集団検診の場合は，検診結果の判定にあたる医師が被検者個々人に関する素因および病歴等について予備的知識がないことが指摘されている（前出東京海上火災事件ほか）。この点については，老人保健法に基づいて行う保健事業としての集団検診においても医師は被検者に「問診」を行うこととされ（前出注15参照），他方労働安全衛生法に基づいて事業者の行う健康診断では「既往歴及び業務歴の調査」,「自覚症状及び他覚症状の有無の調査」を行うべきこととされている（同法66条1項，労安衛則43条1号，2号，44条1号，2号）。このように集団検診においても，十分とはいえないであろうが，医師は被検者の個別的状況をまったく知り得ないことはない建て前になっている。レントゲン写真の読影にかぎらず，医師の医療行為（検診）の結果の判定（異常の有無の確認）は，右の問診や被検者に対する調査を併用して行われたか否かが確認されるべきである（仮に医師にそのようなことがなしえない時間的制約が課せられた客観的状況が認められるときは，当該健康診断はその実施体制自体に適切を欠くものであり，実施義務者の注意義務違反が問疑されるべき筋合いである）。

(5) 定期健康診断の過程で医師と被検者との間で個別的対応の機会（またはそれに等しい状況）が生じる場合がある。たとえば，異常所見を認めた次の段階の処置が問題になる場合であり（その1），被検者から医師に対し自覚症状（病状）について一定の具体的申告がなされた場合である（その2）。

（その1の事例）　医師が定期健康診断の胸部エックス線間接撮影写真に異常陰影を認めたものの，前年度のフィルムと比較し陰影の大きさ等に変化がないものとして精密検査は不要と判定した事例（魚津郵政事務官事件・前出(4)参照）。判旨は，担当医師が被検者亡Aのフィルム読影において異常陰影を発見し精密検査が必要と考え，前年度のものと比較読影を試みたことは医師として「要求される水準を十分に満たすものであった」が，比較読影の段階

では「大量のフィルムを読影するという状況ではなく，認識した個別の検査結果の異常の存在を前提に一般的に医師に要求される注意を払って判断しなければならないものと考えられる。」とし，同医師が，陰影が前年度フィルムと比較して客観的に変化しているのに変化なしと判断し，精密検査を指示しなかったことには過失が認められ，精密検査を行っていれば肺癌を発見することができたとした[16]。

（その2の事例）　定期健康診断（胸部レントゲン撮影）の際，被検者の亡AはB医師に「息苦しさと胸がしめつけられるような痛み」を訴えたが，同医師は糖尿病負荷検査を指示し，胸部精密検査を行う必要を認めず，その約1ヵ月後に同じ診療所でレントゲン撮影をした際にも同医師に「咳きと血痰」を訴えたところ消炎剤，去痰剤を処方され経過観察とされた事例（東京火災海上保険事件・前注10参照）。判旨は，亡Aの胸部腫瘤様陰影に気づきながらも精密検査不要と判断したことに「一般臨床医の医療水準を前提として考えた場合」，過失があったとした[17]。

右の場合の「一般臨床医の医療水準」は，前出魚津郵政職員事件判旨にいう「個別の検査結果の異常の存在を前提に一般的に医師に要求される注意」と同質のものと考えてよいと思われる。いずれも，医師の注意義務違反の有無の判断基準としては，健康診断に通常伴う集団性がないか，その面で考慮

---

[16]　亡Aに対する問題の定期健康診断は昭和62年4月被告（国）の逓信病院によって実施され，同人は平成2年5月肺切除手術を受け同年10月死亡した。本件は亡Aの遺族が国家賠償法1条または民法715条を根拠に国に対し損害賠償を請求した事件である。判旨は，逸失利益の損害賠償請求は棄却したうえで，亡Aが翌年（昭和63年）の健康診断で理由を告げられなかったものの再検査（胸部エックス線検査）を指示されながらこれに従わなかったこと，喫煙量が多かったこと等を斟酌し慰謝料請求の一部のみ認容した。判旨は，本件定期健康診断における医師の検診行為を「公権力の行使」（国家賠償法1条）と認めているのか，それとも使用者責任（民法715条）を根拠に損害賠償責任を認めたものかを，判旨はあえて（？）明言していない。

[17]　亡Aはさらに，2回目のレントゲン撮影の10日後に同診療所の別のC医師から先の糖尿病検査の結果報告を受けた際，「痰を伴った咳が出ること，時折発作的咳が出ること」を訴えたが，同医師はレントゲン写真を見ることなく糖尿病に対する食事療法を指示した。亡Aは同年11月入院先の病院で肺癌により死亡した。判旨はC医師の過失を否定した。また，過失ありとされたB医師の勤務する医療機関に対し従業員の健康診断を委嘱し実施している会社に安全配慮義務違反は認められないとしている。

すべき事情の認められない場合であり，適切な判断といえよう。

まとめ

　本稿では，まず労働災害の被災者の遺族による損害賠償請求事件（労災民訴）に関する最高裁判決の趣旨から，使用者に安全配慮義務違反があるというためには，使用者による労働場所の指定，設備等の供給または労務提供過程における指示・管理に労働者の生命，健康に対する危険が内在し，それが顕在化したといえる場合（「業務要因性」が認められる場合」）でなければならないとした（第1節）。次に，労働安全衛生法が労働者の健康障害防止のために事業者に課している各種の措置をさしあたって健康配慮義務の最低限度の内容を構成するものとしてのべ，これらをその性質上，(a)業務要因性のある危険から労働者を保護する措置として安全配慮義務の内容になるようにべきもの，(b)安全配慮義務または健康配慮義務のいずれかの内容になるべきものとその区別の基準，および(c)健康配慮義務の内容となるべきもの，に3分した。そうして，安全配慮義務の内容となるべき措置にかかわる健康配慮義務は安全配慮義務と同様に労働契約上の信義則を法的根拠にし，それ以外の措置にかかわる健康配慮義務は不法行為法上の注意義務を法的根拠にするものであるとのべた（第2節）。以上の考察を前提に，健康配慮義務の重要な1つである一般健康診断の実施義務者である事業者の注意義務について，国家公務員につき実施された定期健康診断に関して生じた損害に対する国の損害賠償責任の有無に関する最高裁判決を批判的に検討した。その上で，検診を担当する医師に対する検診実施体制上の指示・管理，第三者に検診を委託して行うときは委託契約上の諸条件の支配をとおして，実施義務者である事業者が医師の医療行為の技術および経験知識の専門性の質に実質的影響を与えたと考えられる場合には，注意義務違反を肯定すべきであるとし，さらにこれに付加して若干の問題を論じた（第3節）。

脳血管疾患・虚血性心疾患の業務上外認定に関する裁判例——「共働原因」と「相対的に有力な原因」——

小 畑 史 子

1 問題提起

　脳血管疾患，虚血性心疾患という疾病は，発症の基礎となる動脈硬化等による血管病変又は動脈瘤等の基礎的病態（基礎疾患，基礎疾病）が加齢や一般生活等における諸種の要因によって，増悪し発症に至るものがほとんどである[1]。しかし，この自然経過中に著しく右基礎的病態を増悪させる急激な血圧変動や血管収縮を引き起こす負荷，すなわち『過重負荷』が加わると，その自然経過を超えて急激に発症することがある[2]。

　このような疾病である脳血管疾患，虚血性心疾患は，労基法規則35条別表第1の2，1〜8号の職業病リストに列記されている職業病ではないが，業務による著しい負荷が発症を引き起こしたと認められる場合に，「その他業務に起因することの明らかな疾病」（9号）として，業務上災害と認定する行政処分や裁判例が蓄積されてきた。その過程においては，業務（公務）と発症との相当因果関係の有無を巡り，多くの訴訟が提起されてきた。

　最高裁は，平成9年，大館労基署長（四戸電気工事店）事件判決[3]において，この相当因果関係の問題につき，①基礎疾患等が自然の経過により発症するほど進行していなかったか，②業務による負荷が基礎疾患をその自然的経過を超えて急激に悪化させる要因となりうるか，③他に確たる発症因子はないかに着目して判断を行った。この最高裁の判断と同じく，脳血管疾患，虚血性心疾患の業務（公務）上外認定を巡る訴訟で，業務（公務を含む。以下同じ。）

---

1) 　脳血管疾患及び虚血性心疾患等に関する専門家会議の報告（昭和62年9月8日付け「過重負荷による脳血管疾患及び虚血性心疾患の取り扱いに関する報告書」）。
2) 　前掲注1) 報告書。

が，自然的進行によっては発症を引き起こさない基礎疾患をその自然的経過を超えて増悪させて発症を招いた疑いのあることに注目した下級審裁判例は従来から多数存在した。そしてそれらの裁判例は，大別して，「業務が共働原因となっていれば相当因果関係の存在を肯定できる」という表現を用いる

---

3) 最三小判平成9・4・25労判722号13頁。拙稿「事故二日後に発症した非外傷性脳血管疾患の業務上外認定——大館労基署長（四戸電気工事店）事件」（判例評釈）ジュリスト1155号（1999）277頁参照。労働者が既に重篤な病状に至っていたにもかかわらず公務（業務）に従事せざるを得ず，そのために死亡につながる疾病を発症したようなタイプの脳・心疾患の公務（業務）上外認定のケースについては，拙稿「狭心症発症後の公務と心筋梗塞発症との相当因果関係——地公災基金東京都支部長（町田高校）事件（判例評釈）ジュリスト1151号（1999）134頁参照。

4) 「共働原因」という文言を用いるもの（便宜上，各判決に判決番号を付す。）。
1 泉大津労基署長（第一警備保障）事件（大阪地判昭和61・2・28労判470号33頁，判タ589号39頁）。
2 天満労基署長（つ吉建設出稼ぎ労働者）事件（大阪地判昭和63・5・16労判518号6頁）。
3 昭和郵便局事件（名古屋地判平成1・10・6労判550号65頁）。
4 函館労基署長（北海小型タクシー）事件（函館地判平成1・12・21労判555号46頁）。
5 名古屋西労基署長（西枇杷島交通）事件（名古屋地判平成2・7・20労判567号6頁）。
6 天満労基署長（つ吉建設出稼ぎ労働者）事件（大阪高判平成2・9・19労判570号42頁）。
7 向島労基署長（渡辺工業）事件（東京高判平成3・2・4労判591号76頁）。
8 地公災基金京都府支部長（京都市立下鴨中学校）事件（大阪高判平成5・2・24労判626号67頁）。
9 横浜南労基署長（東京海上横浜支店）事件（横浜地判平成5・3・23労判628号44頁）。
10 渋谷労基署長（三陸運送）事件（東京地判平成5・6・8労判634号30頁）。
11 地公災基金東京都支部長（町田高校）事件（東京高判平成5・9・30労判644号30頁）。
12 地公災基金鹿児島県支部長（牧ノ原高校教員）事件（福岡高宮崎支判平成5・12・15労判666号70頁）。
13 地公災基金京都府支部長（京都市消防局）事件（大阪高判平成6・2・23労判649号14頁）。
14 尼崎労基署長（交安タクシー）事件（神戸地判平成6・3・11労判657号77頁）。
15 尼崎労基署長（交安タクシー）事件（大阪高判平成7・2・17労判676号76頁）。
16 京都南労基署長（北信運輸）事件（大阪高判平成7・4・27労判679号46頁）。
17 横浜南労基署長（東京海上横浜支店）事件（東京高判平成7・5・30労判683号73頁）。
18 山形労基署長（山形交通）事件（山形地判平成7・5・30労判682号76頁）。
19 地公災基金東京都支部長（町田市職員）事件（東京地判平成7・10・26労判686号48頁）。

1 問題提起

もの[4]と,「業務が相対的に有力な原因となっていれば相当因果関係の存在を肯定することができる」という表現を用いるもの[5]と, どちらの表現も用いずに相当因果関係の有無を判断するもの[6]とが存する[7]。

5)「相対的に有力な原因」という文言を用いるもの(便宜上, 各判決に判決番号を付す。)
20 飯田橋労基署長(大日本印刷)事件(東京地判昭和62・12・22労判510号17頁)。
21 地公災基金埼玉県支部長(越谷市職員)事件(東京高判昭和63・6・29労判528号98頁)。
22 社会保険庁長官(興生建設)事件(東京地判昭和63・9・14労判600号78頁)。
23 中野労基署長(旭運輸)事件(東京高判平成1・10・26労判556号81頁(要旨))。
24 大阪中央労基署長(市田)事件(大阪地判平成2・1・26労判556号32頁)。
25 大阪中央労基署長(生口電設)事件(大阪地判平成2・1・29労判556号26頁)。
26 山口労基署長(岡山県貨物運送)事件(山口地判平成3・2・21労判582号20頁)。
27 中野労基署長(第三大祐丸)事件(東京地判平成3・7・16労判593号12頁)。
28 静岡労基署長(三菱電機静岡製作所)事件(静岡地判平成3・11・15労判598号20頁)。
29 泉大津労基署長(朝比奈建材)事件(大阪地判平成4・2・24労判609号77頁)。
30 昭和郵便局事件(名古屋高判平成4・3・17労判618号66頁)。
31 茨木労基署長(関西新幹線整備)事件(大阪地判平成4・3・23労判617号62頁)。
32 加古川労基署長(ケーフルーツ商事)事件(大阪高判平成4・4・28労判611号46頁)。
33 廿日市労基署長(大原鉄工所)事件(広島地判平成4・9・30労判624号55頁)。
34 大阪中央労基署長(第一交通)事件(大阪地判平成4・12・14労判620号25頁)。
35 北大阪労基署長(西部ゴム)事件(大阪地判平成5・1・29労判628号64頁)。
36 山口労基署長(岡山県貨物運送)事件(広島高判平成5・3・29労判649号79頁)。
37 大館労基署長(四戸電気工事店)事件(仙台高秋田支判平成6・6・27労判722号15頁)。
38 名古屋南労基署長(矢作建設)事件(名古屋地判平成6・8・26労判654号9頁)。
39 地公災基金大阪府支部長(松原第四中学校)事件(大阪地判平成6・8・29労判659号42頁, 判タ871号216頁)。
40 仙台労基署長(松下電工)事件(仙台地判平成6・10・24労判662号55頁)。
41 地公災基金静岡県支部長(吉田高校教員)事件(静岡地判平成6・11・10労判672号59頁)。
42 飯田労基署長(信菱電機)事件(長野地判平成7・3・2労判671号46頁, 判タ876号163頁)。
43 名古屋南労基署長(東宝運輸)事件(名古屋地判平成7・9・29労判684号26頁)。
44 半田労基署長(日本油脂)事件(名古屋地判平成8・1・26労判691号29頁)。
45 名古屋西労基署長(富士交通)事件(名古屋地判平成8・3・27労判693号46頁, 判タ916号113頁)。
46 地公災基金愛知県支部長(名古屋市豊正中学校教員)事件(名古屋地判平成8・5・8労判696号25頁)。
47 地公災基金大阪府支部長(吹田市西消防署)事件(大阪地判平成8・7・29労判699

号14頁,判タ927号125頁)。
　48　京都上労基署長(ローム株式会社)事件(京都地判平成8・9・11労判709号59頁)。
　49　地公災基金宮崎県支部長(日向工業高校)事件(宮崎地判平成8・9・20労判711号83頁)。
　50　地公災基金千葉県支部長(匝瑳高校)事件(千葉地判平成8・9・25労判704号97頁)。
　51　西宮労基署長(大阪淡路交通)事件(神戸地判平成8・9・27判タ934号241頁)。
　52　三田労基署長(ニューオリエントエキスプレス)事件(東京地判平成8・10・24労判710号42頁)。
　53　名古屋南労基署長(矢作電設)事件(名古屋高判平成8・11・26労判707号27頁)。
　54　帯広労基署長(梅田運輸)事件(釧路地判平成8・12・10労判709号20頁)。
　55　地公災基金静岡県支部長(吉田高校教員)事件(東京高判平成9・10・14労判727号50頁)。
6)　「共働原因」という文言も「相対的に有力な原因」という文言もどちらも用いないもの。
　神戸労基署長(三輪機工)事件(神戸地判昭和59・2・17労判428号38頁)。
　向島労基署長(渡辺工業)事件(東京地判昭和62・9・10労判504号40頁)。
　武雄労基署長事件(佐賀地判昭和63・9・30労判527号20頁)。
　滝川労基署長(北星ハイヤー)事件(札幌地判平成1・12・25労判556号47頁)。
　加古川労基署長(明貨トラック)事件(神戸地判平成3・10・8判601号6頁)。
　仙台労基署長(森勇建設)事件(仙台高判平成3・11・27判632号70頁)。
　加古川労基署長(明貨トラック)事件(大阪高判平成4・8・31労判624号76頁)。
　地公災基金京都府支部長(京都市立下鴨中学校)事件(大阪高判平成5・2・24労判626号67頁)。
　天満労基署長(近畿保安警備)事件(大阪地判平成6・1・31労判649号34頁)。
　佐賀労基署長(蓮池タクシー)事件(佐賀地判平成6・2・18労民集45巻1・2号50頁,判タ868号181頁,労判679号83頁)。
　西野田労基署長(淀川製鋼所)事件(大阪地判平成6・9・2労判668号15頁)。
　名古屋西労基署長(西枇杷島交通)事件(名古屋高判平成6・9・26労判664号39頁)。
　佐賀労基署長(蓮池タクシー)事件(福岡高判平成7・1・26労判679号81頁)。
　三田労基署長(東日印刷)事件(東京地判平成8・6・13労判698号18頁)。
　北九州西労基署長(東京製鐵九州工場)事件(福岡地判平成8・9・25労判705号61頁)。
　山形労基署長(山形交通)事件(仙台高判平成9・3・17労判715号53頁)。
　地公災基金愛知県支部長(瑞鳳小学校)事件(差戻審)(名古屋高判平成10・3・31労判739号71頁)。
7)　他に両グループの裁判例の混合体とでも呼ぶべき裁判例もある。
　地公災基金鹿児島県支部長(牧ノ原高校)事件(鹿児島地判昭和61・12・2労判495号80頁)(「基礎疾病の増悪について公務の遂行が相対的に有力な原因として作用し,その結果右基礎疾病を急激に増悪させて死亡の時期を著しく早めるなど,公務の遂行が基礎疾病と共働原因となって死亡の結果を招いたと評価できる場合には,右公務の遂行と死亡との相当因果関係を肯認できる」とする)。

1 問題提起

　「業務が共働原因となっていれば相当因果関係の存在を肯定できる」とする裁判例のグループと，「業務が相対的に有力な原因となっていれば相当因果関係の存在を肯定することができる」とする裁判例のグループは，表現の上からは明らかな差異がある。すなわち，前者は，業務が一原因として共に働いているのであれば，それを超えて業務が相対的に有力な原因となっていることまでは要求しないが，後者は，業務が全ての原因の中で相対的に有力な原因であることを要求していると解釈できる。実際，前者の裁判例の中には，「業務が相対的に有力な原因であることまでは要しない」とするものがあり[8]，逆に後者の裁判例の中には「公務が共働原因となっていれば足りるものではない」とするものがある[9]。

　しかし，裁判例を子細に分析すると，両者には，実質的な近似性がうかがわれる。このことを指摘した文献は過去にも存在するが[10]，筆者は，両グル

　　品川労基署長（中央田中電機）事件（東京地判平成1・3・1労判537号51頁）（「共働の原因又は相対的に有力な原因」という文言を用いる）。
　　社会保険庁長官（興生建設）事件（東京高判平成3・4・30労判600号76頁）（「前記職務遂行が本件疾病に対して相対的に有力な原因となっていたとか，右基礎疾患と共働の原因となっていたと認めることはできない」とする）。
　　新宿労基署長（大日本印刷）事件（東京高判平成3・5・27労判595号67頁）（「相対的有力な共働原因」という文言を用いる）。
　　地公災基金香川県支部長（高松市職員）事件（高松地判平成5・11・8労判640号47頁）（「相対的に有力な共働原因」という文言を用いる）。
　　茨木労基署長（関西新幹線整備）事件（大阪高判平成6・3・18労判655号54頁）（「有力な共働原因ないし誘因となって，基礎疾患を急激に…」と判示する）。
　　地公災基金香川県支部長（高松市職員）事件（高松高判平成6・11・1労民集45巻5・6号400頁）（「相対的に有力な共働原因」という文言を用いる）。
　　茨木労基署長（西武運送）事件（大阪地判平成7・3・27労判679号58頁）（「相対的に有力な原因又は共働の原因」という文言を用いる）。
　　堺労基署長（仲川交通）事件（大阪地判平成7・10・23労判687号61頁）（「相対的に有力な原因若しくは共働原因」という文言を用いる）。
8）　前掲注4）・17判決。
9）　前掲注5）・46，49判決。
10）　岩出誠「腎・心臓疾患等の労災認定基準改正の与える影響―改正を導いた裁判例の動向とそれへの影響を中心として」（ジュリスト1069号（1995）47頁）は，過去の裁判例を，「一般的ないし客観的相対的有力原因説」，「ゆるやかな相対的有力原因説」，及び共働原因説に分類し，そのうち「ゆるやかな相対的有力原因説」と共働原因説との

ープの判断枠組みがお互いの間に実質的近似性が生ずることを許容する原因に着目し，そこから両グループの近似性がいかなる点においてどの程度存在するのか，及び両グループの違いが存するのはいかなる点においてかを確定してみたい。

筆者は，両者に近似性が生ずることを許容する原因の第一は，「共働原因」，「相対的に有力な原因」という文言が内容的に幅を持っていることにあり，第二は，業務と「共に働いた」原因か否かを検討される比較対象が何で，業務と「相対的にどちらが有力な原因か」を検討される比較対象が何であるかが一律でないことにあると推測する。そこで本稿ではまず，①従来の裁判例において，業務が「共働」原因であるとはいかなる状態を指していたのか，そして業務が「相対的に有力な」原因であるとはいかなる状態を指していたのかを明らかにし，次いで，②業務が共働原因であることで足りるとする裁判例と，業務が相対的に有力な原因であることを要するとする裁判例とは，それぞれ業務と何とを並列して検討を行っているのかを検討する。その上で第三に③全ての発症原因の中で最も有力な原因が，加齢，日常生活等の自然的増悪をもたらす原因や業務という増悪原因以外のものである場合，それぞれのグループの裁判例によればいかなる判断がなされるのかを検討したい。これらの検討を通して，両者の近似性がいかなる点においてどの程度存在するのか，そして違いが存するのはいかなる点においてかを確定するのが本稿の目的である。

差異がほとんど見られないことになると指摘する。その他，武井寛「脳・心臓疾患に関する業務上外認定（判例評釈）」労旬1240号（1990）24頁，山下幸司「合宿研修中におけるくも膜下出血による死亡と労災認定基準（判例評釈）」（労判663号（1995）6頁），上柳敏郎「脳・心臓疾患と最近の判例動向」（季労175・176合併号（1995）32頁），水野勝「競合的原因と過労死の認定に関する理論的主要問題」労旬1358号（1995）18頁，安西愈「脳心疾患の公務災害認定をめぐる諸問題（上）」労判693号（1996）6頁，石田道彦「過労死をめぐる新認定基準と行政・判例の動向」日本労働法学会誌87号（1996）183頁，上柳敏郎「過労死の業務上外判断」日本労働法学会誌90号（1997）191頁，山川隆一＝荒木尚志「ディアローグ・労働判例この一年の争点」日本労働研究雑誌450号（1997）11頁・山川発言，西村健一郎「船員のくも膜下出血による死亡が業務上の過重負荷によるものと認められた事例（判例評釈）」判評477号（1998）24頁，拙稿・前掲注3）評釈279頁参照。

2 検討

(1) 「共働」原因,「相対的に有力な」原因の意味

業務が「共働」原因であるとはいかなる状態を指すのか。そして業務が「相対的に有力な」原因であるとはいかなる状態を指すのであろうか。

(a) 業務が発症の共働原因となっていることを相当因果関係の存在の要件とする裁判例は,業務の基礎疾患に与える影響の程度がいかに小さくとも,ともかく業務が一原因でありさえすれば,相当因果関係を認めるのであろうか。

確かに,表現上は,業務が発症の共働原因となっていることを相当因果関係の存在の要件とする裁判例は,業務の基礎疾患に与える影響の程度がいかに小さくとも,ともかく業務が一原因でありさえすれば,相当因果関係を認めると解する余地がある。しかし,業務が発症の共働原因となっていることを相当因果関係の存在の要件とする裁判例のうちかなりのものは,業務が基礎疾患を自然的経過を超えて増悪させているか否かを検討している[11]。そのような裁判例においては,業務が,自然的進行によっては発症しないと認め

---

[11] 前掲注4)の各裁判例。

なお,業務が共働原因であることを要件とする裁判例の中で,業務が基礎疾患を自然的経過を超えて増悪させているか否かを中心に相当因果関係の判断を行っているとは必ずしも言えない裁判例には,以下のようなものが含まれている。

①業務・公務の遂行が,病的素因を刺激し又は基礎疾患を急激に増悪させて当該疾病の発症の時期を早める等,その病的素因や基礎疾患と共働原因となって当該疾病を発症させたと認められる場合に相当因果関係を認めるもの。
・地公災基金高知県支部長(越知中学)事件(高知地判平成2・2・22労判571号30頁)。
②業務・公務の遂行が基礎疾病を誘発し又は急激に増悪させて死亡の時期を早める等,それが基礎疾病と共働原因となって死亡の結果を招いたと認められる場合に相当因果関係を認めるもの。
・地公災基金秋田県支部長(大館市教員)事件(秋田地判昭和61・12・19労判496号84頁,判タ629号143頁)。
・四日市労基署長(日本運送)事件(名古屋高判昭和63・10・31労判529号15頁)。
・地公災基金東京都支部長(木場ポンプ所)事件(東京地判平成2・10・11労判571号5頁)。
・地公災基金秋田支部長(大館市教員)事件(仙台高秋田支判平成3・6・19労判603号68頁)。
・地公災基金愛知県支部長(瑞鳳小学校)事件(名古屋高判平成3・10・30労判602号29頁)。

られる基礎疾患を，その自然的経過を超えて増悪させて発症に至らしめたと認められない場合には，そもそも共働原因と認められないのである。すると，そうした，共働原因となっていることを要件とする裁判例においては，少なくとも業務が基礎疾患をその自然的経過を超えて増悪させるほど有力な原因といえなければ，共働原因と認められず，業務と発症との相当因果関係が肯定されないと言える。

　(b)　業務が相対的に有力な原因であることを要件とする裁判例は，業務が最有力原因でなくても，かなり有力な原因でありさえすれば，相当因果関係を認めるのであろうか。

　「相対的に有力な原因である」という表現は，曖昧さを内包している。業務が他のどの原因と比べても一番有力であることを指しているのか，業務が全ての原因の中で，相対的に見て有力な部類に属しているということを指しているのか，判然としない。裁判例の中には，業務が最有力であることまでも要求してはいないと明言するものもあり[12]，公務が過重負荷となったことが認められなかった事例ではあるが，「公務の遂行が相対的に有力な原因にあたると評価して相当因果関係があるものと認めることは困難であり，……血圧のコントロール不良により高血圧症の進展（増悪）を来したことが最も有力な原因であるとみるのが合理的であると考えられる」と判示したものも存する[13]。しかし，それ以外の裁判例は，この点について触れておらず，いずれであるか断言できない。

　(c)　(a)で指摘したように，相当因果関係を肯定するには業務が共働原因となっていることが必要であるとする裁判例のうちかなりのものは，業務が基礎疾患をその自然的経過を超えて増悪させるほどの原因でなければ，相当因果関係を肯定しない。業務が基礎疾患をその自然的経過を超えて増悪させているか否かは，相当因果関係を肯定するのに業務が相対的に有力な原因となっていることが必要であるとする裁判例においてもほぼ必ず検討されている[14]。ところで，これらの，共働原因となっていることを要件とする裁判例・相対的に有力な原因となっていることを要件とする裁判例の中には，それ

---

12)　前掲注5）・30, 32, 49判決。
13)　前掲注5）・30判決。

14) 前掲注5）の各裁判例。
　なお，業務が相対的有力原因であることを要件とする裁判例の中で，業務が基礎疾患をその自然的経過を超えて増悪させているか否かを中心に相当因果関係の判断を行っているとは必ずしも言えない裁判例には，以下のようなものが含まれている。
　①公務とは無関係の他の原因を有していた場合でも，公務の遂行が基礎疾患を増悪させるなど公務が疾病発生の相対的に有力な原因であると認められる場合には相当因果関係を肯定する裁判例。
　地公災基金埼玉県支部長（越谷市職員）事件（浦和地判昭和61・5・30労判528号102頁）。
　②業務が発症の誘発原因たる一過性の血圧亢進の誘因足りうることを認定し，疾病のいくつかの原因，素因のうち，業務が相対的に有力な原因の一つであるとして相当因果関係を認めた裁判例。
　中野労基署長（旭運輸）事件（長野地判昭和62・4・23労判498号57頁）。
　③業務を相対的に有力な原因として，肉体的疲労や恐怖・驚愕などの精神的感動により一過的に血圧が亢進し，これを副因として発症に至ったと認められることが必要であるとした裁判例。
　恵那労基署長（成豊建設）事件（岐阜地判平成2・11・5労判575号45頁）。
　④「業務に起因して基礎的病態が著しく増悪したものとは認められない」事例で，「業務がそれ自体単独で，又は同人の喫煙，飲酒，加齢等の素因と共働し，これらにより相対的に有力な原因となって冠動脈の動脈硬化を招き，或いは増悪させたと認めるに足りない」とした裁判例。
　東大阪労基署長（大喜工業）事件（大阪地判平成1・1・26労判534号48頁）。
　⑤(1)発症の際現に行っていた業務が，業務の内外を問わず，日常経験することが極めて少ないような血圧の上昇をきたすものであることが経験則上理解しうる程度に強度の肉体的または精神的負担のあるものである場合(2)労働者が，通常であれば医師の診察を受けるべきであると判断される程度の身体の不調があるにもかかわらず，他の者ではその業務を代替できないためなど業務上の理由で，休養をとり医師の診察を受けることが事実上期待できない状況で業務を継続した後に当該疾病を生じた場合であって，右身体の不調と頭蓋疾病との間に合理的関連性が認められる場合など，通常人の合理的な判断として，当該業務が相対的に有力な原因となって当該疾病を生じさせたと認めるのが相当である場合には，当該疾病の業務起因性を肯定すべきとした裁判例。
　仙台労基署長（森勇建設）事件（仙台地判平成1・9・25労判551号63頁）。
　⑥「既存の素因ないし基礎疾患を有する者が，一方で地方公務員として勤務するうち，この素因等が原因又は条件となって発症した時でも，公務に従事したことが相対的に有力な原因となって素因等の増悪を早め，あるいは発症を誘発されてついに死亡するに至ったと認められる場合には，公務と右発症との間には相当因果関係が肯定される。……いかなる内容の業務であれ，これに従事することにより何らかの精神的肉体的負荷を被ることは必然であり，また素因等が加齢に伴う自然的経過により増悪していく可能性も当然のことながら否定できないところである。従って，公務と素因等

ぞれ,「業務が基礎疾患をその自然的経過を超えて増悪させているか否か」を検討するものと,増悪の程度を強める修飾語をつけた「業務が基礎疾患をその自然的経過を超えて『急激に』増悪させているか否か」,「業務が基礎疾患をその自然的経過を超えて『著しく』増悪させているか否か」等を検討するものが両方含まれている[15]。増悪の程度を強める『急激に』,『著しく』という文言を用いた表現を採用する裁判例が,共働原因となっていることを要件とする裁判例の中にも存在し,逆にそうした文言を用いない表現を採用する裁判例が,相対的に有力な原因となっていることを要件とする裁判例の中にも存在するのである。このことから,相対的有力原因であることを要件とする裁判例のグループが,共働原因であることを要件とする裁判例のグループよりも,業務が基礎疾患を増悪させた程度について高い水準を要求しているわけではないと言える。ゆえに,この点に関しては,相対的有力原因であることを要件とする裁判例と,共働原因であることを要件とする裁判例とを

の発症との間に何らかの関連性があるというだけでは未だ公務起因性を認めることのできないことは当然で,公務による負荷の程度が極めて軽微なことから客観的に見て死亡の原因は専ら素因等にかかるという時には起因性を否定すべく,既に判示のとおり,公務の遂行が相対的に有力な原因になっている場合に始めて起因性が認められると解すべきものである。」とした裁判例。

地公災基金愛知県支部長(瑞鳳小学校)事件(名古屋高判平成3・10・30労判602号29頁)。

15) 前掲注4)の共働原因であることを要件とする裁判例のうち,業務が自然的経過を超えて基礎疾患,基礎的素因を増悪させたか否かを検討するものは,以下の通り。
3,4,5,7,8,9,10,12,13,14,15,16,19判決。
前掲注4)の共働原因であることを要件とする裁判例のうち,業務が自然的経過を超えて『著しく』・『急激に』・『著しく急激に』基礎疾患,基礎的素因を増悪させたか否かを検討するものは,以下の通り。
1,2,6,11,17,18判決。
前掲注5)の相対的有力原因であることを要件とする裁判例のうち,業務が自然的経過を超えて基礎疾患,基礎的素因を増悪させたか否かを検討するものは,以下の通り。
23,26,29,31,34,40,51判決。
前掲注5)の相対的有力原因であることを要件とする裁判例のうち,業務が自然的経過を超えて『著しく』・『急激に』・『著しく急激に』基礎疾患,基礎的素因を増悪させたか否かを検討するものは,以下の通り。
20,21,22,24,25,28,32,33,35,37,38,39,41,42,43,44,45,46,47,48,49,50,52,53,54,55判決。

全体としてみると,確たる違いは見いだせない。両グループの出す具体的結論に差異があるとすれば,それは「自然的経過を超えて(急激に)(著しく)増悪させる」という文言の意味内容が,両グループで異なる場合であると言えよう。

また,(b)の検討から,相対的に有力な原因であることを要する裁判例には,業務が最有力原因であることを要求しないものが少なくとも複数含まれていることが知られた。共働原因であることを要件とする裁判例は,業務が最有力原因か否かに関心を払っていないが,相対的有力原因であることを要件とする裁判例も業務が最有力であることを要求しないのであれば,業務がすべての原因の中でどの順位を占めることを要求するかについては,両グループの間に絶対的違いは見いだせないこととなる。

以上のことから,①相対的有力原因であることを要件とする裁判例が,発症と相当因果関係があると認める業務の有力さと,共働原因であることを要件とする裁判例が,発症と相当因果関係があると認める業務の有力さ,及び②両グループの裁判例が業務について全ての増悪原因のうちどの順位を占めることを要求するかの二点については,両グループに決定的違いがない可能性を指摘できる。

(2) 業務と並列される対象

業務が共働原因となっていることを要件とする裁判例と,相対的に有力な原因であることを要件とする裁判例は,それぞれ業務と何とを並列して検討を行っているのであろうか。仮に共働原因と相対的に有力な原因が異なる概念である場合,同じものと並列して,一方は業務と共働原因になっていれば業務が相対的に有力な原因でなくとも相当因果関係が認められるとし,他方は業務が相対的に有力な原因となっていなければ認められないとするのであれば,両グループの裁判例の判断基準は明らかに異なると言える。

(a) 業務が共働原因となっていることを要件とする裁判例は,何と業務とが共働しているか否かを検討しているのであろうか。

業務が共働原因となっていることを要件とする裁判例は,ほぼその全てが,業務と基礎疾患(基礎的素因,基礎疾病)とを並列して,両者が共働原因となって発症を引き起こしている場合に業務と発症との相当因果関係を肯定で

きると判示している[16]。被災労働者が基礎疾患を有していて，それを業務が増悪させて発症に至らしめたという状況を，基礎疾病と業務とが共に働いて発症を引き起こしたと表現しているのである。

---

[16] 前掲注4）の共働原因であることを要件とする裁判例が，業務と何とを並列して，両者が共働原因となって発症したと言えるか否かを検討しているか。
　(1) 基礎疾病と並列して共働原因となって発症したと言えるか否かを検討している判決（判決番号で示す。）
　　　　1…基礎疾病
　　　　2…基礎疾病
　　　　4…基礎疾病
　　　　5…基礎疾病（加齢，喫煙等いくつかの要因が競合していると指摘）
　　　　6…基礎疾病
　　　　7…基礎疾病
　　　　8…病的素因や既存の疾病（加齢，日常生活上の負荷のみにより発症に至ったと考えがたいことを指摘）
　　　　9…基礎疾病（加齢，日常生活によっては発症しないことを指摘）
　　　10…病的素因ないし基礎疾患（肥満，加齢に言及）
　　　11…基礎疾病
　　　12…基礎疾患（他に原因を見いだしにくいことを指摘）
　　　13…脳動脈瘤の存在（＝基礎疾患）
　　　14…基礎疾患（肥満，糖尿病）
　　　15…基礎疾病（年齢に言及）
　　　16…病的素因や基礎疾病等（加齢及び日常生活上の負荷）
　　　18…基礎疾病
　　　19…病的素因ないし基礎疾患
　(2) それ以外のものと並列している判決（判決番号で示す。）
　　　　3…基礎疾患，その他の要因（「公務が基礎疾患を増悪させて死亡の時期を早めた場合または公務と基礎疾患が共働原因となって死亡の直接の原因となる疾病を発症させた場合において，公務と基礎疾患の増悪または公務と直接の原因となる疾病の発症との間に相当因果関係が認められる限り，公務と死亡との間に相当因果関係が肯定され，公務起因性が認められるものというべきである。また，公務とその他の要因が共働原因となって基礎疾患を増悪させ，それにより死亡するに至った場合にも，公務と基礎疾患の増悪との間に相当因果関係が存する限り，公務と死亡との間には相当因果関係が認められるものである。」）
　　　17…脳動脈瘤の発生・増悪については加齢等，脳動脈瘤の破裂については高血圧症
　なお，前掲注4）であげた以外の裁判例につき，前掲注11）参照。

2 検 討

(b) 業務が相対的に有力な原因となっていることを要件とする裁判例は，業務が何よりも相対的に有力か否かを検討するのであろうか。

業務が相対的有力原因となっていることを要するとする裁判例は，業務と基礎疾患とを比較するものもあるが，業務と加齢や日常生活等の要因とを比較して，業務が相対的に有力な原因となっているか否かを検討するものの方が多数を占める[17]。業務と加齢，日常生活とは，等しく基礎疾患の増悪原因であるので，後者の裁判例は，業務と他の増悪要因とを比較していると言える。

---

17) 前掲注5）の相対的に有力な原因であることを要件とする裁判例が，業務と何とを比較して，業務がそれよりも相対的に有力な原因となって発症したと言えるか否かを検討しているか。
　(1) 業務と基礎疾患のみとを比較して検討する判決（判決番号で示す。）
　　　　26…基礎疾病
　　　　32…基礎疾患
　　　　33…脳動脈瘤
　　　　42…基礎疾患
　　　　49…基礎疾患
　　　　51…高血圧症
　　　　53…基礎疾患
　(2) 業務と加齢や日常生活等の増悪原因・発症原因とを比較して検討する判決（判決番号で示す。）
　　　　21…食事，運動，血圧，神経の緊張度（ストレスを含む），遺伝
　　　　25…日常生活の起居動作
　　　　27…加齢や一般生活等における諸種の要因
　　　　29…加齢や一般生活における諸種の要因
　　　　30…疾病の諸々の原因
　　　　35…「発症原因の中で（相対的に有力な）」
　　　　36…加齢による自然的要因，日常生活上の行為＝排尿等
　　　　38…加齢その他の原因
　　　　40…日常生活上の多様な出来事
　　　　43…加齢その他の原因
　　　　44…加齢その他の原因
　　　　45…加齢その他の原因
　　　　46…加齢その他の原因
　　　　48…加齢その他の原因
　　　　54…日常生活上存する他の諸々の原因

発症の基盤となる基礎疾患と，その基礎疾患を増悪させることが疑われる業務とを比較するのは，性質の違うもの同士を比較することであるし，増悪原因同士を比較することはできても業務と基礎疾患とを比較することが物理的に可能かどうか疑問がある。加齢や日常生活という要因は，基礎疾患の自然的増悪をもたらす要因であるが，同じ増悪要因として業務とそれらを比較することは可能であるし，業務がそれらと比較して相対的に有力な原因であることを要求することは，意味のあることである。

(c) (a), (b)の検討を前提にすると，加齢や日常生活がもたらす自然的進行によっては発症に至らないはずの基礎疾患を，業務が自然的経過を超えて増悪させ，発症に至らしめた状態を指して，基礎疾患と業務とが共働原因になったと表現することは可能であるし，また，業務が加齢や日常生活上の負荷よりも相対的に有力な原因になったと表現することも可能である。これを医学的知見に引きつけて言い換えれば，基礎的病態に業務による過重負荷が加わって発症したことに着目して基礎疾患と業務とが共に働いて原因となったと表現できるし，基礎疾患が，加齢や日常生活等における諸種の要因によ

　　　55…それ以外の発症の原因
(3) 基礎疾患を含む複数の原因と比較している判決（判決番号で示す。）
　　　20…他の要因及び病状の自然的進行
　　　22…他の要因及び基礎疾患
　　　23…「いくつかの原因，素因（のうち相対的に有力な）」
　　　24…疾病，酒，タバコ
　　　28…身体的素因等
　　　34…業務を含む複数の原因＝心臓疾患，糖尿病，喫煙
　　　37…素因，基礎疾患
　　　39…その他の素因や嗜好，公務外の生活（高血圧等の既往症，年齢，肥満，飲酒，喫煙）
　　　41…加齢，高血圧症等の疾病，日常生活上の多様な出来事
　　　50…基礎疾病や素質的因子等他の要因
　　　52…他の原因（危険因子＝基礎疾患，リバウンド効果，肥満，喫煙，飲酒，疲労，ストレス）
(4) 不明な判決（判決番号で示す。）
　　　31…（諸般の事情を総合的に判断）
　　　47…不明
なお，前掲注5）にあげた以外の裁判例につき，前掲注14）参照。

り自然的経過の増悪をし，業務により自然的経過を超えた増悪をしたことに着目し，業務が相対的に有力な原因となったと表現することもできると言える。

業務が共働原因となっている場合に相当因果関係を肯定できるとする裁判例も，自然的進行によっては発症しない基礎疾患を，業務が自然的経過を超えて増悪させて発症に至らしめたか否かを判断する以上，加齢や日常生活の負荷による自然増悪によっては発症にいたらない基礎疾患であるか，業務以外に増悪原因はあるかという点を検討すると考えられる。このような，加齢や日常生活の負荷，業務以外の増悪原因の有力さの検証を行う点は，相対的に有力な原因であることを要件とする裁判例と同じである。すると，業務が基礎疾患と共働原因となっていることから業務と発症との間には相当因果関係が認められるという表現を用いようと，業務が加齢や日常生活上の負荷よりも相対的に有力な原因となって発症を招いているから業務と発症との間には相当因果関係が認められるという表現を用いようと，どちらの表現を用いる裁判例も，行う判断の経過やその結果は，同一である可能性がある。

(3) 最有力な第三の原因の存在

(1), (2)において，両グループの裁判例が，加齢，日常生活，業務，基礎疾患等の原因を巡り，近似性のある判断を行ってきた可能性を指摘した。それでは，全ての発症原因の中で最も有力な原因が，加齢，日常生活等の自然的増悪をもたらす原因や業務という増悪原因以外のものである場合，両グループの裁判例はいかなる判断をなすのであろうか。

(a) 共働原因となっていることを要件とする裁判例は，業務と基礎疾患以外の第三の原因が最有力であった場合も，業務と第三の原因が基礎疾患と共働原因になっているという理由で相当因果関係を認めるのであろうか。

表現上からは，認める可能性も，認めない可能性も考えられる。裁判例の中には，「公務とその他の要因とが共働原因となって基礎疾患を増悪させ，それにより死亡するに至った場合にも，公務と基礎疾患の増悪との間に相当因果関係が存する限り，公務と死亡との間には相当因果関係が認められる」

---

18) 前掲注4)・3 判決。

とし，更に続けて「なお相当因果関係が認められる場合であっても，当該職員が故意または重大な過失により基礎疾患を発症させ，またはこれを増悪させるなど，災害補償制度の趣旨に反する特段の事情が存する場合には，補償法14条の趣旨に照らし，公務起因性は否定されるべきである」とするものがある[18]。しかしこれ以外の裁判例は，特にこの点に言及しておらず，どちらの可能性も否定できない。

(b) 相対的有力原因となっていることを要件とする裁判例は，業務と，加齢や日常生活等の自然的増悪をもたらす原因以外に，全ての原因の中で最も有力な原因が存在する場合にも，業務が第二順位等かなり有力な原因であるときには，業務が相対的に有力な原因になっているという理由で相当因果関係を認めるのであろうか。

この点も，表現上からは認める可能性も認めない可能性も考えられる。過去の裁判例の中には，基礎疾病の他に発症原因となる他の要因の存在が認められることを一判断材料として，「業務の同人の高血圧症に対する影響は，未だ，他の要因及び病状の自然的進行より以上に，同人の高血圧症を急速に増悪させて脳出血の発症を著しく早め，よって同人に死をもたらす程度のものであったと認めることができない」とするもの[19]や，「狭心症について職務起因性を認めるためには，職務に起因する過度の精神的，肉体的負担が他の要因及び基礎疾患の自然的進行より以上に，その者の既に有する基礎疾患を急速に増悪させ，その結果，狭心症の発症を出現させたものであること，すなわち職務の遂行が当該疾病に対して相対的に有力な原因になっていたことが認められなければならない」とするもの[20]がある。これらは，業務が他の要因より以上に基礎疾患を増悪させていることを業務と発症との相当因果関係を肯定する要件としている。また，業務による負荷の程度や，発症に至るまでの経緯，既往症がないこと，急激な血圧上昇の発生原因となるような素因や嗜好も認められないこと，同人の公務外の生活において，急激な血圧上昇の発生原因となるような精神的身体的負荷をもたらす事由の存在が認められないことを総合して，業務により脳動脈瘤が自然的経過を超えて急激に

---

19) 前掲注5)・20判決。
20) 前掲注5)・22判決。
21) 前掲注5)・39判決。

著しく増悪し，発症に至ったとするもの[21]もある。この裁判例は，公務外の生活において発症原因となるような負荷をもたらす事由が存在しなかったことを，業務が発症を導いたことを基礎づける一判断材料としているが，そのような公務外の事由が存在したときにいかなる判断を行うかについては，明言していない。

　これら以外の裁判例は，この点について触れておらず，どちらの可能性も認めざるを得ない。

　この点は，(1)(b)の，「相対的に有力な原因である」とは「最有力原因である」ことと等しいのかという検討にもつながっていく。

　(c)　以上の検討から，最有力の原因が，加齢，日常生活等の原因や業務以外であった場合に関しては，両グループの裁判例とも，いかなる判断をなすのか確定できないことが知られた。

3　結　論

　2の(1)，(2)の検討から，両グループの裁判例の判断枠組みは，実質的な近似性を許容するものであると言える。すなわち，両グループの裁判例の判断方法は，表現は異なっていても，自然的進行によっては発症を引き起こさない基礎疾患が，業務により，加齢や日常生活等による自然的経過を超えて増悪させられた場合に，他に確たる要因がないときには，相当因果関係の存在を肯定するという限りで，重なる可能性を持つ。

　そこに違いが存するとすれば，それは，第一に，「自然的経過を超えて増悪させる」ということの意味内容が両グループで異なっている場合である。共働原因であることを要件とする裁判例が相当因果関係の存在の肯定のために要求する，業務による基礎疾患の増悪の程度（増悪を表す折れ線の傾斜角度）が，相対的に有力な原因であることを要件とする裁判例の要求するそれよりも低いとすれば，両グループの枠組みはどちらに依拠するかによって結論の変わりうる，異なる枠組みであるといえよう。

　また第二に，相対的に有力な原因であることを要件とする裁判例が最有力原因であることを要求する場合や最有力であることまでは要求しなくてもかなり有力な原因であることを要求しており，共働原因であることを要件とす

る裁判例の要求するレベルと差異があるときには，やはり両グループの枠組みは，どちらに依拠するかによって結論の変わりうる異なる枠組みであると言える。

　第三に，2の(3)の検討から知られるように，業務も自然的経過を超えて基礎疾患を増悪させる要因であったが，加齢や日常生活等の自然的増悪の原因となるものと業務という原因以外の原因が，最有力であった場合に，業務が相対的有力原因であることを要件とする裁判例が相当因果関係を一切認めず，共働原因であることを要件とする裁判例が認める可能性を持つとすれば，そこに差異があることは明らかである。

職業性疾病・作業関連疾病と安全配慮義務

中嶋士元也

はじめに

(1) 安全配慮義務論は，民法，労働法，民事訴訟法学上において「一つの最高裁判決を契機として，短期間のうちにこれほど多く論じられ，またこれほど多くの関連裁判例を生み出した問題はない」[1]と指摘されるほどに，昭和50年最高裁判決（1陸上自衛隊八戸車両整備工場事件・最三小判昭和50・2・25民集29巻2号143頁）の出現以後から平成初期にかけての約15年間は，雇用契約関係に係わる安全配慮義務論争が百花繚乱の観を呈したのである[2]。私自身もこの過程において，この論議に参加した（1987年論説。以下，前稿という）[3]。

もっとも，ここほぼ10年間は，同論争はやや鎮静化している。しかし，これは，必ずしも安全配慮義務をめぐる論議が収束したからではない。現に，

---

1) 奥田昌道「安全配慮義務」（石田・西原・高木先生還暦記念論文集・中巻『損害賠償法の課題と展望』日本評論社・1990）1頁。
2) 比較法研究をも含めた安全配慮義務論の全貌と関連文献及び裁判例を渉猟・紹介しつつ吟味を加えた近時の有意義な文献として，奥田・前掲論文，日本私法学会シンポジウム「安全配慮義務の現状と課題」（特に国井和郎・松本博之・北川善太郎の各教授による報告）（学会誌私法52号・1990），下森定編『安全配慮義務法理の形成と展開』（日本評論社・1988。主要な各種論文等を収録する）3頁以下，和田肇『労働契約の法理』（1990）81頁以下，高橋眞『安全配慮義務の研究』（成文堂・1992）1頁以下，宮本健蔵『安全配慮義務と契約責任の拡張』（信山社・1995）117頁以下等がある。これに対し，安全配慮義務概念の不法行為概念からの独自性に関して疑問を呈する立場からの論説として，新美育文「『安全配慮義務の存在意義』再論」法律論叢60巻4・5号583頁以下（1988）がある。
3) 中嶋「安全配慮義務論争の課題（上）（下）」日本労働協会雑誌338号・340号（1987）（同『労働関係法の解釈基準（上）』251頁以下に収録。信山社・1991）。

その後も雇用関係の過程で労働災害に遭遇した労働者からの安全配慮義務を根拠とする損害賠償請求の訴えは後を絶たず，裁判例は蓄積を重ねている。したがって，それら裁判例に対する評釈の類は依然として数多くみられるところである。しかし，本格的論陣はやや低迷の状況にある。安全配慮義務論争鎮静の主たる原因は，係争事案（実務的必要性）の減少のためではなく，その体系化を図ろうと情熱を燃やした学説の側の各論者が自己の主張をひとまず出し尽くしてしまったにもかかわらず，特に安全配慮義務を司る「債務構造論」ともいうべき基礎理論に関する帰趨（支配的見解の形成）が容易に決しないため，学説側がいささか"疲労気味"の状態にあるためと思われる。したがって，いずれ，同義務の債務構造論争は再燃するものと推測される。

(2) 本稿は，安全配慮義務に関する判例法理の分析と実務規範のあり方を試みた前稿のいわば続論として，前稿後の判例・学説の展開過程を追跡しつつ，これまでの論議においてなお吟味が希薄であった論点・課題につき解釈基準を提示しあるいはその準備作業を行おうとするものである。そして，さしあたりの筆者の関心事は次のようなところにある。

(a) まず，筆者が前稿において考察の対象としたのは，「労働災害」のうち主として労働者の突発的「災害・事故」に関する事案である。そこでは，職務遂行過程に関連する「病弊の蓄積・疾病への罹患」（職業性疾病ないしは作業関連疾病）につき安全配慮義務がこれをいかに把握しうるかの課題については，これを「意識的」に考察の対象から除外した[4]。のみならず，当時の安全配慮義務をめぐる訴訟事案は圧倒的に「災害」に関するものであり，それに対応してほとんどの論者の論述も労務提供過程における「災害的出来事」を想定して組み立てられていたといってよい。もちろん，「災害」と「疾病」とでは，安全配慮義務論の様相に本質的な差異があるというわけではないが，諸論点のうち，特に，義務内容の把握，因果関係，帰責事由，立証法則，時効の起算点において，別異の基準によって処理せざるをえない場面があると思われ，主として「災害」に関して定立された（とみられる）従来の解釈基準は「疾病」の場合には修正が施されるかあるいは別個に設定される必要があるのかどうか，考察を加える価値がある[5]。本稿では，従来の

---

4) 中嶋・前掲書268頁注1)。

はじめに

論議を補強しつつ「疾病」に焦点を当てて論じたい。ただし，本稿では上記諸論文のうち義務内容と因果関係及び帰責事由の問題のみを論じ，立証法則と時効の起算点に関しては，それらが，後述(b)の課題とも密接に関連すると思われるので，予定している次稿で一括して取り扱いたい。

(b) つぎに，従来の安全配慮義務違反問題の照準は，被災労働者の損害賠償請求権（事後救済）の発生要件いかんに当てられていた。しかし，近時労働災害への危険に遭遇した労働者に「平和義務履行請求権」が肯定されるべきかどうか，及び「労務給付拒絶権」が認められるべきか否か，すなわち同義務に対応した形での労働者側の「予防措置権」（事前措置）の存否が次第にクローズ・アップされてきている[6]。この課題のうち特に「労務給付拒絶

---

5) 奥田教授は，ドイツ民法の系譜において，雇用契約に基づく「安全配慮義務（Fürsorgepflicht）」と「特別の社会的接触」を有するに至った当事者の双方または一方に課される「保護義務」（Schutzpflicht）とはまったく別の過程を経て判例・学説上に登場したことを指摘しつつも，右両者の共通点と相違点を分析する。そして，「労働関係における安全配慮義務は，物的設備の危険性に由来する労災事故の場合に限られないこと，広く労務の管理，健康の管理など広汎な拡がりを有していること（職業病の防止や，過労死の問題なども射程に入る），言い換えれば，自己の供給した物または自己の行為から相手方の生命・健康等に被害が生じないように注意すること（これが保護義務に共通のメルクマール）に尽きない」。すなわち，一方で物的危険の防止という「保護義務の尽き果てたところから使用者の固有の安全配慮義務が始ま（り）」，他方で「使用者には，単に自己の行為によって労働者の人身を侵害することのないように振る舞う（不法行為規範のもとでの不可侵義務）のみならず，労働者の健康管理の面で積極的にさまざまの措置をとることが義務づけられる。これは，一般的な保護義務の内容あるいは限度を超えたものといわざるを得ないであろう」説く（前掲論文24，25頁。なお高橋・前掲書10頁以下参照）。これによれば，「物の危険」に対する生命・身体の保護は一般的「保護義務」でも相当程度に救済可能であるが，「自己の行為の危険」からの保護の側面においては，保護義務で処理できる場面は限定的であり，一般的接触関係の範囲を超えて，取り分け雇用関係においてより積極的かつ拡大の措置義務を使用者に講ぜしめるべく要請されるのが安全配慮義務の存在意義であるという理解になる。そして，「物（材料・器具）の危険」からは災害も生じ疾病（粉じん，ガス等に起因する）も生じるが，「健康管理面での積極的措置の要請」は，一回性の災害よりも，むしろ蓄積的な疾病を防止し回避する場合に固有の効能を発揮すると考えられる。つまり，「安全配慮義務」は，どちらかというと職業性・作業関連疾病の予防・回避においてこそよく固有の機能を発揮しうるともみることができよう。一回性の災害のみを念頭に置いて安全配慮義務の骨格と内容を把握しようとすることは，いささか視野を狭くすると思われるゆえんである。

権」に関しては，安全配慮義務・保護義務の母国ともいうべきドイツにおいて新立法たる「労働保護法」（Arbeitsschtzgesetz＝1997）において明文化され，新たな論議が展開されつつある[7]。と同時に，履行請求権・労務給付拒絶権の問題は，安全配慮義務の「債務の性質・構造論」（基礎理論）との整合性ないしは関連性が特に要請されることとなる。これらの課題に関しても，引続き次稿で考察を加えたい。

1　安全配慮義務論の今日的段階

(1)　本稿の目的である「職業性疾病・作業関連疾病と安全配慮義務」との検討に進むに先立ち，これまでにおおよそ確定された安全配慮義務に関する判例理論を中心とした骨格及び前稿において筆者が示した方向性を確認しておくべきであろうが，ここでは省略せざるをえない。それらについては筆者前稿を参照されたい[8]。また，筆者前稿の見解に対しては，その後他の論者からいくつかの批判が提示されたので，それらに応えてもおくべきであろうが，それらに関する本格的応答はやはり他日，本稿で積み残した「立証責任」「時効の起算点」の論点とともに，新たに「履行請求権・労務給付拒絶権」及び「債務構造論」を考察する際に行いたい。

(2)　安全配慮義務に関する論議（判例・学説）は，労働・雇用契約関係につき同義務の存在を明言した昭和50年最高裁判決（1陸自八戸）以降，10年あまりの間に約20例の最高裁判決を通じて，裁判実務の想定する「安全配慮義務」の法構造（いわば原型）がほぼ明らかにされた。すなわち，定義，法的根拠，適用範囲，義務内容，因果関係，立証責任，帰責事由，遺族の慰謝

---

6)　以前より，履行請求権や労務給付拒絶権の問題は一応論じられてきた。下森・前掲書245頁以下（下森），宮本・前掲書369頁以下，土田道夫「安全配慮義務の最近の動向」経営法曹110号（1995）26頁以下。なお，ドイツ民法618条に基づく法的効果の概要として，宮本・前掲書125頁以下，高橋・前掲書13頁以下。

7)　例えば，Vgl. N. Fabricius, Einstellung der Arbeitsleistung bei gefährlichen und normwidrigen Tätigkeiten, 1997 C. F. Müller.；M. Kittner＝R. Pieper, Arbeitsschutzgesetz (Basiskommentar) 1997, Bund-Verlag..

8)　中嶋・前掲書255頁以下参照。

料，附遅滞，時効の諸点の骨格である。これらについては，筆者もすでに整理作業を行っているので，ここでは，前稿以後下された注目すべき最高裁判決のみを付け加えて記しておく。

　(a)　帰責事由（予見可能性・結果回避可能性）　職業性疾病につき通常予想しえない危険まで防止すべき措置をとる必要はなく，振動障害発症の予見可能性が存していても，「社会，経済の進歩発展のため必要性，有益性が認められるかあるいは危険の可能性を内包するかもしれない機械器具については，その使用を禁止するのではなく，その使用を前提として，その使用から生ずる危険，損害の発生の有無に留意し，その発生を防止するための相当の手段方法を講ずることが要請されているというべきであるが，社会通念に照らし相当と評価される措置を講じたにもかかわらずなおかつ損害の発生をみるに至った場合には，結果回避義務に欠けるものとはいえない」（2 林野庁高知営林局事件・最二小判平成2・4・20労判561号6頁）。この2事件判決は，チェンソーなどの使用による白ろう病の発生が使用者の帰責事由に基づくかどうかが争われた事案であり，ある程度予見された職業性疾病の発生・蓄積は使用者の「結果回避義務」にいかなる影響を与えるかという問題を提起した。後に詳述する（2(5)②）。

　(b)　時効　安全配慮義務違反に由来する損害賠償請求権の消滅時効期間は10年と解すべきである（1 陸自八戸）。そして，消滅時効の起算点に関しては，まず「安全配慮義務違反に基づく損害賠償債務は，安全配慮義務と同一性を有するものではない。けだし，安全配慮義務は，特定の法律関係の付随義務として一方が相手方に対して負う信義則上の義務であって，この付随義務の不履行による損害賠償請求権は，付随義務を履行しなかったことにより積極的に生じた損害［第二次的に発生した別個の損害］についての賠償請求権であり，付随義務履行請求権の変形物ないし代替物であるとはいえないからである。そうすると，雇用契約上の付随義務としての安全配慮義務に基づく損害賠償債務が，安全配慮義務と同一性を有することを前提として，右損害賠償請求権の消滅時効は被用者が退職した時から進行するという使用者側の主張は前提を欠き，失当である」（3 長崎じん肺第二事件・最三小判平成6・2・22労判646号12頁）。そうであるとすると，非常に長い年月を経過しつつ徐々に症状が重篤になる事態も少なくないところの，進行性疾患の典型であるじ

ん肺罹患者の損害賠償請求権の消滅時効に関しても次のように解すべきである。すなわち，事後的にみると軽いじん肺から重いじん肺までの過程は一個の損害賠償請求権の範囲が量的に拡大しているに過ぎないとみえるとしても，（じん肺法に基づく管理区分の行政決定上の）各管理区分に基づく各損害は質的に異なり，病状が進行する過程では病状が今後どこまで進行するかを確定することは医学的に困難であるので，じん肺に関する最初の軽い行政決定を受けた時点で，その後の重い行政決定に相当する病状に基づく損害を含む全損害が発生していたと認めることは適当ではないから，消滅時効の起算点を最初の行政決定を受けた時からであるとする原審の判断は適法ではなく，消滅時効の起算点は「最終の行政決定」を受けたときから進行すると解すべきである（4 長崎じん肺第一事件・最三小判平成6・2・22民集48巻2号441頁）。右3・4事件判決は，じん肺という特異な進行を示すと同時に症状に関する行政管理区分の決定というこれまた特異な様相を呈する事案についてのものであるが，しかし，民法学上債務不履行や不法行為に基づく損害賠償請求権の時効論の上での体系的な位置づけにつき論議を呼んでいる[9]。

2 職業性疾病・作業関連疾病における措置義務

(1) 疾病の態様

使用者の安全配慮義務（ないしは類似の義務）違反が民事訴訟で争われた職業性疾病・作業関連疾病の種類・態様としては，次のようなものがみられる。

(a) 数多く裁判例に登場した疾病は，頸肩腕症候群，難聴，振動病，呼吸器疾患，腰痛，循環器系疾患，有機溶剤中毒などである。

(b) その他，各種ガン，ヒソ中毒，放射線障害，マンガン中毒，消化器障害，CO中毒，うつ秒・自殺，などがある。

(2) 義務の一般的範囲

安全配慮義務については，すでに1陸自八戸が災害事故と職業性疾病の双

---

[9] 消滅時効に関する最近の論説として，例えば，辻伸行「安全配慮義務違反に基づく損害賠償と消滅時効規範」上智法学論集39巻3号1頁以下。

2 職業性疾病・作業関連疾病における措置義務

方とに関する包括的な定義を与えていたところではあった。しかし，それに引き続く安全配慮義務違反訴訟は圧倒的に災害事故をめぐって提起されてきたため，同義務の骨格は，主として「一回性の災害事故」を想定して形成されてきたといってよい。

　他方，職業性疾病をめぐる事案にあっても，1陸自八戸出現前後から，使用者には定期検診によって「病気の早期発見に努め，罹患していることが判明した職員に対しては，勤務場所または職務の変更など適切な事後措置をとる」義務（5林野税務署事件・岡山地裁津山支判昭和48・4・24労判181号70頁）や会社独身寮への「入寮者が通常期待できる看護を受け療養することができるよう配慮するべき義務」（6日産自動車事件・東京地判昭和51・4・19労判253号48頁）などが事案に応じて個別的に措定されていたが，これをより一般化すると同時に詳細化した定義を施す判決がその後現れ，そこでは，実定的労働安全衛生法令の趣旨に基づき，使用者は「常に局職員の健康，安全のため適切な措置を講じ，職業性及び災害性の疾病の発生ないしその増悪を防止すべき義務を負っているだけでなく，職業性又は災害性の疾病に罹患していることが判明し又はそのことを予見し得べき職員に対しては，疾病の病勢が増悪することのないように疾病の性質，程度に応じ速やかに就業の禁止又は制限等を行うことはもとより，場合によっては勤務又は担当職務の変更を行う等適切な措置を講ずべき注意義務を負っている」と説かれた（7横浜中央郵便局事件・横浜地判昭和58・5・24判時1085号112頁。それ以前にも同旨の8東京国際郵便局事件・東京地判昭和52・11・28労働法律旬報951号71頁＝国賠法上の注意義務として争われた）。また，上記のような安全配慮義務を履行するに際しての措置をより具体化して，「労働時間，休憩時間，休日，休憩場所等について適正な労働条件を確保し，さらに，健康診断を実施したうえ，労働者の健康に配慮し，年齢，健康状態等に応じて，労働者の従事する作業内容の軽減，就業場所の変更等適切な措置をとるべき義務」を負うとされている（9富士保安警備事件・東京地判平成8・3・28労判694号34頁）。

　これらの定義によれば，「労務（公務）を提供する過程における労働者の生命・身体等を危険から保護するよう配慮する義務」たる安全配慮義務が，「疾病」との係りにおいて機能する場面（範囲）としては，第一に疾病の防止段階，第二に増悪の回避段階（罹患後の措置段階）の二段階が措定されてい

(3) 義務の具体化・類型化

それでは，使用者に要請される上記二つの段階での措置の必要性ないし義務の具体的な内容はどのように設定されるべきかが次の課題である。

(a) 疾病の防止段階

疾病の予防段階における安全配慮義務の特徴は，いうまでもなく，「業務に起因する疾病」に罹患せしめないよう配慮する義務であるというところに見いだされる。つまり，業務外の（私生活上の）疾病を防止する契約上の義務は基本的には使用者には存在しない。この点において，業務上疾病であるか業務外疾病への罹患であるかを問わず，罹患後の労務過程における使用者の配慮・措置義務が機能する第二段階における安全配慮義務とは異なる。従来の裁判例を分析するとき，疾病の防止段階の義務としては，材料自体が有する危険から労働者を保護する義務と作業自体の有する危険性から労働者を保護する義務の二つを分類するのが最も包括的であるが，余りにも具体性を欠く。そこで，この段階での義務設定は，裁判例におけるほとんどが労働安全衛生法令の内容に従ってあるいはそれを斟酌して行われていることに鑑み，本稿においてもその観点からの分類を行いたい[10]。

① 労働安全衛生法令を遵守すべき義務

「労務（公務）を提供する過程」における各種疾病の防止に関して具体的に安全配慮義務違反の成否が問題となる最大の類型は，実定法としての労働安全衛生法（安衛法）及びその付属法令によって使用者（事業主）に各種措置義務が課せられている場合である。

安衛法令では，「労働者の危険又は健康障害を防止するための措置」（特に同法22～23条，25条，27条1項等及安衛法施行令，安衛規則，有機溶剤中毒予防規則，四アルキル鉛中毒予防規則はじめ約10数種の関係省令及び罰則あり），「有害物

---

[10] 岩村正彦「じん肺症と使用者の安全配慮義務」ジュリ825号55頁が析出したところでは，じん肺症が問題となった裁判例において安全配慮義務の具体的な内容として示されたものとしては，①粉じん発生防止のための措置，②粉じんの除去・飛散防止のための措置，③粉じん吸入防止器具を使用させる義務，④安全教育を施す義務，⑤健診・精密検査を受診させる義務，⑥じん肺法による管理区分の決定を通知し，相応の健康管理措置をとる義務などがある。じん肺症以外の事案にあっても，ほぼ同様の義務内容が措定されること，本文記述のとおりである。

の調査」(同法58条＝罰則なし),「労働者の就業に当たっての措置」(安全衛生教育＝同法59条〜60条の２＜一部罰則あり＞,安衛規則35条),「健康の保持増進のための措置」(作業環境測定＝同法65条〜65条の４＜一部罰則あり＞,健康診断の実施＝同法66条〜66条の２＜罰則あり＞,健康診断実施後の措置＝同法66条の３＜罰則なし＞,健康診断の結果通知＝同法66条の４＜罰則あり＞)等が規定されている[11]。　この類型における従来の裁判例にあっては,有機溶剤や四アルキル鉛による中毒症への罹患が典型的なものである。この両者の場合,安衛法に基づき事業者(使用者)には,「事業者が講ずべき措置」に関し詳細な労働省令が定められている(安衛法27条１項,有機溶剤中毒予防規則＝有機則,四アルキル鉛中毒予防規則＝四アルキル鉛則)。

まず,これらの職業性疾病たる有機溶剤中毒の予防諸法規にあっては,「Ｙ社は,Ｘの使用者として安衛法,安衛規則等に定める義務を負っているが,同社の本件作業内容から,同社が有機則に定める義務をも負っているというべきである」。そして,「各規定は,いわゆる行政的な取締規定であって,各規定の定める義務は,使用者の国に対する公法上の義務と解される。しかしながら…右各規定の内容は,使用者の労働者に対する私法上の安全配慮義務の内容ともなり,その規準になる」と判示され,そこでは,有機則を中心とした局所排気装置の設置,適切な保護具の備付け,有機溶剤に関する安全衛生教育の実施,健康診断の実施(身体の異常の把握),必要な作業環境測定,有機溶剤に関する注意事項の掲示等の諸義務が安全配慮義務の内容として措定されるとともにその義務違反が肯定されている(10内外ゴム事件・神戸地判平成２・12・27判時764号165頁。同旨11みくに工業事件・長野地裁諏訪支判平成３・３・７労判588号64頁,12ソニーマグネプロダクツ事件・仙台地判昭和52・３・14労判273号46頁)。

②　安衛法令上の規定を斟酌して措置する義務

裁判例のうちには,安衛法令上の規定を直接契約上の義務内容とすべきであるとはせずに,安全配慮義務につき,同法令等の「趣旨に基づき,その被用者の健康安全に適切な措置を講じ,職業性の疾病の発生ないしその増悪を

---

[11]　安衛法規の概略に関しては,さしあたり,保原喜志夫＝山口浩一郎＝西村健一郎編『労災保険・安全衛生のすべて』(1998) 28頁以下(畠中信夫)参照。

防止すべき義務」と捉える立場がある（13大興電機事件・東京地判昭和50・11・13判時819号93頁，同旨8東京国際郵便局事件）。

　また，安衛法令上の規定を直接契約上の義務内容とすべきか「その趣旨を斟酌する」に過ぎないかについては明言しないが，安衛法令と同様の基準をもってないしは安衛法令所定の危険物質の暴露にまでは至らないが同化学物質が類似の危険を有することを理由に，その予防のための措置を契約上の義務としてを設定してこれを「安全配慮義務」となし，それに対する違反の有無を吟味する手法がみられる。すなわち，「使用者は，たとい（有機溶剤中毒）予防規則等の法令に根拠規定がない場合でも，当該作業場の作業環境，作業に伴う危険などの現実的状況に応じて必要な措置をとるべき義務を要請されるものといわなければならない」と（14東北機械製作所事件・秋田地判昭和57・10・18労判401号52頁＜有機溶剤中毒＞。その他15ワンビシ産業事件・東京地判昭和55・3・10判時960号69頁，16新日本ヘリコプター事件・東京地判昭和57・10・26判時1066号80頁＜四アルキル鉛中毒＞等）。のみならず，安衛法令は「最低限を定めたものであって右内容のみを実施していれば使用者は常に被用者に対する健康管理義務を尽くしたとはいえない」と判示した例もみられる（17住友林業事件・名古屋地判昭和56・9・30労判378号64頁＜ただし，安全配慮義務違反否定例＞）。

　これら判決例にあっては，疾病の防止段階の措置義務として，①有害な化学物質排出の抑制等安全な環境の保持，②安全設備の設置，③保護具の装着，④安全衛生教育・危険性の周知徹底，⑤各種健康診断の実施，⑥作業環境の測定が使用者に措置すべき内容として要請されている。そしてそこでは，右諸要請のひとつないしは総体が「安全配慮義務」の内容を形成するものとして捉えられている。

　右諸事項は，安衛法22，23条及び付属省令（①），同22条及び付属省令（②），22条及び付属省令（③），同59，60条の2及び付属省令（④），同66条及び付属省令（⑤），同65条及び付属政省令（⑥）によってそれぞれ詳細な措置を要求されているものであり，それらはとりもなおさず，少なくとも職業性疾病の防止段階における雇用契約上使用者が負担すべき安全配慮義務をめぐっても問題となるであろう事項をほぼ網羅しているといって差し支えなかろう。

③　安衛法令と契約上の権利義務

ところで，膨大な付属法規をも含めた公法的規定たる安衛法令が雇用契約においていかなる効力を示すかは早くから論議されてきたところである。つまり，安衛法令は私法的効力をも発生せしめるか否かの争いである。そして，安全配慮義務違反訴訟との関連においては，①安全配慮義務違反に基づく損害賠償請求訴訟において，安衛法令が，被告（使用者・事業主）に同義務が課せられることの根拠となるか，②直接的に具体的な契約内容とはならなくても，安衛法令は，被告（使用者・事業主）に同義務を課す場合の「斟酌すべき基準」となりうるか，③安衛法令は，安全配慮義務の履行請求が許容されることの根拠となるか，の三点が課題であるとされてきた。これらの論点に関する裁判例は分かれ，他方多くの労働法学説は安衛法令は公法的規定であると同時に私法的規定でもあり，したがって安衛法令は安全配慮義務の具体的内容ともなると説いてきた。しかし，近時，これらの課題に関して，比較法的考察を含めた総合的検討を行った結果，「わが国の労働安全衛生法は，法の受益者である労働者に，法の義務主体に対して，私法的請求を行う権利を付与する私法的法規ではなく，純粋に公法的な法規である」，したがって「（安衛法令は）公法的な法規であり，その義務主体が，私法上安全配慮義務の主体となることを直接に示すものではな（く）」，安全配慮の義務設定にあたっても，「（安衛法令は）直接安全配慮義務の具体的内容となるのではなくその内容の検討の際に基準となるかまたは斟酌すべきもの（に過ぎない）」との見解を強く唱える立場が登場している[12]。

私も，結論的には，この見解に賛成である。安全衛生法規の私法的性質に関して，比較法的にみると，これを純粋な公法法規であり私法的効力は与えられない（ただし，損害賠償請求訴訟の際の基準となり斟酌される）との法制度をとる国（アメリカ）と，反対に，第一義的には公法的法規ではあるがそれらは使用者の労働契約上の配慮義務によって補充され強化されており，したがって安全衛生法規は直接使用者の契約上の義務を規律するとの法理論が支配的である国（ドイツ），包括的な安全衛生法規には私法的な効力を認めない

---

12)　小畑史子「労働安全衛生法規の法的性質(一)〜(三・完)」法学協会雑誌112巻2号，3号，112巻5号。この問題に関する判例・学説の動向及び本文引用箇所に関しては，同5号648頁以下特に658, 668, 669頁。

が，同法規に付属する安全衛生規則については（これを否定する条項が同規則中に設けられていない限り）私法的効力を付与するとの中間的な制度を採用する国（イギリス）とに分かれている。安全衛生法規の私法的効力付与に否定的ないしは消極的な制度・理論を採用する立場（アメリカ，イギリス）が，安全衛生法規に対し直ちに私法的効力を付与することが適当ではないと考える根拠は，煎じつめていえば，「同法規をもって私法上の契約義務としても措定するならば，むしろ，立法者の意識としても，私法的責任の射程を懸念しそれに拘泥するあまり，独自の行政的考慮に沿ってより広汎かつ効果的な労働災害防止効果のある安全衛生法規を設置することに消極的にならざるをえなくなる」との懸念を有するからであろう[13]。

　筆者は，かつて，「安全衛生関係法令の実行義務は，使用者の裁量などの入り込む余地のない明確な基準であれば，それ自体安全配慮義務の中核的部分を構成すると解してさしつかえなかろう。典型的結果債務として捉えられているといってよい」と把握し，そのことを原告（被災者）側の立証責任を軽減させる方向で反映させる見解を提示した[14]。これに対しては，民事訴訟法学の立場から，「この（中嶋の）見解には，次のような疑問がある。（安全配慮義務の設定につき）物的設備にせよ人的措置にせよ安全衛生関係法令に定めがあるのとないのとで，どうして決定的な差異が生じるべきなのか」[15]と。

　たしかに，私見には再考すべき点があると考える。それは，わが国の安全衛生法令というものの「（公法的）義務・措置の多様性，拘束性の濃淡」にある。これをそのまま契約当事者間の権利義務として設定させるにはあまりに漠然としていて不適切な規定も中核的な規定の中にさえ少なくない（例えば，同法3条，58条，62条等）。そこで，筆者は，「使用者の裁量などの入り込む余地のない明確な基準」であることを高度の契約義務として取り入れる要件と

---

13) 安全衛生法規の私法的効力に関するアメリカ，イギリスの法制度・法理論に関しては，小畑・前掲論文法協112巻2号253頁以下及び同3号377頁以下に詳述されている。またドイツの同問題の状況に関しては，さしあたり，Manfred Löwisch, Arbeitsrecht. 4., Aufl., 1996, S. 332 ff., W. Zöllner = K. G. Loritz, Arbeitsrecht., 4. Aufl., 1992, S. 306. 土田道夫「労働保護法と労働契約との関係をめぐる一考察」法政大学大学院紀要9号（1982）305頁以下，和田・前掲書92頁，高橋・前掲書17頁等。
14) 中嶋・前掲書270頁。
15) 松本・前掲私法学会シンポジウム（私法52号）33頁。

したのであったが，そうすると今度は，付属政省令の膨大な措置内容のすべてをそのまま実現するのでなければ常に安全配慮義務違反に陥るということとなり，それは使用者に不可能を強いるに等しい。それらのなかには行政的取締を通じて時間をかけて行わざるをえない類いの事項も少なくないからである。逆に，安衛法令のみを遵守していたのでは使用者の義務としては足らない場面も多々あろう。つまり，安衛法令以上の私法的義務を使用者に課すことが適当な事案の処理についても留保しておくべき必要がある。このような諸場面を考慮すると，前記①の立場よりも②の立場の方が，民事法上の基準としては適切であるということになる。しかし，その際の義務設定には，安衛法令の内容とおおよそ同一の「趣旨・基準」に基づく措置義務が，多数例において，安全配慮義務としても実質的妥当性を有することに変わりはないであろう。この際の立証責任については，私見への批判にもかかわらず，前稿と同様の見解を維持したいが，ここでは触れない。

(b) 疾病の増悪回避段階

① 健康診断の結果を告知すべき義務

使用者は，安衛法令に基づく（あるいは実質的に同種の）各種健康診断を行った場合に，その結果として，受診した「労働者の健康状態が不良かまたはその疑いがある場合は……遅滞なく（当該）労働者に健康診断の結果を告知すべき義務がある」(18京和タクシー事件・京都地判昭和57・10・7労判404号72頁)。後述のような，使用者が雇用主として自ら講ずべき種々の措置義務のほかに，労働者へも健康の不良状態を通知し，精密検査の受診の必要性を知らしめるとともに労働者自身が健康への留意を行うべきことを覚悟せしめる必要があるからである。労働者の側がこれに応えず，さらなる健康診断を受診しないままにないしは不養生のままに症状が増悪した場合には，使用者は，訴訟において，増悪回避義務の軽減が認められ，あるいは帰責事由が免責され，あるいは損害賠償額算定の際の減額事由の対象となる（2(5)①）。

② 増悪回避義務

増悪回避義務は，すでに疾患を有する（その先行する疾患に業務との因果関係＝業務起因性が存することが前提となるかどうかに関しては争いがある。後述）労働者につき症状が悪化しないよう配慮する義務として把握されている。具体的に課させられる義務は次のようなものである。

(ア) 症状の確認義務・医師の意見の聴取義務

まず,「(労働者の)健康に異常の疑いがある場合には早期にその状態を確認する」義務があり,つぎに「異常が発見されたときには医師の指示に従って」措置する義務がある考えられる(18京和タクシー事件)。後者に関しては,医師の「通院加療中」との診断書がある場合には,同医師の意見を聴取する義務(8東京国際郵便局事件)や「嘱託医による就労能力についての診断結果が明らかになっている以上……(それに)従うべき義務が存した」とされる(19空港グランドサービス事件・東京地判平成3・3・22労判586号19頁。そのほかに,20観光日本事件・大津地判昭和51・2・9判時831号77頁)。さらに,ここにおける三つの義務は,相互に密接に関連し,あるいは段階的に把握されるであろう。

(イ) 軽作業転換義務・適正配置義務・就業禁止義務

ⓐ 従来の多くの裁判例にあっては,ある疾病に罹患した労働者につき,使用者には包括的に軽作業へ転換させる義務・症状に相応した適正な職務に配置する義務・就業を禁止させる義務を並列的ないし包括的に措定し,具体的にはそれらのうちの当該事案にとって必要であった義務内容に対する違反があったかどうかを吟味するという手法がとられている。そもそも安全配慮義務の内容は,雇用過程の「具体的な状況」によって異なる(1陸自八戸事件)ことを前提として設定されたものであるから,労働者の職種,労務内容,労務提供場所,労働者の症状等によって多様であることが予想されるので,一定の義務概念によって外延を画定しつつも,それらの義務内容の具体化は事案によって適切に行うという手法をとるしかないであろう。

ⓑ ただし,その場合,「職業性または災害性の疾病」への罹患がその後の使用者の右諸義務が機能する前提であるかのごとくの表現をする事例(7横浜中央郵便局事件,8東京国際郵便局事件,13大興電機製作所事件・東京地判昭和50・11・13判時819号93頁)と「腰痛症が労災事故によるものであるかどうかにかかわらず…原告に再び腰痛症が発生することのないようにするため…配慮する義務」(21ダイエー事件・大阪地判平成元・2・28労判542号68頁。同旨19空港グランドサービス事件,20観光日本事件)が課せられるとの立場とに分かれる。前者の立場では,使用者の負う安全配慮義務は,あくまでも業務に内在する危険性の発現たる疾病すなわち業務起因性の認められるいわゆる職業性疾病

・作業関連疾病の発生を前提として，それに対する使用者の各種の措置義務の発生を意味することになるが，後者の枠組みでは，職業性疾病・作業関連疾病の発症であるか業務外疾病（いわゆる"私病"）であるかを問わず，使用者には発症後の一定の措置義務が発生することになる。下級審裁判例が，早くより，会社寮内で急性気管支肺炎で死亡した未成年労働者の遺族からの損害賠償請求につき，その業務起因性及びそれを前提とした措置義務違反は否定したが，「仮に入寮者が勤務と関係のない原因に基づき発病した場合であっても……入寮者が通常期待できる看護を受け療養することができるよう配慮するべき義務」を措定し，その違反について肯定していた（6日産自動車事件）。また，本態的高血圧症の保有者に対しても（それは業務に起因しない素因ないしは基礎疾患である），「高血圧症を増悪させ，脳出血等の致命的な合併症を発症させるような精神的及び肉体的負担を伴う業務に就かせてはならない」（22システムコンサルタント事件・東京地判平成10・3・19労判736号54頁）との義務が措定される。

ⓒ おもうに，安全配慮義務は，「使用者の指示の下に労務（公務）を履行する過程の生命・身体の危険」（最高裁）を処理する法概念であり，少なくとも災害事故や職業性疾病のうちの「防止段階」での同義務は業務外事故・業務外疾病には作動しないはずである。しかし，増悪回避段階における義務は，労働者がある病気に罹患しているときには，「使用者の指示の下に行うその後の労務（公務）履行過程における生命・身体の危険」に直接的かつ濃厚に連結する事態であることに鑑み，その発症原因が業務に起因しているといないとにかかわらず，それに対する措置義務は雇用契約における信義則上肯定されるべきである。

ただし，業務に起因した疾病と起因せざる疾病とでは，使用者の増悪回避段階において使用者が負担する安全配慮義務の濃淡（強さ）に影響を与えると解するのが妥当と考えられる。

(ｳ) 継続的健康把握義務・過重業務抑制義務

上述(ｲ)に述べた作業転換や就業禁止義務（後者が安全配慮義務の違反の直接的原因とされた事例はいまだ見当たらないが）とは別個に，一定の心身状態にある労働者に対する労働時間や従前の同一職務における負担軽減の義務を安全配慮義務の内容として設定した裁判例の一群がある。具体的には，労働者の

過重勤務状態から派生するとみられるうつ病への罹患とそれに基づく自殺の事案及び循環器系障害保有者に対する措置義務として特に強調されている。

ここでは，使用者には「（労働者の）労働時間及び労働状況を把握し，同人が過剰な長時間労働によりその健康を侵害されないよう配慮すべき安全配慮義務」(23電通事件・東京地判平成8・3・28労判692号13頁，24川崎製鉄所事件・岡山地裁倉敷支判平成10・2・23労判733号13頁）が課せられると説示するなど，要するに過酷な労働条件（特に常軌を逸した長時間労働，残業，休日労働）を抑制すべき義務として設定されているといってよい（25協成建設工業ほか事件・札幌地判平成10・7・16労判744号29頁，26東加古川幼児園事件・大阪高判平成10・8・27労判744号17頁）。ただし，うつ病への罹患から自殺という過程には「本人の性格や心因的要素」も寄与するところから，被災者たる労働者側にも3割から8割までの「過失」（ここでの過失は，労働者の落ち度を意味するわけではない）がそれぞれ認められ，過失相殺の対象となっている（27電通事件・東京高判・平成9・9・26労判724号13頁，前掲24川崎製鉄所事件，26東加古川幼児園事件）。また，重篤な循環器系の基礎疾患を保有する労働者に対しては，随時的な作業転換義務・適正職務配置義務に至らないまでも，「継続的健康把握義務」(28伊勢市事件・津地判平成4・9・24労判630号68頁）が設定される。

(エ) メンタルヘルスケア

さらに，近時，やはり，うつ病・自殺事案に関しては，被災者に「心身共に疲労困憊」「空しい気持ち」（23電通事件），「精神的重圧」（26東加古川幼児園事件）が顕著であれば，然るべき措置（いわゆるメンタルヘルスケアを意味すると考えてよい）を講ずべき義務が課せられている。

(4) 因果関係・義務違反の事実

職業性・作業関連疾病に関する安全配慮義務は，「使用者の指示の下に労務（公務）を履行する過程における労働者の生命・身体の危険への配慮」すなわち疾病を防止し（第一段階），罹患した場合にはその増悪を回避する（第二段階）義務として設定さるべきものである。

同じく労務の履行過程において発生する労働災害であっても，一回性の災害事故（けが等）の場合には，傷病発生の場所・時間は比較的特定しやすいことは経験則上明らかであるに反し，「疾病」は「蓄積型」の類型であり，のみならず人体は遺伝や素因にも大きな影響を受け，さらに人間は職場生活

のみで生きているのではなく「私生活」の比重も小さくはなく，「疾病」は右諸要素がいわば複合した形で顕在化する。その中から，「職業性ないし作業関連的疾病」のみを取りだして，使用者に対する法律上の問責の対象とすることには，非常に困難が伴うことが多い。

そのような事情を抱えつつ，安全配慮義務論における因果律を探る作業をどのような視点をもって行うかはそれ自体難作業であるが，上述の義務内容の類型に応じてこの課題を検討してみたい。

(a) 疾病の防止段階の因果関係

疾病の防止段階での民事訴訟における因果関係は，次の二点において問題となる。第一は，「業務」と「発症」との因果関係（いわゆる業務起因性）である。第二は，「義務違反の事実」すなわち「使用者の防止行為の不履行」と「発症」との因果関係である。そして，第三に，右前者の因果関係が明らかとなれば，後者の因果関係も事実上推定されることになるかどうかである。しかし，最後者の課題は，立証責任のあり方にも大いに係わることであり，本稿紙幅の関係からも，他日次稿において取り扱うこととする。

① 「業務」と「発症」との因果関係の争点

(ア) まず，安全配慮義務違反に由来する労災民訴における傷病発生の因果関係は，行政官庁から労災保険金を受給するための要件たる「業務起因性」の概念とほぼ同一のものである（29大阪地裁職員事件・最二小判昭和58・11・11労判カード421号21頁，30熊本地裁八代支部廷吏事件・最二小判昭和51・11・12判時837号34頁）。したがって，業務上災害認定法規（労基法75条2項，労基則35及び別表第1の2）が，「業務上疾病」として取り扱っている疾病の場合にはほとんどの裁判例が，被災者（原告）側の格別の因果関係に関する立証活動を要求することなく，両者の間の相当因果関係を認める（例えば，じん肺に関する31日鉄鉱業松尾採石事件・東京地判平成2・3・27労判563号90頁，32同東京高判平成4・7・17労判619号63頁＜33同最三小判平成6・3・22労判652号6頁によって維持された＞等）。

(イ) しかし，労働行政上の業務起因性判断と労災民訴上の裁判所の相当因果関係論が同一の基盤に立たなければならないという要請はもとよりない。

というのも，労働省令による「業務上疾病」に関する規則及び行政認定基準（通達）は，ほぼ医学専門家による医学的知見に依拠して設定され運用さ

れているに対し、周知のごとく最高裁は、「訴訟上の因果関係の立証は、一点の疑義も許されない自然科学的証明ではなく…高度の蓋然性を証明することであり、その判定は、通常人が疑いを差し挟まない程度に真実性の確信を持ち得るものであることを必要とし、かつ、それで足りる」との立場を繰り返し鮮明にし（最二小判昭和50・10・24民集29巻9号1417頁, 34横浜市立保育園事件・最三小判平成9・11・28労判727号14頁），さらに訴訟上の証明（法学的証明）の医学的証明に対する優越性を一挙に押し進め「（原審における医学的本件鑑定は）医学研究の見地からはともかく，訴訟上の証明の見地からみれば（顆粒球減少症）の起因剤及び発症日を認定する決定的な資料ということはできない」（最二小判平成9・2・25判時1598号70頁）と判示するに至っている。ここに至るまでには，すでに下級審裁判例によって，「疫学的因果関係が証明された場合には原因物質が証明されたものとして，法的因果関係も存する」（名古屋高裁金沢支判昭和47・8・9判時674号25頁）とされ，さらには，因果関係の認定方法をかなり緩和し，クロム化合物とがん発生の因果関係につき，「疫学調査委の利用は，訴訟上因果関係を認定する一つの手法に過ぎないから疫学調査の結果，統計学的有意差…が認められなくとも，平均値よりかなり高率であれば」因果関係「認定の一資料とするを妨げない」と説く例（35日本化学工業事件・東京地判昭和56・9・28判時1017号34頁）もみられたところである。

　(ウ)　このような観点からすれば，安全配慮義務違反訴訟においても，次のような処理がなされることも十分可能である。すなわち，労働者Tの電極製造工場でのタール，ピッチへの暴露等の肺がん死に対する因果関係が争われた事案において，Y社は，労基則が「コークスまたは発生炉ガスを製造する工程における業務による肺がん」のみを掲げ，行政解釈（通達＝昭和57・9・27基発640号）が当該事案に係わる「電極製造工場におけるタール，ピッチへの暴露等」による肺がんについては「業務上疾病」とはしないとの見解であることを引用して，当該事案の肺がん死には因果関係が認められないと主張したところ，裁判所は，「認定基準通達の定めの如何は，私人間の本件訴訟における前記因果関係の認定判断に何らの関係を有するものでもない」反面，「亡TのY社でのタール，ピッチ暴露状況は製鉄用コークス炉上等での業務に十分匹敵するもの」であるから，本件訴訟上は「因果関係を肯定するのが

相当である」と判示した（36エスイーシー事件・大阪高判昭和62・3・31労判494号21頁）。そして，安全配慮義務違反訴訟における職業性・作業関連疾病の因果関係の判定につき，労基則別表所定の業務・疾患（疾病）と実質的に「類似の業務」あるいは実質的に「類似の疾患」が認定されるならば，それらが労基法・労基則の規定及び行政認定基準（医学的知見）から外れてはいても，裁判所によって相当因果関係＝法的因果関係が改めて吟味の対象となることを示している（16新日本ヘリコプター事件，前掲34横浜市立保育園事件の第1審たる37横浜地判平成元・5・23労判540号35頁及び38同東京高判・平成5・1・27労判625号9頁等参照）。

②　義務違反の事実と発症との因果関係

(ｱ)　職業性・作業関連疾病の防止段階において，安全配慮義務の内容を形成する措置義務としては，既述のように，材料・空間から生ずる危険に対する保護を目的とするものと作業自体の危険に対する保護を目的とするものに大別され，それが(3)(a)②に示した①～⑥の措置義務に細分化される。のみならず，疾病防止段階の安全配慮義務が「業務に起因する疾病」の発生が責任の前提とされる以上，訴訟に際して「（当該事案に則した具体的な）義務の内容を画定し，かつ，義務違反に該当する事実を主張・立証する責任」を負わせられる（39航空自衛隊航空救難群芦屋分遣隊事件・最二小判昭和56・2・16民集35巻1号56頁）被災者（原告）側としては，「使用者の義務違反＝債務不履行」が「疾病」を発生せしめたという意味での因果関係についても立証すべきこととなる。すなわち「二段階にわたって安全配慮義務の内容を具体化し，その上で義務不履行の事実を詳細に認定する」[16]という多くの裁判例の手法に従うことになれば，この立証は，「法学的因果関係」の証明で足りるとはいえ，医学的事項を濃厚に含む類の事柄に関する事項が多い事情に鑑みて，被災者側にとってなかなかに容易ではない。例えば，原告が，比較的義務の特定が容易と思われるところの，健康診断を行い異常を確認すべき義務の違反を主張したとしても，「ある時点で健康診断をして，血中鉛量，尿中鉛量の増加が認められて，適切な措置をとることによって，発病または重症化を防ぐことができたか否かは明らかではなく，健康診断の欠如が原告の発病と因

---

16)　岩村・前掲論文56頁。

果関係があるとすることについては疑問があるから，健康診断をしないからといって被告に安全配慮義務違反があったとは断定できない」(15ワンビシ産業事件)との判示は，この困難さをよく示している。ことに，労基則別表所定外の疾患ではあるが，しかしがん罹患の危険性は否定しえないような物質の暴露（例えばタール，ピッチによる肺がん，消化器がん）の際には措置義務違反による「発症」の証明はいっそう困難となろう（36エスイーシー事件参照）。

(イ) つぎに，因果関係が，ある事実によって切断された可能性のある場合の取扱いの問題がある。このような事例としては，次のようなものがある。

ⓐ A労働者の死亡につき，Y社の作業場で使用している有機溶剤による肝障害が発生し，それが安衛法令（有機溶剤中毒予防規則）の違反状態に起因することは明らかであるとしても，その肝障害さらにAの直接的な死因であるクリプトコッカス症の発生・死亡と因果関係があるかどうかが争われ，医証も真二つに分かれたが，「経験則上……Aは肝障害に陥らなければクリプトコッカス症に罹患することもなく，死亡することもなかったものというべきであるから，クリプトコッカス症によってその因果関係は切断されない」(12ソニーマグネプロダクツ)。ここでは，むしろ，すべての医学的知見が肝障害からクリプトコッカス症への罹患の科学的可能性を否定していたならば，裁判所によっていかに判定されたかの仮定の問題が残る。その場合には，（クリプトコッカス症への罹患）を「特別ノ事情」（民法416条2項）に対する予見可能性の存在の論理を操作して使用者の損害賠償責任を認めようとしても，具体的には使用者はすぐれて医学的なクリプトコッカス症への罹患につき「予見可能」であったはずだとはとうてい認めることができないからである。

ⓑ つぎに，判例上，うつ病が昂じて自殺という結果を生じた場合の問題が提起されている。この類型では，業務とうつ病との因果関係は「常軌を逸した長時間労働」ないしは「苛酷な負担」を決定的要素として認定されている。したがって，うつ病に関する安全配慮義務違反の事実は「自殺労働者の業務上の負荷ないし長時間労働を減少させるための具体的軽減措置をとらなかったこと」に求められよう。しかし，さらに，うつ病からの自殺には，使用者側にいかなる内容の義務違反が存したのか（疾病防止段階での義務違反なのか，疾病増悪回避段階での義務違反なのか）の認定は見当たらない。「うつ病患者が自殺を図ることが多い」(24川崎製鉄所事件)と認定するのみである。

しかし，自殺という行為そのものに，自殺者の自由意志が介在する場合には，業務と自殺との相当因果関係はもちろん切断されることになろう。うつ病から自殺に至るのは重症のうつ病患者でも3分1の程度であること（24川崎製鉄所事件における医学的知見）をも考慮すれば，業務・うつ病とうつ病・自殺の因果の連鎖はなく，したがって業務（長時間労働）と自殺との「相当」因果関係は切断されているともいえなくはないのである。3ヵ月の「苛酷な」勤務によってうつ病へ罹患したため退職した後1ヵ月を経て自殺したなどの事案（26東加古川幼児園事件）はなおさらその色彩が強くなる。

しかし，これまでの下級審裁判例は，かような切断論をとらず，うつ病による感情障害の中での自殺には自由意志は介在しないと捉え（27電通事件第二審），あるいは，「うつ病に陥り，自殺を図ったことは，被告（会社）はもちろん通常人にも予見することが可能であった」（24川崎製鉄所事件）ことを理由に，安全配慮義務違反の成立を認めている。

この前者の認定は，自殺は労働者の自由意志ではなく，異常精神活動（うつ病）の生理的連鎖反応がもたらしたものとみて，因果関係を肯定するという手法をとる。これに対し，後者の枠組みは，客観的責任要件（因果律）を確定しないままに，主観的責任要件すなわち帰責事由（予見可能性）の操作のみをもって結論を導きだしているとのそしりを免れない。しかし，実は，右手法は，交通事故後の被災者の自殺と事故との因果関係を取り扱った事例では，近時数多くみられる処理方法であって[17]，そこでは，「特別事情」によって生じた損害論（民法416条2項）に依拠することによって[18]，交通事故加害者に損害賠償を命じつつ，因果律の不足，予見可能性の程度の薄さ，被災者の自殺行為への寄与などは，「過失相殺」を行うことによって5割から8割程度の賠償額の減額を言い渡している。やはり「予見可能性」によってことを決しようとするうつ病・自殺関係の安全配慮義務をめぐる事案にあっても，被災者側の過失割合は，3割（27電通事件高裁判決），5割（24川崎製鉄事件），8割（26東加古川幼児園事件）とされている。

---

[17] 判例・学説に関しては，さしあたり，幾代通＝徳本伸一『不法行為法』（有斐閣・1995）146頁以下。

[18] 西村健一郎「過重労働による労働者の自殺と使用者の損害賠償責任」労判747号12頁参照。

たしかに，このような判定手法は，必ずしも不適切ではない（後述(5)）。
(b) 増悪回避段階の因果関係
① 因果関係の個数

これに対し，既往症に対する増悪回避段階における因果関係の問題は，次のように整理できる。第一に，特定の疾病の増悪回避のための措置義務が機能する前段階での既往症（先行症状）自体は業務に起因している必要はない（(3)(b)②(イ)(b)(c)）。第二に，しかし，いったん先行症状が発生した時点以降においては，当該先行症状の増悪・死亡には業務が原因として作用している必要があり（17住友林業事件），しかも，先行症状と同一の症状が悪化したか先行症状から派生したとみられる症状の悪化である必要がある。すなわち，例えば，家庭での引っ越しでギックリ腰を起こした労働者に対しても使用者の安全配慮義務（増悪回避義務）は機能するが，同義務違反を問うためには，その後の腰痛症の悪化は業務が原因であると認めなければならず，かつ，別の症状（例えば頸肩腕症候群）の悪化であってはならない。第三に，使用者の「義務違反の事実」すなわち「使用者の増悪回避行為の不履行」と「症状の増悪・死亡」との間の因果関係が必要である。つまり，増悪回避義務が尽くされていれば，症状の増悪または死亡はなかったであろうと合理的に判断できることが必要である。ここでの判断は，したがって，かなり医学的知見に係わることになる。しかし，常に「自然科学的証明」（医学的知見）が要求されるわけではなく，経験則上の「高度の蓋然性」の存在でも足りることはすでに確立した判例法理である（(a)①(ア)(イ)）。

② 義務の履行の中核

(ア) 問題は，当該症状に対し，使用者がいかなる措置義務を果たせば「増悪回避義務の履行」がなされたと判定できるかということである。職業性疾病・作業関連疾病の義務内容は，画一的ではなくむしろ多岐にわたっていることは既述のとおりであり，((2)・(3)) そこには「行為債務」特有の困難さがつきまとうことは確かである。おもうに，使用者としては，「疾病の態様に応じた現実的かつ合理的措置」をとることが要求され，かつ，それで十分である。事後的にみて望ましかったと判断されるすべての措置内容を講ずる必要はなく，いわゆる「結果債務」を負わせられているわけでもない。しかし，「無理をするな」という程度の抽象的な，あいまいな指示であってはならな

い。各種事案を通してみてみると，中核的な措置として，①嘱託医を活用しその助言に従って作業方法を指示すること（8 東京国際郵便局事件，19空港グランドサービス事件等），②単一の措置ではなく，複合的な措置を講ずること，例えば，「腰痛症を配慮して原告の配置転換を考え，これが原告に受け入れられないと，原告に対して重い物は持たないように注意するとともに，原告が自らの裁量で仕事の範囲を決めてその作業のみを行うことを許容し，（同一職場の同僚に対しても）原告には重量物を持たせないように指示して，原告の作業について重量物の運搬等の必要が生じた場合には他の従業員に協力させる態勢をとり，右協力が可能な人員も配置」した場合などには，「安全配慮義務を十分に尽くしていたもの」と認められること（21ダイエー事件），③そして，最低限の措置としては，過重負担の軽減措置特に作業時間の短縮措置をとること（17住友林業事件，23・27電通事件，24川崎製鉄事件等）が要求されよう。

(ｲ) 反面，被災者側に⒜上司の検診の勧めに従わなかったこと（17住友林業事件），⒝軽減の作業指示を守らなかったこと（21ダイエー事件），などの事情が認められれば，使用者は義務違反の責めを免れよう。

③　循環器系疾患死の場合

(ｱ) さらに，因果関係をめぐっては，循環器系疾患死（世にいう過労死）に特有の論議が提起される。循環器系疾患死に関しては，「業務起因性」＝相当因果関係（労基則35条及び同別表第1の2第9号）についての労基監督署の業務上外認定（行政処分）の基準のあり方及び行政処分を争う行政訴訟等においての判定手法についての論議がやかましいことは周知のところである。行政当局（労働省）は，昭和36年，昭和62年，平成7年の三次にわたって，行政認定基準（通達）を発し，その時々の裁判例（行政訴訟等）の動向や世論による「認定基準は厳し過ぎる」との批判を考慮して，徐々に認定基準の緩和を図っているが，被災者・遺族側にあっては，政府への労災保険給付金等の申請によって労災保険等を受給する道はなお困難であるとの判断から，この道を避けてあるいはこの道と並行的に，使用者の災害惹起の直接的な責任を追及すべく，民事訴訟を提起する傾向を強めている。ちなみに，労基監督署その他の公的機関の業務（公務）上外認定を争う行政訴訟等における「業務（公務）起因性」（相当因果関係論）のあり方関しては，筆者は，ごく最近に私

見を発表したところである[19]。

　循環器系疾患死をめぐる民事訴訟たる安全配慮義務違反を争点とする場合には，行政訴訟等における処理方法とは，特に因果関係論（の一部），帰責事由の判定，損害額の算定（端的にいえば過失相殺）の各論点及びそれらの相互作用において顕著な違いが認められることになろう。概要を示せば，次のごとくである。

　(イ)　行政訴訟等においては，訴訟上の争点は業務起因性（業務と循環器系疾患死との相当因果関係）に絞られるが，その際の実体的判定要素は，第一に，被災労働者の「業務過重性」という要件である。第二に，被災労働者の「血管病変等の超自然経過的な増悪」という要件である。

　ⓐ　まず，行政訴訟等においても同様であるが，循環器系疾患（死）の業務との因果関係が問題とされるほとんどの事例は，被災労働者にすでに循環器系の基礎疾患（高血圧症，狭心症，動脈瘤等の存在）がみられる場合である。したがって，このような事案の類型に右第一，第二の実体的要件とを当てはめて捉えたときには，次のような判断枠組みが主流となっている。すなわち，「被災労働者Ｉの業務と，脳出血発症との間に因果関係が存在するというためには，必ずしも業務の遂行が脳出血発症の唯一の原因であることを要するものではなく，他の原因が存在していても，業務の遂行による過重な負荷（業務過重性）が，自然的経過を超えて右素因等を増悪させ，Ｉの脳出血発症の共働の原因の一つであるということができれば，それをもって足りる」。そして「Ｉの脳出血発症は，同人の基礎疾患である本態性高血圧と，被告における過重な業務とが，共働原因となって生じたものであるというべきであり，Ｉの死亡と業務の間には相当因果関係があるというべきである」と（22システムコンサルタント事件・東京地判平成10・3・19労判736号54頁。同じ枠組みを示す例として，40真備学園事件・岡山地判平成6・12・20労判672号42頁，41石川島興業事件・神戸地裁姫路支判平成7・7・31労判688号59頁，9富士保安警備事件）。

　ⓑ　右の諸例において留意すべきことは，被災者に循環器系の基礎疾患が存する一方で業務の過重性も認められる場合には，相当因果関係の肯定のた

---

[19]　中嶋「職業性循環器系疾患死の因果関係論（続論）」上智法学論集42巻3・4号（1999）32頁以下。

めには「右両者は共働原因として結果に作用することで足りる」との判定基準を提示していることである。行訴等判決においては，「業務過重性が有力な原因でなければならない」（相対的有力原因説）との判定基準をほぼ確立していることからすれば，因果関係論は民事訴訟においてはるかに緩やかに被災者保護のために機能（注19）拙稿参照）しているということができる。その原因としては，民事訴訟においては，客観的因果律のみを争う行訴等におけると異なり，当事者の主観的要件も斟酌される結果，賠償額算定にあたって「過失相殺」の理論を，ほぼ裁判官独自の裁量で駆使できることが挙げられよう。現に，右安全配慮義務違反肯定例にあっては，ほとんどの事案において過失相殺が言い渡されているのである。

ⓒ　つぎに，これらの裁判例において使用者の安全配慮義務違反の事実として挙げられているのは，長時間労働を継続したこと，作業量・残業・宿日直の制限を行わなかったこと，健康診断・健康管理体制の不実施，産業医の判断を仰がなかったこと，年齢・健康状態等に応じた作業内容の軽減等適切な措置をまったくとらなかったことなどである。ここで重要なことは，もっぱら相当因果関係を争う行訴等においては，基礎疾患の保有者のうちでも，「重篤な基礎疾患」を有する被災者の循環器系疾患死の際には，原則的に業務と死亡との業務起因性が否定されると解さざるをえないことである[20]。これに対し，民事訴訟においては，循環器系疾患の発症自体は業務に起因する必要がない（生まれつきの心臓の持病があってもよい）ことに加えて，発症後は安全配慮義務の作用として「年齢・健康に応じた作業内容の軽減等」の保護が与えられ，「健康な者に対するものであれば特別苛酷，過重なものとはいい難いが，被災者の如き危険な体質，要因を持つ者に対する労務指揮としては過重な負担を課するものであったというべく，会社としては……負担を軽減する義務」（17住友林業事件）が課せられることになるから，賠償額算定の際に減額措置は受けるとしても，被災者には一定の賠償額を得る道は優に開けていることになる。

ⓓ　これに対し，安全配慮義務違反否定判決では，おしなべて業務に過重性が認められないことが認定され，あわせて自己の判断で持病の治療を放棄

---

[20]　中嶋・前掲論文58頁。

していたこと，被災労働者から体調不良の申し出がなかったこと，喫煙・飲酒の習慣の継続，予測不可能などが挙げられている（42旺文社事件・千葉地判平成8・7・19労判725号78頁，43友定事件・大阪地判平成9・9・10労判725号32頁等）。

(c) 択一的損害惹起の因果関係

疾病の防止段階にあるか増悪回避段階にあるかを問わず，相当因果関係の存否が問題となる特異な問題が提起されている。次のような事案であった。過去複数の粉じん職場で働いてきたじん肺患者Xらが，そのうちの特定のY企業のみを安全配慮義務違反で訴えた場合に，当該特定使用者の安全配慮の履行義務違反（履行を怠った事実）とじん肺への罹患とが相当因果関係にあり，Y社には損害賠償責任が生ずるか。Y社は，Xらの粉じん歴中においてY社での就労期間が占める割合に応じてY社の責任は限定さるべきであると主張した。判旨は，本件のような，被害者の損害が複数行為者のいずれの行為から生じたかを特定できない場合（択一的損害惹起の場合），複数の職場のいずれにおいても現に罹患したじん肺になりうることが認められる限り，民法719条後段の類推適用によって，じん肺への罹患と複数の使用者それぞれの各義務違反の債務不履行との間の因果関係が法律上推定されるべきであるとした。つまり，Xとしては，じん肺罹患と使用者Yとの間のみの特定的な因果関係を立証できなくても，複数の使用者の各々の債務不履行が現に罹患したじん肺をもたらしうるような危険性を有し，右じん肺の原因となった可能性を主張・立証できれば，使用者において，自らの債務不履行とじん肺罹患との間の一部または全部に因果関係のないことを主張・立証できない限り，使用者はその責任の一部または全部を免れることはできない，と判示した（31日鉄鉱業松尾採石所事件）。この判決は，最高裁で確定した（44同事件・最三小判平成6・3・22労判652号6頁。その他，45前田建設工業等事件・東京地判平成5・8・9労判653号20頁）。

(5) 帰責事由・義務の軽減・過失相殺

職業性疾病・作業関連疾病に関する使用者の安全配慮義務違反の成立を基礎づける要件は，①被災労働者の業務が原因で疾病が発生・増悪したかどうか（疾病の発生・増悪に関する相当因果関係），②疾病は使用者の過失（帰責事由）によってもたらされたかどうか（疾病の発生に関する使用者の責任原因），

③使用者が被災労働者に対して負う責任の範囲はどこまでか（損害賠償の範囲に関する相当因果関係），を基本とする。

これら①②③が原理的にどのように区別され，実際的にどのように機能を分担しあい，またいかなる相互的な作用を営んでいるか，を探究することは一個の問題である。

それらの課題はさておくとして，ここで考察の対象とする右②の「帰責事由」は，本来的には客観的な因果関係の問題ではなく，労働者の生命・身体の危険が予見可能であったのに予見できなかったり（予見可能性の要素），予見して発症・増悪という結果を回避しうる可能性があったのに結果回避措置をとらなかった（結果回避可能性の要素）という事情を使用者の落ち度（過失）とみて，使用者の主観的責任要素とする作用を営むものである。しかし，実際上帰責事由は，①と③を仲介し接合させる機能を果たす要素であり，特に契約の相手方に"配慮する"という性質の義務（行為債務）にあっては，「義務違反の事実」の証明（①の領域に属する）と「過失」の証明（②）とを不可分なものとして判定せざるをえないことも多いので，「帰責事由」問題は，法的因果関係判断の一環をなす問題として捉えて差し支えないともいえるが，一応別個の考察対象としつつ次に記す。

(a) 帰責事由と義務の軽減及び過失相殺との関係

① (ア)まず，安全配慮義務違反の責任を生ぜしめる主観的責任要件としての帰責事由すなわち過失は，予見可能性（ただし，民法416条2項において特別の事情による損害賠償の範囲を画定する基準としての「予見可能性」の概念とは異なる）と結果回避可能性とを基準とするが，それは通常，業務と疾病の相当因果関係を確定し，同義務違反の事実と結果の発生との間の相当因果関係を確定した後に（客観的責任要件），使用者側からの免責の抗弁として審理されるのが通常である。したがって，オーソドックスな判断過程をたどる裁判例は，使用者には「安全配慮義務の不履行がある」と説示しつつも，続いて「予見可能性」の存否の事情（免責事由）を探る。そして，心筋梗塞のため37歳で死亡した被災者Hが体調の不調を会社関係者に訴えることもせず，同様に休暇をも申し出ず，上司・同僚はHの体調不調に気づかず，H自身医師の診察を受けることもなく，Hの妻さえも健康障害を知らず，職務内容もただちに死の結果をもたらすほど過重ではなく，Hは課長補佐という立場上過労によ

る職務の軽減措置を申し出ることは可能であり，上司から検診に誘われた際にはこれを断っていることなどからすると「Hの発病ないし死について，被告会社には予見可能性がなかったものというべく，結局被告の前記生命ないし健康確保義務不履行は，被告の責に帰すべき事由に基づかないものといわねばならない」と判示して，債務不履行責任を否定する (17住友林業事件)。

　(ｲ)　しかし，安全配慮義務のように手段を尽くす行為債務（手段債務）の場合には，義務違反の事実はとりもなおさず予見可能性の要件を満たし，過失が肯定されるとの構成をとる判決例もある。すなわち，「継続的な健康把握く義務を尽くしておれば，本件訓練の時点で被災労働者が労作性狭心症による不整脈で死亡する事態を予見することも決して不可能ではな（く）」，被告会社の主張は「義務を果たさなかった結果として，予見可能性がなかったと主張しているに等しく，論理が逆であ（る）」(28伊勢市事件＝義務違反肯定例)。また，「(被告は) 本人から，何ら体調に異常がある旨の申し出もなされなかったと主張するが，安全配慮義務は，労働者の申し出により初めて生ずる義務ではなく……被告主張の事実が存在したとしても，被告がこれにより免責されるものではない」(41石川島興業事件)。

　②　つぎに，安全配慮義務違反は否定されないけれども，(ｱ)に掲記した諸事情の一部が，単に過失相殺の要因に挙げられる例も非常に多い (28伊勢市消防署事件，9富士保安警備事件＜本人の素因＞，40真備学園事件，22システムコンサルタント事件＜検診の不受診，自己管理の不十分＞)。

　③　しかし，逆に，それらの被災労働者側に存する事情が，使用者の安全配慮義務を機能させずあるいは同義務は軽減されると判断することによって，結局安全配慮義務違反を否定した例もある (42旺文社事件＜上司に「大丈夫」と答えて検診を受けなかった，健康不良であるのに自ら出社した，外形的に何ら異常と認めるべき事情はなかった＞，43友定事件＜休暇申請も体調不良の申し出もしなかった，自己の判断で治療を放棄した，喫煙・飲酒の習慣を改善しなかった＞)。

　④　かようにしてみると，少なくと循環器系疾患死事例にあっては，労働者側に存する事情につき，それが同様の事情であっても，ある例は安全配慮義務違反の責任の成立は阻むことができないとし，ある例は逆にそもそも同義務は機能しないと捉え，その中間には帰責事由たりえないとしたり，損害額の減額事由（過失相殺＝民法418条。ここでの過失とは，不法行為要件としての

過失や債務不履行にいう帰責事由とは異なり，賠償額を減額するに適当な債権者側の事情というほどの意味である）となるに過ぎないと解する例が鼎立していることになる。しかし，これらにうつ病・自殺の事例をも加味すると（27電通事件第二審，24川崎製鉄所事件，26東加古川幼児園事件），個人差が大きく（素因，心因的要素），しかも因果関係や予測可能性に関する画一的な医学的知見を得ることも非常に困難とされる，職業性疾病・作業関連疾病において発生する被災労働者側の事情は，因果関係を肯定し，義務違反の事実を肯定し，使用者の帰責事由の存在をも肯定したうえで，賠償額の算定場面での「過失相殺」の問題として処理する裁判例が多数を占めているということができよう。そして，それは妥当であると思われる。なぜなら，理論的な帰結というよりも，交通事故関係訴訟におけると同様に，場合によっては損害額から7割ないし8割をも減額できるという弾力に優れた実務性を有するからである。

(b) 帰責事由と業務の社会的有益性

最高裁は，林野庁高知営林局事件において，営林署作業員らがチエンソー（自動鋸）などの使用による振動障害（白ろう病）につき，国に対し安全配慮義務違反を理由に損害賠償を請求した事案につき，チエンソー等の使用による右障害に対する予見可能性，結果回避可能性のいずれをも否定して，作業員らの上告を棄却した（2林野庁高知営林局事件）。注目すべきは次のような説示を行ったことである。再び引用すると，「社会，経済の進歩発展のため必要性，有益性が認められるかあるいは危険の可能性を内包するかもしれない機械器具については，その使用を禁止するのではなく，その使用を前提として，その使用から生ずる生ずる危険，損害の発生の可能性の有無に留意し，その発生の防止するための相当な手段方法を講ずることが要請されているというべきであるが，社会通念に照らし相当と評価される措置を講じたにもかかわらずなおかつ損害の発生をみるに至った場合には，結果回避義務に欠けるものとはいえない」し，林野事業を円滑に遂行するためには「林野庁に振動障害を回避するためチエンソー等の使用自体を中止するまでの義務はない」と。

右の判旨は，林野庁によって振動障害防止・軽減のために種々の相当な措置がとられてきたとの認定が前提となっている。右判旨自体に対する賛否は分かれようが，安全配慮義務にも濃淡ないし段階性があり，常に一挙に究極

の保護措置（器具使用中止，就業禁止など）をとらないと帰責事由とされるわけではないとの趣旨と思われる。そもそも，安全配慮義務の法的性質（基本的に，物的環境整備・人的配備に関する手段債務である）を考慮すれば，最高裁の趣旨は理解できるが，最高裁が段階的措置義務の要請を述べるならば，林野庁がチエンソーの弊害を明確に認識してこれを公務上の疾病とすることを人事院との間で折衝に入った昭和40年以降については，国には少なくとも，「使用時間軽減措置の怠慢」が問われて然るべき事例であったと思われる[21]。現に，その後造船所において使用される振動工具（各種ハンマー。チエンソーではない）によって振動障害がもたらされた事案において，「被告会社主張の通達（昭和45年チエンソーに関する操作時間，保護具等に関する基発134号及びチエンソー以外の振動工具の取扱いに関する昭和49年基発608号）発出以前の昭和40年には前記チエンソー使用労働者の振動障害が大きな社会問題として取り上げられるようになったこと及びその後の同振動障害に関する学会等の……説示を総合すると，造船業界の最大手企業である被告会社において，その後遅くとも5年を経過するまでの間には，チエンソー以外の振動工具についても，その使用によって人体障害を生じさせるおそれのあることを予見し得たものというべきであって，昭和49年の右通達発出までの間，これを予見し得なかったとすることは到底できない」とし，作業時間短縮，防振手袋着用等の必要な措置（結果回避措置）を講ずるべきであったと説示して，被災者らの請求を一部認容する判決が出現した（46三菱重工業神戸造船所事件・神戸地判平成6・7・12労判663号29頁。）この判決は，原告ら主張の「安衛法各規定の要件に該当する事実主張があれば，同安全配慮義務の内容は，これをもって特定された」と断定するところに難点はあるが（(3)(a)③参照），結果的に「作業時間短縮」を安全配慮義務の内容に措定して，使用者の尽くすべき手段を最高裁より広汎に設定したのは妥当であったと思われる。

　いずれにせよ，これらは，因果関係の明確な職業性疾病・作業関連疾病への経年的蓄積の責任とそれを免れしめる機能を果たす「社会・経済的有益性」との関係をいかに解すべきかの課題を提起した。

---

21)　中嶋・判例評釈・労経速報1424号15頁参照。

B　雇用政策と労働法の新潮流

米国企業における苦情処理 ADR と社内オンブズパーソン

菅野 和夫

はじめに

　近年，個別労使紛争の増加と共に，その解決制度の改善が重要な政策課題として論じられている。これまでのところは，企業外の公的機関による包括的相談・あっせんサービス（ワンストップ・サービス）のニーズに着目して，労働委員会，労政事務所，労働基準監督署，都道府県女性少年室などの行政機関をいかに活用・再編成すべきか，そして，それら裁判外の相談・あっせんサービスと，民事調停，少額訴訟，仮処分などの司法機関による簡易な判定サービスとをいかに連携させるべきかが，主要な論題となっている。

　しかし，労使関係法研究会報告書[1]が指摘したように，個別労使紛争も，まずは，企業内でその実情に即して自主的に解決されることが望ましく，また企業外での解決が困難な紛争も多々存在する。しかしながら，わが国の企業では，従来は，労使協議制度の発達と対照的に，苦情処理制度は未発達ないし不活発であった。今後は，企業内の紛争解決制度の整備も重要な課題として検討していく必要がある。

　本稿は，近年，様々な苦情処理手続を発達させてきた米国の大企業に着目し，同手続の内容と機能を探ることを目的とする。とりわけ，「社内オンブズパーソン」（Corporate Ombudsman or Ombudsperson）の制度について，その発展の状況とその意義・機能を描写して，わが国の今後の制度整備への示唆を汲み取ってみたい。

　1）　労使関係法研究会「我が国における労使紛争の解決と労働委員会制度の在り方に関する報告」平成10年10月。

1 米国企業における苦情処理 ADR の発達

(1) 苦情処理 ADR とは

ADR とは，「裁判に替わる紛争解決手続」("alternative dispute resolution")の意であり，紛争当事者間の話し合いの仲介，合意達成のためのあっせんや調停，第三者による判定としての事実認定（fact finding）や仲裁，私設の簡易裁判（mini-trial）や簡易陪審裁判（summary jury trial）等々の多様な手続を包含する。ADR は，米国において，1970年代後半以降，民事裁判よりも簡易・迅速・低廉な紛争解決手続を求める運動のなかで形成されたコンセプトであり，実際の制度としても，多方面の紛争分野について多様な形態で発展してきた。かくして，今日では多くのロー・スクールにおいて，ADR は様々な形で授業科目となっている[2]。

雇用労使関係においては，ADR は，組合が存在する企業における労働協約による苦情処理・仲裁手続として1950年代から普及してきた。これは，職場における労働条件や労働関係のルールを包括的に規定した労働協約の下において，労働協約の解釈適用に関するすべての紛争を，労使間のいくつかの段階の協議を経たうえ，最終的には労使が自ら選任する職業的仲裁人の仲裁判断によって解決するという制度である[3]。この手続は，米国労働運動の最大の業績として評価され，今日まで存続している。しかし，組合の組織率低下（98年，13.9％）と共に，この手続で守られる労働者の範囲は縮小してきた。

他方，米国では，最近20年間には，組合のない企業における苦情処理手続

---

[2] 米国における ADR の発展と内容については，野村美明「アメリカにおける裁判外の紛争処理」北大法学論集42巻4号（1993）1065頁以下，太田勝造「アメリカ合衆国の ADR からの示唆」木川統一郎編著『製造物責任法の理論と実務』（成文堂，1994）137頁以下，山田文「裁判外紛争解決制度における手続的配慮の研究――アメリカ合衆国の制度を中心として――(1)」法学58巻1号(1994)45頁以下，Carrie Menkel-Meadow, "Introduction: What Will We Do When Adjudication Ends? A Brief Intellectual History of ADR," *44 UCLA Law Review* 1613（1997）。わが国における ADR を概観した文献として，伊藤眞＝小島武司『裁判外紛争処理法』（有斐閣，1998）。

[3] 中窪裕也・アメリカ労働法（弘文堂，1995）127頁以下，中窪裕也「アメリカ団体交渉法の構造(3)」法学協会雑誌100巻11号（1983）2071頁以下。

が増加してきた。これらの企業内苦情処理手続は，上司や人事部とのインフォーマルな話合い段階，社内のあっせんや判定などの解決手続，外部の第三者によるあっせんや仲裁の手続などを組み合わせたものであるが，雇用関係の紛争について，企業内の手続を省略し，外部の第三者によるあっせんや仲裁のみを利用する企業もある。そのほか，社長直属の苦情相談者であって，中立性と秘密厳守を基本とした「社内オンブズパーソン」をおく企業も増加している。これらは，いずれも，企業のADR利用の流れの中に位置づけられる制度であって，「苦情処理ADR」と称することができる。

(2) 苦情処理ADR発展の現象

米国における苦情処理ADR発展の現象については，様々な調査や見積もりがあるが[4]，最近の大規模な調査としては，コーネル大学紛争研究所（Cornell／PERC Institute on Conflict Resolution）の1997年調査「米国企業におけるADRの利用状況」（"The Use of ADR in U. S. Corporations"）を掲げることができる。この調査は，米国の上位大企業1000社のうち528社について，ADRの利用状況を各企業法務部から郵便および電話で聴取したものである。これによれば，過去三年間に約9割（88%）の企業があっせん（mediation）を，そして約8割（79%）の企業が仲裁（arbitration）を利用している。他の類型のADR手続としては，41%の企業が「あっせん仲裁」（"med-arb"）を，23%の企業が簡易裁判（"mini-trial"）を，21%が事実認定（"fact-finding"）を，そして11%が「同僚による判定」（"peer review"）を利用している。他方，「社内オンブズパーソン」を有している企業は55社（10.3%）であり，労働協約上の苦情処理手続とは異なる企業内の苦情処理手続を有している企業は185社（35.0%）であった。

この調査では，企業の方針として訴訟とADRのいずれを優先かという問

---

4) Mary Rowe, "Dispute Resolution in the Nonunion Environment: An Evolution Toward Integrated Systems For Conflict Management?" in Sandra Geason ed., Frontiers in Dispute Resolution in Labor Relations and Human Resources, Michigan State University Press, 1997, pp. 79-80 は，半分以上の大企業が組合に組織されていない被用者のための何らかの苦情処理手続を有し，そのうち5分の1が最終ステップとして外部の第三者による仲裁手続を有しているとの1989年の調査などを引用して，組合のない企業における苦情処理手続の発達状況を推論している。

いを発したが，できるだけ ADR で解決するとする企業が3割弱，訴訟による解決の補足的手段として ADR を利用するとする企業が約25％，常に ADR で解決するという方針の企業が約15％，常に訴訟で解決するとの企業が6-7％という割合であり，全体的には，企業による ADR 利用の積極的姿勢が示された。また，今後の ADR 発展の見込みについては，多くの企業は，雇用関係と商事関係の紛争ではあっせん・仲裁の利用は増加すると予測し，企業金融と財政的再組織の紛争では利用は減少すると予測している。あっせんと仲裁とでは，あっせんの方が今後の利用の希望が多い。

(3) 苦情処理 ADR 発展の要因

苦情処理手続の整備を含む企業による ADR 利用の背景には，過去20年間における雇用関係訴訟の増加がある[5]。例えば，1990年には雇用差別訴訟の件数は1970年の20倍に達した[6]。1994年の連邦司法会議の報告書 (The Report of the Judicial Conference of the United States) では，連邦地裁への同年の約23万6000件の新規訴訟の20～25％は雇用関係の訴訟であると分析されている。また，行政機関への差別禁止法違反の申立も増加している。1993年には，雇用機会均等委員会に88,000件の告発 (charge) がなされたが，これは前年比22％の増加であった。

雇用労使関係法の法律実務に長年従事し，現在ではハーバード大学行政大学院 (Kennedy School of Government) で労使関係を教えている Jay S. Siegel 氏は，増加した雇用関係訴訟の内容について，概括的には，伝統的労働法の事件（不当労働行為，労災認定，労働基準法違反，協約の履行請求 etc.），諸々の雇用差別訴訟，解雇その他の雇用関係紛争（多くは州裁判所へ）がそれぞれ約3分の1ずつと見積もっている[7]。

雇用関係訴訟の増加は，主として訴訟のコストの大きさの面から企業によ

---

5) Jay S. Siegel, "Changing Public Policy: Private Arbitration to Resolve Statutory Employment Disputes," 13 The Labor Lawyer, pp. 87-88 (1997); David R. Barclay & William A. Carmel, "Benefits of a Resolution-Centered ADR Program", Corporate Legal Times, Vol. 4, No. 37, December 1994, p. 1-2.
6) David R. Barclay & William A. Carmel, "Benefits of a Resolution-Centered ADR Program", Corporate Legal Times, Vol. 4, No. 37, December 1994, p. 1.
7) 筆者による Siegel 氏の1998年9月11日のインタビュー。

る ADR 利用を促進している[8]。また，企業にとっての訴訟のもう一つのコストは，陪審裁判であるという。つまり，陪審裁判の場合は，判断基準が法律論ではなく陪審員の公正さの感覚にあるので，結論の予測が困難であるという[9]。また，雇用関係訴訟では，陪審裁判の場合，原告（労働者）の勝訴率は約3分の2で，それら勝訴事件では1件平均60万ドルの賠償が命じられているとも見積もられている[10]。そこで，公民権法第7編（Title VII）の1991年改正が懲罰的賠償に上限を付しつつ陪審裁判を求める権利を保障したことが，ADR の発達を促進したとも指摘される[11]。

上記コーネル大学紛争研究所の調査でも，最も多数の企業（54％）が掲げる ADR 利用の理由は，裁判に要する時間と費用である。近年の市場競争の熾烈化から，企業は reengineering と restructuring を遂行しており，経営トップは，法務部門に対し法的紛争の処理に要するコストの削減を指令し，このため法務部長は ADR の積極的利用の政策をとってきた。そこで，ADR に詳しい外部の弁護士やコンサルタントをも利用して，ADR 利用の推進に努めてきたのである。このことは，上記調査で「常に ADR によって解決する」との方針を表明した会社は，近年に経費削減の必要性に迫られダウンサイジングを行った超大企業に多いという結果にも現れている[12]。

上記調査で指摘された他の要因としては，雇用機会均等委員会（EEOC），州労災委員会（Workers' Compensation Commission）などの行政機関が事件負担の軽減のために ADR の利用を奨励していることがある。同様に，半分以上の州の裁判所も，裁判所の事件負担を軽減するために ADR の利用を奨励し，あるいは義務づけている。上記調査でも，あっせんを利用した企業の64％が，裁判所があっせんの利用を義務的としているためと回答している。仲裁を利用した企業の93％は，仲裁契約が仲裁の根拠だったと回答したが，

---

8) Siegel 氏によれば，訴訟の提起，証拠開示から始まる訴訟手続の経済的コストは，普通の解雇事件では，会社側は弁護士費用を入れて10万ドルくらい，原告側は5万ドルくらいかかるのではないかということである。
9) Siegel 氏とのインタビュー。
10) David R. Barclay & William A. Carmel, "Benefits of a Resolution-Centered ADR Program", Corporate Legal Times, Vol. 4, No. 37, December 1994, p. 1.
11) Siegel 氏インタビュー。
12) 逆に「常に訴訟を」という企業は，比較的小規模で利潤率が高い企業に多い。

これら仲裁契約の増加の背景には、連邦最高裁が、1974年のAlexander判決[13]で示した、差別禁止を争う権利は仲裁契約によっては奪い得ないとの見解を、1991年Gilmer判決[14]において修正したことがある[15]。

これらの他、コーネル大学紛争研究所の調査結果では、訴訟手続の不確実性を嫌い、紛争解決の手続および結果について企業自身が決定権を保持したいという願望も、ADR利用の一つの要因となっていることが明らかにされている。

企業における苦情処理ADR発達については、従業員の悩みを解消し人間関係を円滑にすることによって生産性を高めたいとの動機や、技術者不足のなかで技術者の養成と有能な人材の保持に役立つとの動機なども指摘される[16]。これは、あっせん、仲裁などの紛争解決手続についてよりも、人事部、苦情相談役などによる非公式の相談手続について当てはまるといえよう。

2 企業内苦情処理ADRの内容

(1) 概　観

米国では、雇用関係に関するADRの流行のなかで、雇用労使関係を専門とする法律事務所も、企業の需要に応えて、雇用関係紛争を解決するための

---

13) Alexander v. Gardner Denver, 415 U. S. 36 (1974).
14) Gilmer v. Interstate / Johnson Lane Corp., 500 U. S. 20 (1991) は、企業年金の受給開始による任意的引退について、年齢差別の法的問題が生じた場合には裁判やEEOCによってではなく私的な仲裁手続によって解決する旨の労働者本人の同意書を、仲裁手続の公正さが保たれていれば有効と判断した。そこで、同判決を契機として、諸々の差別禁止法上の権利遂行を妨げうる公正な仲裁契約とは、どのような要件を備えたものであるのかが重要な法律問題となっている。これまでのところ、同判決の判旨を手がかりとして、契約の明確性と任意性、仲裁人選定の任意性、相当の証拠開示手続、書面による理由付きの裁定判断、などの要件が指摘されている。これを論じるものとして、Jay S. Siegel, "Changing Public Policy : Private Arbitration to Resolve Statutory Employment Disputes" 13 The Labor Lawyer, p. 87 (1997), David R. Barclay & William A. Carmel, "Benefits of a Resolution-Centered ADR Program", Corporate Legal Times, Vol. 4, No. 37, December 1994, p. 1.
15) Jay S. Siegel, *ibid*, at p. 90.
16) MITのオンブズパーソンのMary Rowe氏との1998年9月11日のインタビューおよびA社オンブズパーソンのR. W.氏との同月8日のインタビュー。

ADR の樹立を指導している。例えば，筆者は，New York のある大法律事務所の雇用労使関係部門が主催した雇用関係における ADR セミナーの資料を入手したが[17]，同事務所がそこで推奨しているメニュウは，第一には，拘束力のある仲裁手続であり，事前の契約による強制的仲裁と，紛争発生後の合意による仲裁が，いかなる要件を満たせば労働者の訴訟提起権を否定する効果をもちうるのかが入念に論じられている。また，仲裁の種類として，仲裁人の判断に枠のない通常の仲裁のほかに，「選択幅限定仲裁」("Bracketed Arbitration") や「最終案選択仲裁」("Final Offer Arbitration") などの選択肢が示されている。ADR の第二のメニューとして推奨されるのは，第三者（雇用関係専門家）の援助による交渉 ("negotiation / conciliation") とあっせん (mediation) であり，とくに簡易・柔軟で解決率の高いあっせん手続の有用性が強調される。第三には，企業内での裁判類似のいくつかの手続が提示されている。簡易陪審裁判 ("summary jury trial")，簡易裁判 ("minitrial")，私的裁判 ("private judging") などであり，これにも拘束力をもたせるものともたせないものがあるとする。

(2) H 社のケース

それでは，企業における苦情処理 ADR の具体例を，いくつか見ておこう。まず，企業法務の雑誌に紹介され[18]，上記セミナーでもモデルとして詳しく提示されている航空機メーカーH社（組合なし）のケースである。

H 社の苦情処理手続は，かつては，雇用関係においてなんらかの苦情をもつ従業員が上司または人事部との間で話し合い，解決されない場合には当該部 (department / division) の長が判断を下すというものであった。この判断については，事業部門 (business unit) の長による再判断 (review) を受けられるが，その後は格別の手続も存しなかった。1981年には，これら手続の改善のために，部長の判断に不満な従業員は，会社の雇用機会均等室に調査の

---

17) March 22, 1995 Breakfast Seminar on Alternative Dispute Resolution Sponsored by Winston and Strawns Labor Employment and Law Department, 32 pages.

18) David R. Barclay & William A. Carmel, "Benefits of a Resolution-Centered ADR Program," Corporate Legal Times, Vol. 4, No. 37, December 1994, pp. 2-3.

やり直しを求めることができることとし，同室が部長の判断と別個の勧告を行えるようにした。しかし，この場合にも，事業部門長の再判定に服するというものであった。

　このような改善にも拘らず，H社では，1980年代に雇用関係訴訟が増加していった。そのなかにはカリフォルニア州の裁判所における合計8,750万ドルの賠償判決に至った二つの雇用差別訴訟もある。そして，従業員の調査では，現在の苦情処理手続は，会社側の利益に偏っていて，苦情提起者の言い分を十分に聴く手続とはなっておらず，しかも時間がかかりすぎると見られていることが明らかとなった。そこで，H社は，1993年から，手続の大幅な改善を成し遂げた。新たな手続は，「被用者問題解決手続」（Employee Problem Resolution Procedure）と称され，被用者が自由に効果的に自己の問題を表明し，その解決を求めることができるようにすることによって，高度の技能，士気，生産性を備えた労働力を涵養することを目的とすると謳っている。新たな手続は，従来の第1〜3ステップに三つのステップを加えた次のような手続の流れとなる。

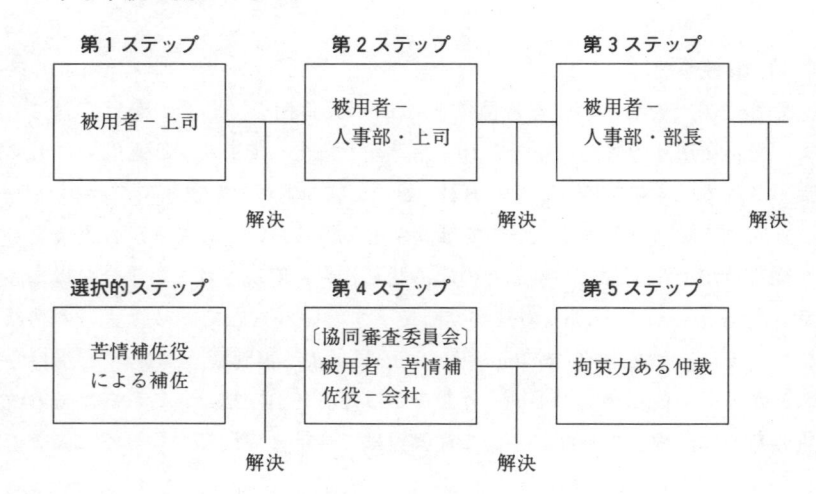

```
第1ステップ         第2ステップ          第3ステップ
┌──────────┐    ┌──────────┐     ┌──────────┐
│ 被用者－  │    │ 被用者－  │     │ 被用者－  │
│ 上司      │    │ 人事部・  │     │ 人事部・  │
│           │    │ 上司      │     │ 部長      │
└──────────┘    └──────────┘     └──────────┘
                      │                  │                 │
                    解決                解決              解決

選択的ステップ      第4ステップ          第5ステップ
┌──────────┐    ┌──────────┐     ┌──────────┐
│ 苦情補佐役│    │〔協同審査 │     │ 拘束力ある│
│ による補佐│    │ 委員会〕  │     │ 仲裁      │
│           │    │被用者・苦情│    │           │
│           │    │補佐役－会社│    │           │
└──────────┘    └──────────┘     └──────────┘
                      │                  │
                    解決                解決
```

　新たな手続では，苦情申立人が部長による判断に不満の場合には，「苦情補佐役」（Executive Advisor）による補佐を求めることができる。苦情補佐役は，上級管理職クラスのスタッフで，人事部がそのリストを作成しておき，苦情提起者がその中から選定する。苦情補佐役は，①当該従業員から苦情の

内容を聴き，それにつき調査して，その妥当性につき助言をし，②適当と考える場合には，苦情の解決のための話し合いを援助し，③苦情処理の次のステップである「協同審査委員会」（Consensus Review Board）につき助言を行う。

協同審査委員会は，役員1名，当該事業部門の他の部の上級管理者1名，人事部の代表者1名の3名からなるパネルであり，苦情提起者，人事部長，会社の雇用機会均等室長によって，予め作成されている候補者リストの中から選定される。この審査委員会の目的は，正式の判定手続の前段として，問題の解決を図ることである。そこでの審査では，証人や証拠を受けつけるが，それらについて格別の手続上ないし証拠上のルールは存しない。苦情提起者は弁護士を伴うことはできず，代わりに苦情補佐役によって補佐してもらうことができる。委員会は，非公開で，両当事者とそれぞれ別個に会見してその言い分を把握し，陳述書と書証を受理し，協同で決定を下す。決定書は当事者にのみ交付される。委員会は，決定において，解雇・レイオフの取消，昇給の実施，人事評価の変更，その他の回復措置を命じることができる。しかし，会社の一般方針を変更させたり，懲罰的ないし補償的な損害賠償を命令することはできない。

協同審査委員会の決定は，会社側には拘束力がある。苦情提起者の方は，決定に不服がある場合には，20日以内に次のステップとしての拘束力のある仲裁手続を求めることができる。問題は，外部の機関による救済を求める権利があるかどうかであるが，制度発足以前から雇用されている被用者についてはこの権利が保持され，発足後に雇用された被用者については仲裁が最終手続であって，訴訟や外部機関への申立はなしえないことが採用の際の同意書によって確認される。

拘束力のある仲裁手続においては，仲裁に付託できる事項は仲裁判断になじむかどうかの観点から列挙されている。また，仲裁に要する費用は当事者間で折半される。いずれの当事者も自ら選任する弁護士を使用することができ，相手方が選定した証人1人とすべての専門的証人に対して証言録取（deposition）を行うことができる。また，相手方に関連の文書の提出を求めることができ，証人および文書の提出を命ずるように申請できる。さらに，仲裁人は，裁定において，当該苦情が依拠する連邦ないし州の制定法の規定

に従った救済を与えることができる。H社での手続を紹介した雇用関係専門弁護士は、この仲裁手続は、上記のような手続的配慮によって Gilmer 判決の訴訟代替要件を十分に満たすであろうと評価している。

上記の新たな手続の実施後1年間（1993-94年）において、H社では、おおよそ3,000件の苦情関連の問い合わせが人事部や雇用機会均等室になされ、298件が正式の申立（complaint）となった。そのうち235件が同年中に処理されたが、うち141件（60%）が当該従業員の満足のいくように解決され、仲裁手続が求められたケースはないという。また、EEOCなどの外部機関への申立が顕著に減少した（154件から3件へ）。

(3) P社のケース

次に、筆者が、1998年の9月に訪問し、ヒアリングと資料入手を行ったP社のケースを紹介する。

P社は、従業員2700人のカメラ・メーカーである。P社は従業員持株制を採用しており、会社の株式の4分の1は従業員が所有している。また、長年、レイオフはしない方針を維持してきて、その旨を会社の雇用・人事関係の方針、規則を示した小冊子（"Personnel Policy Satements and Policy Rules"）において表明してきた。

P社の紛争解決手続は、"Dispute Resolution: Appeal Process Guide" というガイドブックにおいて説明されている。

ガイドブックでは、P社の紛争解決の思想が次のように述べられている。紛争（conflict）は自然に生じるものであり、改革を促すなど積極的に評価すべき面もある[19]。そして紛争解決手続の究極目標は、被用者の各人が自分で紛争を解決できるようにすることである。紛争は、環境いかんによって健全で迅速な解決が可能となるものであり、経営側も開放的で公正な解決を協同で図る責任がある。経営の観点からは、紛争解決は、労働の環境を改善し、生産性を高め、経営者・従業員のパートナーシップを形成し、訴訟を最少限にする、等の点で「経営の発展、人々の発展」という当社の経営理念に資す

---

19) 上記のガイドブックは、不満、心配、対立は誤解、説明・意志疎通の不足、情報不足などからも発生するのであり、これらを取り払ってもなお意見の対立が存在している場合に初めて「紛争」が存在するといえると、「紛争」を定義している。

る。また，紛争は，できるだけ現場に近いレベルで解決を図るのがよい。そして，紛争解決の鍵は，紛争は自分自身で解決するという気持ち，紛争解決を援助する適切な手続・人材が存在していることをよく知っていること，自分の問題を安心して表明できること，紛争解決システムを公正で効率的なものと信頼していること，などである。

上記のような思想によって設置されている手続は，次のチャートに表されている。

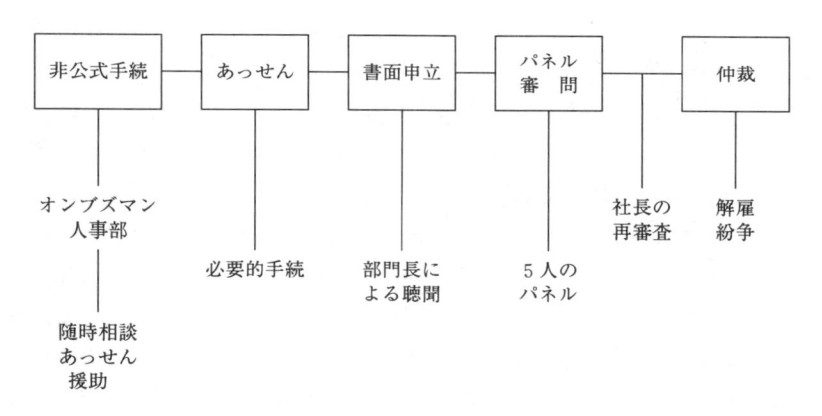

```
┌──────┐  ┌──────┐  ┌──────┐  ┌──────┐  ┌──────┐
│非公式手続│→│あっせん│→│書面申立│→│パネル │→│ 仲裁 │
│      │  │      │  │      │  │ 審問 │  │      │
└──────┘  └──────┘  └──────┘  └──────┘  └──────┘
    │         │          │         │         │
オンブズマン  必要的手続  部門長に   5人の    解雇
人事部                  よる聴聞   パネル   紛争
    │                             │
随時相談                         社長の
あっせん                         再審査
援助
```

最初の手続は非公式のもの（"informal process"）である。紛争解決には，誤解の除去，情報の供与，意志疎通などが必要なので，まず，「オンブズマン」や人事部等が関与して，対話や第三者の援助による話し合い（facilitated discussion）を行うプロセスをおく。90〜95％の苦情（complaints）はこの非公式手続の段階で解決するとのことである。

次の手続は，双方の合意の形成を図る社内あっせん（mediation）である。あっせん員は社内からボランティアを公募し，あっせん員の訓練（外部機関による30時間の訓練プログラム）を受けさせる。全社で約100人があっせん員として登録されているが，実際に活動しているのは約20人である。あっせんは月に2，3件行われ，最近4年間で250件行われた。

あっせんは，2人のあっせん員によって行う（comediation）のが普通である。実際の手続は，両当事者を一緒にして，言い分を聞き，話し合いを支援する手続（facilitated discussion）と，一方当事者から交互に言い分を聞き調整を図る手続（shuttle diplomacy）とからなる。

あっせんや，次の段階の書面による申立の手続では，希望すれば自分の指名する従業員を「不服介添人」（appeal assistant）にして，自分の言い分の伝達を介添えしてもらえる。あっせん員も，あっせん手続で知りえた情報については秘密遵守義務がある。あっせんには，不服申立運営部，人事部，法務部のスタッフも出席する。

次の手続は，書面による申立（written appeal）である。これをするには，あっせんを経ておく必要がある。給料（pay），勤務成績（performance），昇進（promotion），配置（job selection）以外の問題については，当該措置の適切性について関係部の部長の判定をも得ておく必要がある。

申立に対しては，各部に設置される5人のパネラーによる聴問（hearing）が行われる。5人のパネラーの構成は，時間給（hourly pay）従業員の事件であれば3人は時間給従業員から，そして月給制（salary）従業員，役員（executive）から1人ずつとなる。月給制従業員のケースなら，3人が月給制従業員から選ばれる。パネラーになる人々は，ボランティアとして応募しておき，40時間の訓練プログラムを受けておく。パネラーは，申立人が選ぶ。

大部分のケースでは，パネラーが全員一致の決定に至る。給料，勤務成績，昇進，配置に関する苦情のケースでは，パネルの判断が最終的であり，それ以上の社内手続を求める権利はない。ただし，パネルの判断については，社長が裁量的に介入し，その判断を覆すことができる。これは，従業員側が負けたが，特別に情状酌量をしてやるというケースを想定している。

解雇・雇用の打ち切りについては，申立人はパネルの判断に不服の場合には仲裁（arbitration）を求める権利がある。仲裁人はJAMES／END DISPUTEという会社から仲裁人を派遣してもらう。この仲裁手続自身は，会社が費用を負担する。また，申立人は弁護士を自分の負担で付ける（一日約3000ドル）ことができる。申立人が弁護士を付ければ会社もつける。約半分のケースでは弁護士が付けられる。この4年間で47件の仲裁が行われた。

以上が，P社における包括的で入念な企業内紛争解決手続である。これによって紛争を企業の中で解決してしまい，外部に出さないようにすることが図られている。興味深いのは，このような制度にいたる経緯である。

現在の制度の前には，労働組合に替わる組織としての従業員代表委員会（Employees Committee）が45年間存在していた。これが，賃金・労働条件の

交渉を行い，また苦情処理手続を運営していた。ただし，前者の機能については，労働協約の締結はなされなかった。また，後者については，最終ステップは仲裁で，アメリカ仲裁人協会（AAA）から仲裁人の派遣を受けていたが，同協会の仲裁は厳格な手続を要求するものであった。従業員代表委員会は，36人のフルタイムの専従役員を有し，その給与は会社が負担していた。

この従業員代表委員会が全国労働関係法によって禁止された使用者による支配介入行為であるとの告発が，全国労働関係局（NLRB）になされ，NLRBが1990年にこれを肯定する決定を下した。そのような判断を予測して，決定前から，同委員会の委員長が違法とされた場合の代替制度について研究する従業員グループを組織し，検討を行い，人事部もこの検討に参画した。このグループが従来の苦情処理手続に代替する制度として考案した案を実験的に実施してみたうえで，新制度を1995年に発足させたのである[20]。

新制度は，オンブズマン，社内のあっせん，パネルの手続など新たな実験ばかりだった。しかも，これを実行に移したときは，ダウンサイジングの真最中で，4年間で30％の人員（1800人）が削減された。具体的方法としては，1年分の給与，3ヶ月間の給与付きの再就職活動の援助，健康保険の二年間の継続などのパッケージで遂行された。このような困難な状況下で新制度の定着が図られたという[21]。

---

20) なお，従業員代表委員会が担当していた交渉機能の方は，現在，従業員持株行使委員会（Employee Ownership Influence Committee，月一回）が代替している。いずれも，労働者の代表者と使用者の交渉（dealing）と見られれば，再び全国労働関係法の違反とされるおそれがあるので，そのように見られないような制度設計をしているという。

21) P社の近年のダウンサイジング時代に数件の雇用打切り事件について仲裁人として仲裁判断を行った前述のSiegel氏は，以上の新たな苦情処理手続について，会社が基本的にコントロールしながら従業員の利益の擁護を図る従来の従業員代表委員会制度を別な形で復活させたものといえるが，それでも，通常の会社よりも従業員に対してはるかに親切でフェアなものといえると評価している。1998年9月11日の筆者とのインタビュー。

3　企業内苦情処理制度の一種としての社内オンブズパーソン

(1)　社内オンブズパーソン（Corporate Ombudsperson）の概観

近年，米国の組合のない大企業で発達してきた苦情処理手続の概要は以上のとおりであるが，次にはその一環として相当数の大企業で増加してきた「社内オンブズパーソン」（"Corporate Ombudsperson (Ombudsman)"）の制度を説明しておきたい[22]。

社内オンブズパーソンは，政府機関や地方自治体の行政の監視役として発達してきた伝統的なオンブズパーソン[23]とは基本的に異なる。伝統的オンブズパーソンは，政府組織の活動を市民の利益擁護の立場で外部から監視するものであり，調査と勧告の機能を中心とする。これに対して，社内オンブズパーソンは，組織内にあって，正式の調査権限をもたないまま，非公式に，調整的に，相談と問題解決を図るものである。他にも，同様の存在は，大学（学生・教職員），病院，介護施設などに存在し，「組織内オンブズパーソン」（"Organizational Ombudsperson"）とも称される[24]。

わが国では，伝統的なオンブズパーソンの意味で「オンブズマン」という言葉が定着しており，実際上も，一定の機能を果たし，一定のイメージを作り上げている。これに対して社内オンブズパーソンは，いまだ基本的に未知の制度といえる[25]。そこで，筆者は，この制度の日本における導入を図る場

---

22)　以下の記述は，主として，1973年以来 MIT のオンブズパーソンであり，オンブズマン協会の初代会長として社内オンブズパーソン制度の発展に尽力してきた Mary Rowe 氏の "Options, Functions and Skills : What an Organizational Ombudsman Want to Know,"という The Ombudsman Association の小冊子および同氏との1998年9月11日のインタビューによる。

23)　伝統的オンブズパーソンに関する比較研究として，小島武司＝外間寛編『オンブズマン制度の研究』（中央大学出版部，1979）。

24)　Cf., Mary Rowe & Dean M. Gottehrer, "Similarities and Differences Between Public and Private Sector Ombudsman," March 19, 1997 (unpublished paper).

25)　わが国でこれまでこの制度にふれた文献としては，菅野和夫＝諏訪康雄「労働市場の変化と労働法の課題」日本労働研究雑誌1994年12月号12頁，諏訪康雄『労使紛争の処理』（日本労働研究機構，1997）139頁。

3 企業内苦情処理制度の一種としての社内オンブズパーソン

合には，伝統的オンブズパーソンとの区別を明確にしつつ，その地位と機能を平易に表現するために，「社内苦情相談役」というような訳を充てるのが適切であると考える。しかし米国での制度それ自体を紹介しようとする本稿では，「社内オンブズパーソン」という言葉を使い続けることとする。

　社内オンブズパーソンは，企業に雇用される者であるが，企業によって中立性（独立性）を保障される。このためにトップ（代表取締役社長）直属の高い地位を与えられることが多い。キャリアを積み上げた被用者の引退前の最後の地位としている企業も多い。また，この中立性と並んで，相談者・相談内容についての秘密の厳守を基本的な倫理とし，このために外部に対する証言拒否権の主張，相談データの抹消などの制度的，技術的な工夫が行われる。その機能は，従業員やその他の企業関係者の悩み，苦情，意見を非公式に受け付け，情報提供と相談を行うことである。そして，必要により，問題解決のための選択肢を提示したり，意志疎通の仲介（shuttle diplomacy）をしたり，依頼されればまれに紛争解決のあっせんを行ったりする。これらの機能のために，必要により企業の人事部，法務部，機会均等室，法・倫理遵守室（compliance office）と協力する。さらに，蓄積した相談データ（個々のケースを一般化したもの）に基づいて会長に対し企業管理のあり方について助言を行う。

　社内オンブズマンが取り扱える問題は，仕事（work）ないしは職場（workplace）に関連した（related）問題の全般とされ，格別の限定が付されないのが通常である[26]。そうした上で，報酬，成績評価，懲戒，人事，安全衛生，差別，ハラスメント，企業倫理，法違反，労働条件，雇用の打ち切りなどの事項が例示されたりする[27]。なお，社内オンブズパーソンは，労働組合のない企業において設けられる場合が多いが，組合に組織されている企業においても設けられており，その場合には，組合の管轄事項（交渉単位に所属する労働者に関する義務的団体交渉事項や労働協約上の苦情処理手続対象事項）は社内オンブズパーソンの取り扱える問題からは除外される。組合がある企業では，社内オンブズパーソンは，組合の管轄を侵害しないように配慮しつつ任務を

---

[26] 後述のA社，UT社，P社の社内オンブズマン紹介冊子のいずれにおいてもそうである。

[27] P社のオンブズマン紹介冊子。

遂行するが，組合がむしろオンブズオフィスに処理を委ねる問題も多いという[28]。

以上が，企業内苦情相談役の一般的な属性と機能であるが，このような人々は企業内での存在であるばかりでなく，企業横断的な専門的職業人として，企業外にオンブズマン協会（"The Ombudsman Association"）という職業人の団体を結成して，倫理綱領（Code of Ethics）と行為基準（Standards of Practice）を制定し[29]，会員のための情報の収集と提供を行い，かつ系統的な教育訓練プログラムを提供している[30]。また，社内オンブズパーソン制度の普及発展のためのPRも行っている[31]。ただし，社内オンブズパーソンは，後記のA社，UT社，P社の例に見るように，当該企業において様々な業務を経験した者から任命される場合の方が多く，しかも任命においては人事労務の経験は必要と考えられていない。むしろ，中立公平性と秘密遵守についての同僚からの信頼が最も重要な資質とされ，オンブズパーソンの任務遂行に必要な様々な技術はオンブズマン協会の系統的な訓練プログラムにおいて修得できると考えられている。

それでは，このような社内オンブズパーソンは，米国の大企業においてどれほど普及しているであろうか。この制度は，あっせん，仲裁などを中心とした苦情処理ADRほどには普及していない。前掲のコーネル大学紛争研究所の調査では，回答企業528社のうち労働協約上の制度ではない（つまり組合がない状況での）苦情処理手続を有しているのは185社（35.0％）であったの

---

28) LT社の社内オンブズマンM.S.氏との1998年9月11日インタビュー。
29) 倫理綱領は以下のとおりである。
  ＊オンブズマンは，特別の中立者として，自己に申告された事柄に関して，申告者の許可がない限り，厳格に秘密を保持する責任がある。オンブズマンの裁量に委ねられる例外は，重大な危害のおそれが現れた場合のみである。
  ＊オンブズマンは，秘密の相談内容に関する記録とファイルを，経営者を含むすべての第三者の検閲から防御するために，あらゆる合理的な手段をとらなければならない。
  ＊オンブズマンは，自己に申告された事柄について，いかなる司法および行政手続きにおいても証言すべきではない。
  ＊オンブズマンは，助言をするときには，すべての当事者に公平な行動または方針を示唆する責任がある。
30) 101と呼ばれる初級コース，202と呼ばれる中級コース，その後の様々な専門的コースが設けられている。

に対して，社内オンブズパーソンを有している企業は55社（10.3％）であった。また，オンブズマン協会は，1997年の年次報告書では，207人の会員と90名の準会員（associate member）を有している。この団体は社内オンブズパーソンとして活動している人々をほぼ網羅しているので，その会員数から社内オンブズパーソンを有する企業のおおよその数を推測できるが，超大企業の場合，数名のオンブズパーソンを有しているケースがあることに注意する必要がある。

社内オンブズパーソンの設置の動機は企業により多様であるが，次の三つが主要なものといえる。第一は，訴訟コストの回避のための ADR の一種としての導入である。例えば，次に紹介する UT 社では，オンブズパーソンに寄せられる相談の約1割が，適切に処理されなければ訴訟に発展しうるものと観測されている[32]。同社および A 社，P 社では，他に，企業内苦情処理 ADR としてのあっせん，仲裁等の手続も設けられており，オンブズパーソンはこれら社内 ADR の一環としても位置づけられているのである。

---

31) なお，米国でのオンブズパーソンの団体は7つある。
  ①カリフォルニア大学人集団（California Caucus of Colleges and Universities）――設立は1975年頃と古い。規約，会長などがなく，組織的に最も柔軟な団体である。
  ②大学オンブズマン協会（University and College Ombudsman Association）――設立は1980年頃。
  ③オンブズマン協会（The Ombudsman Association, TOA）――設立は1982年。Mary Rowe 氏が84年まで会長を勤めた。当初は，社内オンブズマン（Corporate Ombudsman）協会と称していた。あらゆる種類のオンブズマンが加入できるが，主としては会社のオンブズマンが加入している。
  ④合衆国オンブズマン協会（USOA）――1970年代に設立された伝統的（classical）オンブズマンの団体。
  ⑤新聞オンブズマン団体（ONO）――1980年頃に設立された。
  ⑥患者代理人協会（Patient Representatives）――病院の患者のためのオンブズパーソンの団体。
  ⑦高齢者ケア施設団体（Nursing Home For The Elderly）。
  これらのほか，矯正施設の，公立義務教育学校の，問題を抱えた子供達の，オンブズパーソンがあり，それぞれ小さな団体を組織している。
32) George Wratney, "The Ombudsman Approach to ADR," (a program paper for the 4th Annual Meeting of the Alternative Dispute Resolution Institute), 1997.

第二は，従業員が気持ちよく働ける職場環境の実現（従業員の定着，生産性の向上）である。これについては，後述のA社，UT社，P社の社内オンブズパーソンは，雇用平等法制の発展により人種・出身国・性などにおいて組織構成員が多様化しそれに伴う摩擦が増大したこと，そして技術者の不足の中で企業がその養成と定着を図っていることを指摘した。上記の三社は，いずれも世界的な大企業であり，給与，配置，昇進などにおいて業績主義，競争的公募，ストック・オプションなどを伴う長期雇用システムを採用している。そして，このような競争的内部労働市場における人事・職場の公正さを担保するために社内オンブズマン制度を置いているのである。

第三に，連邦政府との契約を行う企業の場合には，企業倫理確立の体制づくりのために社内オンブズパーソンを設置するというケースが見られる。後に見るA社およびUT社のケースがそれであるが，同社のみならず，政府契約に依存する企業の一つのパターンであることが，複数のオンブズパーソンによって指摘された[33]。つまり，企業内での法と倫理の遵守体制の確立は，業界の主要企業による自主的ガイドラインのなかで連邦政府との契約の実際上の要件となっており，そのなかに，企業内部における報復のおそれのない不正の申告手続の設置とこれへの適正な対応（不正防止・是正）が重要な要件として設定されている。そして，連邦量刑委員会（United States Sentencing Commission）が1991年に作成した企業犯罪の量刑基準（ガイドライン）には，企業内での効果的な不正防止手続の存在を，不正発見の場合の捜査当局への申告と捜査への協力，関係者の責任の引き受けと並んで，量刑軽減の事由としている（具体的なポイント制）[34]。社内オンブズパーソンは，これらのガイドラインの要請する企業内不正防止手続として利用されているのである。

(2) A社のケース

次は，三つの国際的大企業について，社内オンブズパーソンの制度のヒア

---

[33] Thomas Furtado, *Why An Organizational Ombudsman?* The Ombudsman Association, 1996, p. 20. その他，筆者がインタビューをしたA社およびUT社のオンブズパーソンも指摘。

[34] Lynn Sharp Paine, "Managing for Organizational Integrity," *Harvard Business Review*, Vol. 72, p. 110 (1994).

3　企業内苦情処理制度の一種としての社内オンブズパーソン

リング結果を記していく。まずは，クレディットカード・サービスを行う世界的大企業A社のオンブズパーソンからの聴取[35]の結果である。

　A社のオンブズオフィスは4年前の1994年に設置された。現在では，米国の各地に5人，欧州に2人，その他（香港，シンガポール，シドニー）に3人のオンブズパーソンがいる。設置の契機としては，連邦政府との契約のガイドラインのなかに企業内での報復のおそれのない問題解決手続（Issue resolution channels without fear of retaliation）の設置・運営があったので，これに対応したことによる。それまでの苦情処理手続については，従業員のアンケートでは，かなりの不信感や報復の懸念が表明されていた。そこで，ラインの上司，人事部，法遵守部，法務部などへの苦情提出と並ぶ手続として社内オンブズパーソンへの相談手続を設置した。

　社内オンブズパーソンにとっては，秘密遵守と中立性が最も重要な属性である。秘密遵守のためには，オンブズパーソンと会社との契約で，社長に直属し，社長にのみ報告する立場と秘密遵守義務などを謳ってある。自分はA社に雇われている立場だが，これらの点で，他の被用者とは「わずかながら区別」（thin wall）が施されている。

　オンブズオフィス設置の当初は，これらの属性を実際に確保するために，オフィスの物理的な独立性（防音装置のある相談室，相談者同士が顔を合わせないように待合室と帰路をレイアウト），独立の電話，独立のコンピューター回線などの工夫をした。また，個々の相談ケースの記録については，個人名などを消去するシステムを設定した。1年半経ったところで，この制度をA社の全世界の支社に拡げ始めた。

　当初の2，3年は，秘密遵守，中立性，非公式性の諸特徴をもった手続による問題の健全な解決（sound resolution of issues）を目標とした。そのためにオンブズ・オフィスの存在，オンブズパーソンとは何か，何をするのかを従業員に周知し，それへのアクセスを確保することに力を注いだ。切手不要のオンブズオフィス宛通信用紙や，AT&Tの料金不要の電話番号の設定，社内ニュースでの宣伝などである。制度を全世界に拡げるときには，案内冊子を21ヵ国語に翻訳したり，通訳付きの無料電話の設定を行った。

---

[35]　1998年9月8日 New York 市の同社オンブズオフィスにて聴取。

今後は，問題発生の防止（issue prevention）を目指す。すなわち，オンブズオフィスにこれまで蓄積され，今後入ってくる情報を用いて，問題発生を予測し，警告し，制度的な改革や対応を提案する。これには，会社の経営首脳のみならず，人事部，法務部，法遵守部との密接な連携が必要である。このように，会社トップに対して，秘密を遵守しながら改革のための情報を提供するのが，これから取り組む課題である。また，10年後の様々な環境変化を予測し，会社の基本的な課題とオンブズパーソンの役割を設計することも試みる。このために，会社首脳，従業員，関連部署などから意見聴取を行うつもりである。

　当社の社内オンブズパーソンは，企業内部からの任命を方針とし，企業内キャリアの一段階としている。内部任命によるのは，内部の人間の方が会社の方針，組織，人々，業務内容をよく知っているからである。自分はA社勤続20年であり，オンブズパーソンになったときは勤続16年だった。それまでは，ラインもスタッフも，現場も本社も，経験した。また，9つの業務部門を経験している。これらの幅広い経験がオンブズの仕事に生かされている。ただし，他の企業でオンブズパーソンとして活躍した人なら，当社でも任務を果たすことはできると思われる。オンブズパーソンに任命する上での最も重要な資質は，中立的で秘密を守るということについての同僚からの信頼である。なお，当社の合計10人のオンブズパーソンについては，経歴，学歴，言語，国籍などにおいて多様な人材を任命するように心がけている。

　昨年の統計で見ると，オンブズオフィスに来るケースの43%がライン・マネージャーに委ねられ，また，人事部，あっせん，仲裁の手続などとの連携も行われる。こうして，ラインマネージャー，人事部，法務部，法遵守部とは互いに協力するパートナーシップの関係にある。苦情はむしろそれらの部署に寄せられることが多いが，どこに持ち込むか不明な場合，報復をおそれる場合，会社の対応が不明な場合，人事部を信頼できない場合などにオンブズオフィスに寄せられる。オンブズオフィスに来る相談の典型例は，①上司が私的出費を会社に付けていると部下が疑いを抱き，放置できないと考えたが，上司との関係を悪くしたくないという場合，②自分の部が開発しつつある新製品が法の基準を満たしていないとの疑いをもったが，トラブルメーカーと思われたくないという場合，③上司から点数の悪い人事評価書を受け取

り，説明を求めたが，納得のいく説明がなされないという不満，④新しい上司が説明なしに，また部下の意見を聞かずに，今までのやり方をどんどん変えていき，職場のモラルがダウンしているという悩みを抱いている場合，などである[36]。

　筆者は，従業員が持ち込む苦情をそのまま信用できるかという点を尋ねたが，これについては，関係者に対しては，あくまでも当該従業員が述べている話であり，これは真相解明の調査ではない，と伝えることにしている。また，相談を受けたときには，相手方は当該状況ではどのように言うだろうかと想像する。当事者の言い分の食い違いを想像し，見分けるためには，あっせん員としての訓練を受けるのが役に立つ。オンブズパーソン同士で経験を話し合い，相談し合うことも重要である，とのことである。

　従業員から持ち込まれる相談は，深刻な対立がからむものはそれほど多くない。特に同僚や上司の不正をもち込むケースはそれほど多くない。そのような場合には，具体的な事実を多角的に聞き出し，どの程度根拠のありそうな話かを慎重に検討する。差別の主張の場合には，当該従業員の上司，人事部，法遵守部などに直接もち込む場合，オンブズオフィスに来てそれらに回される場合などがある。

　A社の人事方針としては，当社でもリストラは実施してきたが，向上心があり，チャレンジを続ける限り長期勤続を歓迎する。また，内部の教育訓練プログラムは豊富であり，このようにして養成した有能な人材を逃さないように意を用いている。内部での人事異動も盛んであるが，異動については競争的な公募制（posting）をとっているとのことである。

(3)　UT社のケース
　次は，重機械メーカーのUT社のケースである[37]。
　UT社は，ジェットエンジン，ヘリコプター，エレベーター，エスカレーター，エアコン機器，輸送機器などの重機械のメーカーで，全世界に支社を有するグループ企業である。

---

36)　これらは，A社のオンブズオフィス案内冊子に，仮想相談事例として記載されている。

UT 社には7人のオンブズパーソンがいる。6人はニューヨークにいて米国を，1人はロンドンにいて欧州を管轄している。また，全世界の数十箇所にはディアローグ管理者（dialogue administrator）がいてディアローグ・プログラムの処理を行っている。それは，電話（無料）または所定の用紙によって会社や会社の誰かに対する質問，要望，苦情，意見を伝えるというものである。ディアローグ管理者は，ディアローグによって提起された問題を担当する部署に発信者の名前を伏せて返答を求め，返答を得てから当該発信人に返送する。

ディアローグもオンブズオフィスも，中立性と秘密保持を基本原則とするが，実際上は，より小さく簡単な問題はディアローグによって提起され，より重大でより複雑な問題（例えば法律問題）はオンブズオフィスに寄せられるという関係にある。また，ディアローグ管理者は，一部のケースについては発信人の許可を得て，オンブズ・オフィスに転送する。

これらの制度が作られたのは，1984年に連邦政府と防衛産業の合意によって不正行為防止のためのガイドラインが作られ，その中に企業内での不正行為防止のための報復のおそれのない問題提起の手続の設置がうたわれたことによる。1980年代当初，軍需企業は契約代金の水増し請求などによって国民の非難を受けていた。レーガン大統領は軍事予算を増額するうえで，連邦軍需契約の問題について上院に調査委員会を設置したが，この委員会で多数の証人喚問が行われ，軍需契約の不正が暴かれた。この委員会は12，3項目の改革を勧告した。その中の一つに応えるべく，主要な軍需企業が集まって，不正防止・是正のガイドライン（"Defense Industry Initiatives"）を作成した。このガイドラインによれば，軍需企業は連邦契約についての不正を防止するための申告とこれへの適正な対応手続を樹立すべきであり，また不正行為の疑いがある場合にはそれを調査し，是正し，外部の機関に報告する義務があ

---

37) 1998年9月8日に New York 市にて同社のオンブズマンG.W.氏にインタビュー。なお，同氏の紹介で，同年11月5日には東京にて，同社の法遵守部の責任者であるP. G. 氏（Vice President, Business Practices）にも会い，補足的な情報を得ることができた。同氏は，以前は海軍の法務官で，契約の相手方企業に対する訴訟を担当していた。そして，UT 社における compliance 体制の樹立の際に，その責任者に依頼されたとのことである。

3 企業内苦情処理制度の一種としての社内オンブズパーソン

る。このガイドラインに従って1984年に社内で倫理綱領と，その遵守（不正防止）を司る企業倫理室（Business Practices Office, BPO）へのホットラインなどがつくられた。

このように，UT 社では，当初は，オンブズオフィスは，倫理綱領の確立のための制度であったが，社長がこれら制度を単なる法遵守以上の意思疎通の制度にしようとしたこと（"beyond compliance"）で，1986年にオンブズ—ディアローグ・プログラムへと発展した[38]。なお，上記のガイドラインの考え方は，後に連邦政府との契約の全分野に及ぼされ，今では連邦政府との契約を締結する企業は，同様の不正防止・是正・報告義務を引き受けることとなった。

BPO が入手する倫理綱領違反の情報の約 5 割はオンブズ—ディアローグ・プログラムを通じて寄せられる。他の約 2 割は内部監査（internal audit）によるもの，約 3 割は外部から寄せられるものである。これら情報に基づき，BPO は，倫理綱領違反について昨年度に127件の調査を行った。これらの約 5 ％は BPO が存在しなかったならば訴訟に発展していたであろうものである。

1986年から11年間に，UT 社は，42,000件のディアローグの問い合わせと，数千件のオンブズオフィスへの相談を受けた[39]。ディアローグやオンブズオフィスに寄せられる質問や問題の約半数は，職場におけるハラスメント，差別，不公正な取り扱いその他の悩みである。これらの中には放置すれば訴訟に発展しうる問題もかなり含まれている。また，約 3 分の 1 は，何らかの措置を求めるというよりは説明を求めるというものである。その多くは，法や倫理綱領の違反にかかわるものではなく，会社の方針の変更を求める意見，労働条件についての不満の表明，経営者に対する suggestions などであり，なかには会社に対する賞賛，謝意等も寄せられる。

全体として，約 1 割の問題が取扱いを誤れば訴訟に発展する可能性のある

---

38) ディアローグは従業員（全世界で17万4,000人，4 割が米国国内）のみが利用できるが，オンブズオフィスは従業員のみならず，株主，供給業者，顧客，競争相手，なども利用できる。

39) なお，同社では，1987年から，あっせんと仲裁という ADR の手続を制度化し，1997年 9 月から 1 年間には約200件のあっせん・仲裁が行なわれている。

もの[40]といえる。約1割のケースは上司と部下の関係の問題（ハラスメント，意思疎通の不良，リーダーシップのあり方への不満，等）で，このなかに成績評価（performance evaluation）への不満が入る。典型的には，自分は一生懸命に勤務していて会社の評価もよいと思っていた社員が，ある日突然，上司から勤務成績不良の評価書を突きつけられたようなケースである（"surprise poor performance review" と称される）。

このようなケースでは，オンブズマンの任務は，当該部下の立場になって上司に対して評価の見直しを勧告するというものではない。まず，上司にこの件で不満を伝えたどうかを尋ね，伝えてなければ口頭ないし手紙で伝えたらどうか，あるいは人事部に不満を伝えたらどうかと示唆する。また，オンブズを通じて不満を上司または人事部へ伝えてほしいのか，あるいは自分の名前を出したくなくただ不満を聞いてほしいのか，一般的な話としてどこかに伝えてほしいのか，というように選択肢を示すのである。この場合の被用者の選択は，自分の上司や人事部をどの程度信頼しているか等によって違ってくる。また，オンブズパーソンは，通常は，上司と部下の間に入って争いが解決するようにあっせんすることはしない。

ディアローグで上司などの非違行為が主張された場合には，具体的な事実の指摘があるか否か，あるならそれが真実か否かをさらに検討する。具体的な事実の指摘がないままに上司を非難している場合には，重大な非難なので具体的な指摘をするように返事をし，指摘がなされなければたしなめる返事を出して終わりにする。新たな上司が来て従来の業務運営を刷新しようとしているような場合には，それを好まない部下のフラストレーションがこのような非難となって現れる。

なお，W氏は勤続20年，オンブズパーソンになるまでは勤続14年で，直前の6年間は，現在の社長のスピーチ・ライターの職にあり，旅行なども含め，常に社長と行動を共にしていた。氏の見解では，巨大な企業の場合には，その文化，経営政策，組織を知っており，人的ネットワークをもっていることがオンブズパーソンの仕事に必要不可欠であるので，オンブズパーソンは組

---

[40] 「弁護士に相談すべきかどうか迷ったのですが……」，「EEOCとオンブズのどちらに相談しようかと迷ったのですが……」というような相談とのことである。

織の内部の者がなった方がよいとのことである。氏の場合には，スピーチ・ライターをするには社内の様々な部署から情報を集めなければならなかったので，社内の組織や情報に通じることができ，その経験が非常に役立っている。外部の者をオンブズパーソンに任命した場合には，これらの点で習熟に時間がかかるのではないか。他の会社でオンブズをやった人ならば，比較的小さな会社のオンブズパーソンならやれるだろうが，巨大な世界的企業の場合には組織は極めて複雑で外部の者には理解がなかなか困難であると思う，とのことである。

内部の者がなった場合，十分な中立性を保てるか，秘密保持のための独立性を確保できるかという点については，自分は数年間社長と行動を共にしてきたので，社内では社長に非常に近い人間と見られている。このような場合，社長に近すぎて中立性を疑われかねない点が短所だが，社長の全面的な信頼を得ており，問題があればすぐに社長に連絡して話し合える点は長所である。

オンブズマンとして会社の様々な人々に働きかけながら，中立性と秘密保持を守るのは，微妙なバランスを要する難しい仕事である。それらを確保するのは，結局，オンブズマン自身の見識（integrity）でしかありえない。会社の綱領には，オンブズの仕事の中立性と秘密保持が謳われているが，それは紙に書いた指針にすぎない。

オンブズマンに望ましい資質は，自分が知らないということを率直に認めて他人に相談できる謙虚さ，秘密を守ってくれるという同僚の信頼，そして組織の中での人間関係を円滑にできる能力である。秘密保持のための様々な工夫，カウンセリングやあっせんなどの専門的な技術は，むしろオンブズマン協会の教育訓練や事後的な勉強で身につけることができるのであって，基本的な人間的資質の方が重要である。

(4) P社のケース

社内苦情処理手続について紹介した前述のカメラ・フィルム・メーカーのP社の「オンブズマン」制度については，以下のとおりである。

同社のオンブズマンは当初は5人だったが，前述のダウンサイジングのなかで従業員数に応じて人員が削減されていき，現在は2人である。当初の5人の時には人種，性，専門・経歴等において多様性を確保していた（女性，

黒人，管理職出身，技術者出身，等)。

　オンブズマンは内部任命が妥当である。理由は，内部の者の方が会社の組織・構成員をよく知っているからである。オンブズマンのK氏（男性）は勤続32年，R氏（女性）は29年であり，K氏は従業員代表委員会の委員長，R氏は中間管理職だった。選任に際しては，多数の応募者の中から何段階もの面接による厳しい選考があった。

　企業内オンブズマンは，企業の構成員の諸問題について，中立の立場に立ち，自由にアクセスできるようにし，秘密を保持し，問題解決の方法と選択肢を示す者である。代理人（advocate）でも，裁判官でも，仲裁人でもない。中立性については，会社に雇われていてどうして中立であり得るのかという同僚からの素朴な疑問に，今でも遭遇する。他方，管理者も，中立性とは意見を何も表明しないことと誤解している場合がある。中立性とは，会社と苦情提起従業員のいずれの立場にも組みしないということであって，公正なプロセスのための意見は表明する。中立性を担保するために，オンブズマンは会長に直属している。秘密遵守の方は，職務により知りえた事実については証言しなくてよいというオンブズマン自身の特権でもある。秘密遵守は，当初はなかなか信頼して貰えなかったが，現在では理解されている。中立性も秘密保持も，会社との間の契約であり，その旨会社の案内書（policy）に記載してある。

　オンブズマンは，まず相談者の相談内容を辛抱強く聴き，そのうえで，提起された問題について選択肢を整理し提示する。そして，相談者に自分で選択肢の一つを選んでもらい，その円滑な遂行の仕方を指導する。85％はこのような相談で解決している。しかし，オンブズマンは場合によってはあっせんも行う。管理者もオンブズマンを頼りにしており，事あるごとに相談してくるし，あっせんを依頼してくることもある。人事部長も今ではオンブズマン制度の強い支持者である。また，自分たちが受けた相談に基づいて，会社内の問題の所在を検討し，社長に報告するのも重要な任務である。

　前述の社内の紛争解決手続のいかなる段階でも，オンブズマンのところに相談に来ることができる。人事部，アファーマティブ・アクション室，法・倫理遵守室（ethics compliance office）とは任務を異にするが，これら部署と密接に連携することが必要である。相談は，オンブズオフィスに来るときは

顕名であるべきで,匿名の電話には相手にならない。匿名電話でも相手にするのは法遵守部門のみである(事柄の重要性から匿名でも申立の調査をする)。

(5) ハラスメントのひとつの解決方法としての社内オンブズパーソン

以上が社内オンブズパーソンの実際の姿と機能であるが,社内オンブズパーソンの重要な意義として,それが近年米国の職場で重要な問題となっているハラスメントの解決に必要かつ有用であることが,社内オンブズパーソンのリーダーとして知られる Mary Rowe 氏によって力説されている[41]。同氏は,1973年以来 MIT のオンブズパーソンを勤めるかたわら,オンブズマン協会の初代会長として社内オンブズパーソンの制度の発展に努力し,また多数の論文[42]で社内オンブズマンの必要性と役割を啓蒙してきた。そのなかで,同氏は,ハラスメント問題の適切な解決のためには,対決的な(adversarial)苦情処理手続のみならず,インフォーマルに柔軟に問題解決を図る仕組みとしてのオンブズパーソンが必要であることを次のように論じている。

ハラスメントは,最も広義には「労働環境を不合理に攪乱する意図ないし

---

[41] Mary Rowe, "People Who Feel Harassed Need a Complaint System with both Formal and Informal Options," Negotiation Journal, Vol. 6 pp. 161 (1990); Mary Rowe, "Dealing With Harassment : A Systems Approach," in Margaret S. Stockdale, ed., *Sexual Harassment in the Workplace : Directives, Frontiers, and Resposme Strategies, Women and Work,* Vol. 5, Sage Publications, Inc., 1996, pp. 241-271.

[42] Mary Rowe, "The Ombudsman's Role in a Dispute Resolution System," Negotiation Journal, Vol. 7, pp. 353-361 (1991); Mary Rowe, "Options and Choice for Conflict Resolution in the Workplace," in Lavinia Hall, ed., *Negotiation : Strategies for Mutual Gain,* Sage Publication, 1993, pp. 105-119; Mary Rowe, Ph. D., "Options, Functions and Skills : What an organizational ombudsperson might want to know," Negotiation Journal, Vol. 11, No. 2 (1995) (reprinted by The Ombudsman Association in a booklet); Mary Rowe, "Dispute Resolution in the Nonunion Environment : An Evolution Toward Integrated Systems For Conflict Management?" in Sandra Geason ed., *Frontiers in Dispute Resolution in Labor Relations and Human Resources,* Michigan State University Press, 1997, pp. 79-106; Mary Rowe, "An Effective Integrated Complaint Resolution System," in Bernice R. Sandler and Robert J. Shoop, ed., *Sexual Harassment on Campus,* Alyn and Bacon, 1997, pp. 202-213.

効果をもった攻撃的，威嚇的ないし敵対的な態度」と定義できる。性，人種，宗教，年齢，障害に基づく攻撃的態度を含むが，それに限られず，職場のいじめや嫌がらせをも包含する。このように定義した場合のハラスメントは，米国の職場における重大な問題といえる。セクシャル・ハラスメントひとつをとっても，毎年，職場におけるおよそ5％の男性と15％の女性がその被害を受けていると感じている。人種，宗教その他の理由によるハラスメントもまた広く行われている。しかしながら，ハラスメントについて正式の申立を提起する人々は少なく，職場の労働者の1％にも満たないのではないかと見られる。重要な問題は，これはなぜかである。

氏がこれまで蓄積してきたデータ（1973年～1988年の16年間にMITの内外から持ち込まれた約6000人からの相談）によれば，相談者の4分の3以上の人々は，問題を明るみにしたときの悪い結果（あからさまな報復よりは，上司・同僚からの静かな反発，会社に献身的でないとみられたり，神経過敏とか子供じみていると見られること）や，プライバシーの喪失をおそれている。彼らは，第三者のところへは問題を持ち込みたくないが，そうかといって自分自身で問題を解決する能力をもっていないと感じている。また，当該ハラスメントについて会社に適切な対応をさせるための十分な証拠を持ち合わせていないとも信じている（多くの場合に実際にもそうである）。また半分以上の相談者は，自分自身で思い詰めて，肩こり，頭痛，過食症，集中力喪失，不眠症，食欲不振，いら立ち，などの症状をもつ。また，自分の問題を，他人にはなかなかわかってもらえないと思い，仕事を辞めなければならないかもしれないと言う。これらの相談者は様々な専門家によるカウンセリングなどのサービスを必要としている。そして，上司や機会均等室などを相談相手とすることに不安や不信感をもっている。

そこで，相談者に対して，結局何が希望なのかと尋ねると，4分の3以上の人々は，正式の調査を行うとか，相手方を罰するというよりは，とにかく問題が終わってくれることであると答える。そして，大部分の人々は，相手方に対してどのように自分の気持ちを伝えるか（手紙の書き方，相手との話し合いの仕方，相手の言い分とそれへの答え方）について相談する。なかには，自分やその他の第三者が相手方との間に立って意思疎通を図ってくれるように頼む者もいる。ハラスメントについての一般的な警告や教育を従業員全体へ

の手紙や集会や教育プログラムで行うなどの一般的な対応措置を望む者もいる。他方，裁判所，行政機関，新聞社などの外部の機関に訴えようとする人々や，相手方との対決を望む者，相手方の懲戒処分を求める者は，それぞれ5〜10％程度にとどまる。

　こうしてMary Rowe氏は，ハラスメントは関係者個々人ごとに異なる意味と影響のある極めて複雑な問題であると特徴づける。そもそもハラスメントは，セクシャル・ハラスメントの定義における相手方に「望まれていない」（"unwanted"）性的行為という要件にあるとおり，主観的な現象であるというのである。このようなハラスメントについては，対決的な苦情処理手続や救済手続は，その被害を受けたと感じる人々のごく一部の者に役立つにすぎない。多くの人々にとっては，非公式で柔軟な問題解決の仕組みが必要な選択肢であり，社内オンブズパーソンの制度はその多くの人々のニーズに適合する。ハラスメントの問題は，企業にとっても生産性への悪影響，訴訟への発展可能性，企業イメージの毀損等の点で重大な問題であり，その防止と解決は使用者と被用者の双方の利益となるものであるので，オンブズオフィスの設置とハラスメント問題へのその活用が望まれる，というのである。

おわりに——日本の個別労使紛争解決制度への示唆

　以上，米国の組合のない大企業における苦情処理ADRと社内オンブズパーソンの制度について，若干の概観と個別ケースの描写を試みた。最後に，これら米国の制度がわが国の個別労使紛争解決制度のあり方に与える示唆を探って，本稿を結ぶこととしたい。

　第一に，米国の組合のない大企業における苦情処理ADRの発達については，それが，近年における雇用差別を中心とした雇用関係訴訟の多さと，その企業にとっての負担加重感を背景としていることが特徴的である。つまり，米国では，訴訟に替わる紛争解決手続は，まず訴訟の増加とその企業にとっての負担加重感が生じて，訴訟コストを回避するための手段として発達している側面が大きい。これに対して，わが国の企業では，上司との密接なコミュニケイションや労使協議制などの企業共同体的な紛争回避の仕組みが発達し，また企業外でも行政機関による相談指導の体制が用意され，訴訟回避

の体制が存続してきた。こうしてわが国では，雇用関係訴訟は，最近は増加傾向にあるとはいえ，米国に比較してはるかに少ない。また，訴訟の金銭的コストもはるかに安価といえる。したがって，訴訟コストという側面では，雇用関係をめぐる紛争について企業が自主的に公式・非公式（formal・informal）のADRを発展させる契機は未だ到来していないといえる。

　しかしながら，このような日本についても，裁判とそれ以外の制度が役割を分担する必要があることは同じであり，したがって裁判以外の諸制度の重要性は同じである。そこで，今後の個別労使紛争解決制度については，企業内の制度，私的な外部団体のサービス，行政機関のサービス，裁判所の手続などの，それぞれのあり方と相互の関係を検討していく必要がある。米国では，そのような技術として，また学問として，ADRが発展してきており，多様な紛争解決のモデルを提供しているのである。

　第二に，わが国企業においては，これまでは上司や人事部によって苦情の防止や処理が図られ，企業内苦情処理手続は未発達であった。しかし，近年は，いわゆるリストラクチャリングの中で雇用や賃金をめぐる深刻な苦情や紛争が増加しており，労働団体，弁護士団体，行政機関（労政事務所，労働基準監督署），裁判所などに持ち込まれている。また，今後は，従業員の多様化，従業員内部の利害の対立，業績主義・個別管理による緊張と不満などによって，企業内の苦情の増加が予想されるし，人事評価の不満のように企業内でないと解決しにくい問題の増加も予想される。さらに，平成9年改正の雇用機会均等法によるセクシャル・ハラスメントに関する防止・是正手続の要請や，平成10年改正の労働基準法による新裁量労働制における苦情処理の要請も新たに生じている。要するに，不況という景気循環的要因にとどまらず，働き方・雇用形態・価値観・人事管理等の多様化と，これによる企業共同体の統制力の弛緩化，そして法制度の変化，という構造的要因が，企業内苦情処理手続の充実を要請していると見られる。

　本稿で瞥見した米国企業の苦情処理の仕組みは，このような企業内苦情処理制度の整備の課題について，一つの参考モデルを提供している。ただし，米国の企業内でのあっせん，仲裁は，あっせん人・仲裁人が専門的職業として確立し，その倫理・行為基準と専門教育を司る職業団体の存在を基盤としていることに注意する必要がある。社内オンブズパーソンも同様である。そ

こで，わが国でも，苦情処理 ADR や企業内苦情相談役の樹立のためには，わが国の実情にあった社会的基盤の整備を考える必要がある。

　第三に，示唆的なのは，企業における法の遵守体制としての社内オンブズパーソンである。つまり，企業の不祥事防止のための米国的仕組みとして，政府契約の要件および企業犯罪の量刑基準において企業内の不正防止・是正体制の樹立を盛り込み，社内オンブズパーソンへの通報とそれによる適正な対応を促進しているのである。その背景には，企業による法の遵守については建前と現実の乖離を認めず，企業の営みの表裏両面について法と倫理の樹立と不正の自浄能力の確立を求める考え方がある。UT 社の法遵守の責任者が筆者に対して，「ある日突然ジャーナリズムや公的機関によってスキャンダルが暴露され，調査が開始されて，企業トップの辞任に追い込まれる」という事態を回避するためには，オンブズパーソン制度が是非とも必要である，と語ったのは印象的である。

　第四に，企業内でのハラスメントへの適切な対応手段としての社内オンブズパーソン制度の意義である。わが国では，雇用機会均等法の平成 9 年改正によって企業内でのセクシャルハラスメントの防止と解決の体制づくりが重要な課題となったが，この課題に貴重な示唆を与えてくれると思われる。ハラスメントに対する企業内でのインフォーマルな解決手続の必要性を説く上記の Mary Rowe 氏の見解については，もちろん米国内でも，インフォーマルな解決は，正義の実現＝違法行為の是正をうやむやにしてしまうといった批判がある。しかし，職場における人間関係の非正常化から生じる問題については，わが国においても，プライバシーを守ったカウンセリング的サービスと中立的でインフォーマルな問題解決の働きかけが，大いに必要とされているといえそうである[43]。

　こうして，筆者は，本稿で見た米国企業の苦情処理システムは，①企業内の苦情処理制度の重要性と可能性，②企業における法と倫理の確立の仕組み，

---

[43] Mary Rowe 氏が筆者とのインタビューにおいて，「自分は MIT に来る前には EEOC にいて差別是正のフォーマルな手続を遂行していた。そこで MIT でも，正義を実現するとの信念でオンブズマンの任務を遂行し始めたが，しかし（ハラスメントの問題については）すぐに（公式手続による）正義は機能しない（"Justice does not work."）と思い知った。」と語ったのは印象的であった。

③職場におけるハラスメント問題の解決方法において，示唆的であると考えている。

裁判所の論理・労働委員会の論理
——JR バッジ事件の場合——

松 田 保 彦

はじめに

　JR の国労組合員に対する組合バッジ着用を理由とする一時金の減額支給をめぐる不当労働行為事件に関して，このほど救済申立を認容した神奈川地労委の命令を支持し，これを不当労働行為と認めた横浜地裁の東日本旅客鉄道事件判決（横浜地判平成9・8・7，労働経済判例速報―以下労経速―1652号3頁），ならびにその結論を相当とした東京高裁判決（東京高判平成11・2・24，未収録），それとは反対に不当労働行為の成立を否定して，都労委の救済命令を取消した東京地裁の判決を維持した東京高裁の東海旅客鉄道（新幹線支部）事件判決（東京高判平成9・10・30，労働判例―以下労判―728号48頁）およびそれを支持した最高裁判決（最二小判，平成10・7・17，労経速1685号10頁）さらに JR の不当労働行為を認めて減額分の賃金請求を認容した広島地裁の判決を修正し，結果的には組合バッジ着用のみを理由とする減額は考課査定における裁量権の濫用になるとした広島高裁の西日本旅客鉄道事件判決（広島高労判平成10・4・30，労判749号71頁）が相次いで出された。組合バッジの着用を理由とする一時金の減額が不当労働行為になるかという問題について，その判断に違いをもたらした裁判所と労働委員会の論理を比べて，不当労働行為をめぐる裁判所と労働委員会の考え方を調整することができるかについて，その検討を試みようとするのが本稿の目的である。

1　国労バッジ事件における論点

　これらの事件はいずれも，JR 各社が国鉄労働組合員に対して就業時間中

の組合バッジ着用行為を就業規則における職務遂行義務規定，服装の整装規定および勤務時間中の会社施設内での組合活動の禁止規定に違反するとして，厳重注意などの措置を行い，一時金の減額支給および昇給欠格条項該当者として取り扱ったことを不当労働行為であるとして，労働委員会に救済申立てをし（JR東海事件ならびにJR東日本事件），あるいはバッジ着用等を理由として一時金の減額査定をしたことを考課査定権の濫用および不当労働行為として減額分の賃金を請求をしたものである（JR西日本事件）。

その争点は大きく三つに分かれる。第一は，就業時間中の組合バッジ着用が就業規則における各規定に違反するかという問題であるが，これらの規定はいずれも労働者の職務専念義務を定めたものと解されるから，この問題は畢竟するところ，組合バッジ着用行為が職務専念義務に違反するかどうかということにある。第二はこれと関連して，このようなバッジ着用行為がそもそも就業規則で禁止されている組合活動といえるか，あるいは正当な組合活動として禁止規定の適用が許されないのではないかという問題である。またかりにかたちの上では，バッジ着用が就業規則に反するとしても，なお正当な組合活動として，それを理由とする減給等の措置が労組法7条1号の不利益取扱い，もしくは3号の組合活動に対する支配介入にならないかという問題がある。そして第三は，バッジ着用が正当な組合活動に当たらないとしても，それを就業規則もしくは職務専念義務違反としてこれらの不利益措置を行ったのは，不当，違法といえないかという問題である。そこで次にこれらの論点に沿って，組合バッジ着用をめぐる三つの事件に関する六つの裁判所と二つの労働委員会の判断を見ることにする。

2　国労バッジ事件における裁判所と労働委員会の判断の概要

(1)　JR東日本事件

本件は，会社が国労組合員863名に対して組合バッジ着用を理由として厳重注意あるいは訓告の処分を行い，一時金の減額などをしたことが不当労働行為であるとして，神奈川地方労働委員会に救済申立てがなされたものである。

地労委は，本件組合バッジ着用行為は会社の組合攻撃に対する組織防衛と

してやむを得ずなされたものと思われる事情が窺われると認定した上で，バッジ着用は形式上非違的であるが，具体的に業務を阻害するとの会社側の疎明もなく，それに対する会社側の取り外し指導，処分等の一連の措置はバッジ着用者が国労組合員だけになったことを奇貨として，組合に打撃を加えんがために行われたものと推認せざるを得ないとし，組合との話合いを続けずに直ちに処分を行った等の会社の態度から見て，組合の弱体化を意図した支配介入行為であって，労組法7条3号に違反する不当労働行為であるとした。（神奈川地労委平成元・5・15決定，別時1081号200頁）

会社側が地労委命令の取消しを求めたのに対して，横浜地裁は，勤務時間中の組合活動は原則として労働者の労務提供義務に違反するものとして正当性を有しないが，本件組合バッジの着用は労務提供義務の誠実な履行と矛盾なく両立するから，例外的にその正当性を認められる場合に相当するとし，また職務専念義務に反するということもできないと判示した上で，これまでの会社側の言動，その他の事情を総合して，本件一連の措置は国労に打撃を与え，その勢力を減殺し，組織を弱体化させることを主たる動機とする支配介入行為であり，労組法7条3号の不当労働行為に該当するとして，会社の請求を棄却した。（前掲横浜地判平成9・8・7）

その控訴審において，東京高裁は，本件バッジ着用は企業秩序を乱す恐れのない特別の事情もなく，就業規則の各規定に違反するとした上で，それを理由としてなした使用者の本件における取扱いは，一見合理的かつ正当な面があるものの，全体としては国労組合に対する団結権の否認ないし嫌悪の意図を決定的な動機としてなされたものと認められるとして，初審判決を相当とした。（前掲東京高判平成11・2・24）

(2) JR東海（新幹線）事件

本件は，国労組合員75名に対する就業時間中の組合バッジ着用を理由とする会社の厳重注意，夏期手当の減額支給，賃金規程の昇給欠格条項該当者としての取扱い措置が不当労働行為であるとして，東京地方労働委員会に救済申立てがなされたものである。

都労委は，組合バッジの着用行為はそれが職場規律を乱し，業務運営の妨げになる等のことが認められない限り，正当な組合活動であって，それをみ

だりに禁止すべきでないとし，会社の国鉄時代からの国労に対する態度や組合バッジ着用を禁止するに至った経過などを総合すると，就業規則の禁止諸規定をことさらに前面に押し出し，それに藉口してバッジ着用のみを理由に厳重注意および夏期手当の減額支給をしたことは，組合員に国労に止まることに不安を抱かせることによって国労を弱体化せんとした支配介入行為であると判断せざるを得ないとした。(東京地労委平成元・2・7決定，別時1096号46頁)

その趣旨を上記の論点に即して整理すると，本件における組合バッジ着用行為は正当な組合活動であるから，就業規則の組合活動禁止規定の適用は受けず，それを敢えて適用してバッジ着用者に不利益措置をしたのは，これによって組合の弱体化を図ろうとしたものであり，支配介入に当たるというものである。

それに対して，本件の行政訴訟において，東京地裁は，本件組合活動禁止規定が正当な組合活動には適用されないという解釈は妥当でなく，本件バッジ着用行為は就業規則の諸規定に違反するから，それに対する会社の措置が妥当性を欠くものでない限り，不当労働行為にはならないとして，これまでの経緯からして会社が本件措置に及んだことには無理からぬところがあると判示して，都労委命令を取り消した。(東京地判平成7・12・14，労判686号21頁)その控訴審において東京高裁は，まずこれまでの労使対立の経緯に照らして会社が就業規則により組合バッジの着用を禁止したことには合理性があるとした上で，組合活動が形式的に諸規定に違反するように見えても，実質的に企業秩序を乱す恐れのない特別の事情がある場合はその違反にならないが，本件バッジ着用はかかる事情のある場合に当たらず，職務専念義務に違反し，企業秩序を乱すものであるから，それを諸規定に違反するとして厳重注意ならびにそれに伴う措置を行ったことは不相当であるとは言えないとして，本件控訴を棄却した。(前掲東京高判平成9・10・30)

この高裁判決は最高裁判所によっても支持された。(前掲最二小判平成10・7・17)

(3) JR西日本事件

本件は，国労組合員25名が，会社から勤務成績・態度等が悪いこと，組合

バッジを着用して就業したことを理由として，減額査定を受け，一時金を減額支給されたことを考課査定権の濫用として，損害賠償を請求したものである。

　第一審の広島地裁は，勤務時間中の組合活動には原則として正当性は認められないが，本件バッジ着用行為は労働を誠実に履行すべき義務と支障なく両立して，使用者の業務を具体的に阻害することがなく，職務専念義務にも反しないから，就業規則が禁止する勤務時間中の組合活動に該当しないと判示し，勤務成績・態度等の悪かったことが認められる1名を除いて，裁量権の濫用に該当するとして，原告らの損害賠償請求を認めた。(西日本旅客鉄道事件，広島地判平成5・10・12，労判643号19頁)

　第二審の広島高裁は，本件組合バッジ着用行為が組織防衛的意味合いからなされたものであったとしても，就業規則で禁止された組合活動に当たるとし，他方，職務専念義務は労働者の勤務時間中の全人格的な従属までを求めるものではない(から，組合活動でも例外的に職務専念義務に違反しない場合がある)が，本件のような状況の中で組合バッジを着用する行為は職務専念義務に違反しない例外的な場合には当たらないと判示する。したがってそれを減額査定事由としたことをもって直ちに不当労働行為に該当するとは言えないが，組合バッジの着用は国鉄時代は問題にされなかった等の事情がある上に，その規制は団結権の制限にかかわる事項であるから，これを理由とする減額査定は慎重でなければならず，それは他の事情との衡量の中で相対的に考慮されなければならないとし，(会社側が新たに提出した資料に基づいて)個別に勤務成績・態度を検討し，バッジ着用以外にさしたる減率査定事由の認められない10名については，その損害賠償請求を認容し，他の15名については，会社側の控訴を認めて，その損害賠償請求を棄却した。(前掲広島高判平成10・4・30)

3　バッジ事件における裁判所の論理と労働委員会の論理

　組合バッジ着用に対する処分をめぐる不当労働行為事件においては，バッジ着用を禁止する使用者の行為ならびにその違反に対する不利益処分という二つの行為が判断の対象とされるが，裁判所あるいは労働委員会によってそ

の比重のおき方が異なる。一つは、専ら本件組合バッジ着用行為が就業規則の規定もしくは職務専念義務に違反するか否かを問題とし、そこから直ちに本件における不当労働行為の成否を判断する。第二は、本件バッジ着用行為が就業規則ないし職務専念義務に違反するとしても、違反の程度その他の事情を勘案して、それに対する会社の措置が不当労働行為に当たるかどうかを判断しようとする。前者においては、組合バッジ着用行為に就業規則の規定を適用すること自体を問題として、そこから使用者の不当労働行為意思の有無を判断しようとするのに対し、後者においては、その違反に対する減給等の不利益措置を問題として、そこに不当労働行為意思が認められるかどうかを判断しようとする。どちらかといえば、裁判所は前者の立場を取ることが多いのに対し、労働委員会は両者を総合的に判断しようとしている。

(1) 職務専念義務違反の成否と組合バッジ着用行為の違法性──裁判所の論理

　裁判所の多くは、組合バッジ着用行為はそれが実質的に企業秩序を乱す恐れない特別の事情が認められるとき（電々公社目黒電報話局事件、最判昭和52・12・13、民集31巻7号974頁、前掲JR東海事件、東京高判平成9・10・30、が引用する）あるいは職務専念義務に違反しない例外的な場合（前掲JR西日本事件、広島高判平成10・4・30）を除いては、勤務時間中の組合活動を禁止する規定に抵触し、職務専念義務違反となると判断する。本件においては、国労と会社の間の長年にわたる確執と悪化し続ける労使関係とそれに対する会社側の規律維持の必要性からして、「実質的に企業秩序を乱す恐れのない特別の事情」は認められないとし、またこのような労使関係において組合バッジを着用することは、職場内に組合意識を持ち込み、他組合員を刺激して無用の混乱を起こすから、「職務専念義務に違反しない例外的な場合」に当たらないとしている。

　要するに裁判所は、本件バッジ着用行為が正当な組合活動であるか否かはその職務専念義務違反の判断とは関係ないとするか、あるいは本件バッジ着用行為は職務専念義務に違反するから正当な組合活動ではないとする（前掲JR東海事件、東京地判平成7・12・14）。いずれにせよ、裁判所における不当労働行為の判断に際しては組合活動の違法性を判断すればそれで足りるとし、

あらためてその正当性を判断する必要はないと考えられているようである。

以上から分かるように，裁判所においては，本件リボン着用行為が実質的に企業秩序を乱す恐れのある違法な職務専念義務違反行為であることを判断するに際して，それが組合活動であることを，組合に対して不利な判断材料として用いているところに特長がある。すなわち労使間の長年にわたる確執とその間の組合の行動が本件バッジ着用行為を「結果として」企業秩序を乱す恐れのあるのあるものとする事情として考慮されるのである。

それに対して，労働委員会においては，本件における労使間の長年にわたる確執やその間の使用者の対応といった事情が，裁判所とは逆に，本件バッジ着用行為をもたらした「原因として」，その組合活動性もしくは正当性を判断するに当たっての組合にとっての有利な判断材料として，また同時に本件バッジ着用行為に対する会社側の措置の不当労働行為性を裏付ける背景事情として用いられていることが注目される。

(2) 組合バッジ着用行為の正当性と職務専念義務違反の成否——労働委員会の論理

バッジ着用はそれが職場規律に違反し，業務運営に支障を来す恐れのない場合は正当な組合活動であり（前掲JR東海事件，都労委平成元・2・7決定；前掲JR東日本事件，横浜地判平成7・12・14ならびに前掲JR西日本事件，広島地判平成5・10・12もこの立場に近い。），またそれが単に組合員であることを確認する行為であるに過ぎない場合には（前掲JR東日本事件，神労委平成元・5・15決定），それが形式的に就業規則に違反することをとらえて，会社が不利益取扱いをしたことは，本件における労使関係の状況や会社の組合に対するこれまでの対応等から見て，組合の弱体化を意図した不当労働行為たる不利益取扱いないしは支配介入に当たるとするのが，大方の労働委員会の見方である。

たとえば，「バッジ着用は所属組合員たることを表明する行為であって，団結権の1態様であり，会社の業務を阻害することのない以上，……殊更，不利益に取り扱うことは，被申立人の他意を窺わせるものである。」（西日本旅客鉄道事件，鳥取地労委平成3・3・16決定，別時1108号224頁；同旨，西日本旅客鉄道事件，鳥取地労委平成5・10・29決定，別時1139号3頁），「本件国労バッジ

の着用は，……単に組合所属の表示をするものにすぎ（ず，……その）事実をもって低査定の理由としたことは，行き過ぎであったというほかはない。」（西日本旅客鉄道事件，岡山地労委平成5・9・17決定，別時1136号2頁），「本件……バッジ着用は，その必要性が認められ，その態様も実質的に労務の提供に影響を与えず，業務に支障を生じさせていないのであるから，労働組合の正当な行為として認められ，不当労働行為救済の対象となる……。」（東日本旅客鉄道事件，埼玉地労委平成6・3・30決定，別時1146号4頁），「会社と国労との関係，組合バッジの着用による業務阻害の有無からすれば，（それを）勤務成績の査定に当たってマイナス評価することには疑問がある。」（西日本旅客鉄道事件，島根地労委平成6・5・10決定，1146号118頁），あるいは「本件バッジの着用は，専ら国労組合員であることを確認するための（防衛的な）行為であり，（その）形状等から見ると，会社業務を阻害する虞れがある（とも……）具体的に職場秩序を乱すものとも考えられない（から）勤務時間中における職場内の行為としても，なお正当な組合活動といえる……。」（東日本旅客鉄道・日本貨物鉄道事件，神奈川地労委平成6・7・29決定，別時1154号4頁）とした命令がある。

(3) 組合バッジ着用行為の違法性とそれに対する不利益措置の当否

上で見たように，組合バッジ着用行為の職務専念義務違反の成否については，裁判所はその違法性の判断をもって足りるとするのに対して，労働委員会はその正当性判断を先行させるというように，裁判所と労働委員会の判断方向は対照的である。それに対し，本件組合バッジ着用行為が実質的に，あるいは少なくとも形式的に就業規則の諸規定に反するとした上で，それに対する会社の措置の妥当性を判断するという場合においては，裁判所と労働委員会の見方にそれほどの差は見られない。

たとえば「組合バッジ着用の事情及びその意義からして会社には慎重な対応が求められるところ，会社は，組合バッジ着用者に対して就業規則違反を理由にその行為の程度に比して苛酷ともいえる……経済的不利益を伴う処分等を繰り返した……（ことは）国労の組織弱体化を企図したものである……。」（東海旅客鉄道事件，大阪地労委平成5・5・24決定，別時1131号35頁）とする労委命令と「本件組合バッジを着用することは……職務専念義務違反とな

らない例外に該当するとはいえない（が，……）その規制は団結権の制限に関わる事項であるから，これを理由に本件減率査定事由とすることは慎重でなければならない。」とした上で，「組合バッジ着用行為はそれのみでは減率の理由として相当でないものであり，……本件減率査定には，合理性が認められず，裁量権の濫用に該当する。」（前掲JR西日本事件，広島高判平成10・4・30）とした判旨との間には，その考え方において相通ずるものがある。

4 裁判所の論理と労働委員会の論理の調整に関する試案

　これまでに見て来たように，裁判所は組合バッジ着用行為を，本件の背景事情からして，企業秩序もしくは職場規律を乱す恐れのある行為であると認められるから，会社がこれを禁止し，その違反に対して相当の不利益措置を取ることには妥当性があるとする。それに対して労働委員会は，本件組合バッジ着用行為は企業秩序にも職場規律にも実質的に反しないとした上で，それを殊更に規制し，その違反を理由に組合員を不利益に取り扱う会社には本件の背景事情からして，不当労働行為意思が窺われるとする。第一に，職場内における組合活動が企業秩序を乱し，職場規律に反する違法な行為であり，そこには組合活動としての正当性を認める余地がないとする点で，第二に，裁判所が本件の背景事情を本件組合バッジ着用行為の違法性を認める理由として使っているのに対し，労働委員会はそれを本件バッジ着用行為の正当性ないし会社の不当労働行為意思を推定する根拠として用いる点において，裁判所の論理と労働委員会の論理は全くつながらないように見える。

　しかしながら，この二つの論理はその筋道のどこかの部分に団結権に対する考慮を入れることによってつながる可能性があると思われるので，以下その幾つかについて検討して見ることにする。

(1) 就業規則違反の組合活動に対する措置の妥当性

　前記の広島高裁判決は，ある意味では労委命令——とくに大阪地労委命令平成5年5月24日は本件減額措置の組合に与える経済的効果を強調してその趣旨を強く打ち出している——も軌を一にするといえるが，本件組合バッジ着用を職務専念義務もしくは職務規律に反する違法な行為であるとした上で，

それに対する会社の措置は団結権保障の見地から慎重になされなければならないとして，処分の妥当性を判断する場面で団結権に対する考慮を入れている。これはバッジ着用行為の違法性の判断については，使用者の施設管理権および労務指揮権は団結権によってなんら制限されるものではないとする裁判所の論理に従うが，それに対する使用者側の対応の妥当性を見るに際しては，そうした措置が及ぼす組合活動なり労使関係への影響を考慮するという点で，裁判所と労働委員会の論理の調整を図るというものである。ことに裁判所がバッジ着用の違法性を判断するに当たって，それが組合活動であることを企業秩序なり職務規律違反の蓋然性を高めるものとしていることとの兼ね合いからしても，このような判断枠組みを設けることには合理性があると思われる。

　しかしながら，不当労働行為救済制度の趣旨・目的に鑑みると，この方法は余りにも現実に妥協的であって問題があるとされよう。例えば，広島高裁判決においては，その結論として組合バッジ着用のみを一時金支給に際しての減率査定の理由とするのは許されないとしているのであるから，前段で組合バッジ着用行為を減率査定事由としたことをもって直ちに不当労働行為に該当するとはいえないと言っていることとそぐわない。その間に論理の矛盾があるとまではいえないが，少なくとも不当労働行為ではないと言ってしまうことは制度の趣旨に合致しないと論難される可能性がある。（もっとも私見は，従来の司法判断の枠組み内で同じ結論が導き出せるのならば，裁判所はあえて不当労働行為の判断をする必要はないし，その方が良いとするので，広島高裁の判旨に違和感は覚えない。）あるいはまた，本件のような事例において，例えば会社が本件バッジ着用に対して何ら経済的な損失を伴わない措置を行ったとして，それを労働委員会が不当労働行為に当たらないと言えるかは大いに疑問である。

(2) 職場内組合活動の評価基準の客観性

　使用者は職場内で勤務時間中に行われる組合活動を甘受する義務はなく，たとえそれが業務の運営に支障をもたらす恐れがなくとも，施設管理権もしくは労務指揮権を行使してそれを禁止し，その違反に対しては，一方において，かかる使用者の権利を侵害するものとして，他方においては被用者の労

務提供義務に反する，いわば債務の不完全履行として，処分の対象となし得るとするのが，裁判所における考え方である。このように見て行くと，裁判所には——企業内組合がわが国における実態であることを考えた上での——憲法における団結権保障に対する配慮が全くないように見える。しかしながら必ずしもそうではない。

　最高裁判所はこれまで職場内組合活動が許されるのは「実質的に企業秩序を乱す恐れのない特別の事情」もしくは「労働組合に施設を利用させないことが当該物的施設につき使用者が有する権利の濫用であると認められる特段の事情」（国鉄札幌事件，最三小判昭和54・10・30，民集33巻6号647頁；済生会中央病院事件，最二小判平成元・12・11，民集43巻12号1786頁）のある例外的な場合に限られると判示している。しかしいかなる場合にかかる「特段の事情」が認められるかについては，これまでのところ最高裁は明確な基準を示していない。そこでこの「特段の事情」の有無を検討するに当たって，団結権に対する何らかの配慮を示すことは十分可能であると思われる。たとえば，実質的に企業秩序を乱す恐れがないと認められる「特段の事情」として，その行為が客観的に見て企業秩序を乱す恐れがないにもかかわらず使用者がその権利を濫用して組合の弱体化を図ろうとしているというような場合を想定することができる。ここで行為をその目的・態様等から客観的に見るというのは，それが組合活動であるからといって殊更に有利にも不利にも特別扱いをしないという意味であると解される。（前掲広島地判平成5・10・12及び横浜地判平成9・8・7のスタンスはこれに近い。）前記済生会中央病院事件判決において，組合が労働時間中に職場集会を開く必要性があることは特段の事情に当たらないと最高裁が述べているのは，そのことを判示したものと思われるのである。

　その意味では，上記東京地裁判決ならびに東京高裁判決が本件組合バッジの着用行為が労使間の対立や組合の併存状況からして企業秩序を乱す恐れがあるとして，そこに特段の事情を全く認めなかったことには疑問なしとしない。これまでの最高裁の論理からすれば，本件組合バッジ着用行為を，少なくとも「裸の行為」として客観的にその企業秩序紊乱性を判断すべきであったのに，これらの判断には使用者側（および他組合）の嫌悪感ないし主観的な感情が考慮すべき事実として受け入れられている。もしも本件バッジ着用

行為が組合活動でなかったならば違った結論になっただろうと思わせるような裁判所の判断には，やはり疑問が残る。

(3) 組合活動に対する不利益措置における動機の競合

組合活動に限らず一般に使用者による被用者に対する不利益処分に関する不当労働行為事件においては，裁判所はまずその不利益処分が正当な事由に基づくものであるか否かを判断し，そこに妥当性が認められないとなって，初めて不当労働行為の成否を検討する。他方，不利益処分が正当な事由によるものであると認められると，不当労働行為の成立が否定される場合が多い。したがって，実質的にはいずれの場合も裁判所が不当労働行為の成否に関して判断する必要はないことになる。不当労働行為の絡んだ事案に関する裁判所の判断枠組みは，それが民事事件として直接裁判所に訴えられた場合であると労働委員会の命令に対する司法審査の場合であると，異なるところはない。不当労働行為制度の下における司法審査制度が一種の覆審制（trial de novo）であることからすれば，これを敢えて異とするには当たらないが，少なくとも使用者が被用者の組合活動をその直接的理由として不利益取扱いをしたといった事案の場合は，不当労働行為制度の趣旨・目的に対する何らかの配慮が望まれる。

それは，被用者の組合活動を理由とする不利益処分に正当事由があると認められる事案においては，動機競合事件における相当因果関係説あるいは決定的動機説の判断方法を採り入れることである。（上記の裁判所の判断方法は実質的には否定説に立つものともいえるから，かかる提案は単に法解釈もしくは立証方法の対案を示すに止まり，裁判所の論理を否定するものではない。）すなわち，職場内組合活動を専ら被用者の行為としての側面から捉えて，職場内規範に照らしてその違法性の有無を判断する裁判所のアプローチとそれを専ら組合員の行為としての側面から捉えてその正当性を検討し，それに対する使用者の措置の不当労働行為性を判断しようとする労働委員会のアプローチをともに前提とし，そのいずれかに決定的な動機があるかを見ようというものである。

JR各社における国労組合員の組合バッジ着用行為に対する会社の厳重注意，一時金の減額等の措置については，一方においてバッジ着用行為が会社

の諸規則に違反し，職員の職務専念義務に反する行為であるから，かかる不利益措置には正当事由があるとしても，他方において，同時にそれが組合バッジ着用という組合活動あるいはバッジ着用者が国労組合員であることを理由とする不利益取扱いであると認められる場合には，そのいずれの見方が優るかを相当因果関係の存否あるいは決定的動機がいずれにあるかによって判断する。すなわち，バッジ着用者が国労組合員でなかったならば，会社はこうした不利益取扱いはしなかったであろうと推定できる（だけの心証が与えられる），あるいは国労を弱体化しようとすることが決定的な動機であると推認されるならば，そこに不当労働行為の成立を認める。JR東日本事件東京高裁判決は，こうした考え方に立っていると見ることができる。逆にもしそれが国労バッジでなかったとしても，あるいは着用者が国労組合員でなかったとしても，会社は同じ取扱いをしたであろうとの心証が得られるならば，不当労働行為の成立は否定されることとなる。

おわりに

　以上，JRバッジ事件を素材として，裁判所と労働委員会の判断の筋道の間に，何とか折り合いをつけようと試みて来た。しかしながら，わが国における不当労働行為に関する複線的救済制度が1種のねじれ現象を起こしているところへもって来て，JR事件を素材に用いるというそのこと自体がいわば歪んだ曲面に真っすぐな定規を当てようとするようなものであろうから，所詮それは木に竹を接ごうとする空しい試みだったのかも知れない。
（追記：なおJR東日本事件については，東京高裁判決に対するJR東日本からの上告受理の申立てに対して，最高裁判所は，民訴法318条1項の事件に当たらないとして，不受理決定を下している。最一小決平成11・11・11）

Re-examination of Employment Security in Japan in Light of Socio-economic Structural Changes

Takashi ARAKI

1. Introduction

Japan's unemployment rate reached a record-high (4.1%) in April 1998 (see Figure 1). The Economist claimed that "soon, and for the first time, Japan will have a higher jobless rate than America-a telling moment in the shifting fortunes of the two economies."[1] The telling moment came

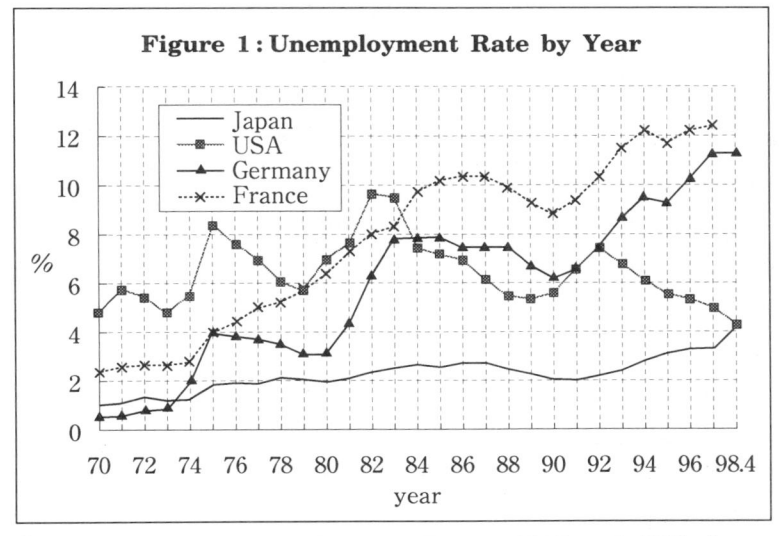

Figure 1: Unemployment Rate by Year

(Ministry of Labor, Employment Report 1997 and JIL's home page on Labor Statistics)

---

1) *The Economist*, p. 19 (June 20th 1998).

at the end of the year. In December 1998, the unemployment rate in the USA was 4.3% and in Japan it was 4.4%. Japan's unemployment rate in June 1999 further deteriorated to 4.9%. The news media interpreted the bankruptcies of the nation's top brokerage firms and banks over the last two years as symbolic incidents indicating the end of Japan's lifetime employment practice.

An academic survey conducted in 1994[2] had already confirmed this trend. The retention rate[3] of male white-collar workers was 78.9 percent at age 30, 70.0 percent at age 40, 66.2 percent at age 50, 57.9 percent at age 56 and 33.6 percent at age 60. This survey indicates a high separation rate in the 20s and the late 50s. Nearly 20 percent of workers in their 20s changed jobs and only one third of male white-collar workers remained with the same company until the age of 60 or the mandatory retirement age.

In contrast to these figures, the Annual White Paper issued on July 7, 1998 by the Ministry of Labor confirmed that 80% of Japanese employers still intend to maintain a policy of long-term employment until the mandatory retirement age, and 60% of employers will continue to do so in the future.

How should we interpret this puzzling situation? Is it nothing but a gap between the Japanese people's ideal

---

2) Nihon-gata Koyo System Kenkyu-kai Hokokusho (A Report by the Study Group on the Japanese Employment System, chaired by Prof. Takeshi Inagami), p. 5 (Ministry of Labor, 1995).

3) The proportion of workers who stayed with the same company compared with the number of workers employed at the same time when they were hired fresh out of school.

and market reality? Notwithstanding the Japanese employers' and employees' hopes, is the market requiring the abandonment of the Japanese lifetime employment practice? Some employers and economists who admire American style mobility and flexibility attribute Japan's sluggish economic recovery to the Japanese lifetime employment practice because it hinders structural changes in industries and workforce supply to new industries or venture businesses. Should the Japanese labor market be like the American labor market? To what extent should Japan introduce labor mobility? What are the merits and demerits of the long-term employment system? How do employment mobility and employment security affect the whole system of employment? What is the role of labor law in such a transformation period? This paper aims to provide some discussion materials relating to these questions.

2. Features of Regulations on Employment Security in Japan

Before addressing these issues, the features of Japanese employment security regulations[4] should be summarized. Sometimes these features are misunderstood by foreign observers.

From a legal perspective, the Japanese workforce is divided into two groups : employees hired under open-ended contracts and those under fixed-term contracts. Regular

---

4) For the dismissal regulations in advanced countries, see R. Blanpain & T. Hamami (ed.), *Employment Security* (Peeters Press, 1994).

employees are normally hired under open-ended contracts and enjoy high employment security according to case law. By contrast, non-regular employees, such as part-time or temporary workers, who are mostly hired under fixed-term contracts, enjoy a very limited employment security. Therefore the Japanese workforce consists of highly protected regular workers and less protected non-regular workers. According to the most recent data[5], regular employees make up 76.4% of the Japanese workforce and non-regular workers make up 23.6%[6].

2. 1. Case Law Protection for Regular Employees

The most significant feature of Japanese law concerning the dismissal of regular employees is that there is no legislation generally prohibiting dismissals without just cause[7]. Unlike European countries, restrictions on dismissal have been provided for by case law[8].

---

5) Somu-cho (Management and Coordination Agency), Rodoryoku Tokubetsu Chosa (Special Survey on the Labor Force), February, 1998.

6) Since it is often said that the coverage of lifetime employment is confined to only about 30 percent of the Japanese workforce, some foreigners misunderstand that the rest must be hired under the unstable fixed-term contract. This is not the case.

7) Apart from the prohibition of discriminatory dismissals and other special protections for pregnant workers and for victims of work-related injury, Japanese legislation affords an employer the freedom to dismiss workers without just cause. However, unlike the American "at will" doctrine, the Labor Standards Law generally requires 30 days advance notice or an advance notice allowance in lieu of the notice (LSL Art. 20).

2. Features of Regulations on Employment Security in Japan

Immediately after WWII, when there was a shortage of food, lack of employment opportunity, and a superfluous workforce, dismissal meant the loss of livelihood for many workers. Even after the long-term employment practice took root in the 1960s, dismissal was detrimental to seniority, which was a decisive factor for beneficial working conditions under the seniority-based personnel and wage systems. Dismissals also put employees at a serious disadvantage because finding a new equivalent job was extremely difficult in Japan's inactive external labor market.

Faced with these circumstances, Japanese courts accumulated precedents that a dismissal without just cause is regarded as an abuse of the right to dismiss and that such a dismissal is null and void. This interpretation was endorsed by the Supreme Court[9] and has become an established case law rule. If the employer's exercise of the

---

8) For details of dismissal regulations in Japan, see Yasuo Suwa, "Flexibility and Security in Employment : the Japanese Case", 6 *The International Journal of Comparative Labour Law and Industrial Relations* pp. 229 (1990) ; Tadashi Hanami, *Managing Japanese Workers*, 29ff. (Japan Institute of Labor, 1991) ; Kazuo Sugeno (translated by Leo Kanowitz), *Japanese Labor Law*, 395 (Washington University Press, 1992) ; Takashi Araki, "Flexibility in Japanese Employment Relations and the Role of the Judiciary", in Hiroshi Oda (ed.), *Japanese Commercial Law in an Era of Internationalization*, pp. 249 (Graham & Trotman, 1994) ; Tadashi Hanami, "Japan" in *supra* note 4, 187 ; Kazuo Sugeno & Yasuo Suwa, *The Internal Labour Market and its Legal Adjustments* (JIL Forum Paper No. 4, 1995).

9) The *Nihon Shokuen* case, Supreme Court, April 25, 1975, *Minshu* vol. 29, no. 4 p. 456.

right to dismiss is judged to be abusive and, therefore, invalid, the employer is obligated not only to give the employee back pay during the period of dismissal but also to reinstate him or her.

A recession triggered by oil crises in the 1970s led Japanese courts to establish new rules on dismissals for economic reasons. By then the longterm employment practice had taken root in Japanese corporate society, and major companies facing economic difficulties refrained from resorting to economic dismissals directly. After careful consultation with their enterprise-based unions, they chose to take various cost-cutting measures to avoid dismissals as much as possible. The unions, for their part, cooperated with management in carrying out relocation and transfer programs designed to avoid economic dismissals.

The courts adopted the practices formed between major companies and their unions as the general rules concerning economic dismissals. Namely, the courts set out the following four requirements for dismissals for business reasons to be allowable : 1) a personnel reduction must be based on business necessity ; 2) every possible measure to avoid layoffs must be attempted, such as a reduction in overtime, attrition and non-replacement, solicitation for voluntary retirements, transfers, etc. ; 3) the selection of employees to be dismissed must be made on an objective and reasonable basis ; 4) the employer must faithfully consult with unions or employees.

In this manner, not only dismissals for individual reasons but also those for economic reasons are significantly restricted by case law.

2. 2. Limited Protection for Non-regular Employees with Fixed-term Contracts

Unlike European Continental countries, in Japan there is no requirement for objective reasons in order to conclude fixed-term contracts and no restriction on their renewal. The sole legal regulation on fixed-term contracts is that the term should not exceed one year[10]. Since renewals are not regulated, however, it is possible to renew a one-year contract ten times, for example.

Since Japan enjoyed long-term economic growth until the 1970s, fixed-term employees have had their contracts renewed repeatedly. In the economic downturn, however, those fixed-term employees were deprived of jobs when their employers refused to renew their contracts. This raised the question of social protection for these employees. On this issue, the Supreme Court[11] held that in the event that the fixed-term contracts were repeatedly renewed so that they were indistinguishable in reality from indefinite-term contracts, the refusal to renew the contract is tantamount to dismissal and thus the theory of abusive exercise of the dismissal right should apply by analogy. As a result, the employer is required to show just cause to ter-

---

10) Amendments to the Labor Standards Law in 1998, effective as of April 1999, made fixed-term contracts not longer than three years allowable in exceptional cases for newly hired workers with high-levels of professional knowledge or expertise in technology and workers older than sixty.

11) The *Toshiba Yanagi-cho Factory* case, July 22, 1974, *Minshu* vol. 28, no. 5 p. 927.

minate repeatedly renewed fixed-term contracts.

Nevertheless, the protection of fixed-term employees is still inferior to that of regular employees with indefinite-period contracts. The Supreme Court[12] held that it is allowable for an employer facing economic difficulties to terminate the employment of fixed-term employees before asking regular employees to retire voluntarily.

2. 3. Characteristics and Current Issues of Employment Security in Japan

Viewed from a comparative perspective, employment security regulations in Japan have several important characteristics.

2. 3. 1. High Protection for Regular Employees against Economic Dismissals

Individual dismissals are universally restricted in most countries, with some reservations in the United States. However, attitudes towards economic dismissals are very different from country to country even in European countries[13]. One of the features of Japanese case law is that it restricts economic dismissals more severely than other de-

---

12) The *Hitachi Medico* case, Supreme Court, Dec. 4, 1986, *Hanrei Jiho*, no. 1221 p. 134.

13) For instance, compare unrestricted economic dismissals in Sweden with highly regulated economic dismissals involving works councils in Germany. See Clyde Summers, Worker Dislocation : Who Bears the Burden? A Comparative Study of Social Values in Five Countries, 70 *Notre Dame Law Review* 1033 (1995).

2. Features of Regulations on Employment Security in Japan

veloped countries.

Because of the aforementioned case law on economic dismissals, typical employment adjustment in Japan follows the time-consuming procedures illustrated below (Chart 1). Economic dismissals are allowed only as an *ultima ratio* and Japanese employment practices provide many alternatives, so employers are forced to exhaust many options before resorting to dismissals.

Chart 1 : Typical Employment Adjustment Procedures

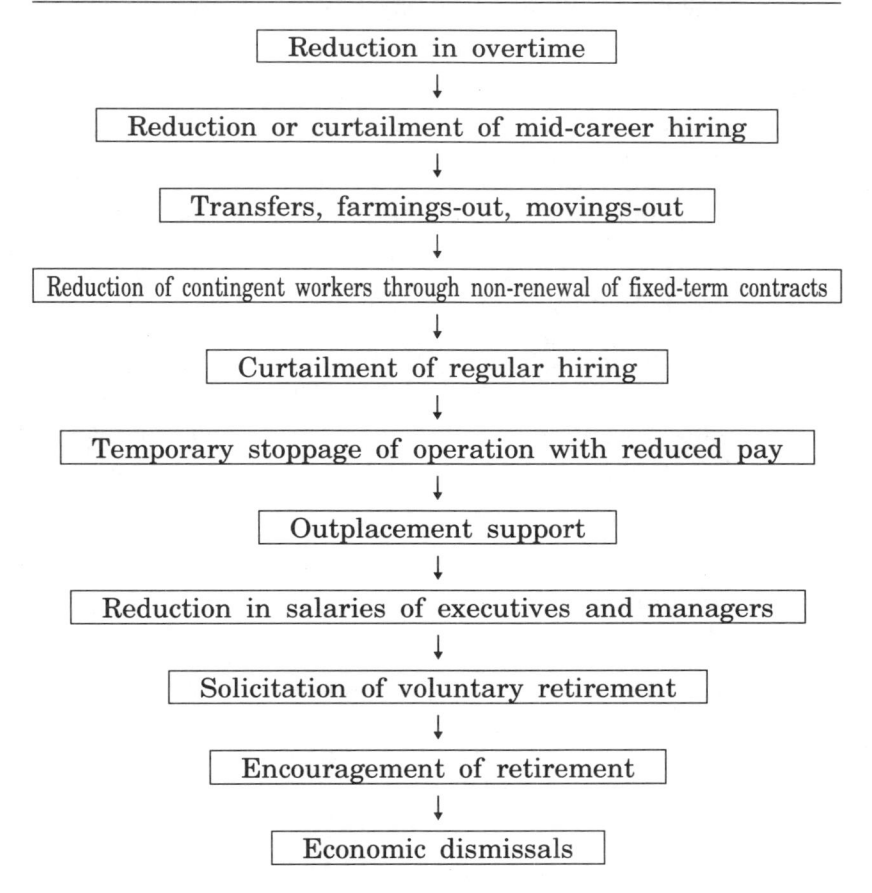

```
                    Reduction in overtime
                              ↓
         Reduction or curtailment of mid-career hiring
                              ↓
              Transfers, farmings-out, movings-out
                              ↓
 Reduction of contingent workers through non-renewal of fixed-term contracts
                              ↓
                 Curtailment of regular hiring
                              ↓
          Temporary stoppage of operation with reduced pay
                              ↓
                    Outplacement support
                              ↓
         Reduction in salaries of executives and managers
                              ↓
              Solicitation of voluntary retirement
                              ↓
                 Encouragement of retirement
                              ↓
                     Economic dismissals
```

This time-consuming process becomes a heavy burden for Japanese employers facing global competition where speed is vitally important in management strategy.

2. 3. 2. Remedies for Abuse of the Right to Dismiss

Another feature of case law on dismissals is its very protective remedies. In many countries, unjust dismissals result in payment of damages. By contrast, under the abuse of the right to dismiss theory in Japan, the employer is obliged not only to pay wages during the *whole* period of dismissal[14] but also to reinstate the dismissed employee, as the dismissal is null and void.

As a result, if a dismissal is held to be abusive, the employer cannot dissolve the employment relations with the employee no matter how much the employer pays the employee. However, after prolonged litigation, it is naturally difficult for both the employee and the employer to return to normal employment relations not only because the human relations between them have deteriorated, but also because the workplace circumstances may have completely changed and the worker's skills may have become outdated. Therefore, it is not surprising that after dismissal litigation most reinstated workers leave the company within three years.

Thus, some academics argue for the introduction of an alternative remedy for wrongful dismissals in the form of

---

14) Since there is no cap on the payment for lost wages, when a worker has spent ten years to win a case, the employer is obliged to pay wages for ten years, though the worker's intermediary incomes can be deducted to the extent of 40% of his/her wages.

the payment of money while allowing for the dissolution of employment relations[15].

2.3.3. Lack of Transparency and Effectiveness

Since restrictions on dismissals are provided by case law whereas enacted laws maintain employers' freedom to dismiss, the current regulations lack transparency with respect to the rules governing dismissals. Foreign-affiliated firms in Japan sometimes dismiss their employees without much thought and are shocked to have their actions held illegal by a Japanese court.

More problematic is the cost of litigation. In order to take advantage of the case law protection against dismissals lacking just cause, a dismissed employee must bring the case to court. Unlike European countries, Japan has no special court for labor-related issues. Therefore all employment-related cases must be filed in ordinary courts. In Japan, partly due to the high cost of judicial procedures in terms of money and time, and perhaps partly due to socio-cultural and psychological reasons, it is not easy for individuals to litigate[16].

---

15) E. g. Fumito Komiya, "Kaiko Seigen Ho (Japanese Law of Dismissal)" *Nihon Rodo Kenkyu Zasshi* no. 446 pp. 29 (1997).

16) The number of labor-related cases newly filed to local courts (first instance) in 1996 was 2,211 including provisional disposition cases. This number is extremely small compared to the number in Germany (about 627,935 cases at the labor courts (first instance) in 1995) or in France (about 156,327 cases at labor courts (first instance) in 1991). Cf. Hiroya Nakakubo, "Procedures for Resolving Individual Employment Disputes", *Japan Labor Bulletin*, vol. 35 no. 6 p. 5 (1996).

2.3.4. Combination of High Protection for Regular Employees and Low Protection for Non-regular Employees

Until very recently, European continental countries have restricted not only unjust dismissals but also the utilization of fixed-term contracts. In the United States, the "employment-at-will" doctrine is, though undergoing modification due to the impact of wrongful termination lawsuits, still maintained as a principle and there are no regulations on fixed-term contracts.

Japan locates itself between the two. Since there are no regulations on objective reasons to conclude fixed-term contracts nor restrictions on their renewals apart from limited case law protection, Japanese employers have utilized them frequently to introduce numerical flexibility into the Japanese labor market[17].

3. Structural Changes Affecting Employment Security

Current structural changes surrounding employment re-

---

17) Takashi Araki, "Accommodating Working Conditions to Changing Circumstances: A Comparative Analysis of Quantitative and Qualitative Flexibility in the United States, Germany and Japan", in C. Engels & M. Weiss (ed.), *Labour Law and Industrial Relations at the Turn of the Century: Liber Amicorum Prof. Dr. R. Blanpain*, pp. 509 (Kluwer, 1998).

18) Takashi Araki, "Changing Japanese Labor Law in Light of Deregulation Drives: A Comparative Analysis", *Japan Labor Bulletin* vol. 36 no. 5 pp. 5 (1997).

lations inevitably affect the value and social consciousness of employment security[18].

3. 1. Individualization and Diversification of Employees in a Changing Labor Market

First, the state of the Japanese labor market has changed. The traditional labor law was designed under a labor market with surplus workers. However, it is expected that Japan will soon have a labor shortage because of the continuously declining birth rate. In the long-term, a labor shortage increases the employees' bargaining power and it can decrease the relative value of employment security. Furthermore, other values such as self-determination or the individuals' freedom of choice can surface as values that are more important for employees.

In a similar vein, the traditional image of weak, homogeneous, less-educated workers who need the government's mandatory and universal intervention is fading, and a new type of worker who is more independent, individualized, with a high-level of education and various orientations is emerging. Currently more than half of the Japanese workforce are white collar workers. Employees, including male full-time workers, especially in the younger generation, have become more individualistic and private life-oriented.

Second, the expected labor shortage requires more utilization of women and older workers. Since the mid 1980s, Japan's employment policy has strongly encouraged women and older persons to enter and remain in the labor market by enacting a series of new laws: the Equal Employment Opportunity Law of 1985 and its amendment in

1997, the Child Care Leave Law of 1992, the Childcare and Family Care Leave Law of 1995, and the Older Persons' Employment Stabilization Law of 1986 and its amendment in 1994. The shortage of labor and government policy will inevitably lead to diversification of the workforce[19].

Third, the previous pyramid shaped labor force structure with more younger and fewer older workers is adopting a barrel shape with fewer younger and more older workers. In spite of the expected long-term labor shortage, this structural change of the workforce causes a surplus of middle-aged and older workers. Since those workers are paid more than their current contribution under the seniority-based wage system, under the current long-lasting recession, they are the target of downsizing. Currently, Japanese firms have not resorted to direct economic dismissals; rather, they have favored other softer means such as solicitation of early retirement and transfers to related firms with or without maintaining a contractual relationship with the original firm (so-called *shukko* or *tenseki*). However, if the recession continues, it will not be surprising if they resort to massive economic dismissals.

3.2. Socio-economic Changes Surrounding Employers

Japanese employers facing intensified global competition

---

[19] However, Japan has not adopted a policy of promoting the introduction of unskilled foreign workers to compensate for the labor shortage.

are being compelled to reconsider traditional employment practices. To compete with resurgent American industries and rapidly growing Asian industries in the global market, Japanese industries have launched restructuring and re-engineering policies. In particular, the case law constraints on swift numerical adjustment of personnel are increasingly recognized as a heavy burden for them.

In addition to such external pressure, internally the industrial structure is shifting more to service industries. The information revolution has also accelerated the reform of corporate structures from a pyramid personnel structure with multi-layered middle management to a flat or network type structure, which makes intermediary supervisors redundant. Moreover, and most importantly, corporate governance is changing. Japanese firms' long-term management focus has been protected by their relationship with their banks and by cross-shareholdings held by friendly firms. Japanese banks are in the midst of turmoil and friendly firms facing financial pressure have started to dissolve cross-shareholdings. Cross-border investment after financial deregulation may further change Japanese-style corporate governance.

4. The Practice of Long-term Employment: The End or Modification?

In light of the aforementioned structural changes, it is certain that mobility will increase in the Japanese labor market. However, whether the Japanese labor market will ever be as mobilized as the American labor market is questionable.

According to Professor Yoshio Higuchi, a leading labor economist, the current increase in the unemployment rate is attributable to two factors[20]. First, non-regular employees, who are responsive to economic fluctuation, made up the main section which increased the total labor force in the early 1990s. However, recently these non-regular employees have become unemployed. Second, although small and medium-sized enterprises had absorbed surplus workers pushed out from larger companies because they were short of more able workers, they are now staring to streamline their workforces.

The Ministry of Labor Annual White Paper of 1998 reports that turnover rates have increased in younger generation and women workers but not in regular employees. Though the aforementioned 1994 survey[21] confirms mobility in the 20s and the late 50s age groups, stable employment is secured in the age groups between 30 and 50.

It is true that more and more regular employees are moving away from their original companies before reaching the mandatory retirement age. However, it is not through dismissals but through transfers to related companies, so-called *shukko* or *tenseki*. The recent increase in *shukko* or *tenseki* indicates not a collapse but a modification of the long-term employment practice. It is no longer secured within a single company, but within a group of affiliated companies.

---

20) Saikin no Rodo-shijo to Koyo Mondai (Round Table Talk-Recent Labor Market and Employment Issues) *Eco-Forum* vol. 17 no. 1, p. 4, 7 (1998).

21) See supra note 2.

These arguments and surveys lead us to a hypothesis that mobility is increasing amongst non-regular employees and peripheral groups in regular employees (20s and late 50s age groups), but the core system of long-term employment, though decreasing in its scope, is still being maintained. As such, current changes in employment practices in Japan should be regarded as gradual modifications rather than the collapse of the practice of long-term employment.

5. Employment Security as a Key Concept Governing Employment Relations

Whether long-term employment is secured or not affects all aspects of the employment system. While long-term employment gives both employers and employees an incentive to invest in firm-specific skills, short-term employment gives no such incentive. Personnel management under long-term employment adopts a seniority-based wage and promotion system, whereas under short-term employment, spot wages and hiring from the external market is common and reasonable. Employment security leads to an internal labor market, and the internal labor market makes decentralized collective bargaining efficient and functional. This is the main reason that enterprise unions and enterprise level bargaining are prevalent in Japan[22].

The employment policies of nations are formed to adapt

---

22) Takashi Araki, "The Japanese Model of Employee Representational Participation", *Comparative Labor Law Journal* vol. 15 p. 143, 144f (1994).

to the realities of their respective employment systems. In Japan where long-term employment is deep-rooted, the state's employment policy has not been to combat already existing unemployment but to prevent unemployment by providing various subsidies for employers to maintain their employees[23].

In short, employment systems are formed on the basis of the extent of employment security. When the degree of employment security changes, this inevitably affects other aspects of employment relations. As such, the extent to which lateral mobility is introduced in Japan requires careful consideration.

6. Merits and Demerits of the Current Long-term Employment System

In light of the above, it is necessary to re-examine the merits and demerits of the current long-term employment system in Japan.

6.1. Demerits of long-term Employment

6.1.1. Demerits for individualized and diversified Employees

First, under the long-term employment practice, individuals' freedom to choose and their right to self-determi-

---

23) Takashi Araki, "Promotion and Regulation of Job Creation Opportunities, National Report: Japan" International Society of Labour Law and Social Security, Promotion and Regulation of Job Creation Opportunities (Proceedings of XIV World Congress of Labour Law and Social Security, Theme I), pp. 385 (1994).

6. Merits and Demerits of the Current Long-term Employment System

nation are infringed or restrained. Since employment security means a lack of quantitative or external flexibility, Japanese employers have introduced qualitative or internal flexibility[24]. Courts have endorsed employers' strategies to compensate for numerical rigidity. For instance, Japanese courts allow employers to transfer their employees based on business necessity without obtaining an individual's concrete consent. Transfers entailing relocation and changes in job-contents are commonplace. Separation from one's family by a transfer is regarded as a matter of course and it is thought that the consequent inconveniences should be endured by employees[25].

Another example of qualitative or internal flexibility is the case law concerning "reasonable modification of work rules." According to the Labor Standards Law, when work rules drawn up by an employer prescribe more favorable working conditions than those in an employment contract, inferior terms in the contract are invalidated and replaced by the better terms prescribed in the work rules (Art. 93, Labor Standards Law). The Law, however, remains silent regarding the effect of work rules that set more inferior terms than those in individual contracts. With regard to this issue, the Supreme Court has established a unique rule, giving the "reasonable modification" of work rules binding effect on all employees, including those opposed to the modification[26]. Despite severe criticism asserting the

---

24) Takashi Araki, *supra* note 17.
25) The *Toa Paint* case, the Supreme Court July 14, 1986, *Rodo Hanrei* no. 477 p. 6.

lack of legal grounds for recognizing such binding effect, the Supreme Court has repeatedly confirmed this rule and it has become established case law[27]. Underlying this ruling is a consideration of employment security and the need for the adjustment of working conditions or qualitative flexibility. In order to maintain employment security entailing rigidity in quantitative or external adjustment, the Japanese employment system has relied heavily on internal flexibility, sometimes ignoring individual will and choice. This system is beginning to be perceived as irrational by some employees as individualism among employees increases.

Second, long-term employment coupled with a pay system that balances in the long term is irrational for those who choose short-term employment or those who move to another company. It is common practice among Japanese firms to provide a retirement allowance. The rate of the allowance offered progressively rises in accordance with the length of service. As a result, the decrease in retirement allowance is very large for those who change jobs in

---

26) The *Shuhoku Bus* case, the Supreme Court Dec. 25, 1968, *Minshu* vol. 22 no. 13 p. 3459.

27) The *Takeda System* Case, Supreme Court, Nov. 25, 1983, *Rodo-Hanrei* no. 418 p. 21 ; The *Omagari-shi Nogyo Kyodo Kumiai* case, Supreme Court, Feb. 16, 1988, *Minshu* vol. 42 no. p. 60 ; The *Dai-ichi Kogata Haiya* case, Supreme Court, July 13, 1992, *Hanrei-Jiho* no. 1434 p. 136 ; The *Asahi Kasai Kaijo* case, Supreme Court, March 26, 1996, *Minshu* vol. 50 no. 4 p. 1008 ; The *Daishi Ginko* case, Supreme Court, February 28, 1997, *Minshu* vol. 51 no. 2 p. 705.

6. Merits and Demerits of the Current Long-term Employment System

Fig.2 Rate of Decrease in Retirement Allowance Due to Job Change (Males in enterprises with 1,000 and more employees in manufacturing)

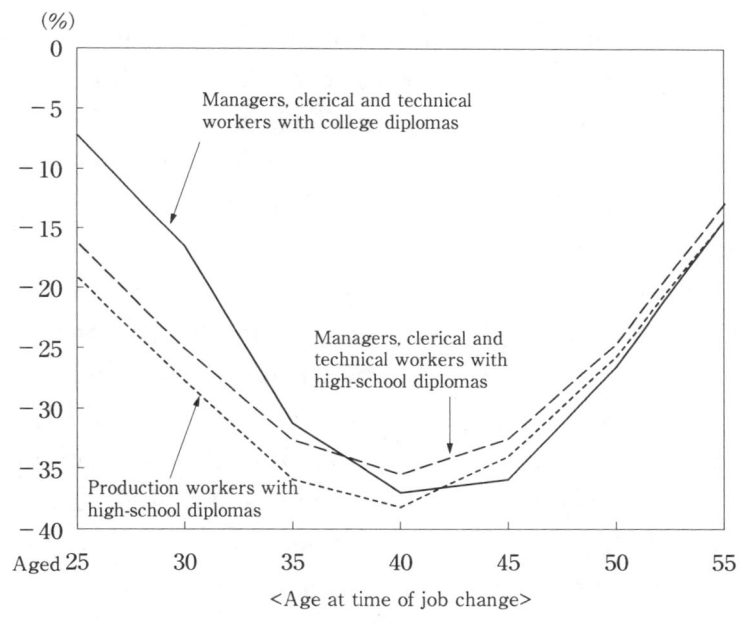

[Figure 2: Line graph showing rate of decrease (%) in retirement allowance by age at time of job change (25 to 55), for three groups: Managers, clerical and technical workers with college diplomas; Managers, clerical and technical workers with high-school diplomas; Production workers with high-school diplomas. All curves dip to their lowest around age 40 (approximately -35 to -38%) and rise toward age 55.]

<Age at time of job change>

Source: Estimated by Labour Economy Affairs Division, Ministry of Labour, from Ministry of Labour, *Basic Survey on Wage Structure* and Executive Office of Central Labour Relations Commission, *General Survey on Wage Situation* : *Survey on Retirement Allowance, Pension and Mandatory Retirement System*.

mid-career because the length of employment is segmented into relatively short periods (see Figure 2).

The current long-term balancing system where a worker is paid less than his/her contribution to the employer in his/her 20s and 30s and is paid more (or receives the unpaid portion) in his/her 40s and 50s is especially disadvantageous to women employees who quit their job when they give birth and raise children.

6.1.2. Demerits for Employers

As mentioned above, Japanese employers have compensated for the lack of quantitative or external flexibility by introducing qualitative or internal flexibility. However, qualitative or internal adjustment is time-consuming and might not be effective enough to cope with intensifying global competition.

Increasing performance-based wage systems require a fair and effective evaluation system. However, in the internal labor market, developed under long-term employment, the labor market's function of evaluating an individual's price in the process of the hiring transaction is not available. To conduct a proper evaluation, employers must train supervisors or evaluators to master fair and consistent personnel evaluation. They are required to explain the evaluation schemes and major criteria for evaluation and to provide dispute resolution systems as well. Such procedural costs to guarantee the fairness and effectiveness of performance evaluation in the internal labor market will place a heavy burden on Japanese employers.

6.1.3. Demerits for Society

First, maintaining high employment security leads to the high cost of labor. This may cause the de-industrialization of Japan. Second, high employment security for regular employees leads employers to utilize more non-regular employees, such as part-timers, dispatched workers (temporary workers) and independent contractors, whose working conditions are normally less favorable than regular employees. Third, employment security for the current workforce may result in new candidates being deprived of employment opportunities.

6.2 Merits of the Long-term employment System

6.2.1. Incentive to invest in human capital

The most significant merit of the long-term employment system may be that it provides employers with the incentive to train and educate their employees. Under short-term employment, employers have no incentive to invest in training, and thus employees must bear the cost of training by themselves. This will lead to a divided workforce consisting of a small number of highly motivated, skilled employees and the remaining majority of less motivated, unskilled ones. One option is to rely on public vocational training like many European countries, but this may be less effective in an era of rapid technological innovation. In this sense, in-house training developed under long-term employment relations can be evaluated as a more effective scheme to enhance the skills of the workforce in its entirety.

6.2.2. Cooperative Labor and Employment Relations with high Morale

Under the long-term employment system, it is reasonable for all members to cooperate because each shall be reciprocated for his/her own conduct, as "repeated game" theory shows. Japan's teamwork is underpinned not solely by cultural factors but also by the long-term employment practice. If an employer dismisses a worker without justification, it could develop into a major dispute with the labor union. It could also have an adverse effect on the morale of other workers who believe that the employer would not resort to dismissals unless they themselves commit a serious breach of faith. This would inevitably affect the cooperative employment relations between labor and management, a factor which has been essential to the competitiveness of Japanese companies[28]. As a consequence, the company would also face difficulties in recruiting able personnel.

A survey by the Social Economic Productivity Center (Shakai Keizai Seisan-sei Honbu) suggests there is consensus concerning these merits of the long-term employment system among Japanese employers (see Figure 3). In the author's view, in the 21st century, these merits continue to be essential in employment relations in Japan where human capital is the sole asset.

6. 2. 3. Employment Security and Protection of Terms and Conditions of Employment

In Japan, where employment security has been believed to be the center-piece of employment relations, the fact that protection of terms and conditions of employment pre-

---

28) The so-called "lean production system" named by the MIT group (J. Womack et al, The Machine That Changed the World-The Story of Lean Production (1990)) as a feature of the Japanese production system is effective only when stable labor relations are secured.

6. Merits and Demerits of the Current Long-term Employment System

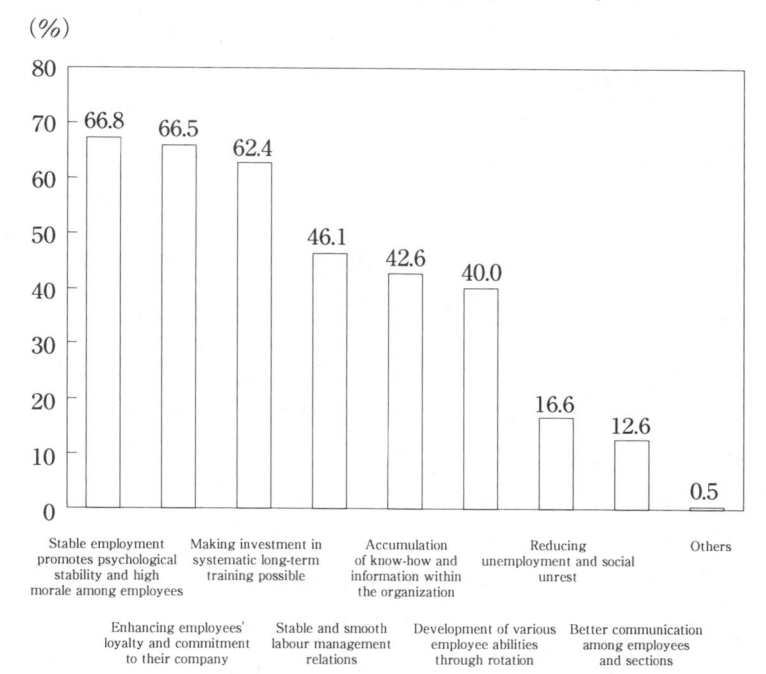

Fig.3 Merits of Lifetime Employment System

(%)
- Stable employment promotes psychological stability and high morale among employees: 66.8
- Enhancing employees' loyalty and commitment to their company: 66.5
- Making investment in systematic long-term training possible: 62.4
- Stable and smooth labour management relations: 46.1
- Accumulation of know-how and information within the organization: 42.6
- Development of various employee abilities through rotation: 40.0
- Reducing unemployment and social unrest: 16.6
- Better communication among employees and sections: 12.6
- Others: 0.5

Source : *Current Situation and Problems of Japanese Human Resource Management System*, Social Economic Productivity Center.

Note : Multiple answers.

supposes employment security is overlooked. However, a comparison with the employment-at-will system in the United States makes the importance of employment security evident[29]. Under the at-will system, an employer has the right to terminate an employee for a good reason, a

---

29) Clyde Summers, "Comparative Perspectives" in S. Estreicher & D. Collins (ed.), Labor Law and Business Change, pp. 140-141 (1992).

bad reason or for no reason at all. Therefore, terms and conditions of employment are subject to at-will modification by the employer. If the employee rejects the proposed modification, he or she is simply dismissed. Where no employment security exists, no protection of terms and conditions of employment exists.

7. Increased Employee Mobility and Challenges for Japanese Labor Law

It is certain that changes are taking place in the Japanese long-term employment practice. Among the younger generation, lateral movement between jobs is not at all rare. Some people prefer self-determination and risk-taking to employment security. However, various institutions in the employment system formed under the long-term employment practice are interdependent. They are not prone to change overnight. In that sense, long-term employment has not yet ended but is undergoing modification. Considering the various merits of the practice of long-term employment, the role of labor law is not to simply increase numerical flexibility but to accomodate balanced flexibility.

The Japanese employment system has relied too much on internal or functional (qualitative) flexibility and excessively restricted external or numerical (quantitative) flexibility. Given the changed circumstances surrounding contemporary employment relations, a new balance between the two types of flexibility needs to be struck. For instance, traditional employment relations with internal (qualitative) flexibility has required, at least to some extent, the sacrifice of individual self-determination. In accor-

7. Increased Employee Mobility and Challenges for Japanese Labor Law

dance with the individualization of the Japanese workforce, it is necessary to decrease the internal (qualitative) flexibility to respect individuals' choice, and to compensate for the decreased internal flexibility, it is required to increase external or quantitative flexibility.

In other words, the problem of the traditional Japanese employment system is that it provides only two options: one is a "regular employee model" coupled with employment security and high internal or functional flexibility; the other is a "non-regular employee model" which simply provides external or numerical flexibility. What is required in the future are numerous employment models with various combinations of internal (qualitative) and external (quantitative) flexibility.

This requires several labor law reforms. First, the case law rule governing dismissals should be enacted in legislation. Currently as it is only regulated by case-law the rule is problematic in terms of transparency. Second, current case law concerning unjust dismissals provides only two rigid, all-or-nothing resolutions. If the dismissal is regarded as an abuse of the right to dismiss, full compensation and reinstatement are provided for. However, if it is found to be a valid dismissal, there will be no compensation at all. There should be another more flexible resolution such as recognizing dissolving employment relations on the condition that the employer should pay certain compensation to the dismissed. Third, the current four requirements for economic dismissals might be reconsidered in order to adapt to the changing labor market situation. Fourth, labor market regulations should be reformed to accommodate increased labor mobility. In particular, the function of employment placement services, including private agencies, or employee dispatching services should be enhanced. Fifth, new rules are necessary to regulate employment security on transfer of undertakings or other organizational changes of corporations. Sixth, an individual labor dispute resolution system should be established since labor mobility inevitably increases individual labor disputes.

Future employment relations will be accompanied by increased external flexibility. The reforms should be designed to cope with the changing environment of employment relations. It is by no means enough to leave everything to the functioning of the external labor market and negate the role of labor law. The role of labor law remains important in Japan. It determines and controls the optimum combination of the two types of flexibility (internal v. external) and keeps the whole labor market and employment relations flexible and capable of adapting to changing socio-economic circumstances.

Guidelines for Multinational Enterprises, Forever?

The OECD Guidelines, 20 years later

Roger BLANPAIN[1]

Introductory remarks

More than twenty years have past since discussions on the role of multinational enterprises and their impact on economic and social policies were at the forefront of public attention. Negotiations, between all involved parties, Governments, Employers' Associations and Trade Unions, lead to a. o. the 1976 Guidelines for Multinational Enterprises, recommended by the OECD and the 1977 Tripartite Declaration of Principles concerning Multinational Enterprises and Social Policy, adopted by the Governing Board of the ILO.

The question arises whether these Guidelines, as far their objectives, content and follow up are concerned, are

---

[1] The author is Professor of Comparative and European Labour Law at the K. University of Leuven, Belgium. He was from 1977 to 1987 member and later head of the Belgian Delegation to the IME Committee of the OCDE, which is responsible for the clarification of the OECD Guidelines and the ongoing evaluation of their relevance.

still relevant today and tomorrow, now that we are at the dawn of the XXIst century.

For indeed, since the 1970's, the scenery has dramatically changed, as well political, economical and social. Especially and utmost, the world of work has undergone tremendous developments.

I. FACTORS INFLUENCING THE WORLD OF WORK

Here, various factors are at play, which are interrelated and aggravate each other greatly, namely:

1. the globalization of the (market) economy;
2. the demographic explosion;
3. the information technology.

These factors are well known, but their impact is often underestimated and many fail to appreciate that they are almost totally beyond the control of the local and national actors, be they governments or social partners. and also of the international or regional (*e. g.* European) authorities.

A. The globalization of the (market) economy
   1. No boundaries

Since the fall of the Berlin wall (1989), Eastern and Central Europe have opened their doors to a freer market system, and before that India and China. Some 3 billion more people have joined a world-wide system in which fewer and fewer national borders block the free movement of money, information, technology, goods and services. Companies can and do invest world-wide wherever market conditions are best.

2. Rigid policies

Moreover, globalization contributes to a disassociation between "money" on the one hand and services/goods on the other. Of the billions of dollars which are continuously "internetted" around the globe, only some 10% are used for the payment of products and services. The rest of this enormous money stream, which no one controls, is a product in itself. Money and its derivatives are a growing business. Governments have to follow a strict budgetary and financial course; spend only as you earn, otherwise the financial markets might punish them.

The European Monetary Union is evolving in accordance with the same logic: Member States need to keep inflation below 3% and aim for a deficit of less than 3% of the current budget with a total debt of at most 60% of the national GDP.

3. Less room for social policies

The consequence of all this is that there is less room left for social policies that might burden public expenditure. On the contrary, public debt has to go down. This means cutting in public jobs and reducing social security benefits, including pension and sickness benefits.

B. The demographic explosion

This explosion refers to two phenomena. One has to do with the fact that every hour 12,500 new babies are born, which adds 1 billion more inhabitants to our planet every 10 years. As the population trend in Europe is rather one of stagnation, the relative share of Europe is shrinking to about 5% of the world population, signifying at the same time that there are hundreds of millions ready to work under conditions which are much lower than the ones we, in our advanced economies, consider to be normal standards.

A second feature has to do with the fact that many of us will get older. People in the 21 st century, certainly in the advanced economies, will live on average close to 100 years or even longer. This happy development has negative implications for our social security budgets, especially in the area of pensions/guaranteed income and the medical sector, but also positive implications for the world of work. Care of the elderly people will prove to be a rapidly expanding work-provider.

C. Information technologies
1. From Fordism to Gatism

Information and communication technologies are by far the most important factor of all. This follows an historical pattern. The development of our societies has always been technologically driven, at the pace of the agricultural society and horses until the 18th century, since then on the basis of machines, of electric and steam power in the in-

I. FACTORS INFLUENCING THE WORLD OF WORK

dustrialised societies, and today and tomorrow in the orbit of the information revolution. This technological development is all-pervasive, dominating and dramatically affecting our societies in general and the labour markets in particular.

We have been catapulted, forcefully and brutally, out of the industrial society into what may be termed an information society.

Indeed, only yesterday Fordism was still riding high in the industrialised world. It lasted triumphantly for some thirty years (1950-1980) and was characterised by the following features:
* almost everyone who could work had a job, neatly "tailored";
* almost everyone earned a "reasonable" salary and was
* a brave "consumer".

There was enough money to finance transfers for the benefit of the sick and the handicapped, to pay for pensions, to support (some) unemployed and the like

Employers and trade unions regularly programmed - with success - social progress. Everyone had a place on the labour market, often colourless and boring, but could see himself and especially his children grow in the system. The children would study, do better and climb the social ladder. There was a "social arrangement" in which employers and employees could find common ground : economic growth on the one hand and social progress on the other were monitored collectively by employers and trade unions, including through collective bargaining, often with the consent of or in concertation with the welfare state.

Consumption then was geared to we would now call rather primary needs. Everybody wanted a TV, a refrigerator, a car, a roof over his head. Our society was one of consumers, targeting useful things : "a society of the useful". Steady consumption made the economic machine run smoothly.

Those glorious thirty years are definitively behind us. "Fordism" is over ; "Gatism", named after Bill Gates of Microsoft, is ushering us in a new world. Freer, but less secure.

2. Tertiarisation

This move into the information society is as drastic, brutal and fundamental as the transition from the agricultural society to the industrial society in the 19th century, when our (great)-grandparents were driven from the barn and the field into the sweatshops and the cities.

More than that. In those earlier (industrial) days, we were merely moving from one sector to another : from the primary sector to the secondary, from agriculture to manufacturing. An analysis at first sight may lead us to conclude that today we are massively stepping into the third

I. FACTORS INFLUENCING THE WORLD OF WORK

sector: the services. This is evidenced by less than 10% of the economically active population left in agriculture, less than 30% in manufacturing and 50% or more in the service sector.

However, things are not that simple. There is much more to it: at present, sectors are merging into each other. What we are really experiencing is a tertiarisation of agriculture and manufacturing on the one hand and a (partial) industrialisation of services on the other. All this is obviously the result of the massive and creative introduction of new technologies, especially of information-communication technology, where in the form of bits - not atoms - knowledge is stored, manipulated and transmitted world-wide without significant costs.

As a consequence, the source of economic value is shifting from the material to the non-material. Where previously wealth had to do with the yield of land (agriculture) and underground deposits (mining) and yesterday opulence was the result of produced goods, today and tomorrow, wealth means knowledge, inventions and intellectual property. What are involved are "things" which the customs officer does not see pass through national borders; the newer wealth has to do with "invisibles", which pass underground, above the ground, through satellites and are sent around the world on the information highways.

New technologies are likewise replacing traditional raw

materials, such as copper as a medium for transporting bits with fibres, which are cheaper and lighter to install and, equally important, perform better.

A couple of examples may serve to illustrate our reasoning more clearly. Take the cost structure of a pound of butter or a car. Only 20% or less of the cost of making butter relates to the agricultural work; 80% or more goes to research and development, including genetic engineering, storing, marketing, distribution and the like. The cost of a car is less and less related to the financing of the chassis or to paying the assembly-line workers involved, of whom there are fewer every day, but results from expenditure/investments for conception, design, R&D, intellectual property, marketing, distribution, licences, financing, insurance... all services, many of which can be operated over information-communication highways.

Products and goods, agriculture and manufacturing, are thus in the grip of "services". Even more, it is clear that goods and services go hand in hand. Industry remains the motor of the economic machine, but is *de facto* "service-driven".

Now, it is plain that these services have become so varied, so specialised, so rapidly evolving and so demanding, that a single enterprise cannot simply house all the services it may need and maintain them at top-level quality. Moreover, they are not needed constantly, but only at specific points in time. On top of that, these services can be very expensive, since top quality commands top rewards. And lastly, they can be provided via the information highways from anywhere, even from the other side of the globe, at possibly only 10% or even less of the cost at home.

3. Externalisation

All this means that enterprises externalise the services concerned and/or obtain them on the outside market. The fact that other undertakings will provide a service has the great advantage - in this ever more competitive world, where quality has to improve continuously and cost go down permanently - that services are ordered only when needed and that the enterprise pays only for what it gets. This contrasts with in-house services provided by the enterprise's own employees, where staff are paid according to the time they spend in the company, during which they are at the service of the company. You pay them for their time. When I buy external services as and when I need them, I pay only for what I get. This may prove to be a lot cheaper, as I can let the market operate between competing service-providers and contract with those who deliver the service (the sub-product) cheapest and fastest. Total quality, at the best price, just-in-time!

4. Outsourcing

This major movement, driven by the tertiarization of industry and agriculture, goes logically hand in hand with the "big bang" of the (bigger) companies. These may literally explode. Enterprises are engaging in outsourcing, entrusting tasks they used to do themselves to other enterprises which can provide them better and more cheaply. A vast subcontracting exercise is carried on. Gone are the days of enterprises that controlled raw materials, having their own coal and ore mines, their own railway system and so on up to the final product, including its distribution. Outsourcing is in.

India's software export industry, worth more than $1 bn a year, has become one of the most dynamic sectors of the Indian economy, fuelled by demands of offshore clients for low-cost, high quality products and services. There are now more than 700 software companies in India. In 1995, 104 companies out of the Fortune 500 outsourced their software development to India.

5. Chains of SMEs

Enterprises are evolving, to a larger extent than before, into co-ordination centres of out-sourced services and activities. A car is the (international) result of the input of perhaps hundreds of companies, possibly spread around the globe. Enterprises are becoming part of one or preferably more networks, are federations of "bits and pieces of activities" in which especially smaller SMEs, legally independent but economically linked up on the basis of "tooth and nail" agreements, deliver services and/or (sub) products to one or more of the co-ordinating centres. Most of the time, the outsourcer retains the economic power; if needed, for reasons of price, quality or just-in-time delivery, the out-sourcer can change subcontractors and choose

I. FACTORS INFLUENCING THE WORLD OF WORK

them, eventually, from a global panoply of bidders. Performance is no longer for the benefit of another department within the company, but for a client: we get chains of SMEs, looking for and performing for clients, always on the move. A client, working for other clients, eventually around the globe.

These SMEs in turn will also subcontract, will have certain tasks performed by other enterprises and grow, while networking.

6. Industrialisation of services

If agriculture and manufacturing are yielding more and more to the grip of "services", the latter, in their turn are at least partly becoming more industrialised, that is provided in a more automated, mass-produced and uniform way. This is certainly the case with banking and insurance, which already operate partly in an industrial, i. e. tailorized basis, but also with fast-food and hotel chains (franchising included), culture (CD's, videos) and leisure, sports and other activities.

Summing-up: transcending all barriers

The world of work is exploding and has become more volatile. The reasons are well known: globalization, demographic trends and the introduction of new technologies, especially the communication-information technologies. We are entering a new world. It immediately becomes clearer why developments in the globalized, non-material market economies are totally transcending the nation/state and its political authorities, paralysing the social partners in their traditional role and making enterprises dash from one chore to the next. Nothing is stable any more; one thing it is safe to say is that safe jobs are becoming a rarity.

The consequences of these developments are manifold and have far-reaching repercussions on the nature of enterprises, on the kind and number of jobs, on labour law and industrial relations systems, on HRM and, plainly on society at large.

The hierarchical enterprise, the pyramid with the MD and the board atop the descending ranks of the managers, the middle managers, the foremen and the white- and blue-collar workers at the bottom of the pile, organised like an army or a governmental organisation, belongs to the glorious years of Fordism, i.e. to the past. Labour relations in those enterprises were subordinate, tended to be more uniform, collective, controllable and controlled, including by way of collective bargaining.

Now, networking is the key word. People-relations, inside as well as outside the enterprise, are becoming less hierarchical and more lateral: working more as equals, on the basis of capability, according to the value one can add and in teams. Work will thus be performed in networks, in teams, which may extend over different formal enterprise structures; employed by company A but partly performing in the laboratory of company B. People will be able to work if they can bring added - non-material - value and will be paid accordingly.

The worker of today and tomorrow will thus perform in one or more networks, on his own, but mostly as part of a team, in the framework of shorter or longer projects, for which he will be contracted. The worker will have to assemble and monitor his own portfolio of work, most often as an independent worker and in a sense becoming his own employer. Labour relations will at the same time be less collective, less uniform, more free, less controllable and controlled. Collective arrangements will be mere frameworks or simply fade away.

The old, hierarchical enterprise, where someone could start his career as a lift attendant and eventually end up as the managing director at the top of the pyramid is definitely becoming an oddity in the landscape of work. Enterprises will be composed of a small core of permanent staff; the rest will probably be more peripheral workers, who will deliver specific services as part of teams, evolving in their own networks, possibly across boundaries and regions.

II. RELEVANCE OF THE GUIDELINES

In order to evaluate the relevance of the guidelines let's consider their objectives, spirit, content and follow up, in order to see whether the still suit the needs of the day and tomorrow.

A. Objectives and spirit
In the Introduction to the OECD lines, the Member

Governments give the general framework, the underlying philosophy and the tone of the Guidelines.

They first concentrate on the importance of the contribution of multinational enterprises and the problems to which their operations may give rise as follows: 'Multinational enterprises now play an important part in the economies of Member countries and in international economic relations, which is of increasing interest to Governments. Through international direct investment, such enterprises can bring substantial benefits to home and host countries by contributing to the efficient utilisation of capital, technology and human resources between countries and can thus fulfil an important role in the promotion of economic and social welfare. But the advances made by multinational enterprises in organising their operations beyond the national framework may lead to abuse of concentrations of economic power and to conflicts with national policy objectives. In addition, the complexity of these multinational enterprises and the difficulty of clearly perceiving their diverse structures, operations and policies sometimes give rise to concern'. (paragraph 1).

In paragraph 2 Governments indicate their goals: 'The common aim of the Member countries is to encourage the positive contributions which multinational enterprises can make to economic and social progress and to minimise and resolve the difficulties to which their various operations may give rise. In view of the transnational structure of such enterprises, this aim will be furthered by co-operation

II. RELEVANCE OF THE GUIDELINES

among the OECD countries where the headquarters of most of the multinational enterprises are established and which are the location of a substantial part of their operations. The Guidelines set out hereafter are designed to assist in the achievement of this common aim and to contribute to improving the foreign investment climate.'

The introduction also deals, among others, with the nature and the binding character of the Guidelines, their relationship to national law, a (non) definition of the multinational enterprise, the relevance of the Guidelines for national enterprises and the use of dispute settlement machinery.

There is no doubt that these objectives and spirit are as valid today as they were 20 years ago: promotion of the positive contribution international investment and trade can make, prevent abuse of economic power, conflicts with national policies and making MNE's transparent. If there is one thing one could say, is that these aims and their spirit as even more relevant today than 20 years ago, since the enormous progress international direct and indirect investment has made over the last decennia.

It has to be underlined again that the guidelines constitute good behaviour for all, as well domestic as multinational enterprises, whenever relevant.

Regarding transparency, multinational enterprises are asked to provide quite detailed information on the enterprise as a whole, as follows :

Disclosure of Information : 'Enterprises should, having due regard to their nature and relative size in the economic context of their operations and to requirements of business confidentiality and to cost, publish in a form suited to improve public understanding a sufficient body of factual information on the structure, activities and policies of the enterprise as a whole, as a supplement, in so far as is necessary for this purpose, to information to be disclosed under the national law of the individual countries in which they operate. To this end, they should publish within reasonable time limits, on a regular basis, but at least annually, financial statements and other pertinent information relating to the enterprise as a whole, comprising in particular :

(i) the structure of the enterprise, showing the name and location of the parent company, its main affiliates, its precentage ownership, direct and indirect, in these affiliates, including shareholdings between them ;

(ii) the geographical areas' where operations are carried out and the principal activities carried on therein by the parent company and the main affiliates ;

(iii) the operating results and sales by geographical area and the sales in the major lines of business for the enterprise as a whole ;

(iv) significant new capital investment by geographical area and, as far as practicable, by major lines of business for the enterprise as a whole ;

(v) a statement of the sources and uses of funds by

II. RELEVANCE OF THE GUIDELINES

the enterprise as a whole;
(vi) the average number of employees in each geographical area;
(vii) research and development expenditure for the enterprise as a whole;
(viii) the policies followed in respect of intra-group pricing;
(ix) the accounting policies, including those on consolidation observed in compiling the published information.'

B. Content

The Guidelines contain, in addition to an introduction, which constitutes an integral part of them, eight sections, namely:

1. General policies;
2. Disclosure of information;
3. Competition;
4. Financing;
5. Taxation;
6. Employment and Industrial Relations;
7. Science and Technology
8. Environment

From the labour relations point of view the Introduction and the chapters on disclosure of information and self-evidently employment and industrial relations are of particular importance.

As far as employment and industrial relations are concerned, the Guidelines cover the following points:

- freedom of organisation and collective bargaining;
- information to employees;
- standards of employment and industrial relations;
- training and employment of the local labour force;
- reasonable notice and consultation in case of major changes in their operations;
- discrimination in employment;
- unfair influence in bona fide negotiations with employees;
- access to real decision makers.

These guidelines retain after 20 years their full use and value. The guidelines which have come most in the limelight over the years have undoubtedly to do with the information, and reasonable notice and consultation in case of major changes. These continue to be utmost relevant as the Renault case (1997), involving the closing down and collective dismissals of more than 3,000 employees in Vilvoorde, Belgium, has clearly demonstrated.

One which could come more to the forefront today is the guideline concerning training. This needs no extensive elaboration. In the new world of work and in the information society, lifelong training becomes a must and is an investment whereby society, the enterprises and employees all win. Indeed, the only weapon workers as well as self employed have to retain a worthy place on the labour market are their skills, which have to follow technical developments on foot and focus on problems solving and communication; skills related as well to "savoir faire", as "savoir être".

C. Binding character and follow up

The observance of the Guidelines is voluntary and not legally enforceable. This seems today even more in line with legal developments than 20 years ago. The role of mandatory legislation gives indeed more and more way to self-accepted, agreed upon rules of behaviour, in line with ideas of subsidiarity and proportionality, which have now a. o. been enhanced in the Treaty of Amsterdam, changing the treaty of the European Community.

Moreover, the procedure of clarification of the Guidelines has proven extremely useful, since once the most important problems were clarified in the earlier years of the guidelines, new requests for clalrification have practically not been introduced. The IME Committee remains a forum where Governments and involved parties can exchange views on experience under the Guidelines. In the Renault case, the Belgian Government could rely on earlier clarifications and discuss the case as well in the Belgian Contact Point as in the OECD. It remains a continuing task for Governments and social partners to continue to propagate the Guidelines and to continue to make them known to the ever expanding international community. In this framework, a declaration of acceptance by the multinational groups of the Guidelines would merit renewed attention.

CONCLUDING

There is no doubt that the guidelines for MNE's have made a substantial contribution to economic and social welfare over the years. This contribution has not always been spectacular as to much attention has been given to the bad cases, which were few after all, given the growing importance of international investment.

The reason for the success of the Guidelines is that they do provide in a flexible way standards of behaviour, giving companies confronted with situations which are not always very easy to cope with, clear guidelines of what to do in a societal recommendable way. That has been and will be their greatest merit.

Employment versus Self-Employment: The Search for a Demarcation Line in Germany.

Manfred WEISS

1. THE CONCEPTUAL FRAMEWORK

1.1. THE CATEGORIES

According to the German legal structure working people traditionally are divided into three categories: employees, self-employed persons and employee-like persons. The decisive category for being an employee for a long time has been subordination. Self-employment is characterized by the lack of such subordination. The employee-like person is self-employed but economically speaking in a comparable situation as an employee. These distinctions have wide-reaching consequences. The employee is not only covered by the protective standards of labour law but also automatically included in the very complex social security system, thereby insured against the risks of age, health and unemployment. Self-employed persons are lacking all this protection, even if nowadays under certain conditions they are entitled to apply for membership in the social security system. If a self-employed person is considered to be employee-like, this person enjoys at least some protective labour standards. The core of these protective measures (for example protection against dismissals or guarantee of remuneration in case of sickness), however, does not apply. And since these persons are self-employed, they are not covered by the social security system: it is up to them to provide for insurance against the risks of life.

Before discussing the demarcation line between 'employee' and 'self-employed' it seems to be necessary to cope with two questions. First it should be clarified whether the protective systems of labour law and social security law apply at least in principle to all employees in the same way or whether significant differences are made between typical and atypical forms of employment. This clarification is necessary to understand the impact of the notion of 'employee'. Secondly the concept of 'employee-like' person has to be specified in order to explain the difference between this group of persons and employees in a strict sense. This information is a necessary precondition to fully understand why it is still important to know whether somebody is only 'employee-like' or a real 'employee'.

1.2. THE PRINCIPLE OF UNIFORM TREATMENT OF THE EMPLOYMENTRELATIONSHIP

The question is to be asked whether from the point of view of legal protection full-timers who are employed for an indefinite period are treated differently compared to part-timers, to temporary employees or to employees on fixed term contracts. At least in principle the answer under German law is no. These groups all are covered by the very same statutory protection as the full-timers for an indefinite period. Therefore, at least from a legal point

1. THE CONCEPTUAL FRAMEWORK

of view the fragmentation between core groups and peripherical groups of employees is less dramatic than in many other countries.

A closer look, however, shows that there are differences. For employees on a fixed-term basis the protection against dismissals of course does not help once their term is over: termination is an automatic consequence without any need to declare a dismissal. Temporary workers according to law have at least in principle an indefinite employment-relationship with their hiring-out agency. But for reasons not to be discussed here there are no collective agreements covering their working conditions. For them the mechanisms of workers' representation only to a limited extent fulfil their function. They are not really integrated into the workforce of the users' enterprises and therefore, in many ways, treated as second class employees[1].

Since 1985 there is an explicit statutory provision guaranteeing the equal treatment of part-timers compared to full-timers. In addition the European Court of Justice has helped to equalize the conditions of full-timers and part-timers under the label of indirect sex discrimination[2]. Re-

---

1) For further details see WEISS M./SCHMIDT M, Germany, in: BLANPAIN R. (ed.), Temporary Work and Labour Law of the European Community and Member States, Deventer/Boston 1993, pp. 121 et seq. (pp. 127 et seq. and pp. 147 et seq.)
2) For an overview see PFARR H., Mittelbare Diskriminierung von Frauen, Neue Zeitschrift fuer Arbeitsrecht (NZA) 1986, pp. 585 et seq.

cently, however, the legislator has defined the tresholds for the scope of application of the Act on Protection against dismissals and in reference to the term of notice in a way which leads to a lowering of the protective level for part-timers: they are not counted as full persons but only with a certain percentage (working a maximum of 10 hours a week 25 percent, a maximum of 20 hours 50 percent and a maximum of 30 hours 75 percent). Thereby it is possible to hire quite a number of part-timers without passing the treshhold[3]. More important, however, is another distincton: part-timers who work less than 15 hours a week and whose income does not exceed a certain level (which is regularly adapted; presently 620 German Marks per month in West Germany and 520 German Marks in East Germany) are excluded from the automatic coverage by the social security system. Therefore, these employees have become very attractive for the employers: no contributions for the social security are to be payed. This means significant cost reduction for the employers (who otherwise have to pay half of the contributions) and practically an equalization between gross wage and net wage for the employees. Since in view of the demographic development and due to the growing expenses of the health care the

---

3) It, however should be added that in the period between 1985 until this recent amendment the treshhold structure was even worse: marginal part-timers did not count at all.

4) For 1998 the contributions for retirement insurance amount to 20, 3 percent and for the unemployment insurance to 6, 5 percent of the monthly remuneration. The contribution to the health insurance differs for different categories of employees.

1. THE CONCEPTUAL FRAMEWORK

contributions have to be steadily increased[4], this marginal part-time employment is chosen by more and more employers to escape this duty. The ever increasing number of marginal part-timers amounts to several millions: exact figures are not available[5]. There is a very heated debate on the question whether and in how far this group of employees should be integrated into the social security system. Those who favor a change stress the need of social protection especially of this group. Those who plead for the maintenance of the exclusion point out that otherwise these people either would remain to be unemployed or pushed into a totally uncontrolled black market. The recent EU-directive on part-time work evidently does not decide this question: the problems of social security are left out there. And the European Court of Justice has confirmed this exclusion of marginal part-timers as being compatible with the present EU-law[6].

The system of vocational training in Germany is governed by a specific statute, the Act on Vocational Training of 1969. According to this law apprenticeship is organized as a dual system, training in the enterprise combined with education in special schools for vocational training. Technically speaking, apprentices are not 'employees'. But according to section 3 of the Act on Vocational Training, the rules and principles governing the employment contract

---

5) About 70 percent of them are female.
6) See judgements of the European Court of Justice of 14 December 1995 (C-317/93 and C-444/93), ECR 1995 I, pp. 4625 et seq. and 4741 et seq.

are to be applied, except in cases where the Act expressly states an exception, or when the application of labour law would not be compatible with the nature and the aim of the apprenticeship. This exception is loosing more and more of its relevance. Therefore, it is fair to say that the legal regime (including social security) for apprentices is practically the same as it is for normal 'employees'.

1.3. THE DEMARCATION LINE BETWEEN 'EMPLOYEE-LIKE' AND 'OTHER SELF-EMPLOYED' PERSONS

From the very beginning in Germany the dichotomy between self-employed being totally excluded from labour law and social security law on the one side and employees being fully covered by those protective standards on the other side was not accepted as a satisfactory solution. This is why the third category of employee-like persons was invented to classify those who are self-employed but whose economic situation nevertheless resembles much more that of an employee than an autonomous self-employed. The criterion used to distinguish this group of self-employed from other self-employed is 'economic dependency'. The notion 'employee-like' persons, defining this group of individuals, was developed by the courts. The notion was not very clear. The situation improved in 1974 when in section 12 a of the Act on Collective Agreements a statutory definition of 'employee-like' persons was provided. According to this definition individuals are economically dependent and need to a certain extent social protection if they fulfil the following conditions: first they have to perform

1. THE CONCEPTUAL FRAMEWORK

their contractual duties themselves and essentially without the help of employees; secondly, the major part of their work must be performed for one person or institution or more than half of their income must be paid by one person or institution. It should be stressed that 'person' or 'institution' in this sense may also mean a group of companies: the individual working for different enterprises within a group is considered to only work for one institution in the sense of this definition. For artists, writers and journalists there is a specific definition: for them it is sufficient if more than one third of their income is paid by one person or institution.

Perhaps more important than this definition is the fact that since 1974 when this statutory provision was passed it is possible that these employee-like persons may be covered by collective agreements which normally only is possible for employees in a strict sense. Thus at least theoretically by collective agreements standards for them could be developed which also in core areas would equalize their position with the one of real employees. Up to now this legal possibility only is used to a very marginal extent which can be neglected here[7]. The reason is very simple: this group of persons is difficult to unionize. Therefore trade unions are not interested to take care of their protection.

---

7) For details see KEMPEN O.E./ZACHERT U., Tarifvertragsgesetz, 3rd edition, Koeln 1997, section 12 a, number 4

The main statutory privileges 'employee-like' persons enjoy are mainly two: disputes between them and their contractual partners are to be settled by labour courts and not by ordinary courts; as far as minimum standards for annual vacations and holidays are concerned they are treated in the same way as employees. In so far they are treated in a more favourable way than other self-employed individuals.

Two groups of 'employee-like' persons are treated by law separately: commercial agents and homeworkers. As far as commercial agents are concerned there is a separate statutory definition in view of their status as being 'employee-like'. The first precondition is that the commercial agent is contractually prohibited to work for other enterprises or, in view of the kind of volume of his or her work, is factually unable to work for other enterprises. The second condition is low income: they are only 'employee-like' persons if their income, on the basis of the contractual relationship, over the last six months did not exceed on average of 2.000 German Marks. This figure can be adjusted to the price and wage level by Government decree. It however has to be stressed that different from other 'employee-like' persons commercial agents never can be covered by collective agreements: they are not included in the definition of section 12 a of the Act on Collective Agreements.

For the homeworkers, as a specific group of 'employee-like' self-employed persons, there is a special statutory

1. THE CONCEPTUAL FRAMEWORK

regulation. The first Act on Homework dates from 1911 but the actual statutory regulation originates from 1951 and has since been amended several times. The latest and most important amendment took place in 1974. A homeworker is anybody who works, be it alone or with the help of family members, for another person or institution at a place of his own choosing whether it is an apartment, a house, or some other place, and who leaves the utilisation of the result of his or her work to the person or institution he or she is working for. The Act also applies to individuals who, in a place of their choice, with at most two other people (non-family members) helping them, are working for another person or institution leaving the utilization of the result of their work to the other person or institution. It makes no difference whether the raw materials are provided or not. The level of protection for this group of 'employee-like' persons is very similar to the level 'employees' in a strict sense enjoy : the rules merely are adapted to the specific situation of these people, essentially characterised by working in isolation. Therefore, in some respect they provide even better protection than it would be the case for normal employees. The most important difference to all other groups of 'employee-like' persons is the fact that homeworkers automatically are included in all branches of the social security system. Different from all the other employee-like persons homeworkers are integrated into the works council system. Whether, however, in actual practice this protection is very helpful for them may be doubted. In this respect they are in a similar position as the temporary workers in the user's company.

1.4. THE DEMARCATION LINE BETWEEN 'EMPLOYEE' AND 'SELF-EMPLOYED PERSON'

Under German law the employment relationship is considered to be a contractual one. This excludes all relationships which are not voluntary but where the individual is forced to work (for example a prisoner in prison), and-more important-where the relationship is based on instruments of public law (for example civil servants or judges). These groups are governed by specific statutory provisions focusing on their function and status. They-at least in principle-have nothing to do with labour law and with the overall social security system.

There is still no statutory definition for the notion of 'employee'. It only is defined in a negative way by the fact that the notion of "self-employed" is defined in section 84 of the Commercial Code. This reads: "He who essentially is free in organizing his work and in determining his working time is presumed to be 'self-employed' ". Thus personal freedom is the main characteristic of being self-employed. This is why the traditional definition of 'employee' implies just the opposite of personal freedom, i.e. personal subordination.

For a considerable time the notion of 'personal subordination' was accepted as a helpful and valid tool to define an employment relationship. Personal subordination was always understood to differ from mere economic dependency on the employer. Therefore the question whether a person is an employee had never anything to do with the salary the individual is earning. This distinction between mere personal subordination and economic dependency is still valid. But meanwhile the problem is that nobody knows any more what personal subordination really means. The traditional view of an individual simply obeying his or her employer's orders in determining the organization of his or her work, or his or her working time, does not correspond with the fact that management by objectives has become the modern pattern, leaving the individuals more and more freedom in deciding how and when they carry out their work. Working time flexibility has become the rule, rather than the exception[8]. And it definitely does not correspond with the concept of autonomous or at least semi-autonomous groups which as an implication of the lean management philosophy have become an essential feature of an efficient modern company. Therefore it is necessary to discuss the question whether and in how far Germany has succeeded to adapt the criterion of 'subordination' to the reality of today's working life.

2. THE NEED FOR REFORM

2.1. THE ATTEMPT OF REDEFINITION OF THE CONCEPT OF SUBORDINATION

Already in the early sixties the problem arose whether a

---

8) See BOSCH G., From 40 to 35 hours: Reduction and flexibilisation of the working week in the FRG, International Labour Review 1990, pp. 611 et seq.

leading medical doctor in a hospital can be an employee, even if he autonomously decides what medical treatment is necessary, and how and when it has to be administered. The choice was either to exclude such a medical doctor from labour law or to include him and redefine the notion of personal subordination. The Federal Labour Court decided the latter[9]. It considered the fact that the medical doctor's capacity to work was almost totally absorbed by the hospital as sufficient for categorizing the relationship as one of 'personal subordination'. This case not only shows the inadequacy of the traditional notion but it also indicates the start of a very controversial debate on the notion of 'employee' which still is going on.

The first wave pushing for intensification and acceleration of this debate dates back to the mid-seventies. The decisive actors were the so called free collaborators of the mass media. These individuals had contracts with newspaper enterprises, radio stations etc. to work for them as journalists, musicians and suchlike. But according to the contracts on which these relationships were based, these individuals were expressly defined as not being employees but self-employed. When the economic crisis of the seventies started to affect the budget of the mass media, and when these so-called free collaborators thus had to face the fact that they could be dismissed without the protection provided by labour law, many of them claimed that

---

9) See Federal Labour Court, Judgement of 27 July 1961, Arbeitsrechtliche Praxis (AP), § 611 BGB Aerzte, Gehaltsansprueche.

2. THE NEED FOR REFORM

in reality they were employees in a strict sense.

In the course of these law suits the notion of 'subordination' was redefined in order to cover quite a few persons who according to the traditional understanding would have remained to be left out. First of all the Federal Labour Court made it perfectly clear that it is not up to the parties of the individual contract to define the legal character of the relationship just by labeling it in a certain way. Whether labour law and social security law is applicable or not, depends on the content of such a relationship. Legally speaking there is no possibility of escaping the constraints of labour law and social security law just by mutual agreements if the facts implied by the contract are not covered by such an agreement. In actual practice, however, it quite often is done. As long as it is not questioned in court nothing happens. The recourse to the content of the relationship implies that the factual structure of such a relationship is to be evaluated. And here of course the question arises what 'personal subordination', as a criterion to distinguish an 'employee' from a 'self-employed', could possibly mean.

The Federal Labour Court has turned the notion of personal subordination into a very complex structure consisting of a wide range of elements which have to be combined and evaluated as an entity[10]. Thus it is always up

---

10) For all details see HILGER M. L., Zum "Arbeitnehmer-Begriff", Recht der Arbeit (RdA) 1989, pp. 1 et seq.

to the courts to determine whether in a particular case the combination of factors indicating the status of an 'employee' is sufficient or not. Since the period when the collaborators of mass media were in the forefront of the discussion the Federal Labour Court has had many opportunities to further develop and specify this concept by testing it in situations which are characteristic for the modern working pattern dominated by the service sector. It, however, is still far from being clear or transparent. Some factors which are indicating the status of an 'employee' are among others: the enterprise expects the individual to be always ready to accept new tasks; the individual is not free to refuse tasks offered by the enterprise; the individual is to a certain extent integrated into the organizational structure of the enterprise; the work is performed by means belonging to the enterprise etc. There is not a single element which could be considered as the decisive one. It always needs an overall perspective in each individual case. The underlying perspective of all these different factors is the following: to what extent is the situation of such an individual comparable to the one of those whose status as employees is not questioned at all? More important, however, is the fact that the notion of 'personal subordination' is not abolished as the decisive criterion, it is merely adapted to the ever changing new circumstances.

2.2. THE NEW QUALITY OF THE CHALLENGE

The traditional model of an employment relationship has been the factory where employees cooperate in a coherent organisational structure. This is the perspective which led

2. THE NEED FOR REFORM

the Federal Labour Court to the conclusion that the integration into the organizational structure of the enterprise is one of the relevant factors to indicate the existence of an employment relationship. The problem, however, is that this traditional model is rapidly eroding. First of all there is an increasing externalization of functions by way of outsourcing. Secondly new information and communication technologies allow to an increasing extent a relocation of work-performance by so called tele-work. The "virtual factory" and the "virtual office" are becoming characteristic features of today's and especially of tomorrow's reality[11].

The pressure of cost reduction has become a decisive element in today's management strategies. In order to remain competitive enterprises look for ways to get rid of the constraints of labour law and social security law. Instead of employing agents an insurance company concludes contracts with self-employed agents. In the construction industry more and more bricklayers, electricians, floor-tilers and even crane drivers are considered to be self-employed. In the transport industry truck-drivers to an ever increasing extent offer their services as self-employed. In the case of the crane driver the crane and in the case of the truck driver the truck quite often is leased to or even owned by these individuals. Experts of information and communication technologies offer their services as self-employed. Hotels and restaurants to an increasing extent are relying on

---

11) See LINNENKOHL K., Die Virtualisierung der Arbeitsbeziehungen, Betriebs-Berater (BB), p. 45 et seq.

self-employed persons for all kind of services. In the health sector the self-employed nurse is a widespread phenomenon. In education, in banking, in engineering and even in manufacturing (self-employed mechanics) this trend is to be observed everywhere[12]. The number of one person self-employed activities is rapidly increasing. In short and to make the point: the contractual patterns stepping out of the traditional employment-relationship have become a mass phenomenon: It is no longer a problem of merely some atypical cases.

The advantages for the contractual partners of these self-employed are evident. They do not have the normal employer's responsibilities under labour law or under social security law. Even if they pay higher wages, they still have less labour costs. Since the self-employed has to handle him- or herself taxes etc., the companies contracting with them can reduce their infrastructure to manage personnel affairs. Under German tax law they in addition have better possibilities to manipulate taxes. They transfer all the risks of work performance to the self-employed (for example the risk to get sick). On the other hand the self-employed may reach a higher net income: this may increase his or her motivation which again is another advantage for the contractual partner. Which ever the advantage for the self-employed may be, the price to be paid

---

[12] For details see SITTE R., Neue Ansaetze zur Eindaemmung der "Scheinselbstaendigkeit", Soziale Sicherheit 1997, pp. 88 et seq. (89 et seq.)

2. THE NEED FOR REFORM

is high: the loss of social protection. It has to be stressed that in view of the unemployment situation the newly 'self-employed' often have no choice but to accept this pattern.

Whether all those who are contracting as self-employed really are self-employed in a legal sense, is of course very doubtful. There is a widespread assumption that most of them in reality are 'employees'. Therefore, the notion of 'fake self-employed' has been invented to illustrate the phenomenon. The question, however, is whether this problem can be resolved by recourse to the notion of 'subordination'. The complexity and intransparency of this notion in its new version as developed by the courts makes it extremely difficult to draw a clear-cut demarcation line. In addition it may well be questioned whether it makes sense at all to determine the level of protection by recourse to 'subordination'. Even if this would be possible, it may well be doubted whether the courts can resolve the problem. After all they only can intervene if they are called upon. This, however, only happens in very rare cases. The efficiency of other presently existing instruments of control have turned out to be very low. In view of the budget situation which implies further reduction of personal and other resources there is no hope to the better.

This new challenge has led to a very controversial discussion on the future of labour law and social security law in Germany as such. The spectrum of the controversy is wide. On the one end are those who are interested to reintegrate all such so called self-employed under the umbrella of labour law and social security law[13]. Especially the latter plays an important role. It is considered to be totally inadequate that the social risks in the very end are transferred to the community : the social security system is deprived of necessary contributions and the danger that these persons will have to be supported by the safety net of the welfare system remains. On the other end there are those who would like to further restrict the notion of 'employee' and facilitate the status of 'self-employment'[14]. For them the cost reduction for enterprises is the decisive criterion. Therefore, they are pleading for a new 'culture of self-employment' in order to stimulate the lasting recovery of the economy and of the labour market.

2. 3. RESPONSE BY AN ALTERNATIVE APPROACH

Since autonomy, creativity, working time flexibilty as well as the freedom to decide on the work peformance as such are becoming more and more important features of the modern working reality a relevant group of scholars is on search for a new criterion, not fully replacing but at least amending the traditional category of "subordination". The key notion in this context has become entrepreneurial risk[15]. The decisive perspective is the fair balance between

---

13) For this view see BUSCHMANN R., Rechtsprobleme der Scheinselbstaendugkeit, in DAEUBLER W. et alii (ed.), Arbeit und Recht, Festschrift fuer A. Gnade, Koeln 1992, pp. 129 et seq.

14) For this view see ZOELLNER W. /LORITZ K. G., Arbeitsrecht, 5th edition, Muenchen 1998, pp. 46 et seq.

15) See WANK R., Arbeitnehmer und Selbstaendige, Muenchen 1988, pp. 125 et seq. as well as WANK R., die "neue Selbständigkeit", BB 1992, pp. 90 et seq.

2. THE NEED FOR REFORM

entrepreneurial risks and entrepreneurial chances. If an individual is in a contractual relationship which puts on him or her entrepreneurial risks but which due to 'subordination' does not allow him or her to make use of entrepreneurial chances, he or she is considered to be an 'employee'. If, however, the individual is only subordinated to an extent, which allows him or her to act as an entrepreneur on the market and to make use of his or her own chances, he or she is considered to be 'self-employed'. Again it is of course difficult to determine which of the two alternatives are given in a specific case. Therefore again indicators are offered. Factors indicating an 'employee' status are the following: the individual has no entrepreneurial organizational structure on his or her own, the individual has no collaborators (family members not included) but works on his or her own, the individual does not dispose on business rooms of his or her own, the individual has no business capital on his or her own, the individual has only one contractual partner for whom he or she works, the individual does not act on the market on his or her own, the individual is not free to choose the location of work, the individual is rather restricted in his or her disposition on working time, the individual does not have clients of his or her own and finally the individual is not free in determining the price for goods or services. By contrast the lack of these factors would indicate 'self-employment'. For some it is also an indication of self-employment if the entrepreneurial risks were taken voluntarily. This, however, is a very doubtful category in view of high unemployment where many people do not have a choice to opt for alternatives.

This new approach is by no means less complex than the redefined category of 'subordination' as sketched above. Again no single factor is the decisive one: in each individual case an overall evaluation is necessary. Therefore, it is very doubtful whether it might be a helpful tool in actual practice. Leaving these practical difficulties aside for a moment, it, however, should be stressed that the normative implications of the two approaches are significantly different. A recent empirical study by the Federal Labour Office's research institute[16] has examined the group of those who are in the twilight zone between 'employee' and 'self-employed'. The sample consisted of 938000 people, identified by a set of predefined criteria. According to the approach of redefined subordination as developed by the Federal Labour Court 48 percent were considered to be without any doubt self-employed and 19 percent to be employees. For the remaining 33 percent an appropriate categorization was not possible. Taking the alternative approach of entrepreneurial risks and chances only 30 percent fell undoubtedly into the category of self-employed and 44 percent were 'employees'. Again for the remaining 26 percent a well-founded classification into one of the two categories is not possible. This result shows clearly that the alternative approach would imply an extension of the notion of 'employee' and at least to a certain extent might

---

[16] Empirische Befunde zur "Scheinselbstaendigkeit", NZA 1997, pp. 590 et seq.

2. THE NEED FOR REFORM

lead to a reintegration of so called 'self-employed' into the employment relationship.

2. 4. THE LEGISLATIVE PROJECTS

The intransparency of the present definition as developed by the Federal Labour Court and as contested by the alternative approach has led to activities to involve the legislator to provide a statutory definition of 'employee'. In this context two strategies have to be distinguished: the attempt to codify the law of the employment contract as a whole on the one side and the attempt to merely focus on the definition of the 'employee' in reference to social security on the other side. The initiative of a comprehensive codification has a long history. So far, however, it has remained a much too ambitious and therefore futile attempt, even if it got a new support in the course of German unification[17]. The much more modest initiative to merely focus on a statutory definition has many more chances to be accomplished.

As far as the codification of the law of the employment contract as a whole is concerned, there are presently two approaches, one intitiated by the State of Saxony[18] (repre-

---

17) See the draft elaborated by a group of professors: Arbeitskreis Deutsche Rechtseinheit im Arbeitsrecht, Welche wesentlichen Inhalte sollte ein nach Art. 30 des Einigungsvertrages zu schaffendes Arbeitsvertragsgesetz haben?, Gutachten D zum 59. Deutschen Juristentag, Muenchen 1992.

18) Entwurf eines Arbeitsvertragsgesetzes des Freistaats Sachsen, Bundesrats-Drucksache 293/95.

senting the Christian Democrats' view) in 1995 and one initiated by the State of Brandenburg[19] (representing the view of the Social Democrats) in 1996. The Saxonian draft defines the employee as somebody "who performs his or her work according to orders or to contractual constraints in the context of an organization not determined by him or her. Persons who voluntarily choose to be entrepreneurs are not employees." This definition very much takes up the criterion of 'subordination' and emphasizes in addition the element of contractual freedom. In so far the Brandenburg-draft is very similar. It, however, adds two presumptions: "He or she who is not free to essentially determine the work performance and the working time, is supposed to be an employee. The proof to the contrary is excluded. He or she who works for somebody else without collaborators of his or her own and without business capital of his or her own, is supposed to be an employee. In this case the proof to the contrary is possible." In other words: this definition tries to introduce a combination between the traditional 'subordination' approach and the new approach focusing on entrepreneurial risks." However, as already mentioned, these drafts do not really have a chance to be passed in the near future.

Therefore, much more relevant is the more specific project limited merely to the statutory definition in reference to social security. This draft was initiated in 1996 by the

---

[19] Entwurf eines Gesetzes zur Bereinigung des Arbeitsrechts des Landes Brandenburg, Bundesrats-Drucksache 671/96.

States Hesse and Northrhine-Westfalia and taken up by the Social Democratic Party in the Federal Parliament[20]. It presently is in the center of the discussion. According to this draft 'employees' are especially those, who "(1) are not employing collaborators (family members excluded) in performing their work; (2) normally only work for one contractual partner; (3) perform work which is typical for 'employees' and (4) do not appear on the market on the basis of an entrepreneurial activity." If at least two of these four indicators are given in a specific case "there is a presumption for an employment relationship. The proof to the contrary, however, is possible." This definition more than anyone before abides to the new approach of entrepreneurial risks and chances. Its goal is clear: to bring as many as possible under the roof of the protective standards of social security law. By introducing a presumption it also tries to simplify the very complex pattern developed by scholarly literature in order to provide a workable concept. The possibility of proof to the contrary may, however, turn this goal into a futile attempt[21].

3. EVALUATION

There is no doubt: the traditional category of 'subordination' as decisive criterion for the employment relationship has come under attack. The turn to the notion of entrepreneurial risks and chances indicates a change of

---

20) Entwurf eines Gesetzes zur Bekaempfung der Scheinselbstaendigkeit, Bundesrats-Drucksache 696/97.
21) In the meantime this law has been passed. Its implications on labour law, however, remain to be unclear.

paradigm. In the meantime, however, there is a growing literature trying to demonstrate the inadequacy also of this new approach[22]. And it has to be admitted that in many cases the new approach might lead to similar deficiencies as the old one. None of both and not even a combination of both seems to provide a satisfying answer in view of the variety and the dynamics of working relationships which are developing presently and in the future.

The problem, however, goes much deeper. The core of the controversy after all is the extent of protection to be provided. It may be doubted very much whether this problem can be resolved by focusing on the definition. Of course, in the present legal situation the definition is the decisive tool in determining the scope of application of protective standards. As far as the core of protective rules in labour law and protection by social security as a whole are concerned, the demarcation line decides on 'all or nothing'. It, however, may well be doubted whether such an 'all or nothing' approach still is the right answer[23]. Therefore, it seems to be necessary to change the focus. The starting point has to be the kind and extent of protection needed in a specific contractual relationship. Protective rules then are to be developed for specific types of activities. Thereby protective standards focusing on the

---

22) See for example ROMME O., Unternehmerrisiko, Zeitschrift fuer Arbeitsrecht (ZfA) 1997, pp. 251 et seq.

23) These doubts are also expressed by HROMADKA W., Arbeitnehmerbegriff und Arbeitsrecht, NZA 1997, pp. 569 et esq. (pp. 577 et seq.)

3. EVALUATION

particular economic and social needs of specific groups could be elaborated. Their specific situation could be taken into account. This -to just give an example- might lead to very different rules for tele-workers compared to rules for persons who are in a franchise relationship. And of course it might lead to an erosion and reconstruction of labour law and social security law as a whole[24]. Such an effort would include a close examination of the question in how far the adequate protection also might be provided by mechanisms of other legal disciplines (commercial law, law on unfair competition etc.).

In elaborating appropriate protective schemes it would be necessary to reflect the possibilities of protection by collective instruments. Here it is evident that patterns developed for the traditional industrial worker of the traditional factory cannot simply be transferred to the highly fragmented and very heterogenious workforce of today and tomorrow. It especially has to be understood that in many cases due to work performance in isolation collective action cannot play the same role as in the traditional environment. All this of course must have implications for the kind of statutory protection to be provided for these groups.

In concluding one might say that the concept of subordi-

---

[24] For such a perspective see also SIMITIS S., Le droit du travail a-t-il encore un avenir?, Droit Social 1997, pp. 655 et seq. (pp. 663 et seq.)

nation symbolizes a discussion which seemingly is focusing on the demarcation line between 'employment' and 'self-employment' but which in reality has to do with the adequate degree of protection. Rephrased this way it is nothing else but the discussion on the future of the welfare State model and its new face. The problem is evident: satisfying answers are not yet in sight.

Developing Competitiveness and Social Justice: the Interplay between Institutions and Social Partners

Keynote address
at the 11th World Congress
of the International Industrial Relations Association
Bologna, 22-26 September 1998

Tiziano TREU

1. Premise. A global reflection.

Today "speed" has assumed a dimension unknown in the past. The pace of work is increasing more and more, thanks to the development of technology, which allows communications in real time, unthinkable until only a few years ago. Consequently, the time for study and analysis is also undergoing considerable change. In all the sciences- and the social sciences are no exception-ideas may become too old before the ink dries. The challenge is open: sometimes the usefulness of a generalised comparison extended to all geographical contexts, even though profoundly different, is contested. In brief, there are elements which lead us to doubt the basis of contributions inspired by global reflection, in a context where time seems to frustrate, in advance, all attempts to draw a balance.

Harder still was the task of trying to foresee, three years in advance, the emerging issues in the field of industrial relations. We were certainly aware of this difficulty when, in the spring of 1995, we tried to outline the themes of discussion at the 11th World Congress of the International Industrial Relations Association. At the time, we decided not to address one specific issue, but to choose an approach or, rather, an imperative: to reconcile competitiveness and social justice, which has always been a critical issue in all discussions concerning labour and employment matters. Even if from a specific perspective: that of the relations between the institutions and the social partners.

Over the last three years, at the impressive speed at which events now take place, so much has changed in the culture and practise of industrial relations, throughout the world. Nevertheless, the papers submitted for this year's Congress do not disavow the approach decided three years ago and set forth in the scientific programme, which is the blueprint of this Congress. The need to proceed with a global reflection-including a number of countries, a variety of disciplinary approaches, a plurality of economic and political contexts, featuring different levels of development-seems even more urgent.

Basically, the global reflection will also concern industrial relations as a scientific methodological approach for examining employment and labour matters, focusing on the role and activities of the social partners and their interactions with the public institutions. Far from highlighting the twilight of industrial relations, the papers produced for this Congress are proof of the surprising vitality of the employers' associations and trade unions, which dis-

1. Premise. A global reflection.

claims certain ill-omened forecasts, in respect of the survival of what we may still call industrial relations, i. e. a framework of regulated relations between the employers' associations and the trade unions.

Of course, there are national contexts or local situations where, for a variety of reasons there has been a visible weakening of either the employers' or the employees' role. But it would be wrong to infer from this that the challenge of globalisation, which has now firmly asserted itself, has removed the premises for the collective, as well as individual, bases of labour relations, thus depriving the social partners of their *raison d'être* (Gunningle, 1995). Although there is the need of profound reform, as a consequence of the widespread internationalisation of the key institutions of industrial relations, such as collective bargaining, a mature and stable system of industrial relations may be considered a factor of progress and development.

And this is precisely why the intensification of globalisation and the consequent delocalisation strategies adopted by the enterprises require good industrial relations systems, in the areas wanting to attract investments. A stable social climate and the availability of skilled human resources, capable of meeting the investors' expectations — both of which are determined by the actions of the social partners — are decisive factors for guiding decision-making. Not to speak of the circumstance, increasingly and empirically confirmed, of the importance of a good climate of industrial relations to keep employees motivated and, therefore, committed to maintaining and increasing their company's productivity levels (Delbridge et al. 1997). The non

-contrasting nature, as well as the necessary complementarity, of efficiency and social justice is now taken for granted even in the analyses of prestigious international institutions, such as the World Bank, according to which the success of modernisation depends not only on the individualisation of employment relations, but also on enhancing the importance of solidarity (Valkenburg, Zoll, 1995).

Obviously, global reflections—from the point of view of the comparison of many national situations or local contexts—are useless if they do not establish certain analytic priorities. And those set forth three years ago, during the planning phase of this world congress, are still useful today. Despite the "speed" factor, which makes these periodical meetings between scholars and practitioners increasingly difficult to plan beforehand, the papers received for the Congress confirm the continuing usefulness of the issues singled out at the time. Here, I will present an overview of these issues, taking account of the wealth of analysis and research documentation produced for the Conference, obviously highlighting the role that the social parties may play, together with the institutions, in reference to a broad range of issues.

2. The end-of-the-century challenge: combining economic growth and employment.

There is a reason why we are still obliged to acknowledge that employment is an absolute priority, not only for governments but also in the dialogue between the social partners, in many countries, and especially in Europe. The struggle against unemployment is increasingly a

2. The end-of-the-century challenge: combining economic growth and employment.

struggle against long-term unemployment, which may become virtually irreversible, giving rise to cases of social exclusion, which are a grave hazard for a country's economic and social cohesion. In the European Union, a considerable effort is being made by the member countries, who have even constitutionalised the joint commitment for employment in the Treaty of Amsterdam of 1997, as part of a logic of convergence, supported by the provision of quantified criteria for assessing the fulfilment of some joint objectives (Biagi, 1998).

The critical point to be addressed is the relationship between long-term unemployment and low educational and professional skills and training. The lesser the qualifications, the longer the period of unemployment. This is why most Governments are focusing on the young, to prevent these potentially irreversible cases of unemployment. Training may produce interesting results, in terms of job creation (but they may hardly be considered spectacular, especially in transition economies: Nacsa, 1998), although the success of the training programmes (and, in general, of all active labour policy measures) seems to be inversely proportional to the trainees' age.

One cannot help agreeing with who (Suwa, 1998) rightly reminds us how difficult it is to retrain persons who are half way through their career and over 50 years of age. A dramatically widespread situation, also because the investments required for training entail extremely high costs, which are not always justified by the success of the retraining programmes. Among other things, this type of action is proof of the importance of developing suitable techniques for promoting training, exactly like any other educational programme.

The one true motivation is to reasonably count on feasible job opportunities. But one cannot underestimate the impact of age, also in view of the population ageing trends, which requires the rethinking of training strategies when the beneficiaries are no longer eligible for this measure (Auer, 1998).

The consensus on the usefulness of training as an employment strategy does not rule out the fact that it must be thoroughly and carefully reconsidered. First of all, by acknowledging how a large part of an employee's skills are acquired by means of the *learning by doing* process (Erickson, Jacobi, 1998), and this process may be fully successful only if the employee is assured a relative degree of job security. Albeit without underestimating the great consensus on the concept of employability and, therefore, the requirement that all workers be really employable, i. e. continuously trained to carry out a number of different tasks, even in different enterprises or branches of the state admministration, it is precisely the evaluation of the convenience of training investments directly by the private sector which highlights the need of a convinced and collaborative (in brief, motivated) attitude by the beneficiary concerned. This may hardly take place when the employee is faced with job insecurity or does not have career perspectives.

It is a significant fact that the experience made in the US has confirmed the convenience for enterprises as a cornerstone of the training programmes' success. This leads

2. The end-of-the-century challenge: combining economic growth and employment.

to the need of achieving a combination of flexibility and security—therefore, the adaptability frequently recalled at the EU level—capable of making effective the employability needed in the more general context of active employment strategies, capable of addressing the mobility induced by the progressive integration of the economy and the progress of technology (Cohen, Zaidi, 1998). At the same time it is necessary that the enterprise in question is engaged in a globalised confrontation, which means that it must search for a competitive edge, because it is being continuously confirmed that it is precisely these economic actors which are especially resorting to training investments (Picot, 1998).

The "speed" factor mentioned at the beginning fully justifies the recommendation (Suwa, 1998) to avoid excessive specialisation in the training approach, to prevent the precocious obsolescence of the employees' skills. Too specific a training exposes the employees concerned to a process of rapid obsolescence, therefore it really is expedient to review the adequacy of basic training programmes to enable the employees to take an active part in problem-solving, according to a methodologically tested approach. At the same time, the training measures must be related to specific groups of workers, in order to achieve important results in respect to equal opportunities as well, which make the impact of equality policies very immediate and direct (Chicha, 1998).

There is no dearth of experiences confirming the key importance of the co-operation between the State and the social parties, in respect of the definition and the management of training measures (Vincent, 1998). Perhaps this has been the most fertile sector for agreements, dating back to the 1970s in many countries and paving the way for even more significant concertation (i. e. trilateral) arrangements in the following decades (Tallard, 1998). A long process, which has engaged and continues to engage the social actors, who may effectively interact in conditions of consolidated representativity: which explains why these practises encounter so many difficulties in countries where there is a transition to the market economy (Simonyi, 1998).

The joint effort by the institutions and the social parties is increasingly aimed to fight unemployment-also by means of training—to contrast the extremely high costs of unemployment. These costs must be considered in both financial and human terms, due to the loss of freedom of individuals, the increased risk of social marginalisation, the worsening of health conditions and the consequent increase of mortality rates, the drop of motivation and the deterioration of social relations, not to mention the increase of race and gender based inequalities (Mitchell, Burgess, 1998). We may certainly agree with the need to study this phenomenon according to a more comparative approach (Oaklander, 1998), also to involve the social parties on a transnational level, as recently requested at the European Union level.

It is precisely at this level that one of the most interesting experiments is currently in progress (Goetchy, Pochet, 1997). The purport of the guidelines defined at the extraordinary European Council on employment, held in

2. The end-of-the-century challenge: combining economic growth and employment.

Luxemboury in November 1997, must not be underestimated (Barbier, 1998), also because the inevitable broadness inspiring the Community perspective does not rule out the strategic importance of the local area initiatives, where the social parties and public authorities have often given convincing proof of concerted actions (Jepsen, Meulders, 1998). The key role played by the social parties, and widely experimented in the last few years (Coldrik, 1995), especially with regard to the use of the structural funds (Wulf-Mathies, 1995), for the improved use of training to promote employment (Freedland, 1996), has been broadly reconfirmed, as part of an exercise concerning the early implementation of the Treaty of Amsterdam (Biagi, 1998).

Training may now be included among the industrial relations issues (Stuart, 1996), since triangular inter-relation in subject matters is an expanding practise, internationally. It is universally recognised that training matters are the privileged field for experimenting collaboration between the social parties (Noble, 1997). Training as a measure of employment policy tool is becoming more and more widespread, albeit with alternate success (Hayes, Stuart, 1996), less so in the US (Osterman, 1995; Macduffie, Kochan, 1995) compared to Japan (Kawakita, 1996), the latter showing a certain interest in the Italian experiments (Genda, 1998).

The consensual approach of the social parties seems indispensable to enable the Governments to pursue the likewise jointly acknowledged need to update labour market regulations, in order to maximise the job-creation potentials of the economic system. The discussion is also increasingly (and appropriately) de-ideologicized, in respect of the unproductive distinction between "good" jobs and "bad" jobs (Houseman, 1995; Dore, 1997; Tilly, 1997), which shows that scarce attention is being paid to the continuous changes in the labour force and the ensuing job diversification (Fredman, 1997).

We cannot underestimate the growing job insecurity, due to globalisation (Standing, 1997), which is a premise for the profound rethinking of the foundations of labour law (Bellace, 1996). Nevertheless, it is necessary to foster co-operation and convergence to enable the use of various forms of employment—different from full-time and open ended employment contracts—albeit under a sort of joint supervision by the social parties.

The unemployment emergency, in a number of countries at least, has paved the way for intensifying synergetic relations between the social parties and the public institutions. The awareness that economic growth in itself is not sufficient to solve the problem of unemployment has accelerated a process of convergence, which may involve a large number of countries, as in the European Union, according to a model of increasing co-operation and convergence. A model which may be attentively assessed in other regions of the world featuring similar challenges. This development of tripartite commitments—always supported by the ILO and, recently, by the G8 jobs meetings—is undoubtedly one of the most interesting and promising experiences made at the close of this century, as a response to the unappeased protectionist or delocalization desires, which risk to oppose and estrange various areas of the world, in respect of labour market competition.

3. A turning point for modernisation: the public employment sector and small and medium enterprises.

At the end of the 1990s, the turning point is especially perceptible in the public employment sector, which in several countries has assumed an innovatory role, even faster and more significantly than the private sector. The convergence in several countries between the public and private sectors is mainly a consequence of the privatisation and reorganisation of many services, with very interesting implications for labour law also (Morris, 1998).

There are at least four profiles of this evolution in the public sector worthy of being underlined: (a) the process of devolution of responsibility; (b) the increasing decentralisation of wage determination; (c) employment and wage flexibility; (d) financial and administrative decentralisation (Madsen, Andersen, 1998). Moreover, one cannot forget that the changes under way in the human resources policies in the public sector are, undoubtedly, the consequence of improving efficiency and quality of the services supplied, which, in turn, has consolidated wage flexibility, favoured by the increased individualisation of wages, increasingly based on merit, supported by the decentralisation of collective bargaining (Bregn, 1998). The above mentioned elements are profoundly innovatory, compared to the previous culture which prevailed in the public sector, inspired by the principles of equality, equity and conformity to procedures (Dell'Aringa, 1998).

Industrial relations in the public employment sector are undergoing significant changes in developing countries also (Pant, 1998), even though proceeding quite slowly. Sometimes, they are the result of the process of European integration which, however, has produced less significant results than the private sector, to date (Keller, 1998). All in all, one cannot reply in a negative manner to the question posed as the theme of the Forum 2 of the Congress ("Restructuring public sector: mission impossible?"). The trend is continuing toward a participatory system of industrial relations, grounded on the autonomy of the parties concerned, engaged in the implementation of joint human resources management policies (Cocozza, 1998).

However, these innovations based on the decentralisation /devolution of operating aspects continue to clash with or to be slowed down by the central Governments, which insist on maintaining the power to set the basic policies. A sort of *coercive isomorphism,* whereby, despite the devolution of responsibility in the handling of labour relations, the central Government continues to ideologically pursue certain schemes, attempting to impose them on the peripheral administrations, when, on the contrary, it is necessary to promote strategies of *mimetic isomorphism*, i. e. imitative mechanisms to replicate the best *managerial practises* (Kessler, Purcell, Shapiro, 1998).

It is interesting to note that also the small and medium enterprises (SME) are going through a period of transition, from old practises to innovative models. To the point of justifying the parallel with the image of the two-faced

3. A turning point for modernisation: the public employment sector and small and medium enterprises.

ancient Roman god Janus: the two faces of SMEs, one looking toward the future, open to the perspectives of increased employment and productivity, the other looking back to the past, symbolising the old fashioned way of handling business and human resources (Galin, 1998).

The confirmation of the potential of SMEs to create jobs, additional (although not large-scale) employment, make these enterprises extremely interesting. Even though the most recent researches have confirmed another well-known characteristic, i. e. the scarce maturity of the system of industrial relations and, in general, the presence of less attractive working conditions, compared to the larger enterprises (in terms of health and safety at work, working hours, wage levels, etc.). SMEs continue to be attractive from a job-creation point of view, albeit not for the more qualified workers, for the reasons mentioned above. From this follows their limited contribution to innovation and, consequently, their greater vulnerability on the market (Fashoyin, 1998).

A certain paternalism, sometimes bordering onto outright authoritarianism, fuelled by the employer's presumption of being capable of doing everything by himself, which has always been a characteristic feature of relations in SMEs, is late in disappearing. However, in a growing number of countries, industrial relations in SMEs also take place at inter-firm level, where the relative employers' organisations play a decisive role in the improvement of the styles of human resource management. A curb on the exercise of the entrepreneurs' powers (Golzio, 1998) which, however, not always translate into the actual modernisation of relations between management and labour, like I mentioned before in respect of the public employment sector (Haddad, 1998).

There is no doubt that a part of the compeitive advantage of SMEs lies in the level of "under-regulation" of the working conditions (Corradetti, Tomada, 1998), which has been confirmed also for widely differing contexts, such as Latin America (Fuentes Puelma, 1998) and the Balkans (Grozdanic, Djordjevic, Djekic, 1998). Empirical evidence, however, is showing us more and more that small and medium entrepreneurs are making an effort to experiment good practises in the management of human resources, to improve the quality of employee information and consultation, no longer resorting to a purely paternalistic attitude (Gollan, Davis, 1998).

Undoubtedly, industrial relations in SMEs suffer acutely from customer oriented practises, which subordinate competitiveness to the employees' capacity to entertain high quality relations with their clients. The protagonism or, in any case, the full enhancement of individual skills leads to the individualisation of employment relationships, which is also promoted by modern human resource management techniques. This should not necessarily constitute a threat for the unions, and likewise the obituary of industrial relations in SMEs, mentioned in the theme of Forum 3 of the Conference, appears to be quite premature (Frenkel, Korczynsky, Shire, Tam, 1998). Although it is difficult for a small or medium entrepreneur to consider the unions as a *constructive sparring partner* (Navrbjerg S. E., Lubanski N., 1998), the trend towards more balanced relations with the representatives of employees (with the exception of micro-enterprises with 15/20 employees) is a relevant trend (Weber, Verma, 1998).

To counterbalance the concentration of "atypical" forms of employment, which is characteristic of SMEs and, hence, the logic of employment precariousness and insufficient protection of employees' rights, a key role is played, once again, by training (at the management level also), rather than by legislation or by the (weak) protection offered by collective bargaining at this level (Wong et al., 1997). The development of a management culture grounded on the enhancement, and not the abuse, of the characteristics of SMEs, in terms of flexibility in the use of human resources, might contribute to the development of the full potential of a sector of the economy which is essential for all contexts, even in developing countries, where this profile is even more at risk.

4. The challenge of the quality of life and work.

Compared to the issues addressed in the preceding paragraphs, the perspective of reconciling the quality of life and work poses the same problems. The era of privatisation, reorganisation and deregulation in which we are living, in fact, is a context where female participation in the labour market has undoubtedly increased, but it has also become more vulnerable (Purcell, 1998). Women are more and more exposed to change, and, if no corrective measures are adopted, corporate strategies well probably affect the working conditions primarily of female employees (Lehto, Sutela, 1998).

One cannot deny the family friendly nature of certain measures, such as part time employment, the annualization of working hours, parental leaves, job sharing, flexitime, or the fact that various forms of "casual" employment (Albelda, 1997) may contribute to combine family and professional responsibilities, especially of female workers (Burgess, Stracham, 1998). The crucial issue, however, is another one. Most of these solutions, in fact, may end up in less attractive employment conditions (as in the case of SMEs: lower wages, unskilled labour, etc.) and, therefore, in a further example of gender-based discrimination.

The picture which emerges is not reassuring. The intensification of global competition in itself increases the risks of the inexorable erosion of living and working standards. One can hardly imagine a counterbalancing effect in a context of industrial relations, given the traditional under-representation of female workers in the trade unions (Sinclair, 1996), with visible effects even on collective bargaining itself (Bergamaschi, 1998). Therefore, one may realistically imagine a broad segment of the female labour force increasingly burdened by anxiety, fatigue and guilt (Edwards, 1998).

But this is not enough. "Squaring the circle", like the theme of this Forum 4, is even more difficult if one considers the problem of the ageing population which, in many societies, is throwing further responsibilities on the shoulders of families, and since the trend for male workers is to work more hours a day, this means an additional burden for the female workers. A situation which, although not totally unknown, is at least a novelty in respect of the dimensions it is assuming (Barrera, Horstman, 1998), both for the delay of the Governments to deal with the issue, by means of "active old age" measures, most of which have still to be implemented, and because of the rooted conviction that the responsibility of care should lie primarily with the families (Maeda, 1998).

Albeit in so difficult a context for overcoming gender-based differences, in respect of reconciling work and family, we must consider the important function of measures such as part-time work, whose incidence is increasing, and not only because of the employees' expectations. Enterprises, too, are concerned to reduce fatigue and stress, to increase motivation and skills, flexibility and loyalty (Haines, Guérin, St-Onge, 1998). And it is precisely in a framework of participatory industrial relations that working conditions may improve, in view of reconciling work and family (Mankidy, 1998), since women are not less motivated than men in exercising a stronger role in the definition of their working conditions (Ramsay, 1998).

However, the issue of careers, and the continuous negative impact that gender-based differences produce in this respect remains unchanged (Eaton, 1998; Auer M., 1998), which confirms the substantial and ongoing subordination of women on the labour market. We cannot give in to pessimism, however, if we take account of the limited (although non-neglectable) effects of the equal opportunities policies (Singh, 1997), especially in the field of training (Green, Zanchi, 1997). It would seem expedient, in fact, to further explore the research trend aiming to identify the business case, to strike a balance between working life and family responsibilities. As in multinational corporations, which are very sensitive to establishing a good balance between working conditions and living standards of their expatriate employees, so as to enhance to the full their professional potential, in an environment which is far away from the one they prefer or are used to.

A more family-friendly corporate environment could be decisive to assure quality to employment relationships (beyond a purely contractual perspective), and it is on quality that the success or lack of success of the enterprise itself depends. Employees who are anxious for their family at home—either young children or elderly parents, who are on longer self-sufficient—are certainly not in the best conditions to express maximum motivation. And the employees' loyalty, their total devotion, which is more and more necessary, may be obtained by means of non-conventional motivation techniques, which go beyond the perspective of simple wage increases. One has also to take into account the changes in the family structure; it is no longer the patriarchal family, where the parents' functions were often carried out by the elderly members of the family, according to a spirit of solidarity with the adults in the prime of their working life. To help employees, also with regard to the multiple needs of their family life, is a key element of a successful human resource management strategy, an area where the reconciliation of apparently unreconcilable interests may have positive effects, in the name of a goal—competitivity—which, ultimately, is a joint goal.

5. Towards the globalisation of industrial relations?

It is the challenge of globalisation which concerns the actors and experts of industrial relations, who are fully aware of the risk entailed by increasing globalisation, in respect of wage cuts and working conditions. But if industrial relations can hope to play a key role for the future, this can only consist in the attempt to address this challenge and create a link between the interests of the underemployed or unemployed and of employees with relatively secure jobs (Visser, 1998). Even though the organisation of the unions on an international level is important (Leftwich, 1998) and capable of producing real solidarity in the event of industrial action, as the recent experience in Australia (Sonder, Hosking, 1998) has confirmed, it is not sufficient to determine a corresponding globalising effect on industrial relations.

In recent years, there have been long discussions on another solution for reconciling globalisation and social justice : to set up a "social clause" system, so that developing countries are not obliged to enjoy the benefits of trade liberalisation at the expense of their workers (Hanami, 1997). We are all too well acquainted with the firm opposition of non-industrialised countries, in respect of establishing a connection between free trade agreements and compliance with minimum labour protection standards, so I need not go into the subject exhaustively here. The struggle against *social dumping* must be accompanied by a fight against protectionist strategies, which, to date, has prevented any significant developments in the World Trade Organisation (Ern Ser, 1998), giving rise to contrasts and distrust on a regional scale also (Morgado, Valenzuela, 1998), so much so that APEC (Pacific, Asia) and CARICOM (Caribbean) have proved unable to reach a sufficient consensus even to discuss the matter (Coulthard, 1998).

The substantially unsuccessful discussions, to date, on a world-wide "social clause" is no good reason to stop talking about the issue, also taking account of the important conclusions reached on 18th June 1998 at the 86th Session of the ILO, which adopted a Declaration on fundamental principles, which may lead to more effective actions. At long last, in fact, the binding nature of the fundamental rights sanctioned by the Constitution and the Declaration of Philadelphia has been recognised, requiring their compliance also by the member countries who have failed to ratify the relative conventions (Myrdal, 1998). A really innovatory solution (Trebilcock, 1998), invoked for a long time (Hepple, 1997), also to firmly contrast the scourges of child labour (Creighton, 1997) and forced labour. An important step forward in the life of this organisation, which may now further strengthen its prestige by better defining a more defined mission.

Nor can we forget solutions which seem to be attracting a growing interest, such as *social labelling* or rules of good social conduct, or the new techniques for defining ethical behaviours susceptible of certification, such as SA 8000 (*Social Accountability 8000*), which are grounded precisely on the regulations produced by the ILO. Voluntary and consensual solutions which, especially with re-

5. Towards the globalisation of industrial relations?

gard to the latter, may become effective if supported by large-scale training actions. One cannot forget the importance of an altogether minimalist approach, such as NAFTA (Erickson, Mitchell, 1998), which provides for compliance by the three member states (Canada, USA and Mexico) of their domestic regulations, thus excluding, for the time being at least, any ambition of homogenisation (Adams, Singh, 1996).

Perhaps transnational collective bargaining is not a short to medium term perspective (Brighi, 1998), but we cannot underestimate some really important convergence trends, such as the humdreds of agreements entered for the early implementation of the 1994 EU directive on the European works councils (Marginson, 1998). Quite a success for a legislation technique for promoting transnational industrial relations, which could be repeated in the forthcoming future, in view of the establishment of the European company, destined to operate in a very promising environment, such as the monetary union. The context of EMU will probably foster decentralised collective bargaining (Knudsen, Lind, 1998) highlighting the different enterprise performances (Traxler, 1997), while at the same time increasing the speed of the process of convergence of social and employment policies.

Today, we may prudentially say that industrial relations are experiencing a process of *emergency of convergence* (Mitchell J. B. D., 1998), because of globalisation, since the relative incentives are so strong that they give rise to actual emergencies. An example is the style adopted by the multinationals, a vehicle of convergence in human resources and industrial relations policies. The frequent use of *expatriate managers* shows that the larger groups are not willing to leave the management, especially of industrial relations, in the hands of the local managers.

The process of contamination, however, cannot be avoided, and will produce a generation of *human resources managers* with an international experience, with a similar —or even homogeneous—backgrounds, giving rise to similar managerial styles (Chua, Saba, Pucik, 1998), a sort of *collective management*. And since we are witnessing a strong trend towards forms of employment, very similar types of *contingent work*, despite the regulatory framework, the social parties should try to acquire a more leading role in this process, so as to govern it in a spirit of consensus.

To state the need of regulating the effects of globalisation, with regard to industrial relations, means to uphold the fairness of competition based on *fair labour standards*. Achnowledged at the recent *G8 jobs summits* of Kobe (1997) and London (1998), this kind of objectives, universally recognised, at least in principle, should be achieved on a voluntary and consensual basis, i. e. once again, with the decisive participation of the social parties. The logic of convergence, more than homogenisation and harmonisation, seems to be acquiring definite contours at European Union level too, where, albeit in an institutonal situation which has developed and consolidated itself over a longer period of time compared to other geographical areas, we are confronted with a process of integration originally based on a trade liberalisation agreement.

6. Industrial relations and democracy: a new mission.

Industrial relations are not only required to perform a function of modernisation, in various respects, as we have seen in the preceding paragraphs. The role of the Governments and especially of the social parties in the countries in transition towards a market economy, is to take up the glove to consolidate the new democratic system implemented at the political level and to transfer it to the workplace. Carrying out this "democratising" function is turning out to be a harder task than had originally been expected. Sometimes, as in the Central European countries for example, there is a "simulated model" of industrial relations, composed of actors with an absolutely uncertain and questionable representativeness, grounded on a mistaken concept of pluralism, since it is often based on extremely fragmented organisations where the old union guard attempts to survive. An often confused situation, caused by the drastic impact of the new laissez faire policies imposed also as a consequence of the pressure of the international financial institutions (IMF, World Bank), which have produced situations bordering on the most savage forms of capitalism (Kollonay Lehoczky, 1998).

The government of transition could not obviously be entrusted solely to the social parties (Matey, 1998), while they were still engaged in a lengthy process of reorganisation. In such conditions, it is the State's responsibility to establish minimum conditions for the exercise of trade union rights (Vodovnik, 1998), without giving in to the allurement or temptation of giving silent support to the process of de-unionisation, to foster investments from abroad. This situation of uncertainty and unstability is typical not only of the Central European countries, but also of Latin America, albeit less exasperatedly so, where there are social concertation practices lacking any effective impact or with hardly credible contents, in this case also because of the lack of representativeness of the actors involved (Raso Delgue, 1998; Coutinho Garcia, 1998).

Especially in the former Soviet-bloc countries there is a sort of *trasformative corporatism* (Iankova, 1998), i. e. a contradictory collaborative/conflictual model, which confusedly combines collective and individual interests, in constant unstable balance between state control and laissez-faire. The failure of mass privatisation, basically due to the lack of foreign investments, has created situations of confusion also with regard to the property of enterprises, which obviously hinders the establishment of stable industrial relations (Casale, Vaughan-Whitehead, 1998). Moreover, it may determine the conditions for a distorted growth, reflecting torments of an ethnic nature, allowing the violation of fundamental rights and even legitimising forms of forced migration (Grozdanic, 1998).

With reference to the East European context, the estabishment of a truly pluralistic system of industrial relations seems to depend on the role which the European works councils, set up in EU enterprises operating with the East, will be able to play Euro-councils style forms of representation could contribute to fill the gap between the discredit managers from the state-owned companies and

6. Industrial relations and democracy: a new mission.

unions precociously weakened as a consequence of too many compromises with the previous regime (Bain, 1998).

Other contexts are even more fragile and immature to claim that the experinences of concertation or tripartite social dialogue is something more than just "institutional ornaments", as in francophone Africa (Kester, Oumou Maiga, 1998) or India (Bhattacherjee D., 1998), where the prevalent risk is the "ossificaton" of the "stronger" interests, represented by the traditional social parties, with the marginalisation of the representatives of consumers, environmentalists, anti-racist or women's emancipation groups. Better results are being achieved in South Africa, where the local labour law tradition has managed to play an intelligent filtering role, in respect of the automatic introduction of foreign models (Albertyn, Rycroft, 1998).

In the transition economies also negotiating for economic growth and social development is far from being a lost battle, according to the theme of a Forum 6 workshop. Social dialogue is itself a factor of competitivity (Sarfati, 1998; Traxler, 1998), especially the more the unions are involved in operating according to a logic of "institutional incorporation", i. e. made jointly responsible by a mature political system which does not aim to marginalise them (Hassel, 1998). Thus, the democratising role which industrial relations may play is of great importance, even though it cannot be successfully fulfilled without a clear strategy by the Government.

7. Towards the year 2000: the role of social concertation.

As I pointed out at the beginning of this paper, the speed of change makes it increasingly difficult to make analyses and forecasts are less and less reliable. Only 10 years have passed since the fall of the Berlin Wall and we are already at the end of the century, at the eve of a new millenninm. Without the risk of rash haste or illusory predictions, we may state that the most important practise which the industrial relations of today are leaving in inheritance to the next millennium is social concertation. Apart from the limitations which it undergoes in the transition economies, due to the scarce representativeness of the social actors, there is no doubt that Europe may send out to the rest of the world a strong message of the re-emergence and reassertion of social concertation, which has been adopted in a number of countries as an indispensable factor for achieving a competitive edge (Regini, 1998).

Over the last 15-20 years, concertation has suffered an oscillatory trend, alternating stages of expansion and contraction. The implementation of European monetary union promises a new expansionary trend, because the initial laissez faire policies should be replaced by the Governments' attempt to rigorously contain the cost of labour. The absorption of any asymmetrical shocks may be more successfully achieved in a neo-corporativist environment, as the Dutch and Austrian experience have proved, when these countries have called to govern the process of re-

7. Towards the year 2000: the role of social concertation.

alignment of their industrial relations systems with the German mark (Crouch, 1998).

Pro-labour governments are not sufficient to guarantee the success of concertation (Refeldth, 1998), although they may undoubtedly support it. The incentive to social deregulation initially introduced by the European monetary union, with the enterprises intent on focusing on their own interests, may be followed by the trend to re-regulation, which is already under way, if one takes into account the spread of the so-called "territorial pacts" (Eire, Finland, Italy, Spain and Portugal), the Community initiatives (directives) on social issues and the new European-wide multilateral monitoring procedure in employment matters (Goetschy, 1998).

By adopting a concertation framework such as the one outlined in the Agreement on Social Policy attached to the Treaty of Maastricht, subsequently incorporated into the new Treaty of Amsterdam, one may project into the future plans of radical change and adaptation of labour regulations. We do not need to devise new techniques for increasing the precariousness of employment relations, to respond to the incessant requests of flexibility. The challenge is much more complex and consists in creating the *adaptability* (not simply precariousness), on which the enterprises may fashion a new reliable and motivated labour force, certain of its employment perspectives, in a framework of continuous training. The challenge of globalisation cannot be won only by means of *outsourcing* or *insourcing* as mass practices, and there are many enterprises which, substantially going back on their footsteps, are reconsidering the return of previously outsourced functions (Marsden, 1998).

The achievement of efficiency depends on new forms of employment, new forms of management and, therefore, on the participation of workers (Markey, 1998), which may also be developed at micro-level, so as to constitute an added value (Munkeby, Handsen, 1998), continuously sought as part of the revised version of *corporate governance* (Goodijk, 1998). Employee participation, which may also be direct (O' Kelly, 1998), as long as it is not alternative to participation through the representative bodies (Markey, Pomfret, 1998). is a guarantee that the democratic system will not contrast with the management's interests. On the contrary, it may become a factor for ensuring greater efficiency and competitiveness (Zammit, 1998), also in transition economies (Kreissig, 1998). This is probably the combination of elements which the social parties and the Governments will be experimenting at the dawn of the next millennium.

REFERENCES

Adams R.J., Singh P. (1996), *Early experience with NAFTA's Labour side accord*, in Comparative Labor Law Journal, vol. 18, N. 2, p. 161 ss.

Albelda R. (1997), *Improving women's employment in the USA*, in Industrial Relations Journal, vol. 28, N. 4, p. 275 ss.

Albertyn, Rycroft (1998), *What is distinctive about South African labour law? An analysis of the historical choices and hidden assumptions of South African labour law*, in Proceedings of the 11 th IIRA World Congress, Bologna.

Auer M. (1998), *The work-family challenge from a career theory perspective*, in Proceedings of the 11th IIRA World Congress, Bolo-

REFERENCES

gna.

Auer P. (1998), *Labour markets, labour market policy and organisational change*, in Proceedings of the 11th IIRAWorld Congress, Bologna.

Bain T. (1998), *The role of works councils in the pluralistic industrial relations systems in central and eastern Europe*, in Proceedings of the 11th World Congress, Bologna.

Barbier J.-C., *Can European Union's involvement in employment policies in Europe be enhanced?*, in Proceedings of the 11th IIRA World Congress, Bologna.

Barrera S., Horstman B. (1998), *Work and family life in India: productivity perspective of ability and opportunity enhancement*, in Proceedings of the 11th IIRA World Congress, Bologna.

Bhattacherjee D. (1998), *The evolution of pluralism in industrial relations: India in a comparative perspective*, in Proceedings of the 11th IIRA World Congress, Bologna.

Bellace J. (1996), *Labour law for the post-industrial era*, in The International Journal of Comparative Labour Law and Industrial Relations, vol. 12, N. 3, p. 189 ss.

Bergamaschi M. (1998), *Il genere nella contrattazione collettiva in Italia*, in Proceedings of the 11th IIRA World Congress, Bologna.

Biagi M. (1998), *The implementation of the Amsterdam Treaty with regard to employment: co-ordination or convergence?*, in Proceedings of the 11th IIRA World Congress, Bologna.

Bregn K. (1998), *Incentive pay in the Danish public sector*, in Proceedings of the 11th IIRA World Congress, Bologna.

Brighi C. (1998), *Contrattare su scala globale: il ruolo delle parti sociali in un contesto transnazionale, accordi commerciali internazionali e clausole sociali*, in Proceedings of the 11th IIRA World Congress, Bologna.

Burgess J., Strachan G. (1998), *Enterprise bargaining and women's employment conditions in Australia*, in Proceedings of the 11th IIRA World Congress, Bologna.

Casale G., Vaughan-Whitehead D., *Privatisation routes in central and eastern Europe: diriving to differentiated labour relations?*, in Proceedings of the 11th IIRA World Congress, Bologna.

Chua R.S.K., Saba T., Pucik V. (1998), *Developing international managers: a suggested framework*, in Proceedings of the 11th IIRA World Congress, Bologna.

Cocozza A. (1998), *Relazioni industriali e gestione delle risorse umane nei processi di trasformazione delle pubbliche amministrazioni in Italia*, in Proceedings of the 11th IIRA World Congress, Bologna.

Coldrik (1995), *The social partners guidelines for recovery and employment*, in Transfer, vol. 1, N. 4, p. 569 ss.

Cohen M.S., Zaidi M.A. (1998), *Labor shortages and pay across national borders*, in Proceedings of the 11th IIRA World Congress, Bologna.

Corradetti S., Tomada C.A. (1998), *Relaciones laborales en la pequena y mediana empresa: tensiòn y integraciòn entre lo individual y lo colectivo*, in Proceedings of the 11th IIRA World Congress, Bologna.

Coulthard A. (1998), *Minimum labour standards in the Asia Pacific Region: the role of APEC*, in Proceedings of the 11th IIRA World Congress, Bologna.

Coutinho Garcia F. (1998), *La crisi asiatica e le sfide della concretizzazione sociale nel Brasile*, in Proceedings of the 11th IIRA World Congress, Bologna.

Chicha M.T. (1998), *Formation en entreprise et égalité en emploi: des stratégies efficaces*, in Proceedings of the 11th IIRA World Congress, Bologna.

Creighton B. (1997), *Combating child labour: the role of international labour standards*, in Comparative Labor Law Journal, vol. 18, N. 3, p. 32 ss.

Crouch C. (1998), *The unloved but inevitable return of neocorporatism*, in Proceedings of the 11th IIRA World Congress, Bologna.

Delbridge R. et al. (1997), *Managing human resources for business success: a review of the issues*, in International Journal of Human Resource Management, vol. 8, N. 6, p. 857 ss.

REFERENCES

Dell'Aringa C. (1998), *Reconciling multilateral interests: the restructuring of employment relations in public services*, in Proceedings of the 11th IIRA World Congress, Bologna.

Dore R. (1997), *Good jobs, bad jobs and no jobs*, in Industrial Relations Journal, vol. 28, N. 4, p. 262 ss.

Eaton S.C. (1998), *Career as life path: tracing work and life strategies in firms of the future*, in Proceedings of the 11th IIRA World Congress, Bologna.

Edwards C. (1998), *Squaring the circle: quality of work and family life. Industrial relations in a wider context*, in Proceedings of the 11th IIRA World Congress, Bologna.

Erickson C., Jacoby S.M., *Embedding the employer: training and work-organization practices of private employer in California*, in Proceedings of the 11th IIRA World Congress, Bologna.

Erickcson C.L., Mitchell J.B. (1998), *Labor standards and trade agreements: U.S. experience*, in Proceedings of the 11th IIRA World Congress, Bologna.

Ern Ser T. (1998), *Globalisation and social justice: towards an optimum position for transnational industrial relations*, in Proceedings of the 11th IIRA World Congress, Bologna.

Fashoyin T. (1998), *Into the unknown: managing human resources in small and medium-sized businesses: a review*, in Proceedings of the 11th IIRA World Congress, Bologna.

Freedland M. (1996), *Vocational training in EC law and policy education: employment or welfare?*, in Industrial Law Journal, vol. 25, N. 2, p. 110 ss.

Fredman S. (1997), *Labour law in flux: the changing composition of the workforce*, in Industrial Law Journal, vol. 26, N. 4, p. 337 ss.

Frenkel S.J., Korczynski M., Shire K., Tam M. (1998), *Front-line work: a challenge to unions*, in Proceedings of the 11th IIRA World Congress, Bologna.

Fuentes Puelma C. (1998), *Los principios de la flexibilidad normativa laboral y su relacion con la pequena y mediana empresa latinoamericana*, in proceedings of the 11th IIRA World Congress, Bologna.

Galin A. (1998), *Into the unknown or the Janus syndrome? The possible darker side of managing the humam resource in small manufacturing enterprises*, in Proceedings of the 11th IIRA World Congress, Bologna.

Genda Y. (1998), *Job gains and losses in Japan: a comparison with Italy*, in Japan Labor Bulletin, january, p. 4 ss.

Green F., Zanchi L. (1997), *Trends in the training of male and female workers in the United Kindgom*, in British Journal of Industrial Relations, vol. 35, N. 4, p. 635 ss.

Goetschy J. (1998), *European integration and industrial relations developments*, in Proceedings of the 11th IIRA World Congress, Bologna.

Goetchy J., Pochet P. (1997) *The Treaty of Amsterdam: a new approach to employment and social affairs?*, in Transfer, N. 3, p. 607 ss.

Gollan P., Davis E.M. (1998), *The implementation of HRM best practice: beyond rethoric*, in Proceedings of the 11th IIRA World Congress, Bologna.

Golzio L. (1998), *The organizational forms and the human resource management in the small firms: the Italian experience*, in Proceedings of the 11th IIRA World Congress, Bologna.

Goodijk (1998), *Corporate governance and workers' participation*, in Proceedings of the 11th IIRA World Congress, Bologna.

Grozdanic S.S. (1998), *Pluralist industrial relations and democratic development in central and eastern Europe-Recent trends and perspectives*, in Proceedings of the 11th IIRA World Congress, Bologna.

Grozdanic, Djordjevic, Djekic, *Development of SME in Serbia*, in Proceedings of the 11th IIRA World Congress, Bologna.

Gunnigle P. (1995), *Collectivism and management of industrial relations in greenfield sites*, in Human Resource Management Journal, vol. 5, N. 3, p. 24 ss.

Haddad C (1998), *Labor participation in modernization at small and mid-size firms: research findings from the USA*, in Proceedings of the 11th IIRA World Congress, Bologna.

REFERENCES

Haines V., Guérin G., St-Onge S. (1998), *Part-time work in a work-family balancing context: impressions and workplace effects*, in Proceedings of the 11th IIRA World Congress, Bologna.

Hayes J., Stuart M. (1996), *Does training matter? Employee experiences and attitudes*, in Human Resource Management Journal, vol. 6, N. 3, p. 3 ss.

Hanami T. (1997), *Globalization of employment and social clauses*, in Japan Institute of Labour Bulletin, february, p. 4 ss;

Hassel A. (1998), *Interest variety and organisational cartels: pluralist versus corporatist forms of trade union organisation in Germany and the UK*, in Proceedings of the 11th IIRA World Congress, Bologna.

Hepple B. (1997), *New approaches to international labour legislation*, in Industrial Law Journal, vol. 26, N. 4, p. 353 ss.

Houseman S.N. (1995), *Job growth and the quality of jobs in the US economy*, in Labour, special issue, p. 893 ss.

Iankova E.A. (1998), *Transitions to democracy and market economy: transformative corporatism in eastern Europe*, in Proceedings of the 11th IIRA World Congress, Bologna.

Kawakita T. (1996), *Japanese in-house job training and development*, in Japan Labour Bulletin, vol. 35, N. 4;

Keller B. (1998), *Public sector employment relations in Germany. In the Bermuda triangle of modernization, unification and Europeanization*, in Proceedings of the 11th IIRA World Congress, Bologna.

Kessler I., Purcell J., Shapiro J.C., *The evolution of new forms of employment relations in the UK public services: the limits of strategic choice*, in Proceedings of the 11th IIRA World Congress, Bologna.

Kester G., Oumou M. (1998), *Beyond the twentieth century: beyond tripartism. An African and European trade union challenge for democracy*, in Proceedings of the 11th IIRA World Congress, Bologna.

Knudsen H., Lind J. (1998), *The outcome of EU directives and the consequences for the system of market regulation in Denmark*, in

Proceedings of the 11th IIRA World Congress, Bologna.

Kollonay Lehoczky C. (1998), *Transitory countries — The common features of industrial relations*, in Proceedings of the 11th IIRA World Congress, Bologna.

Kreissig (1998), *Employee participation and new forms of management in East germany and Russia*, in Proceedings of the 11th IIRA World Congress, Bologna.

Jepsen M., Meulders D. (1998), *Are local initiatives the answer to unemployment?*, in Proceedings of the 11th IIRA World Congress, Bologna.

Leftwich H.M. (1998), *Union structural and strategy choices: the challenge of a global economy*, in Proceedings of the 11th IIRA World Congress, Bologna.

Lehto A.M., Sutela A. (1998), *Competitiveness and gendered changes in working life*, in Proceedings of the 11th IIRA World Congress, Bologna.

Macduffie J.P., Kochan T. A. (1995), *Do US firms invest less in human resources? Training in the world auto industry*, in Industrial Relations, vol. 34, N. 2, p. 147 ss.

Madsen J.S., Andersen S.K., *Modernisation and collective bargaining - a cross national study of the public sector in Europe*, in Proceedings of the 11th IIRA World Congress, Bologna.

Maeda N. (1998), *Life cycle effect of the extended household structure on women's labour force participation in Japan*, in Proceedings of the 11th IIRA World Congress, Bologna.

Mankidy J. (1998), *Quality of work-life and industrial relations: linking the inevitables*, in Proceedings of the 11th IIRA World Congress, Bologna.

Marginson P. (1998), *The Euro company and Euro collective bargaining*, in Proceedings of the 11th IIRA World Congress, Bologna.

Markey (1998), *Efficiency, new forms of management and participation*, in Proceedings of the 11th IIRA World Congress, Bologna.

Markey, Pomfret (1998), *Management attitudes to consultation in Australia and the USA*, in Proceedings of the 11th IIRA World

REFERENCES

Congress, Bologna.

Marsden D. (1998), *New and old sources of labour market segmentation*, in Proceedings of the 11th IIRA World Congress, Bologna.

Matey M. (1998), *Social dialogue. Tripartite model in central and eastern Europe: example of Poland*, in Proceedings of the 11th IIRA World Congress, Bologna.

Mitchell J.B.D. (1998), *Emergence of Convergence?*, in Proceedings of the 11th IIRA World Congress, Bologna.

Mitchell W.F., Burgess J. (1998), *Eight propositions for achieving full employment: an australian perspective*, in Proceedings of the 11th IIRA World Congress, Bologna.

Morgado Valenzuela E. (1998), *Nuevas expresiones de los vinculos entre las relaciones de trabajo y los procesos de integracion y libre comercio en America*, in Proceedings of the 11th IIRA World Congress, Bologna.

Morris G. (1998), *Restructuring public services: the implications for labour law*, in Proceedings of the 11th IIRA World Congress, Bologna.

Myrdal H.-G. (1998), *The ILO tripartite declaration on multinational enterprises. Its origins, achievements and prospects*, in Proceedings of the 11th World Congress, Bologna.

Munkeby, Handsen (1998), *Adding value through broad participation — The Norwegian enterprise development 2000 programme*, in Proceedings of the 11th IIRA World Congress, Bologna.

Nacsa B. (1998), *Creating new jobs through training and retraining: a failure in the present so far*, in Proceedings of the 11th IIRA World Congress, Bologna.

Navrbjerg S.E., Lubanski N. (1998), *Human resource management and trade unions: conflict or co-operation*, in Proceedings of the 11th IIRA World Congress, Bologna.

Noble C. (1997), *International comparisons of training policies*, in Human Resource Management Journal, vol. 7, n. 1, p. 5 ss.

O' Kelly (1998), *Direct participation and new forms of work organisation in Europe*, in Proceedings of the 11th IIRA World Congress, Bologna.

Oaklander H. (1998), *The new unemployment in the United States*, in Proceedings of the 11th IIRA World Congress, Bologna.

Osterman P. (1995), *Skill, training and work organization in american establishments*, in Industrial Relations, vol. 34, N. 2, p. 125.

Pant R.M. (1998), *Globalisation, competitiveness and social justice: a study of selected Indian public sector units (PSUs)*, in Proceedings of the 11th IIRA World Congress, Bologna.

Picot G. (1998), *Training, computer technology and international competition*, in Proceedings of the 11th IIRA World Congress, Bologna.

Purcell K. (1998), *Flexible employment and equal opportunities: compatible or contradictory?*, in Proceedings of the 11th IIRA World Congress, Bologna.

Ramsay H. (1998), *Gender & democracy at work*, in Proceedings of the 11th IIRA World Congress, Bologna.

Raso Delgue J. (1998), *El dialogo social y las politicas de adjuste en America Latina a la vigilia del siglo XXI*, in Proceedings of the 11th IIRA World Congress, Bologna.

Refeldth U. (1998), *Le retour des pactes sociaux et du néocorporatisme en Europe*, in Proceedings of the 11th IIRA World Congress, Bologna.

Regini M. (1998), *Different trajectories of social concertation in 1990s Europe*, in Proceedings of the 11th IIRA World Congress, Bologna.

Sarfati H. (1998), *The labour market flexibility vs. jobs: a challenge for social dialogue*, in Proceedings of the 11th IIRA World Congress, Bologna.

Simonyi A. (1998), *New models of professional training and changing labour relations in Hungary*, in Proceedings of the 11th IIRA World Congress, Bologna.

Sinclair D.M. (1996), *The importance of gender for participation in and attitudes to trade unionism*, in Industrial Relations Journal, vol. 27, N. 3, p. 239 ss.

Singh R. (1997), *Equal opportunities for men and women in the EU: a commentary*, in Industrial Relations Journal, vol. 28, N.

REFERENCES

1, p. 68 ss.

Sonder L., Hosking B. (1998), *Waterfront reform in Australia; domestic conflict and the internationalisation of industrial disputes*, in Proceedings of the 11th IIRA World Congress, Bologna.

Standing G. (1997), *Globalization, labour flexibility and insecurity: the era of market regulation*, in European Journal of Industrial Relations, vol. 3, N. 1, p. 7 ss.

Stuart M. (1996), *The industrial relations of training: a reconsideration of training arrangements*, in Industrial Relations Journal, vol. 27, N. 3, p. 253 ss.

Suwa Y. (1998), *Career is property: basic strategy or impossible dream?*, in Proceedings of the 11th IIRA World Congress, Bologna.

Tallard M. (1998), *La formation, point d'ancrage de la construction des compromis sociaux depuis 1970*, in Proceedings of the 11th IIRA World Congress, Bologna.

Tilly C. (1997), *Arresting the decline of good jobs in the USA?*, in Industrial Relations Journal, vol. 28, N. 4, p. 269 ss.

Traxler F. et al. (1998), *Globalisation, collective bargaining and performance*, in Transfer, vol. 3, N. 4, p. 787 ss.

Traxler F. (1998), *Collective bargaining between competitiveness and social justice*, in Proceedings of the 11th IIRA World Congress, Bologna.

Trebilcock A. (1998), *What future for social clauses? Differing institutional approaches*, in Proceedings of the 11th IIRA World Congress, Bologna.

Valkenburg B., Zoll R. (1995), *Modernization, individualization and solidarity: two perspectives on european trade unions today*, in European Journal of Industrial relations, vol. 1, N. 1, p. 119 ss.

Vincent C. (1998), *Genèse du sistème français de formation professionnelle continue: entre Etat et partenaires sociaux*, in Proceedings of the 11th IIRA World Congress, Bologna.

Visser J. (1998), *Globalization and informalization of labour: is there an organized response?*, in Proceedings of the 11th IIRA World Congress, Bologna.

Vodovnik Z. (1998), *The role of the State in promoting social dialogue (The different role in EU and eastern countries)*, in Proceedings of the 11th IIRA World Congress, Bologna.

Weber C.L., Verma A. (1998), *The 'flexibility' of small and medium-sized establishments: evidence from Canadian establishments*, in Proceedings of the 11th IIRA World Congress, Bologna.

Wong C. et al. (1997), *Management training in small and medium-sized enterprises: methodological and conceptual issues*, in International Journal of Human Resource Management, vol. 8, N. 1, p. 44 ss.

Wulf-Mathies M. (1995), *The Structural Funds and employment*, in Transfer, vol. 1, N. 4, p. 533 ss.

Zammit (1998), *Efficiency vs democracy in the workplace. Self-management at Malta drydocks-A postscript*, in Proceedings of the IIRA World Congress, Bologna.

The Implementation of the Amsterdam Treaty with regard to Employment: Co-ordination or Convergence?

Marco BIAGI

1. Introduction: A fundamental question

The subject of this paper is a first examination of the implementation of the new Treaty of Amsterdam title on employment. Taking into consideration the first year of the early implementation of the Treaty itself (with regard to the formal ratification), the theme will be discussed focusing on the question of the essence of this first trial run of implementation. In other words, one might wonder whether we are confronted simply with a co-ordination of the Member States' employment policies or rather with a logic of convergence triggered by the Commission's proposals and sustained (at least in part) by the decisions made by the Council and the European Council.

The question does not hold a formal value only but assumes a fundamental significance. The first implementing phases of a Community Treaty tend to acquire the value of a precedent, which if not binding then certainly of notable importance for the subsequent application of the provisions contained in it. Despite the fact that at first glance the terms "co-ordination" and "convergence" might appear similar in meaning, while not clashing, I intend to highlight this distinction of terms, and clarify that the dramatic urgency regarding employment in Europe has determined two exceptional practices; one unequivocal, the other not openly declared but equally practised. In the first case here, I refer to the early implementation of a Treaty not yet in force; in the second to an effective limitation of the autonomy of Member States. It is evident that while the former practice is, by its nature, of transitory importance, the latter could become established hereafter affirming a competence of the Community authorities possibly beyond the limits foreseen by the Treaty.

In order to answer the question at hand I will proceed firstly with a reading of the literal provisions of the new Treaty, drawing from them the first hermeneutic indications. Therefore, it seems necessary to monitor the implementing procedure and what will happen with the interaction among the different Community institutions and with the national authorities, above all examining the dialogue with the Italian government. Then I will look at the present practice and will offer an examination a year after the signing of the Treaty. Lastly, I will finish highlighting the fact that one cannot speak of simple co-ordination but rather about a policy of convergence, even if this policy is still in the early stages, which is in line with the spirit of the new Community provisions.

Some objections could be raised as to the role exercised by the European Commission that sometimes seems to have taken on a role of censor (regarding the employment policies of single governments) which was not provided in the Treaty. This role instead of being a stimulus might create obstacles in the good running of the internal policies, rather than making it easy the practice of multilateral monitoring among the Member States. It is therefore this multilateral peer pressure that could lead to a logic of convergence and thus, in the years to come, result in a new chapter of developments that are mature and convincing.

2. The new provisions of the Treaty: various inspirations in one Title

The new article 125 (following the numbering of the consolidated version of Treaties), begins establishing that "Member States and the Community shall, in accordance with this title, work towards developing a coordinated strategy for employment...". The idea is confirmed by the following article 126.2 where we can read that "Member States having regard to national practices related to the responsibilities of management and labour, shall regard promoting employment as a matter of common concern and shall coordinate their action in this respect within the Council..." Such a formula is confirmed again in article 127.1 which assigns the Community the task of contributing "to a higher level of employment by encouraging cooperation between Member States and by supporting and, if necessary, complementing their action", thus guaranteeing in this context that "the competences of Member States shall be respected". These provisions that concern the national prerogatives can be linked to the second part of article 129 which proclaims in conclusion that the coordinated measures on employment "...shall not include harmonisation of the laws and regulations of the Member States". This is a very precise rule of closure.

Together with this first normative *corpus*, substantial in its very nature, exists a second one concerning the procedure. Having recognised in the above-mentioned terms the autonomy of the Member States, the Treaty establishes in article 128. 2 that the Council "...shall each year draw up guidelines which the Member States shall take into account in their employment policies." In this respect, "each Member State shall provide the Council and the Commission with an annual report on the principal measures taken to implement its employment policy..." (article 128. 3). It is what has been termed *national action plans for employment* (NAP) upon which the Council "...shall each year carry out an examination of the implementation of the employment policies of the Member States in the light of the guidelines for employment". (article 128. 4).

According to the Treaty, in other words, the Council examines NAPs taking into consideration the guidelines already defined and "if it considers it appropriate in the light of that examination, make recommendations to Member States". (article 128. 4). This is a very important political sanction because it could place a national government into great difficulty internally with public opinion. One understands well the consequences of a possible "recommendation" bearing in mind the great impact that even

2. The new provisions of the Treaty: various inspirations in one Title

basic documents of analysis of the Commission assume, primarily with regard to the task of the Council (*see infra* § 4). In any case, as the subsequent article 128.5 provides, "on the basis of the results of that examination, the Council and the Commission shall make a joint annual report to the European Council on the employment situation in the Community and on the implementation of the guidelines for employment".

Curiously the norm under examination puts at the beginning (article 128.1) what should logically come after that is summarised. Besides receiving the yearly report of the Council and the Commission, the "European Council shall each year consider the employment situation in the Community and adopt conclusions thereon" which then serves the Council in defining the guidelines for the following year. The cycle repeats in this way every year. It seems that only one hypothesis can be determined - limiting the national sovereignty i.e. the Council deciding that a Member State has distanced itself too far from the guidelines established regarding employment. But if the act of handing out recommendation (obviously decided without the consensus of the Member State concerned and hence adopted by a majority Council) were so, it would result in an *extrema ratio* of rare practicability.

The logic of co-ordination or co-operation is better highlighted in the third part of the Title in question where the two final rules deal with the moment of multilateral collaboration. So article 129 gives the Council the power to "adopt incentive measures designed to encourage cooperation between Member States and to support their action in the field of employment through initiatives aimed at developing exchanges of information and best practices...". Mention is made of "comparative analysis" and the need to promote "innovative approaches", evaluating the experiences accomplished and making reference to "pilot projects". The significance of the above mentioned norms is made more consistent with the opening expressions of the Title that recall a spirit of collaboration: exchanges of experiences, work in common, comparison in research of the most efficient measures

In the same way we can evaluate the creation of the Employment Committee (article 130) that has an advisory function which is called upon to promote a co-ordination among Member States regarding employment matters. In this early phase of implementation of the Treaty the Committee, made up of two members from each Member States, plus the Commission, coincides with the Employment and Labour Market Committee set up by the Council decision of December 20 1996. It is superfluous to refer into details to this decision as the Treaty of Amsterdam simply reflects its content. Such a committee (in place since January 1997) fulfils the task of monitoring the employment situation and employment policies in the Member States and the Community. In addition the Committee may "formulate opinions at the request of either the Council or the commission or on its own initiative..." (article 130).

Therefore it is evident that with the Title on Employment of the Amsterdam Treaty there is a co-existence of rules characterised by a certain diversity of thought: some are inspired by a general philosophy of co-operation, whereas others indicate what is necessary in terms of joint action (the guidelines) and having sometimes a sanctioning effect (the recommendation handed out eventually to one of the Member States). Finally some instrumental indications exist to accomplish the collaborative moment, exemplifying forms of co-operation and identifying one instrument (the Employment Committee). It is not surprising that all this is producing a practice that is difficult to evaluate.

3. From Amsterdam to Luxembourg and beyond: the first semester of implementation

The European Council of Amsterdam (June 16 1997) adopted a resolution on "Growth and employment" in which (§ 6) the Heads of State and Prime Ministers were in favour of the immediate implementation of the newly signed Treaty before the ratification of the Member States. Even though agreeing with this important political option, caused by the dramatic state of unemployment in the European Union, one cannot help but notice that from a strictly legal point of view we are dealing with a "very controversial procedure" (Weiss 1998, p. 9). A kind of emergency procedure that should have been administered with high caution.

The Commission - highly skilled and convincing in performing its various functions in social affairs - already managed on October 1 1997 (COM (97) 497 final) to advance its own proposal for the 1998 employment guidelines. In that document the main points were presented that in a few months were to become the measures addressed to the Member States, above all the four "pillars", i. e. entrepreneurship, employability, adaptability and equal opportunity.

In particular the Commission's document had already identified the main objectives to propose to Member States. Shortly afterwards these objectives have been formalised at the European Council on Employment (Luxembourg November 20-21 1997) which defined the guidelines for 1998. Firstly, the commitment of tackling youth unemployment and to fight long term unemployment, provided in guideline 1 ("Member States will ensure that every unemployed young person is offered a new start before reaching six months of unemployment in the form of training, retraining, work practice, a job or other employability measure") and in guideline 2 ("Member States will ensure that unemployed adults are also offered a fresh start before reaching twelve months of unemployment in the form of training, retraining, work practice, a job or other employability measure, or more generally, by accompanying vocational guidance").

Furthermore the Commission concentrated right from the beginning on the transition from passive to active measures on employment. So it was established the principle

3. From Amsterdam to Luxembourg and beyond: the first semester of implementation

(destined to become guideline 3) according to which "Member States will endeavour to increase significantly the number of persons benefiting from active measures to improve their employability. In order to increase the numbers of unemployed who are offered training or similar measures, it will, in particular, fix a target, in the light of its starting situation, of gradually achieving the average of the three most successful Member States, and at least 20%".

It is worth remembering that the Commission's proposals and, subsequently, the decisions of the Luxembourg summit, included a large number of topics. The guidelines, as written in the formal document that listed them at the Council of Social Affairs on December 15 1997, number no less than 19. In the context of this paper, it is not necessary to go through all the guidelines, even though this might be of great interest.

It is however advisable to note that there is a clear difference between the first three guidelines, mentioned above and the others. The first case deals with obligations of a quantitative nature that Member States have decided to undertake. Whereas in the second one the term guideline reflects a simple indication. In other words the Commission, the European Council and the Council agreed to specify some criteria of convergence alluding to the provisions from the Maastricht Treaty relative to the creation of the Monetary Union.

Thus the three "criteria of convergence" regarding employment are as follows:

(1) to offer every young person, before reaching 6 months of unemployment, the possibility of entering the labour market by way of training or other employability measures;
(2) to offer every adult, before reaching 12 months of unemployment, an equal opportunity;
(3) to increase the number of people who benefit active employment policies including at least 20% of the unemployed.

This is perhaps the most important moment of the implementation of the Amsterdam Treaty in the field of employment. The Commission had no hesitation whatsoever in proposing a strategy of clear convergence, gaining insight, at least in part, from the experience of the Monetary Union model. At the political level, both the European Council and the Council (not to mention the Employment Committee that analysed the proposals) accepted this decision, even if there was perhaps no full knowledge of the binding (and very demanding) nature of the tasks undertaken with the first three guidelines.

The Italian government agreed fully with this decision. It was hoped in fact that "the strategy of employment co-ordination established by the Amsterdam Treaty transforms into a plan of convergence" (Competition and social cohesion in Europe, 1998). And to demonstrate this point

3. From Amsterdam to Luxembourg and beyond: the first semester of implementation

further, it added: "It furthermore deals with developing gradually but with certainty a culture of convergence in a way not dissimilar to what happened and is happening in economic and monetary policies". This is therefore unconditional support, although not completely aware of all the subsequent effects and obligations. Further on in the same document it is mentioned that "one will not necessarily have to or will be able to apply indicators of quantitative order". Not only this, but it added that the three guidelines recalled (and at that point proposed by the Commission) should not have impeded "the Member States from independent research in order to achieve an appropriate balance between preventive action and action of reinsertion of the long term unemployed, as well as the discretion in the identification of measures to be adopted (work experience, training and others)".

In any case the Social Affairs Council of December 15, 1997 (to which an express mandate from the European Council of Luxembourg, December 12-13 1997, was assigned: for the second time in a matter of weeks the Heads of States and Governments looked into this topic, although limiting itself to the confirmation that had been established in the summit at the end of November) was very clear in requesting Member States not only to observe the logic of measurability of the first three objectives but also in proposing "national objectives quantified whenever possible and appropriate". And it indicated the objective of presenting "a national plan of action for employment to communicate annually to the Council and the

Commission", along with a "report on the ways of putting such a plan into practice". It was the Employment Committee agreeing with the Commission to present the plans before April 15 1998, while the date for delivering an implementation report was fixed for July 31 1998.

4. The preparation of the National Action Plans for Employment and the Cardiff European Council

A few months were conceded to the Member States for the preparation of the NAPs; in practice from mid-January to mid-April. While the Treaty of Amsterdam speaks expressly of the guidelines (article 128. 2), the concept of detailed plans prepared conforming to the guidelines represents a practice decided by the Council on the Commission's proposal. It was not easy for Member States to reorganise all their employment policies and to present them drafted according to the new guidelines. Although using different technical expressions, the NAPs consisted of documents summarising measures *already* adopted or, in any case, decided by the Member States.

It is precisely this first phase of implementation that has in fact demonstrated that, in the first semester, Member States can no longer modify the general lines of employment policies in order to answer the input of the Community guidelines defined at the end of the previous year, even though the problem may have arisen acutely during the first year. If in future the guidelines, even revised ones, do not undergo substantial alterations, the national Governments will be able to consider them when

4. The preparation of the National Action Plans for Employment and the Cardiff European Council

styling the national programmes at the beginning of autumn in the context of the budget of the incoming year.

For the preparation of the Italian NAP, the Commission proposed a preliminary meeting with the Italian government that was held in Rome on February 19, 1998. Similar meetings were organised with other Member States. This element of assistance or of support is here reported to emphasise the task undertaken by the Commission in this first phase. The intensity of the Commission's action is surely explainable by the success of the above mentioned communication of October 1 1997, obtained at the European Council and the Council: a success rarely achieved, at least to such a great extent, and that explains the subsequent dynamism in the first semester of 1998.

The national plans for employment were examined in mid-May 1998 at a special meeting of the Employment Committee to which the Commission presented a communication (From Guidelines to Action: the National Action Plan for Employment) where there was a first evaluation of NAPs. In this case too it is not my intention to examine the merit of the document. It is of more interest to emphasise that the Commission mentioned, in relation to different guidelines as implemented by various NAPs, those Member States that had offered a description of the most convincing measures on the subject. Although not making judgmental comparisons, the absence of reference by the Commission to a Member State in relation to one specific point was considered an implicit criticism. This type of approach has generated, in Italy's case, an internal controversy almost as if the Commission had already decided to propose to the Council a recommendation to remind Italy of its Community obligations regarding employment (Rampini 1998 ; Biagi 1998).

The European Commission regretted that "the majority of NAP had been drafted as documents to formulate general policies rather than as operative instruments". Furthermore it observed that only four Member States (France, Spain, Luxembourg and Great Britain) had understood fully the sense of the *preventive approach* in identifying the implementing measures of guidelines 1, 2 and 3, so as to affect not so much the stock of unemployment but rather the flows.

The Commission again took the opportunity to underline (in the context of a very detailed analysis obviously referring to all guidelines), with particular reference to guideline 3 that a number of Member States had not offered convincing descriptions of measures adopted in their policies. Since once again the governments that had instead presented a convincing NAP were mentioned, it is evident that the Commission was addressing those national cases that had not yet come up to scratch.

It is not difficult to understand that this kind of exercise puts on national governments a very strong pressure. The perspective that Community authorities pass a nega-

4. The preparation of the National Action Plans for Employment and the Cardiff European Council

tive judgement (above all the Commission, since it is unlikely that the Council reaches such a conclusion) becomes a deterrent for national Governments.

In reference to this I would like to point out another kind of practice, much closer to the logic of co-ordination than convergence. Obviously all NAPs circulate within the Employment Committee. These documents are full of examples, information and thus, highly useful. In the above mentioned meeting of mid-May 1998, an exercise of significant interest was carried out, whereby there was a kind of cross examination among Member States. Italy was questioned by representatives of the Netherlands and Portugal while later Italy participated in questioning Belgium and Germany with the collaboration of Sweden and Spain. A very interesting discussion followed that saw all representatives of the Employment Committee dedicated to the exchange of the best practices.

The Employment Committee, in analysing the NAPs, did not address individually the Member States but made general order evaluations. In the document drafted in preparation of the Cardiff European Council, the Employment Committee underlined the limits of the experience in progress, emphasising for example that the efforts of Member States regard above all the employability and entrepreneurship, with a lesser importance given to adaptability and equal opportunities. Not only but the Committee underlined that the distribution of resources in relation to specific guidelines was vague in many respects, but also that they were not sufficiently specified. These indications were very meaningful, but no comparison or classification among Member States was made.

As the meeting of Cardiff (15 and 16 June 1998) approached, international observers expressed their opinions about the experiment in motion (Smith 1998), correctly defining it as a system of peer pressure finalised to coordinate the employment policies of Member States.

The European Council of Cardiff dedicated a large part of the work to the theme ofemployment. In the Presidency Conclusions we read that, "the progress achieved in this field delights everyone and urges Member States to continue the concrete application of the plans of actions as quickly as possible with a continual evaluation and updating". Apart from the inadequate expression used by the drafters (it is difficult to be delighted about the progress achieved concerning employment in the European Union), the message is to continue the implementation of NAPs. It is equally important to remember the auspice addressed to the Social Affairs Council and the ECOFIN Council which "should continue to collaborate so to exchange the best practices, to develop a common evaluation of Member States actions plans for employment and to examine the employment guidelines for 1998 in preparation of the European Council of Vienna and future European Councils". No mention was made about the evaluations of single NAP at the European Council of Vienna due to be held in December 1998.

5. From Cardiff to Vienna: monitoring or evaluating the national policies?

In the second half of 1998 it will be possible to answer the basic question (convergence or co-ordination). In fact by July 31, the Commission has requested the Member States a report about the implementation of NAPs. Such an implementation report will constitute, along with the NAP, the "annual report on the principal measures taken to implement its employment policy in the light of the guidelines for employment" which each Member State must provide the Council and the Commission (article 128. 3). This means that, at least in the first year of application, there are two documents to bring to the attention of the Commission, which will then, on this basis, release its own communication on October14and will help the Council with the preparation of the joint report (article 128. 5).

It seems useful to speak more in depth about this point. The Commission in fact taking note of NAPs, drafted a questionnaire addressed to various Member States in order to make it easier the preparation of their own implementation report. Distributed on June 15 1998, the national governments once again had only a few weeks to draft the new document, after further bilateral meetings with the Commission (with the Italian government on June 26) to illustrate the same questionnaire and to clarify bilaterally the exercise in progress. The questionnaire is divided in two parts: in the first there are questions posed to all Member States; in the second the questions are addressed to each Member State in particular. In the former case the themes dealt with are of a general character (e. g. the role of social parties, transformation of NAP into budget commitments, contribution of the Social Fund to the financing of the various measures, methods of monitoring in the application of the plan and the likes).

The second part of the questionnaire (as regards Italy) is dedicated to the requests of specific clarification. Again as an example, what the Regions' role will be in the programme of personalised interviews of a preventive nature for the long term unemployed (guidelines 1 and 2), following the institutional devolution from national to regional authorities of public employment services as pre-announced in the NAP. From other questions arise the problem of appropriateness of the measures adopted as instruments in the fight against unemployment (e. g. training and work contracts) with reference to the fact that guideline 1 requires the adoption of measures that confront the problem of the young unemployed within the first six months. In other words the fact is challenged as to whether a series of measures, even if listed under the first three guidelines, are actually offered to those who have been unemployed for a period longer than the 12 months stipulated. It is easy to understand immediately that beyond the request of clarification, the Commission exerts a highly crucial role, not hesitating to highlight the possible inadequacies of the measures adopted observing the decisions taken at the Luxembourg summit.

The suggestion is to conform and adapt domestic employment policies to the guidelines agreed at the Community level. The purpose is completely transparent in the general part of the questionnaire (i. e. common to all Member States), where it is asked to distinguish better between the initiatives launched before starting the drafting of the NAP, those announced in the same NAP and finally those applied after the adoption of NAP. Each Member State should operate such tripartition in the context of an employment policy arranged between Autumn 1197 and Summer 1998. It seems that national government could be in trouble to respond to this kind of requests. For example in the Italian case only in autumn 1998, in preparation of the 1999 budgetary law, it will be possible to adopt new measures in order to better conform to the 1998 employment guidelines. Such a problem (typical of many Member States) is considered as real by the Commission.

From the outline of the 1998 joint report on employment, as circulated by the Commission in July 1998, it seems that this report will deal with each Member State in a very detailed way. A minimum of at least three pages will be dedicated to each Member State and the national situation will be examined, focusing also on the capability of accomplishing the NAP objectives.

6. Eurowatching or convergence?

From what has been said it seems difficult to agree with the opinion (Blanpain 1998) that the Treaty of Amsterdam would not have brought about any innovation whatsoever with respect to Community competence on employment, legitimising once again a kind of Eurowatching, i. e. a strategy of observation incapable of influencing the national choices. To the point of requesting the non ratification of the Treaty for fear that, conversely, it would consolidate anti-European options.

The reality is that what is happening is certainly a very interesting experiment (Goetschy, Pochet 1997) and that following the summit of Luxembourg a significant impact is foreseeable (Barbier 1998). A clear step forward, following the first monitoring strategies agreed in the fundamental Essen European Council (Auer 1998).

The reservations expressed in this paper do not concern the fact that the co-ordination of the national employment policies have turned out to be a pursuit of a convergence among Member States. Nor are doubts raised about the interesting exercise of benchmarking that, thanks again to the services of the Commission, is carried out in relation to different themes (above all in the Employment Committee), even if the search of indicators for this kind of evaluation has not already achieved the necessary results. Support and agreement cannot be offered to the methodology adopted by the European Commission, based on a sort of ranking system in the evaluation of various Member States in implementing the 1998 employment guidelines. It is advisable that this line is reviewed, not only since it is not confirmed in the Treaty, but also because it could be harmful to the development of the convergence process itself.

References:

Auer P. (1998), Monitoring of Labour Market Policy in EU Member States, in Auer P. (ed.), Employment Policies in Focus, MISEP, Berli, p. 232 ss.

Barbier J.-C. (1998), Can European Union's involvement in employment policies in Europe be enhanced?, in Proceedings of the 11 th IIRA World Congress, Bologna.

Biagi M. (1998), Lavoro, le promesse della ricetta Italia, in la Repubblica, 3 giugno 1998.

Blanpain R. (1998), Il Trattato di Amsterdam e oltre : la fine del modello sociale europeo?, in Diritto delle relazioni industriali, vol. VIII, N. 1, p. 11 ss.

Competitività e coesione sociale in Europa : per una politica di convergenza sull' occupazione. Posizione del Governo italiano in preparazione del Consiglio Europeo straordinario sull' occupazione, in Diritto delle relazioni industriali, vol. VIII, N. 1, p. 119 ss.

Consiglio Europeo straordinario sull' occupazione (1998), Lussemburgo, 20/21 novembre 1997, Conclusioni della presidenza, in Diritto delle relazioni industriali, vol. VIII, N. 1, p. 122 ss.

Goetschy J., Pochet P. (1997), The Treaty of Amsterdam : a new approach to employment and social affairs?, in Transfer, N. 3, p. 607 ss.

Preparation of the Cardiff European Council (1998), Opinion of the Employment and Labour Market Committee on the 1998 National Employment Action Plans, 8733/98 Limite.

Rampini F. (1998) ; L'Europa accusa, in la Repubblica, 30 maggio 1998.

Smith M. (1998), Sign of progress in EU campaign for more jobs, in Financial Times, 12 giugno 1998.

Weiss M. (1998), Il Trattato di Amsterdam e la politica sociale, in Diritto delle relazioni industriali, vol. VIII, N. 1, p. 7 ss.

Towards a Revolutionised Working Life

The Information Society and the Transformation
of the Workplace
The Japanese *kaisha* as a Harbinger of the Future?

Reinhold FAHLBECK

1. Introduction. Purpose

This article will present thoughts about the possible design of working life if we were faced with the option of "starting from zero". More precisely, the purpose is to ponder the design of working life in the era of the information society. The article presents a scenario, an attempt to pinpoint the future. The article is not confined to "employers-employees" but covers working life in its entirety.

The author tries to be independent of prevailing labour market structures and perspectives and also of the traditions that have shaped today's structures. To the extent possible the author tries to discuss issues free from links to the present system. Evidently, it is no easy task, indeed an impossible one, to adopt a completely independent stance but the ambition is nevertheless to present a perspective that is as unbiased as possible.

The article will use the terms "buyers of labour" and "sellers of labour". In so doing the article is completely value neutral and the terms are used is a strictly technical way, with no hidden meaning. Those who ask for manpower are "buyers of labour" and those who offer their own labour are "sellers". Reference can be made to employers looking for employees but any other kind of demand for or supply of labour is also included, for example independent contractors, contract work, subcontracting or hiring out or manpower.

Other terms would be preferable. The "employer-employee" dichotomy is not suitable, however, for the simple reason that the article is not confined to employment relationships. The dichotomy *"value provider—value receiver"* (alternatively *"value seller—value buyer"* or *"value giver—value taker"*) would be more appropriate than "buyer of labour—seller of labour". Those who work do provide/create/give/sell new and additional value whereas their opposite party receives/buys/takes these newly created values. However, introducing such new terminology might confuse the reader and create difficulties rather than enlighten.

2. Points of departure

Three points of departure set the article in motion. These are closely related. They can be looked upon as describing a basic pattern for the possibilities for and the degree of independence and self-realisation of individuals in working life.

2. Points of departure

Table 1 illustrates how buyers and sellers of labour interact professionally and privately in two main respects, i. e. if they live and work together and how their legal and personal relations are structured.

Table 1. Relationship between "buyers" and "sellers" of work

	Agrarian Society	Industrialised Society	Information Society
Where?	live and work together. work and private life intertwined	live separately but work together. work and private life separate	live and work separately. work and private life partly intertwined
How?	status-relationship. work : family duty. strongly hierarchical	contractual relationship. work : commodity. strongly impersonal	contractual relationship. work : transfer of knowledge. strongly mutual

Table 2 illustrates what factors have represented value during the same three phases and how these factors find expression.

Table 2. Factors representing wealth and value-adding factors

	Agrarian Society	Industrialised Society	Information Society
Wealth factor	land (real estate)	capital (money)	people
Value-adding factor	manual work : muscle power	combination of means of production : machine handlingpower	knowledge and creativity : brain power

Table 3 illustrates the role of capital during these same three periods.

Table 3. Capital

	Agrarian Society	Industrialised Society	Information Society
Owners	family	buyers of work	sellers of work
Shape	land	monetary capital (physical capital)	human capital (intellectual capital)
Purpose	maximising family survival	maximising monetary capital	maximising quality of life

The tables call for some explanations. The agrarian society is the society where a majority of the working population is rural and depends for its livelihood on farming, forestry and fishing. In the industrialised society the majority of the population is engaged in manual and/or mechanical manufacturing industry. The information society, finally, is a society where the majority of the working population is engaged in clerical work and service work. Heavy dependence on data and information technology is characteristic features of the information society and the same is increasingly true with manufacturing industry as well.

Table 1 focuses on the individual relationship between buyers and sellers of labour. A characteristic feature of the agrarian society is the close personal relationship between them and also the strict subservience of the seller to the "master". The industrialised society sees a depersonalisation of the relationship but the seller remains sub-

2. Points of departure

jected to a strict regime of buyer supremacy despite the fact that the seller can sever the bonds at any time by simply terminating the contract. In the information society personal contacts and closeness are based on what the parties agree upon at any given time. So is their interdependence but typically there is a close professional relationship although this relationship is mutual and the seller is frequently holding the trumps. Work at common work sites depends less on personal interaction and increasingly on co-operation based on data and information technology. Distance work is becoming increasingly prevalent, in particular teleworknig.

Table 2 illustrates factors that represent and create wealth in economic life. Land is what exists in the agrarian society, that and nothing else. Cultivating land creates wealth, that and nothing else. In the industrialised society money becomes the factor that represents wealth; "everything" can be bought and sold for money on a free market. A complicated interaction between the means of production (raw material, work and capital, i.e. money, real estate and equipment) emerges. In the information society capital (i.e. money and equipment) becomes less important and the importance of raw material is drastically reduced. Knowledge and creativity are primarily what count. These are primarily individual. Though organisations are also said to possess knowledge this is so basically only in the sense that individuals are knowledgeable and that structures are created that allow individual knowledge and creativity to come to the fore.

Table 3 highlights various aspects of the role, form and purpose of capital. Private ownership hardly exists at all in agrarian societies. Those who "own" the family land at any given time are more often than not prohibited from selling it on the open market. By and large capital is not marketable and closely attached to the family. The transition to industrialism means that capital is liberated in the sense that it becomes marketable and offered at a free market. Capital represents power and is typically restricted to a fairly small stratum of society. The information society sees a further liberalisation of capital and its dissemination to an increasingly wide part of the population. Everyone becomes a "capitalist". The aggregated power of traditional capitalists over "capital" diminishes since the relative role of capital in the shape of such wealth that can be dominated by individuals, primarily money and equipment, becomes increasingly less significant. Possession and control of capital is increasingly atomised as knowledge and creativity increasingly comes to represent the relevant capital.

In a way the three tables mirror a historical development. Still, all these three kinds of societies are represented on our planet today. All countries have a past as agrarian. Many still are, indeed accounting for well over fifty per cent of world population. Some countries have stepped into the information society. Most OECD-countries belong here, with the exception of the last admitted countries (e.g. Mexico or the three countries in central Europe).

2. Points of departure

The tables are close related. In a more profound sense they all mirror the degree of independence enjoyed by individuals in society. Thus seen the three tables represent a movement from a state of less independence towards a state of more independence. It is, to phrase it differently, an evolution towards increased liberty, a kind of human liberation. This raised level of independence in turn reflects the fact that average wealth increases as economies move from the agrarian towards the information society. Increased private prosperity results in a bigger potential for independence. The tables illustrate this process of liberalisation.

Elements from both the agrarian and the industrialised societies remain in the information society but their relative importance diminishes gradually. To an even greater extent than the industrial society a manifold of activities with radically divergent structures already has, and will increasing will, become the hallmark of the information society. That, inter alia, means that the information society is a highly pluralist society.

The evolution towards the information society also means an evolution towards decentralisation and flexibilisation. Giant accumulations of capital either held by private individuals or invested in specific enterprises and projects are characteristic of the industrialised society. This, already in itself, represents both centralisation and standardisation. Knowledge, on the other hand, is primarily held by the many and knowledge is never completely standardised. As a result the spread of information that goes hand in hand with the information society already in itself represents decentralisation and flexibilisation, quite apart from such additional moves in that same direction that people living in information societies might deliberately decide to make.

3. The role of capital versus the role of work

Central to a discussion about the design of tomorrow's working life is the interplay between capital and work. This is neither new nor original. It has always been that way. However, the information society brings a new angle to the issue. The question is first and foremost which contribution to economic life, capital or work, is to be accorded priority?

The answer is quite simple, a truism perhaps even. Only work can create new values. Capital, regardless of shape-be that land, buildings, equipment or money-does not per se increase in value. Only when human work is added will an increase in value result. "Capital" in itself is dead. Nothing material has any intrinsic value, only work or the fruits of work can turn it into something of value. "Capital" is created by humans and ruled by human labour. The bulk of capital is collective, even if owned by private individuals or institutions, e.g. private investment funds or pension funds.

It most certainly is true that this ranking of capital and work is not always visible in actual life. As always before

3. The role of capital versus the role of work

capital still seemingly takes precedence over work. In agrarian and industrialised societies the fairly obvious principle of work's precedence over capital is rather fictitious, to put it mildly. That principle belongs to the lofty world of ethics-if at all recognised-rather than to the actual world of day-to-day realities. Individuals have always been in a critical position since the prime "capital" at their disposition are their bodies and muscles only and that "capital" is not all that valuable in most instances since it is uncomplicated and can easily be substituted. However, the evolution away from "muscle power" via "machine operation power" towards "brain power" represents a crucial change. To a great extent this shift also entails a shift in relative power and in the balance of power in society. Whenever the "capital" of sellers of labour is easily substitutable and consequently only scantily individualised buyers of labour enjoy a considerable advantage. The information society changes all that since the relevant "capital" increasingly is personal, vested in individual knowledge and creativity. These are far less substitutable. As a result the precedence of work over capital will become more easily understandable and recognisable.

Indeed, the dualism between capital and work is illusory. It is predicated on a chain of basic misunderstandings, i.e. (1) that capital is given precedence over work, that (2) work is considered from an economic angle only and that (3) work is looked upon as a means of production, a commodity.

"Business is the pursuit of the potential of human beings, who are the focal point of society. Capital is not money but people." That is part of the core message of a Japanese company when introducing its basic philosophy. The company further stresses that its equity is very small. Necessary capital can be borrowed so the role of equity is limited. "The ideal (equity) is zero and will not change in future, whatever business economic theories may say." The reason is that "capital rests in human beings". These ideas antedate the information society but seem well suited for it[1].

4. Whose Company?

Against this background the obvious question is: who owns the company, shareholders or those working for the company? From a legal perspective the answer is as easy as it is obvious in all countries based on private ownership and a market economy: the shareholders.

Who are they, the shareholders? Suffice here to state that those who work for the company are not shareholders in that capacity alone. Holding of shares and contribution of work are two different things. They can be combined

---

[1] Statements by Idemitsu Inc, one of the leading petroleum companies in Japan. The ideas are presented in a publication by the Asian Productivity Organization: *Top Management Forum: Human-Centered Management* (Tokyo, 1993, ISBN92-833-2130-8), at p8 and 74. It should be added that the idea that the ideal equity capital really is zero does not form part of the theme of this article. The quote from Idemitsu serves to illustrate the superiority of human capital over monetary capital.

4. Whose Company?

but they are not necessarily so.

The company belongs to the shareholders. But is that is satisfactory answer in a scenario for tomorrow's working life? Hardly. Though by all likelihood the legal answer will remain unaltered for the foreseeable future many considerations indicate that another answer would better suit the situation.

For decades after WW II companies have been looked upon as an arena for a number of actors, primarily shareholders/owners, employees (but not others working for the company), suppliers, customers, credit institutions and the government. Management is looked upon as a basically neutral actor whose task it was to strike a balance between these various actors and their often competing interests. The actors all have a relationship with the company but their contracts differ radically. The shareholders have a "soft" contract whereas the other actors have a "firm" contract in the sense that they are legally entitled to specific performance by the company of their claims whereas shareholders face the risk of non-performance. Shareholders, to put it differently, risk loosing their contributions, which is not the case with other actors. It is quite another matter that companies sometimes default on their obligations nevertheless, e.g. because of bankruptcy.

This model does not lack value but it threatens to obscure essential matters at the same time. A look at the typical big Japanese company provides an interesting way of approach. Just like everywhere else company law in Japan put shareholders firmly in command. For a variety of reasons companies are not run in accordance with existing company law, however. Though it is true that neither company law nor labour law in Japan provide for any far-reaching employee participation, much less actual power, in the running of companies, Japanese companies more often than not are effectively run by their employees and are de facto "employee owned".

Many, indeed most, big Japanese companies belong to a business group. Cross-ownership within the group is prevalent. At the same time no parent or holding company controls the group[2], every member company of the group instead holding shares in every other group member company. This environment has produced a kind of "employee governance".

Employee rule is obvious in a variety of ways. To mention just one, company boards present a splendid illustration[3]. Japanese company boards comprise a substantial

---

2) A ban on holding companies was introduced during the American occupation of Japan after the war; see e.g. Oda, Hiroshi, Japanese Law (Butterworths, London, 1992), p347 et seq.. The creation of the *keiretsu* can be regarded as a circumvention of the prohibition. However, the *keiretsu* produced a radically different result; no longer "one owns everyone and everything" but rather "everyone owns everybody and everything" or, perhaps cynically stated, "no one owns anyone or anything".

A cautious easing of the ban on holding companies was introduced in 1997.

number of members, some thirty people or even more. With few exceptions all members are career employees. The exceptional outsiders usually represent the bank, insurance and/or trading company of the group. The career members have worked all their professional life for the company, starting at the bottom of the ladder and working their way upwards. The younger among them are still active as line managers. With only some very rare exceptions the CEO is one of these career employees. To recruit a CEO from outside is virtually out of the question. Executive managers have very little contact with outside, non-group, shareholders. One reason is that few, if any, outside investor hold an important share of company equity. Quite understandably the loyalty of managers focuses on the working community that the company represents. Their professional achievements have all been devoted to that community and all their colleagues are part of it. In this sense executive management in reality represents the employee community rather than the shareholder community.

---

3) For discussions about the composition and size of Japanese company boards see e.g. Araki, T, Joint Consultation, *Comparative Labor Law Journal*, volume 15, 1994, Abegglen, J, & Stalk, G, KAISHA. The Japanese Corporation. How Marketing, Money, and Manpower Strategy, Not Management Style, Make the Japanese World Pace-Setters (Basic Books, New York, 1985), Clark, R, The Japanese Company (Yale University Press, 1979), Oda, H, Japanese Law (Butterworths, 1992) or Shirai, T, editor, Contemporary Industrial Relations in Japan (University of Wisconsin Press, 1983)

Can information society companies be expected to emulate this Japanese model? The Japanese model is in no way a response to the exigencies of or a consequence of the information society. It would seem, however, that the model is ideally suited for the information era. The model is a living expression of the fact that the employees are at the core of company life and that monetary capital must allow these "company members" to take precedence. It seems like a fair bet that those working for companies-"company members", as it were—will claim for themselves a role in company decision-making that reflects the crucial contribution of their knowledge and creativity.

How secure efficiency and control? How prevent complacency, cronyism, corruption and personal connections that trump the broader interests of the company, other actors or markets? How find necessary capital for company growth? How justify that members are given precedence over shareholders when shareholders—after all—do contribute capital that can be lost because of member decisions?

Members in companies where they have a strong, perhaps even decisive, influence are no less interested in efficiency than "outside" shareholders of a profit maximising type. Members want employment protection, good remuneration for their work, stimulating jobs. Members work primarily for themselves, not for "outside" shareholders. Typically, member involvement in the company is long-range. Internal models for competition and rewards can ensure that only those best qualified are promoted to the

4. Whose Company?

top. Members are also profit maximises, albeit putting quality of life maximising ahead of money maximising. In addition, product-, credit-and stock markets will be no less severe and implacable in making allocations here than elsewhere.

Crucial in order to legitimate and maintain strong, perhaps decisive, member influence is that member contribution and risk taking can be seen as more important to companies than that of shareholders. Shareholders contribute money and put that money at risk. The importance of their contribution is closely linked to the supply of capital and the risk involved. In times of shortage of capital or in turbulent times these contributions are noteworthy enough. However, the relative importance of monetary capital has diminished considerably and it can be expected that this trend continue concurrently with the continued advance of the information society. In addition, the legitimacy of shareholder capital has diminished drastically. Shareholder capital is overwhelmingly investment capital, not risk (or venture) capital properly. Funds, in particular pension funds, have increasingly become the dominant supplier of equity capital. The functional difference between suppliers of equity and other commodities has dwindled. So has the willingness on the part of most investors to take risks.

Concurrently, members' knowledge and creativity gain in importance and consequently their contribution to companies, both in absolute and in relative terms. The risk that members face is less economic and more personal than that of equity providers. Though it is true that members also face the risk of losing money when companies fail, such losses may be covered by state insurance schemes, e. g. insolvency insurance. The dominant risk for members deals with health, physical as well as mental. Lost capital can always be recreated. Lost health often cannot, and neither can lost enthusiasm and creativity. Often enough member losses are irretrievable and irreversible and thus much more painful that those of equity suppliers. Quite apart from the issue whether human enthusiasm, creativity and health may not perhaps be more important that capital in the first place!

5. The company and its members

Companies will increasingly rise and fall with their members. This is the main reason why it can presumed that members will demand to have a decisive influence over decisions in companies. But who are these members?

At the present time there seems to be a strong tendency towards a dualisation of members in companies. On the one hand there are those employed permanently, on full time and with mutual expectations that they will remain with the company for long periods of time. This is the core (primary) workforce. On the other hand there are all the others, the "atypical", peripheral or contingent workers (the secondary workforce)[4]. These members are employed- e.g. on fixed time contracts or as part-time employees-, temporary workers (hired-in people), self-employed people, contract workers or what not. They provide numerical flexibility. But increasingly they also provide knowledge, experience and expertise that are not otherwise available at the workplace. Long gone are the days when the atypical workers were predominantly unskilled performing only menial tasks[5].

In Japanese companies only core employees count. This model might spread but that would be neither desirable nor fortunate. Non-core people already account for a considerable portion of members and their share can be expected to increase. If "core employees" were the only members to be included in the group of influential members the legitimacy of member claims to a decisive role would be severely undermined.

But the risk for such an evolution must not be exaggerated. A growing portion of contingent members is highly creative people with specialised skills. It can hardly be expected that these people will put up with a shadowy role as secondary members.

---

4) It no longer makes much sense to call this workforce atypical, contingent, peripheral or secondary. The size and ubiquity of the 'atypical' workforce turns the designation into an anachronism. This workforce is neither atypical nor peripheral, contingent or secondary any longer.

5) For example, temporary work agencies are rapidly expanding into professional work, e.g. accounting, engineering or information technology. Even highly specialised areas like legal work have become niches for some temporary agencies. See e.g. articles on temporary agencies in Europe, Japan and the USA respectively in the International Herald Tribune, June 13-14, 1998, at p18.

This means that fresh and innovative thinking is called for to redefine the group of members that count. It can be expected that today's limitation to employees, in particular "core" employees, will be abandoned. There is a need for a new actor's model!

6. A new actor's model

In a study of labour market regulation and ways of functioning in the USA I arrived at the conclusion that it is suitable and pertinent in the US context to distinguish between a total of twelve actors (or constituents)[6]. They are: (1) ndividual employers (self-employed and those employing others), (2) employer organisations, (3) people looking for work, (4) employees, (5) union members, (6) unions, the public at large (third parties) in three distinct roles, i. e. as (7) consumers, as (8) producers (potential entrepreneurs/investors) and as (9) citizens, and finally the state, in turn appearing in three roles, as (10) executive, as (11) legislator and as (12) judiciary. All these actors take part in the balancing between competing interests in the labour market in a very conspicous way. US interest balancing considers all these actors in a very determined and deliberate way.

US thinking here might serve as a model. Of particular importance are the sensitive issues of the balancing of

---

[6] For a summary in English of this study see Fahlbeck, The Demise of Collective Bargaining in the USA. Reflections on the Un-American Character of American Labor Law, *Berkeley Journal of Employment and Labor Law*, Volume 15 (1994).

6. A new actor's model

shareholder versus member claims and the internal balancing inside the member group (actors 1—i.e. the self-employed—and 4 above).

With regard to shareholders a division into two groups looms at the horizon, i.e. passive and active shareholders or, in other words, investment shareholders and risk taking shareholders (entrepreneurs and venture capitalists). Passive shareholders seem rather much like all other suppliers; cf. section 4 above. Their role in running companies is insignificant. As a consequence their legitimacy as an actor entitled to a role of any considerable influence is quite small. Besides, by and large these investment shareholders are not really interested in assuming a responsible role in company affairs. The role of investment shareholders is primarily linked to the stock market. They "vote with their feet". They withdraw their support if their expectations are not met. By doing so they fulfil an enormously important role as actors in the stock market and—by extension—as examiners and appraisers of companies[7]. But this is a completely different role than that of actually taking part in the running of the company.

---

7) The explosive growth of stock market capitalisation as well as holdings of equity funds in recent years amply illustrate the awesome and overwhelming importance and power of "fund capitalism". "Everyone" in the industrialised world is rapidly in the process of becoming a shareholder, either directly or indirectly. See e.g. articles in Newsweek, April 27, 1998, pp33-42, or in Times Magazine, April 27, 1998, pp36-44.

Active shareholders, the entrepreneurs and the venture capitalists, on the other hand, evidently enjoy considerable legitimacy as influential decision-makers. However, on close observation, their legitimacy is based primarily on their active participation in company affairs, not on their equity position per se. Just like other members they are involved in company affairs and contribute by their knowledge and their creativity to company fortunes. This is what confers legitimacy.

Perhaps a two-category share system should be aimed at. Investment shareholders buy shares with limited voting rights, perhaps preferential shares with limited risk. Active shareholders, on the other hand, hold shares that give full voting rights but carry a concomitant risk.

Concerning members a reorientation also looms at the horizon. Of particular importance is the distribution of influence between employed and non-employed members (whatever their capacity may be, e.g. free-lancers, consultants, self-employed, contract people, temporary members). Non-employed members typically have contracts with companies that are either for fixed periods or easily terminated (or both). But experience demonstrates that non-employed members often remain in contact with companies for prolonged periods of time. Often enough they are also highly qualified. It seems only fair that many non-members are also included in the group of members that count.

Perhaps some kind of "member assemblies" will come into existence. These—or a committee elected by the "company member assembly"—might become a forum for inter-member communication and consultation as well as a body for contacts with management. "Member assemblies" might conceivably bring about profound changes in the actor's model. Such "assemblies" might well become the nucleus of crucial decision making at places of work. It is true that co-operation between all actors is necessary for company survival and success. Consumer and capital markets in particular are formidable allocators of resources. However, participation by these "outside" actors is doomed at the very outset without active participation by members. That is the way it has always been but not until the advent of the information society does this become a reality that dwarfs everything else.

7. Management

It is obvious that management techniques will be profoundly affected by higher education levels of members and by increasing company dependence on the knowledge, creativity and enthusiasm of members. Many management theories must be abandoned. Authoritarian, centralised and rigidly pyramidal management techniques will come tumbling down first, together with systems that allow for far-reaching unilateral and discretionary decision making by management.

Companies based on exchange of information, participation, co-determination and flat decision making structures that additionally provide ample room for individual initiatives seem called for. A philosophy based on the idea of bottom > up rather than a top > down is another part of the information society company. Management techniques will increasingly focus on members, *human-centered management*.

Voices from the world of the Japanese *kaisha* may again be fruitful.

Management means "management through meeting of minds" and of crucial importance is "the ... dialogue with individual workers in order to bring different ways and approaches of thinking into a single line. Workers are not treated as mere employees but are business partners sharing the fate of the company. In this context they are encouraged to own company stock." It is also true that "every worker is an entrepreneur ... and human resources management emphasizes the aspect of entrepreneurship development."[8]

Another voice sounds like this. "It should be stressed that ... each worker is a top manager. As long as the basic policies of the company are followed, each is responsible and accountable for his assignments, free from intervention by others, which often requires a high level of decisionmaking. Idemitsu's pol-

---

8) Op. cit. note 1 supra, at p11. The company is Kyocera, a leading producer in Japan of electronic components and equipment.

icy in human resource development is that workers should be developed by assigning jobs that seem to go beyond their current capabilities. This is risky and they often make mistakes, although such mistakes are taken as education costs. ---From this point of view, under the saying 'Every one of you is a business manager' employees are entrusted as far as possible with work over and above their abilities. This is a form of nurturing employees. It also means mistakes are made, but company thinking is that from the point of view of human nurturing this comes at a reasonable cost. Another company saying is: 'Mistakes are a precious tuition fee'".[9]

In this perspective co-determination by members does not represent a threat to the established management. Co-determination for members is a prerequisite for top management legitimacy. It also becomes a necessity to enable managers to satisfy demands from outside actors.

8. Labour unions

As we all know labour unions have played a pivotal role in the industrialised society, in particular during its formative years. Unions have been of enormous importance in improving the working and living conditions of working people and in promoting values such as the humanisation of working life, the dignity of human work and the reduction of differentials in pay and status of different catego-

---

9 The Idemitsu company. Op. cit. note 1 supra, at p9 and 75.

ries of employees. Buyers of labour have had to swallow that unions came into existence as a response to the conditions that they managed to impose on sellers of labour, in particular during the infancy of industrialism. However, unions have declined dramatically in many countries that have entered into the information age. In France and the USA, for example, union density in the private sector is below ten per cent and still declining. Many observers are of the opinion that unions are a thing of the past without any real relevance in the information society.

It seems rather obvious that sellers of labour in the information society are less in need of a collective voice than those in the agrarian or industrialised society. Workers are better educated and their relationship to buyers of labour are often in their favour. This would translate into declining union density rates in the OECD countries. By and large this is also the case but the picture is far from unequivocal. Furthermore union density rates should be fairly low in OECD countries. That, however, is far from always the case. Much to the contrary these countries differ considerably, some countries close to one extreme of the spectrum (e.g. France and the US, with very low unionisation rates) and some others to the opposite extreme (e.g. the Nordic countries, with unionisation rates in Sweden well above the eighty per cent mark).

What are the reasons for such differences? What would happen if these countries started afresh without unions and without existing arrangements in favour of unions or

8. Labour unions

against them? These questions are intimately linked to existing structures and regulations in the labour market. Existing structures are not easily changed. This is in particular so when-as here-these structures are concerned with power and balancing of power. Consequently it does not make much sense to discuss these questions solely from the perspective of what might be needed in the information era, disregarding today's power structure.

The point of departure for an answer must be that workers should have true freedom of choice to become union members or to refrain from membership. In turn, true freedom of choice implies that societies provide for alternative routes to obtain such services and benefits that unions traditionally provide. This, inter alia, would mean that countries provide for minimum wages, allow workers to resort to industrial actions without union fiat, put information and consultation channels at the disposal of members even in the absence of unions, grant unions small or no privileges (with the possible exceptions of unions that have established a contractual relationship with the company) or refrain from statutory rules or other arrangements that induce workers or employers to become members of labour market organisations. In short, societies should take a truly neutral stance regarding ways for workers to relate to other actors in the labour market, primarily employers.

Obviously true freedom of choice is limited if-and to the extent that-legislation in a country gives workers a strong self-interest to join unions. An extreme example is legislation to the effect that unemployment benefits are fully financed by government grants and only unions members are entitled to such benefits. Less drastic is a system of a similar kind but open to all employees. Rules on co-determination may channel employee participation through unions or not. And so may rules on, for example, safety and health work at places of work, participation in important decisions concerning the running of the company and provisions on derogation from statutory rules or veto rights for workers. Legislation in the various countries provides samples of statutory rules that are favourable, unfavourable or neutral to unions.

Broadly speaking union density rates seem to be low and declining in countries where workers enjoy true freedom of choice. France and the USA are, again, prime examples. Sweden, again, represents the opposite pole. True freedom of choice is scant, indeed largely illusory in Sweden. This is so both from a legal and from a practical point of view. Those who opt for non-membership face a number of more or less legal-usually less legal-pressures and punishments, e.g. lower pay and ostracism.

Attempts to analyse factors that affect union membership positively or negatively are precarious and fraught with uncertainties. Still, in an article that has not yet been published, I have endeavoured to assess the impact of twenty factors. Each factor has been assigned a numerical value, ranging from a high of $+6$ to a low of -6.

This means that the highest score possible is +120 and the lowest −120. Table 4 summarises the findings for three countries. The table makes it abundantly clear that Sweden and the USA are at opposite extremes.

Table 4. Summary of factors that influence unionisation rates

	Very positive +6	Positive +3	Neutral 0	Negative −3	Very negative −6	Total score
Japan	7(+42)	3(+9)	5(0)	4(−12)	1(−6)	33
Sweden	17(+102)	1(+3)	2(0)	—	—	105
USA	6(+36)	2(+6)	3(0)	4,5(−135)	4,5(−27)	1,5

It is obvious that there is an enormous difference between Sweden and the USA concerning the attitude of the government towards unions, regardless of whether the total scores in this table are absolutely accurate or not. Sellers of labour obviously enjoy much less freedom of choice to join unions or not in Sweden than they have in the USA. It is not far-fetched to consider Swedish regulation to express a patronising attitude towards people and their ability to take care of their own interests.

Characteristic of the information society is the increasing importance of knowledge and creativity. These qualities are individual and have only scant relationship to standardisation and collectivisation. The core idea of unions—to monopolise labour supply, to take labour out of competition—does not look overly compatible with labour supply patterns in an information society. This strongly suggests that unions will face increasing difficulties to assert themselves even in countries (like Sweden) where the legislator grants them extreme privileges.

To question the role and benefit of unions in an information society comes easy. Due to the increased importance of individual knowledge and creativity sellers of work will become increasingly independent and self-reliant. Increased personal individualism will follow suit. Unions will stand to benefit from nothing of all this. Nor will unions benefit from easily anticipated changes in the market place. Product output will become much more varied and adjusted to the needs and wishes of each customer. This will result in less rigid price structures and lead to increased emphasis on maximising income rather than minimising cost. This, in turn, will make unions more expendable from the point of view of sellers of labour.

Section 6 discusses a new actor's model. As was stated there is a need to allow non-employed members a voice at the place of work as well. Unions do not represent these members. This is also an argument for questioning the role and legitimacy of unions.

It might also happen that unions find themselves in a stronger position than today in this sector of the economy since companies will be even less capable of influencing prices of their products, inducing them to focus on cutting costs instead. Thus, labour costs in factory work face increasing downward pressure.

Furthermore, it is a fact that important portions of atypical workers face working conditions that are far less favourable than core members[10]. This is true regardless of whether they are employed in factory work or perform information sector type jobs. Indeed atypical members rather than core employees might represent the true potential for unions in the information society!

9. Product markets

It is part and parcel of the very notion of the information society that the emphasis in the economy shifts from products to services. Services, in turn, are less standardised than products. In addition, demand for products also becomes less standardised. To an increasing extent buyers ask for products that meet their specific needs. Long past is the time when-as Henry Ford wanted it-everyone could get his car in the colour of his liking provided that everyone wanted a black car.

The evolution towards an increasingly individualised demand structure for goods and services goes hand in hand

---

10) Just one example to illustrate. During the summer of 1997 the American company United Parcel Service (UPS) was the target of a massive strike. An important issue at stake was the situation of part-time employees. Hourly wages for part-timers were only half those of full-time employees despite identical work-tasks. Cf. e.g. The Economist, August 16th, 1997, p27, "No part-time explosion".

with a concomitant individualisation of labour supply. It is no wonder that sellers of labour become more discerning and specific as consumers when their demand for work becomes so. It is probable that the truly decisive factor for increased flexibility in working life is changes in consumer demand patterns.

10. Flexibility

If it is accurate to maintain, as was done in section 9, that flexibility in working life is primarily dictated by changes in consumer demand patterns then it can safely be predicted that the evolution towards a more flexible working life has just started. It is no bold guess that demand patterns will become increasingly individualised and specific. This, in turn, requires an increasingly flexible work organisation to satisfy these demand patterns. The two will walk hand in hand.

Increased education, knowledge and creativity also lead towards a more flexible working life. Members will find standardisation, routine and monotony increasingly unpalatable. Continued education and recurrent professional training in conjunction with various kinds of schemes for time off-*sabbaticals*-point in the same direction and so do programs for job rotation. Personnel policies of Japanese companies in all these respects (with the exception of sabbaticals) have already been very influential in the world and will become increasingly so.

Distance work will mushroom as will member expectations to combine private and professional life. "Work centers" may come into existence to provide distance workers with the opportunity to work for their respective companies while at the same time keep in contact with their kids in the annexed child care center. A "work center" might become the equivalent in the information era to the factory in the industrialised period. A factory is part of the sphere of buyers of labour and in the factory all sellers of labour work for the same buyer. The "work center" is part of the sphere of sellers of labour and those who work there do so for different buyers, regardless of the kind of contractual relationship that exists between them and the buyers.

Remuneration for work will also be affected. As the importance of education, knowledge and creativity increases so will expectations that differences in these respects are reflected in differences in pay. Whereas seniority has traditionally been the most important factor for pay in Japan, many big Japanese companies have recently turned to an "annual wage system". This system is based on a thorough and careful evaluation of members' contributions to the company. Annual wages are allowed to fluctuate upwards and downwards. It can also be expected that reward systems based on company profits will become common.

For a long period of time the tremendous and stupefying growth in collective and individual wealth that is one of the characteristics of "capitalist" systems has lead to increased flexibility. This can most readily be seen in the reduction of working hours and the concomitant choice between longer hours and more money or the opposite. There is every reason to believe that continued growth in wealth will continue to result in ever more flexible solutions in working life.

11. A revolutionised working life?

The model here presented means that those working for companies-members-will have a strong, indeed decisive, say in the running of companies. The model might appear both far-fetched and revolutionary. This model is light-years away from both the traditional "capitalist company" where owners wield supreme and unchallenged power and the planned economy company, the hallmark of communism.

The contrast to a state controlled, planned economy is by far the biggest. In a planned economy decision making structures are extremely centralised and concentrated to a small group of people. These people are not subjected to any kind of external control nor are they faced with the exigencies and the ruthlessness of markets, be that a consumer, a credit or a stock market. History tells us that planned economies result in the utter exploitation of people, both materially and mentally, in the most degrading and humiliating way.

Strong ownership direction may also result in limitations of members' participation. However, experience demonstrates that even owner-controlled companies can allow for far-reaching participation by members. A 1996 study

11. A revolutionised working life?

analyses degrees of employee participation in a number of OECD countries[11]. The study shows that employee participation is highest in Japan. The USA comes second. This might surprise since the USA is a country where ownership supremacy is strongly advocated.

It is particularly noteworthy that neither of these two countries has legislation that provides for employee participation. Participation does not follow any legislative mandate. It has emerged as an expression of sound and prudent management techniques or, if you prefer, as a result of a Solomon balancing of company actors. In Japan this development occurred before the advent of the information society. Characteristic for Japanese management techniques has also been emphasis on skill formation already at shop floor level (cf. section 7). Skill and participation have gone hand in hand.

For long American management techniques were the contrary. Ownership control has dominated. A drastic change has taken place in recent years, partly as a response to the Japanese challenge. Legislation has played no role at all. There simply is no legislation in the USA on employee participation. Nor is employee involvement channelled through unions to any great extent. The union-

---

11) Fröhlich, D, & Pekruhl, U, Direct Participation and Organisational Change: Fashionable but Misunderstood? An Analysis of Recent Research in Europe, Japan and the USA (European Foundation for the Improvement of Living and Working Conditions, Dublin, Ireland, 1996, ISBN92-827-6673-X9.

isation rate has declined to slightly below ten per cent in the private sector. An important factor, besides the Japanese challenge, seems to be the advent of information society and the concomitant transformation of the American working population.

Experience from Japan and the USA points towards the future. Deep and far-reaching employee participation in these countries perfectly fit the emerging patterns of the information society. It seems safe to assume that participation will be even deeper and more comprehensive in mature information societies. At the same time participation should include not just core employees but all members in the company.

To conclude. The Japanese kaisha appears to have features that are indeed harbingers of things to come elsewhere as well. The fact that much of the characteristics of the kaisha seem to be under attack at the present time[12], indeed even to some extent eroding, does not diminish its potential. Perhaps a shake-up is needed to realise its full potential by liberating it from its smugness and restore to

---

12) See e.g. an article in The Economist, May 9th 1998, at p73: *Mitsubishi: The diamonds lose their sparkle*. The theme of the article is that "(T) he Mitsubishi group possesses all the advantages that once made corporate Japan seem unstoppable. That is why it is in a mess". The main explanation for this purported "mess" is conservatism and complacency within the group and its various entities. Reinhold Fahlbeck, Towards a Revolutionised Working Life?

monetary capital some of its lost ground. Once through this face-lift the kaisha has all the promise of becoming palatable even outside those isles where it originates.

Labor Law Amendment to Reform the Korean Industrial Relations

SOHN Chang-Hi

Introduction

On March 13, 1997, the long-awaited labor law amendments were passed in the National Assembly and followed by additional amendments in February 20, 1998 after a drawn-out debate and much publicized surrounding politics. These amendments were heralded by the Kim Young-sam administration as the final piece in its comprehensive political and economic reform agenda, as it was hoped that the changes will fundamentally stamp out the authoritarian and undemocratic industrial relations and labor law of the past military regimes.

However, the 1997 amendments seems to be marred by the residue of the general strike and the negative public opinion generated by the previous labor law amendments passed during the dawn session in December 26, 1996, which consisted only the representatives of New Korea Party (government party) which held quorum of the National Assembly. In stark contrast with the administration's jubilant sentiment, labor leaders have expressed their bitter dissatisfaction with a number of core issues covered by the 1996 · 1997 amendments including the reluctant legalization of plural unions, prohibition of wage payment to full-time union organizers, institution of dynamic working hours, and endorsing of dismissal due to managerial reasons. They are outspoken saying that the amendments are totally biased in favor of the Management side, so another set of labor law amendments should be made from now on. On the other hand, the management side, as if rebutting the labor's demands, asked for another legislation that aims to overcome the national economic crisis falled on since November, 1997. Cons and pros on labor law amendment will remain in debate for a considerable period of time in future.

Nonetheless, the recent changes of the Korean labor law must be evaluated as a progressive step-forward as it did indeed withered the labor-suppress policy of the authoritarian military regimes that reached to peak by the time of 1980 amendments. In addition, the fact that the amended labor law now includes specific mechanisms aimed at installing flexibility into the labor market is a enough sign demonstrating the 'transition' of time. The New Industrial Relations Concept (Apr., 1996) of President Kim Young-sam that initiated the labor law amendments was correct and justifiable by identifying as its goals to enhance competitiveness of Korean enterprises in the world market and to improve the workers' quality of life. The proposal put stress on the harmonization of the Korean labor law with internationally accepted labor standards and practices as the necessary mean to attain its goals. In this respect, The proposal has a privilege to be credited as a timely expression of trend toward democratization and globalization, as it explicitly focused on the guarantee of workers' basic rights and attainment of labor market flexibility. It will not require long duration of time to find out how many of the above mentioned amendments will prove to be faithful to this promise or expectation. Only after such a determination is made, can the labor sector substantiate its argument that the government actions aimed at making the labor market more flexible for the sake of enhancing Korea's competitiveness has overshadowed the other goal of guaranteeing the basic right of the labor.

It is clear that the labor law reform is a necessary step to correct the authoritarian and antidemocratic industrial relations of the past decades. However, it should be kept in mind that substantially legal reform by itself may not fulfill this objective. Without the meaning change of behaviors of the parties concerned without self-initiated establishment of voluntary fair-rules by the labor and management, 'downward' labor legislation is apt to foster an inclination to depend more on none-voluntary legal procedures set up by the government, and make labor and management victim of 'legalism'.

I. Pursuit of Change and Reform

Industrial relations refers to a particular form of human relationship that is characteristic of industrialized society. It may be effected by various aspects of the society that constitutes the context under which it exists. They are the particular timing of industrialization, the stage of development, the characteristics of elite groups leading the industrialization the legal framework and labor practices and the traditional sense of values which may directly or indirectly have influence in the said society

In the case of Korea, the process of industrialization that began in 1962 transformed the once poverty stricken country into the model of high paced industrialization that became envy of the world. It was achieved during the decades of 1970s and 1980s led by relentless group of economic technocrats backed by the strong support of the government, vigorous entrepreneurs and hard-working laborers.

During the process of rapid (compressed) industrialization, the rule of development autocracy that was rationalized under the doctrine of 'develop first, distribute later' and national security superceded everything. Of course, Industrial relations could not be an exception to that rule. As a result, industrial relations in Korea has been in chains of the traditional Confucian value consciousness and restrictive legal framework which lack the balance of power between the parties yet maintaining much of the authoritarian nature even after entering 1990s. But it was soon discovered that Korea was no exception to the historical truth that it is impossible to suppress the publics only with the rationale of traditional cultural concept of totality, industrialization, and national security. can not rule the mind and act of the people of industrial society in which people behave in individuality.

Changes of environmental context that brought about reform movements consisted of the waves of democratization internally and globalization externally.

I. Pursuit of Change and Reform

(1) Wave of Democratization

The Citizens' Democratic Struggle, which reached its height on June 10, 1987 forced the ruling Democratic Justice Party's Presidential Candidate Rho Tae-woo to announce what has become known as the June 29th Declaration. Rho's Declaration elevated the demand for democratic change over all aspects of politics, economy, and the society as a whole. Politically, this wave of democratization put Kim Young-sam into presidential power on February of 1993, whose civilian government promised comprehensive democratic innovation in the fields of politics, economy, civil service, army that started from the corruption purge.

As for the labor, the remarkable quantitative increase of labor force along with the qualitative change of workers gave spur to the perception of working class desire for well-off life and the right consciousness claiming for more human-like treatment. Accordingly, labor movement enhanced demanding for democratic industrial relations and better quality of life through the guarantee of workers' basic rights. In sum, they started speak aloud farewell message to the old fashioned authoritarian system and practice of industrial relations and legislative and administrative restrictions.

(2) Wave of Globalization

The end of the Cold War marked by the falling of the Berlin Wall in 1989 initiated the wave of economic globalization that makes political boundaries virtually meaningless. Institutionally, this wave of globalization launched the World Trade Organization (WTO), and as for trade among nations, a debate started whether to add the social clause to trade agreements that would link the internationally authorized labor standards and the basic rights of workers with commodity and service trades. Meanwhile, Korea gained membership into various international organizations including ILO in 1991 and OECD in 1996. And her status as a bona fide international participant has been enhanced. As such, Korea can no longer maintain ambiguous position hitherto against the world-wide trend of modernization of industrial relations in terms of reforming her industrial relations structure and labor law system.

After entering into the 1990s, international bodies such as the United Nations Commission on Human Rights, ILO, IMF, ICFTU, and OECD have exerted pressure on the Korean government to address this issue by amending the labor law to reflect more democratic nature. It is evident that this sort of outdoor pressure functioned as one of the determinants on recent labor law amendments in Korea.

(3) The Government Pledge

From its inauguration in 1993, the administration of Kim Young-sam pledged to reform Koreas industrial relations. As such, the new 5-year Economic Plan included reorganization of industrial relations as one of its major tasks and in terms of policy agenda,, the administration disposed the priority on amendment of the existing labor law (Apr. 1993). In line with this spirit, the Presidential Commission for Promotion of Globalization included 'the globalization of industrial relations system and practices' as the second among its 12 major action plans (Jan. 1995). Nevertheless, government failed to materialize into any affirmative actions, as the administration showed little willingness afterwards while most Korean believed that stable industrial relations is the prime keyword for further economic development and social stability. Reform of labor law and industrial relations became a public mandate for the new civilian government.

At last, after a long period of hesitation, President Kim Young-sam put forward his Vision for the New Industrial Relations in April 1996, which motivated a big change in Korean labor law system. This New Vision was in fact an acknowledgement of the essential social necessity to change the nature of Korean industrial relations from the one characterized by 'opposition and conflict' to the one of 'participation and cooperation' in line with the international standards.

The Kim Dae-jung administration inaugurated in January 1998 also launched the Presidential Commission on Labor Relations (Tripartite Commission) that represents Labor, Management and Government to tackle on labor issues through social consensus building.

II. Passage of the Amendments

1. From 'New Vision' to the First reform attempt
   (1) Kim Young-sam's Vision for A New Industrial Relations

The recent legislative action to amend the labor law in Korea began with President Kim Young-sam's declaration of his Vision for A New Industrial Relations on April 24, 1996. On that day, the president Kim invited over 220 guests representing various segments of the Korean society to the Blue House where he proclaimed that in order to enhance the quality of life for workers and to increase competitiveness of Korean economy and enterprises in the era of globalization with unlimited competition toward the 21st century, we must move forward to change the nature of our industrial relations from that of opposition and conflict to that of participation and cooperation through a decisive reform measures. The Vision was based on the following 5 basic principles : i) maximization of common good for labor and management, ii) participation and cooperation, iii) mutual recognition of freedom and responsibility, iv) value of education and respect for human dignity, and v) adaptation of system and consciousness to the international standards. To establish a new industrial relations based on these basic principles, the president Kim noted that the employers must eliminate its authoritarian management practices and instead embrace notions such as transparent management and investment on employees to their satisfaction. In response, the labor trade unions must change their attitude toward management from reckless struggle-first with blind distribution demand to the more rational and productive approach. As for the role of government, it should eliminate the excessive restriction on the industrial relations and act as a mediator fair to labor and management. In sum, the president Kim asked each sectors of the society to bring about the Grand Consensus in order to institute a new industrial relations in Korea.

II. Passage of the Amendments

In retrospect, the president Kim Young-sam's proclamation was no less than his expression to dissociate from the past military governments authoritarian labor law system. However, it is regrettable that such general expression on reform failed to deploy into the actual law amendments to the full extent.

(2) Discussion at the Presidential Commission on Industrial Relations Reform (May 9 · Nov. 12, 1996)

Soon after the proclamation of the New Vision, the Presidential Commission on Industrial Relations Reform was launched with the mandate to form an institutional framework that will implement Kim's Vision. The Commission undertook its task for 6 months starting from May 9, 1996. During the first phase of its work the Commission focused its efforts on preparing the outline of labor law amendments supposed to be the basis of the new industrial relations. Prior to this work, the Commission agreed to i) set the scope of amendment to 5 statute laws : Labor Standards Act, Trade Union Act, Labor Dispute Adjustment Act, Labor Relations Commission Act, and Labor-Management Council Act, ii) set the objective of amendment guaranteeing enhanced basic rights for workers, and fostering more flexibility in the labor market, iii) match the content of amendments with the internationally authorized standards, and iv) take unanimous form of agreement among representatives of labor, management and public in its proceedings.

Although the Commission worked vigorously with study, research, hot discussions and several public hearings to seek the unanimous agreements by the three-sides (representatives of labor, management and public) on various issues, they reached to consensus only about minor issues to their great dismay. Consequently, the Commission's final report to the president Kim was not a unified recommendation, but rather a hodgepodge recommendation reflecting respective positions taken by the three-sides.

The Commissions failure to form a consensus is attributable to three reasons. Firstly, both the labor and the management, sticking to their self-interest extravagantly, lacked in recognizing the historic significance of labor law reform. Secondly, the president Kim's vague directive that the law shall be amended upon consensus of the labor and the management, whatever they agreed, induced both sides they can reject any proposals as far as they don't think favorable. Thirdly, both sides didn't have enough ability to bring about necessary consensus among their constituents.

As a result, the Commission submitted a report to the president on Nov. 12, 1996 which included following agreed points: i) legalization of political activity by labor unions, ii) setting the founding date of a labor union as the date of application accepted, iii) giving the union representative the authority to sign up the collective labor contract, iv) termination of government agency's authority to investigate labor unions activities, v) elimination of regulations that induce in-house labor unions, vi) prohibition of unofficial concerted actions, vii) allowing compulsory arbitration only in water, electricity, gas, petroleum, and telecommunications industries, viii) enhancement of independency and

II. Passage of the Amendments

neutrality of the Labor Relations Commission, ix) extension of the scope of Labor Standards Act to small enterprises, x) flexible working hours, discretionary working hours, pre-determined working hours, xi) paid annual/ monthly leave, and xii) introducing the protective measures for hourly work. Practically speaking, these are rather less-important minor agreements. Meanwhile, the Commission failed to reach a consensus on following points, which were seen as the core issues on industrial relations debate: i) prohibition of multiple labor unions, ii) prohibition of the third party intervention, iii) union membership of discharged employee, iv) definition of labor federation, v) emergency order by the court on unfair labor practices, vi) remuneration to the full-time union organizers, vii) wage payment during strike, viii) replacement workers during strike, ix) scope of public work, x) agreement mandate at the labor-management council, xi) dynamic working hours, xii) dismissal due to managerial reasons, xiii) payment during business suspension, xiv) early payment of severance pay, xv) dispatched work, and xvi) right to organize for civil servants and teachers.

For the above mentioned non-agreed points, the idea of the public members in the Commission was that enhancing the guarantee for basic rights of workers in the field of collective industrial relations while enlarging the flexibility of labor forces in the field of individual labor relations.

(3) The Amendment Proposal by the Government (Dec. 10, 1996) and its Abnormal Passage in the

National Assembly (Dec. 26, 1996)

Upon Commission's report to the president, the administration formed the Task Force on Industrial Relations Reform Implementation comprised of officials from various related agencies. The Task Force formulated amendment proposals for the 5 labor Acts, which was reviewed by the Cabinet and presented to the National Assembly on Dec. 10, 1996. This amendments proposal had characteristics somewhat different from the recommendation made by the public members of the Commission. That is to say, the former was rather conservative approach in their guarantee of workers' basic rights and liberal approach in fostering flexibility in the labor market in comparison with the latter. Immediately, the labor resisted to that amendment proposals with a warning of possible general strike.

Political chaos began in early morning of Dec. 26, 1996 when the special session of the National Assembly composed only of New Korea Party members passed the amendment proposals in surprise-attack. The covert passage brought about immediate and total protest of the labor sector. The administration was charged with violation of the democratic due process in addition to severe criticism on the Amendments for its unbalanced content. The labor retaliated with a general strike, and various sectors of the society including scholars, religious leaders, civic leaders led vehement protest demanding nullification of the Amendments and re-reform of the labor law. Finally the president Kim Young-sam apologized to the public promising re-revision.

In sum, the Amendment of Dec. 26, 1996 was short-lived

II. Passage of the Amendments

in the face of the national opposition. The reasons may be explained as follows: i) covert political maneuver staged by the New Korea Party at the end of the year, ii) postponing 3 more years to allow to set up multiple upper labor organization, iii) underestimating the significance of the labor resistance, iv) misjudgement to the public sentiment without due consideration, v) the president Kim's careless statements at the new year press conferences, neglecting the importance of quick response to be shown in vital situation, and vi) indecisive attitude of the administration and the ruling party in coping with the general strike threat without consulting neither the opposition party nor the labor unions. Some more additional reasons could be added to why the working class resisted. Firstly, the delay of multiple union recognition was a matter of life and death for the Korea Federation of Trade Unions, secondly, legalization of the dismissal due to managerial reasons expected to undermine severely the job security, especially, of the white collar workforce, and thirdly, implementation of dynamic work hours would be disadvantageous to the blue collar workforce whose income could be drastically reduced. Besides, negative evaluations from outsides by international organizations such as ILO, ICFTU, IMF, ETUC, as well as AFL-CIO and the Washington Post were burdensome to the Kim Young-sam administration.

2. The Second Reform
   (1) Public Apology of the President Kim Young-sam (Feb. 25, 1997)

At the new year press conference on Jan. 7, 1997, the

president Kim Young-sam proudly stated that the '96 amendments have transformed the Korean industrial relations structure into more advanced form, and that although it requires sacrifices by both labor and management, considering the present economic situation, all must share and endure the burden. However, after meeting with the Cardinal Kim Soo-hwan on Jan. 17, 1997, he realized true reason of the public discontent with the '96 amendments and felt deeply the necessity of re-amendment that ended up with his frank apology to the public on Feb. 25 and signaled another amendment work shall be carried out.

(2) Agreement of the political parties on the Second Labor Law Reform (Mar. 8, 1997) and its Passage in the National Assembly (May. 10, 1997)

Prior to his public apology the president Kim met with heads of political parties where he admitted that it is wrong not recognizing the upper labor organizations in plural in spite of its social existence as such, and stated that he will postpone the enforcement of arrest warrant issued for those union officials who led the strike in protest of the labor law amendments, officially signaling his willingness to amend the labor law again.

After some political maneuver, both the ruling and opposition parties successfully reached a consensus on amendment measures, which was passed by the National Assembly on Mar. 10, 1997. The new amendments that 'nullifying' the First Amendment (Dec. '96) and took a form of 'enacting' new laws may be evaluated substantially as a 'softening modification' over the First Amendment in terms of the 24 dispute issues including the following revisions: i) immediate recognition of multiple upper labor unions, ii) allow the unit union officers to take office in the upper labor organizations, iii) adjusting the scope of permissible substitute workers during strike, iv) ban on strike demanding payment for the striking period, v) limiting maximum working hours 12 hours per day under the dynamic working hour system, and vi) 2-year postponement of legalizing dismissal due to managerial reasons.

However, apart from amendments mentioned above, the labor side remained in dissatisfaction because the new legislation maintained the same stance with '96 Amendments, and ILO is also criticizing the unresolved issues, especially about the rights to organize for civil servants and teachers.

(3) Things to be Kept in Memory through all the Course of amendments

The original labor laws set up in 1953 was based on liberal autonomic industrial relations. But it was a legislation aiming at somewhat demonstration effect in the midst of confrontation with North Korea under the context of the Cold War. Since then, major labor laws amendments took place eight times during the military regimes. All the amendments were nothing but ad hoc behind-the-curtain improvisations influenced by political power groups. Furthermore, those amendments were protective when workers appeared as an individual, and restrictive when appeared as a collective body. In this aspect, the recent amendments leaves many lessons to us.

Firstly, the 6-month debate in the Commission on Industrial Relations Reform, revealed almost all the problems of Korean industrial relations comprehensively for the first time. Now we realize what's the problem and what kinds of options to choose henceforth.

Secondly, excessive adherence to self-interest among all the parties involved made them not to recognize the historic significance of the amendments, which marred labor laws amendment based on social consensus. Especially the 'all or nothing' approach by the labor and management plagued the entire productive negotiation process aiming at participatory and cooperative labor relations. Both parties refused to negotiate in good faith on core issues such as dual unions and dismissal due to managerial reasons.

It is evident that Korean industrial relations is still overshadowed by opposition and conflict. Even if taking into consideration that the president Kim's initial promise was to make into law whatever the labor and the management agreed, and also the promise might be just 'calculated' one on the premise that the labor and the management will not agree easily, the both parties cannot escape from the criticism that they failed to match with the public interest. Furthermore, they must be held primarily responsible that they gave a free-hand to the government in amending labor laws, despite the contents of that amendments was far less impressive than those of the public members' proposals, while they failed to agree on the core issues in debate.

Thirdly, the interest conflict among various ministries of the government and among political parties was no better than that between the labor and management. When looking at the approach by the government to address this issue, one can not help but wonder if they even have a slightest idea and concept of 'democratization' and 'globalization'. From various government ministries such as the Ministry of Finance and Economy, Ministry of Education, and other agencies could not eradicate their sense of attachment to regulatory powers. And the fact that the opposition parties kept silence until the last moment made people quite depressive.

Fourthly, had the Government adopted the Commission's recommendations on the three core issues regarding legalization of plural unions, limitation on the use of substitute workers during strike, and narrowing the scope of compulsory arbitration in the course of Dec. '96 Amendment, it is probable that the reaction from the labor sector and the general public would not appeared so vehement opposition even though measures for flexible labor market such as dynamic working hours and legalization of dismissal due to managerial reason were introduced.

Fifth, totally speaking, the labor, the management and the Government showed much lower level of understanding for the historic significance of the labor laws amendments and reluctant approach to reform through the enough discussion and deliberate legislative process.

3. The Third Reform with New Acts Added (Feb. 14, 1998)

The financial crisis in Nov. 1997 began to push Korea into an economic unforeseen pitfall. In following few months, the Korean government sought an emergency aid from the IMF under which Korean economic policy is outlined and put into practice. IMF's diagnostic measures requested the flexible labor market. Business restructuring became essential means to survive. Employment adjustment in which dismissal of redundancy is the last resort, is unavoidable. Together with shut-down of many thousands small and medium enterprises, it led to the massive unemployment problem (unemployed: 556,000 persons in 1997, 1,700,000 persons in 1998, unemployment rate: 2.3% in 1997, 7.9% in 1998). Consequently, how to maintain the job security, how to tackle the unemployment problem and how to extend the social security network became main concern of recent labor legislation.

The third amendment of the Labor Standards Act focused on the article 31 and 31-2 regulating dismissal due to managerial reasons. This time, the concerned amendment provided more in detail that in the case of mergers and acquisitions of business to prevent further managerial deterioration, dismissal may be justifiable. Even where dismissal due to managerial reason is permissible, discriminatory dismissal based on sex is explicitly prohibited, workers representatives should be notified 60 days prior to the dismissal and the management should have consultation with the labor about how to evade the dismissal if possible and how to set up the benchmark for the dismissal.

And the management shall endeavor to recall the dismissed employees in the case of future job opening.

The Employment Insurance Act was amended to enhance its scope of coverage to all the work-places with at

II. Passage of the Amendments

least 1 employee from Oct. 1, 1998 and raised the minimum level of unemployment benefit and the length of the duration. It also provides vocational training subsidy together with several kinds of living assistance for the unemployed.

Enacting the Dispatched Workers Protection Act, despite protest from the labor sector for a long time, is indicative of the legal system adjusting to the changed reality of the current labor market, similar to that of the Japanese experience.

The Wage Claim Guarantee Act was enacted letting the Wage Payment Security Fund to make wage payments on behalf of employers unable to provide such payment due to financial reasons. This Act may subdue the feeling of insecurity among workers failed to get their wages.

On the other hand, in the area of labor legislation on collective industrial relations, the long time debated two hot issues are spotlighted recently by law. One is the Civil Servant Workplace Council Act, which offer civil servants in central and local governments consulting chances to better their working environment, to elevate job efficiency and to dispose their grievances at workplace Councils. Another one is legislative schedule legalizing the Korea Teachers Union was fixed on Oct. 31, 1998 at the Tripartite Commission on the labor relations. These two legislative action is a evidence showing Korean labor law is gradually getting near the international standards of labor law.

III. Significance and Content of the Newly Amended Labor Law – referring mainly to Mar. '97 Amendment

1. Significance

The Labor Law in Korea has been amended 9 times since its first enactment in 1953. However, it has always been the case that amendments were legislated unilaterally by the regime in power without any consultation to gather the public sentiment on the issue. Furthermore, they were in no way meant to pursue the goals of democratization or globalization of industrial relations in Korea. Therefore, in comparison with the previous revisions, the 1997 amendment deserves good remarks in that it was legislated after series of long discussions among representatives of all concerned parties and social groups, as well as 6 public hearings led by the PCIR on the main issues, and the process was the first in history to have put through public scrutiny and was the result of unified recommendation by both the ruling and the opposition parties. Aside from the question of its actual merits, it doesn't necessarily be denied that the amendment was the last step in a series of democratic reforms provoked by Kim Young-sam Administration.

Cons and pros unavoidable about the contents of the amendment. But, at the very least, it is fair to say that '97 Amendment is a little step forward in the right direction, if not the big advance.

However, it will take some time to see if the newly amended labor law can function as an effective means in

III. Significance and Content of the Newly Amended Labor Law-referring mainly to Mar. '97 Amendment

promoting the participatory and cooperative industrial relations in which the basic rights of workers are strengthened and the flexibility of labor market is enhanced as the president Kim Young-sam proudly self-praised. It seems that the situation has not improved under the new administration of President Kim Dae-jung.

2. Content

The Mar. '97 Amendment followed the basic directions previously proclaimed by Kim Young-sam : i) to incorporate internationally accepted standards and practices but with adjustments tailored by the particular Korean circumstances, ii) to keep balance and rationality as the reform basis. As for the industrial relations in collective sense, irrational regulations and practices are to be eliminated to lay foundations for voluntary negotiation by the labor and the management. And as for the industrial relations in individual sense, excessive restrictions are to be moderated for the purpose of enhancing a more flexible labor market, iii) for the purpose of ensuring participatory and cooperative industrial relations environment, concerned act shall be amended. The above general principles maintained as in the past, but the four labor acts were 'amended' in a form of "enactment" as follows ;

(1) Building up base for voluntary negotiations
① Trade Union Act and Labor Dispute Adjustment Act are unified in the name of Trade Union and Labor Relations Adjustment Act.
② Multiple unions are legalized.

③ Prohibition on labor unions political activities, third party intervention, limitation on labor union dues are eliminated.

④ Wage agreement may extend up to 2-year duration like the other collective bargaining agreements.

⑤ Duty to bargain in good faith and ban on abusing of authority during negotiation.

⑥ Emergency order by the court to obey adjudication rendered by the Labor Relations Commission in case of unfair labor practices.

⑦ The scope of substituting workers during strike readjusted.

⑧ The government agencies authority to investigate unions activities

(2) Moderating restriction in the labor market to foster more flexibility

① Dismissal due to managerial reasons are legalized under 4 conditions : i) imminent managerial necessity, ii) exhaustion of all other means to evade dismissal, iii) setup a rational and equitable standard for dismissal, and iv) bona fide consultation with workers representative.

② Dynamic working hours, flexible working hours and discretionary working hours introduced.

③ Early payment of severance pay and severance pay insurance system introduced.

④ Protection of short-time workers.

⑤ Specially designated holiday may replace annual/monthly leave with pay.

⑥ Regulations covering minimum working hours for

special industries are relaxed, while payments during business suspension could be paid on the ordinary wage base.

(3) Eradication of unreasonable system and practices

① Payment for full-time union officials shall be banned, as a unfair labor practices from Jan. 2002.

② Worker's strike action requesting wages for striking period shall be regarded illegal.

③ Clarifying the establishment date of trade union as the date when the application paper received by government agencies, while explicit enumerating reasons for the rejection of certificate of union establishment report.

④ Bestow on labor union representative the legal power to sign up collective agreement concluded in addition to the authority to negotiate on behalf of union members.

⑤ Labor unionist claiming his dismissal is without just cause may maintain his union membership until the National Labor Relations Commission render an adjudication.

⑥ Either party concerned may terminate the collective agreement by giving notice to the other party three months in advance of the date he wants to terminate the collective agreement.

(4) Rationalization of concerted action and dispute adjustment

① Duty to refer the labor dispute to the adjustment of the Labor Relations Commission prior to the industrial action.

② Striking workers are prohibited from occupying the

production facilities or installations related to important businesses.

③ Compulsory arbitration is forcible only to the essential public services such as railroad, water, electricity, gas, oil, hospital, banks, telecommunication services.

④ Prohibition of strike by site-working blue collar civil servants is lifted.

⑤ Dispute on interpretation or adaptation of collective bargaining agreement may refer to the Labor Relations Commission.

(5) Reasonable Re-organizing the Labor Administration
① Enhancing the independency of the Labor Relations Commission.
② Securing the fairness and neutrality of the Labor Relations Commission.
③ Improving the professional capacity of the Labor Relations Commission.

(6) Base-building for the Participatory and Cooperative Industrial Relations
① Enacting 'Act Concerning the Promotion of Worker Participation and Cooperation' which replaced the old 'Labor Management Council Act'.
② Enlarging the scope of matters subject to consultation.
③ Newly providing matters subject to council's resolution.
④ Workers' members may request relevant documents to the employer.

⑤ Rationalizing the way of electing workers' members. Labor union represent all the employees at enterprise level only when the union is formed by a majority of workers.

IV. Evaluation and Prospect

1. Evaluation

Whether and how much the new labor law will contribute to establish the new Korean paradigm of industrial relations based on participation and cooperation and thus eventually enhance workers' quality of life and competitiveness of business will differ depending on the standpoint of the evaluator. The answer will remain the same if one ask how much successful is the new amendments in the amidst of worldwide-stream of democratization and globalization in creating a new model of industrial relations in Korea.

Let's listen first to the Government voice which sounds somewhat self-complacent. The president Kim Young-sam, as he proclaimed '97 Amended Acts, praised enthusiastically, the new laws and said since that laws are reflective of the spirit of his New Vision of Industrial Relations, our industrial relations will change from the conflict-prone mode to the cooperative mode which will make both the labor and the management live in peace.

The business sector also showed similar positive responses. For example, Korean Employers Federation evaluated that both business and labor participated through two-way dialogue in the legislative action, and that new labor law enhanced the employers' action range to adapt rapidly changing labor market environment, and that it laid the foundation upon which healthy industrial relations may develope, and that the new laws are expected to contribute for the progress of Korean economy.

However, the reaction of the labor sector is very vehement. They insists, the Mar. '97 legislation is no different than its predecessor, Dec. '96 Amendment. They said that it's the second labor-killing law, and that it gave up the premise of the original objectives of the Vision, which promised guaranteeing the basic rights of the workers and enhancing the quality of life for workers, and instead it turned out that the amendment process was nothing but a back-room political compromise.

Reaction from the academia is not so favorable either, while there are some who would comment favorably the legalization of multiple unions, adoption of dynamic working hours through mutual agreement, and enlargement of obligatory items to be consulted and some items to which labor and management must reach agreement at the labor-management Council.

In retrospect, the failure of the Presidential Commission on Industrial Relations Reform to lead out the consensus among concerned parties on the core issues instigated government to expedite its own legislative process without listening to the others. The Commission failed to lead all the way through the process. As a result, the final piece of legislation lost its sense of balance. Of course, in meeting the demand for more flexible labor market, both management and labor had better to set their stance in proactive way. Therefore, legalizing dismissal due to managerial

IV. Evaluation and Prospect

reasons, introducing the dynamic working hours and flextime practices could demonstrate the merits of its own. However, this is not to say that they should be adopted immediately without any filtering devices. Think about the case of dismissal due to the managerial reasons. Prior to the incorporating into the provision over statute law, there already exists a series of the Supreme Court rulings allowing that kind of dismissal as far as it fulfilled the necessary legal conditions. Naturally one may doubt the necessity to regulate by the specific legal articles.

It is true that the flexible labor market is essential for Korea to compete in the global market. However, the flexibility of labor-force disposition can not be the sole determinant of Korean economic competitiveness. One must not forget that the more important factor to be considered is 'the flexibility of technology'. In terms of collective industrial relations, drastic weakening of workers' basic rights should not be linked to reduction of workers' desire to participate and cooperate.

Despite the new labor law cannot carry out the drastic reform with all its defects, I would think it as a small step to make us think of the true reform which may bring about a more democratic and global industrial relations in Korea.

2. Prospect

Although the labor law amendments are indispensable to industrial relations reform, the reform is not satisfied fully with the amendments alone. Since the actual industrial relations is continuously moving human relationships, they can hardly be governed by the rule of static law. Even though the task of democratizing and globalizing industrial relations is still to be ongoing matter, we must realize that there exist an inherent limitation on the part of laws and regulations in bringing out the change from conflict and opposition to participation and cooperation. The excessive expectation and dependency on law is very dangerous. Because it makes us more lean on the law and legalism prevails.

However, since the labor law has quite a remarkable leading function in practical industrial relations, the work changing the 'existing' law into the 'should-be' law is to be continued. In relation to that work, we must keep a premise in our mind that in the course of promoting the democratization and the globalization, the labor laws and labor administration should be oriented not to control but adjust and assist in a fair stance the industrial relations. As the New Vision put the stress on that neither the over-regulation nor the over-protection help the labor and the management to build up a healthy cooperative industrial relations. Matching with the international accepted standards and practices is mandate. It is not the time yet to predict whether or not the newly amended labor laws will keep pace with this directive. When we remind the lacking of sense of balance in recent labor law amendments, it seems quite probable that another requirement for law reform will be put forward in near future. So meanwhile, stiff and rigid interpretation and application should be avoided.

IV. Evaluation and Prospect

There are no evidences to conclude that the state of industrial relations in Korea has worsened since the labor law amendments were enacted. Despite the warnings given by the labor sector, the number of labor disputes with industrial action between 1997 and 1998 remain under 100 cases. Surely the economic crisis raided at the end of last year is partly attributable to this figure, but it can also be said that these trends may be the results of the mutual recognition of both labor and management that their survival depends on cooperation, not opposition.

From the experience, it is clear that the best way to induce cooperation is not through the strength of law, but the independent voluntary establishment of rules by the actors themselves. In Korea, it can be said that only rules over industrial relations have been enacted by the government. As exemplified by the 10-year period covering from 1971 to 1980 in the history of Korean industrial relations when not only the concerted activities but the rights to negotiate were taken away by the government. The tradition of Korean industrial relations has not given any opportunities to initiate self-imposed rules over their affairs. Through such historical experience, we recognize that the stable development of industrial relations is made feasible through promises made among actors and their willingness to stand by their words.

Like any other social arrangements, certain set of rules are necessary to establish stability. It is especially true for the case of industrial relations which is forged not based on familiar or fraternal relationships. So, where there are mutually agreed rules which all parties are abiding by, settlement of disputes and conflicts will become far easier to resolve. Recognizing the merits of self-initiated rules independent of laws and regulations in effectively resolving labor disputes as well as to establish stability in industrial relations will foster basis for labor-management self-governance and brighter future for the Korean industrial relations.

Early Ideologies of French Unionism

Jacques ROJOT

INTRODUCTION

Tadashi Hanami has been a pioneer in discussing an enlarged understanding of Labor Law. His publications have dealt with all areas of the law, evidently, but also with Human Resource Management and Industrial Relations. He is also a renowned scholar of comparative Industrial Relations. Foremost is the role played by the unions in Industrial Relations. In Japan, ideology has played an intriguing role in the different union federations and their evolution over time. Very present, at some junctures in SOHYO, it has been put somewhat to the background in RENGO. One would of course would not dare discuss Japanese Unions in a Liber Amicorum devoted to the very best specialist of Japanese Industrial Relations. Therefore, this paper aims to present the early ideological strands of French unionism, in order to open the ground to later comparative work[1].

---

1) An earlier version of this paper has been discussed at the meeting of the working group on Industrial Relations Theory of The Dublin European Conference of the International Industrial Relations Association on August 29, 1997. the comments of the participants to the meeting are gratefully acknowledged.

A translation problem occurs first, which is not unusual in dealing with the Japanese and the French language. In French the English word "union" is translated by the French world "syndicat", thus "unionism" would normally translate as "syndicalism" even though one should be aware that in English, at least in the American usage, "syndicalism" has a meaning different from the one of generally known "unionism"; it is understood as something akin to what would be called in France "revolutionary unionism". Revolutionary unionism is precisely an essential part of our topic.

Second, while researching the paper, it was found out that there is relatively little interest, with a few marked but rare exceptions nevertheless, in the joint fields of labor ideologies and the history of the Labor Movement, seen from an industrial relations perspective. Whilst numerous professional works from the part of Historians deals with the history of strikes, of the Working Class, of social mobility, of socialism and the like, few focus on the unions' ideologies themselves and their impact on the Labor Movement, with a decidedly industrial relations angle, except under the guise either of discussions of very specific technical points or of very broad general descriptions. Furthermore, some of the few who came to write about our subject have not been trained as professional historians. Neither is the present writer, and, of course, the Industrial Relations point of view is the object of the paper and will be adopted. The interest here is mainly focused on the ideologies and their impact on labor unions, not on History, its methods and their application to the field of labor. This explains why many of the sources used are not drawn from works authored by Academic Historians. Besides, the matter seems controversial and the appropriateness of the field seems hotly debated among professionals, as witnesses an introduction by one of them for the book of another one[2]. The former, reflecting upon his qualifications for having being offered to write the introduction by the latter "as an activist and an historian" notes that "nobody ignores the fact that (...his qualifications. as such...) were sometimes challenged by certain political and "academic moguls" ("mandarins" in French)". Thus, it appears, on the one hand that the field is beset with academic rivalries, and on the other hand that some of the work around labor historical aspects is of an activist nature, and called upon to prove, or disprove, the rightfulness of present day ideologies, which its authors either subscribe to or despise. This can be further pointed out by the fact that, often, books and papers reporting the life and work of such or such past important figure in the development of labor ideologies either glorify him or vilify him, often depending on the ideological angle adopted by the author[3].

Also, within what appears to be an ideological minefield, what we want to outline here is not only focused on an

---

2) Introduction by J. Maitron to R. Brècy, La grève générale en France, Paris, E. D. I., 1969
3) For instance, in the case of Proud'hon, one author goes to great pains to demonstrate his working class origins, and the revolutionnary depth of his insights, whereas other works dismiss him disdainfully as a "petit bourgeois".

Industrial Relations perspective, but is indeed strictly our own interpretation of data. When other published work is used and quoted, as it is often the case below, it is our own understanding of this work which is offered. Besides, we adopt a presentation based on types of ideologies, across history, and not a chronological outline, for the ease of understanding. Our concern is with Industrial Relations, not History, and we trace ideologies across time instead of following historical events. This however, can distort the perception of the succession of historical events. Finally, for briefness sake, we assume a reasonable knowledge of French general history from the part of the reader.

After some general comments, we shall review the strands of ideology that we consider as the most influential on unions and briefly conclude.

GENERAL COMMENTS:

Several points must probably be emphasized before proceeding directly to an analysis of the various ideologies, in order to draw the broad framework within which they developed.

First, there is no strict division of work between political and union activity, in the early period of the industrial revolution, which would be better called evolution for it developed rather slowly. Instead one is confronted to a nebulous galaxy of social reformers and a mix of interwoven economic and political concerns such as the universal franchise, wages and conditions, the Republican Political System, etc.

GENERAL COMMENTS:

Second, a high degree of confusion reigns: on the one hand, individuals pass through parties and ideologies: one may well begin as an anarchist, become later a blanquist, and die a communist[4]. Pelloutier, for instance, the important figure who created the Labor Exchanges, was first a Guesdist, then a libertarian socialist and ended a revolutionary syndicalist. On the other hand it appears that it is not sure that the theoretical and ideological frameworks put together by the theoreticians and which some of the activists of the time claimed to follow were well known and mastered in their intricacies by some of their practitioners and followers.

Third, it is well known that industrialization was slow and late in France, much more so than in other developed countries of the times[5]. G. Noiriel[6] for instance, notes that until the late 1880's it is still the old economic sectors which are prevalent in the economic growth of the country. Agricultural production remains its essential element. Industry is divided into two sectors: a small modern one, concentrated and dynamic (mining, railroads, heavy metallurgy) and a traditional one, resting on tradi-

---

4) Multiple examples of such changes can be found in the notes by Dubief, presenting original texts from revolutionary unionists, Dubief, H., Le Syndicalisme Révolutionnaire, Paris, Armand Colin, 1969.
5) See for instance E. Hobshawn, L'ère des révolutions, Paris, Fayard, 1969.
6) Noiriel, G., Les ouvriers dans la société française-XIX°-XX° siécle, Paris, Editions du Seuil, 1986.

tional craft activities based on work at home and the dispersion of industry among rural areas. Whatever the much debated reasons for that state of affairs, it has resulted in the existence of a huge mass of small owners-peasants and the persistence of a large number of independent handicraftsmen, or highly skilled employed craft workers masters of their trade, spread among semi-rural areas and budding industrial centers with various and changing economic status and conditions of work. Within these industrial centers coexist a growing number of unskilled factory workers, employed skilled craft workers, self-employed handicraftsmen, low ranking civil servants, small shopkeepers, petty proprietors, artisans, the latter hovering between poverty and self-employment at the rhythm of the economic crisis of the XIXth Century. Thus, in France, took place a slow development by successive strata of a non-homogeneous population of workers, coming from a diversified industrial proletariat issued from different socio-economic backgrounds, constituted by successive waves of former farmhands, part-time peasants, migrants workers, women, crafstmen and former self employed handicraftsmen, resulting into a segmented, diversified Working Class[7]. This, in our view, was conducive to a dual consequence for the development of French Industrial Relations: on the one hand the persistence of a divided labor movement and, on the other hand the coexistence of diver-

---

7) As noted for instance by Lorwin, Val R., <u>The French Labor Movement</u>, Cambridge, Harvard University Press, 1954 or Sellier, F., <u>La confrontation sociale en France-1936-1981</u>, Paris, P. U. F., 1984.

gent ideologies issuing from and/or responding to differing needs of different segments of the working population. Noiriel[8], for instance, recalls that in the elections of 1848, 1851 and 1852, workers whose workplace was set in rural areas voted massively for the conservative candidate.

Fourth, an aspect often neglected should in our view be underlined and put in its rightful place. Workers and Unions ideologies should not be the only ones to be taken in account. The labor movement was facing a strong employer's ideology. It contained notably two important elements among others: full fledged economic liberalism, at least on the labor market if not on the product market when faced with foreign competition, and a concept of authority as sovereign. On the one hand, in the triple revolutionary heritage the emphasis here is put on "Liberty" or freedom, (among the other elements: fraternity, well forgotten by all, and equality, privileged by the other side). The consequence is full fledge liberalism. Whilst, in 1848, freedom, from political restraints with the universal franchise but also freedom of enterprise, constituted a common ground for both employers and workers, after the days of June, it was clear that it meant also a free market for labor, from the point of view of the employers, to be treated as a commodity like others. The freedom of contract was written in the constitution[9]. Individual rights

---

8) op. cit.
9) Lieberman, S., <u>Labor Movements and Labor Thought-Spain, France, Germany and the United</u> States, New-York, Praeger, 1986, p. 184.

were then protected and collective rights ignored, relaying the revolution's Le Chapelier Acts forbidding collective organization for "pretended" common interests, in the name of individualism.

On the other hand the central concept of power of the entrepreneur is of foremost importance, with its consequences: the right to manage, and the absolute authority flowing from it. M. Crozier[10] provided a penetrating picture of the French attitude towards authority, within his classic model of the bureaucratic vicious circle, held by everyone whether at the top or way below. It is absolutist, omnipotent, and universalistic. The holder of authority should know no limits to the extent of his power and no constraints in his way of exerting it, beyond narrowly interpreted legal ones, difficult to enforce in any case in a relationship of subordination, such as the one between employer and employee. Subordination was indeed the central element of the contract of employment, with which the Revolution and Empire replaced the "Ancien Régime"'s system of (theoretically) reciprocal duties hierarchically ordered. Because of its absolute nature authority cannot be shared or compromised and must remain sovereign, actually and symbolically. Procedural rules are unnecessary because the authority is absolute and concepts of fairness are as irrelevant as concepts of commutative justice. The idea of checks and balances, of due process, as well as the one of institutionalized countervailing power, or of sub-

---

10) Crozier, M., <u>Le phénoméne bureaucratique</u>, Paris, Le Seuil, 1956.

stantive limitations, is foreign to it. This concept of absolutism is both offensive and defensive: offensive because its holder has boundless authority upon others below him, and defensive because authority confers total autonomy and freedom of interference from the part of others. He who has authority has no account to give to anybody for his actions.

The model is easily applicable to the employment relationship and it permeates employers and managerial thought and behavior, to this day[11]. This, together with the consequences of the lateness and slow pace of industrialization drove the employers and the administrative elite ruling the country to an opposition stance to the lower classes which prevented it to manage the transition towards the integration of a middle Class within the "bourgeoisie"[12].

It is striking here to draw a parallelbetween the wall thus erected between the "bourgeoisie" and the working

---

11) See, for instance, Rojot, J. "The Development of French Employers' Policies towards Unions", Labour and Society, vol. 11, n° 1, Jan. 1986; "France", in M. J. Roomkin (ed.), Managers as employees, Oxford, Oxford University Press, 1989; "Human Resource Management in France", dans R. Pieper (ed.), Human Resource Management: An International Comparison, Berlin, De Gruyter, 1990; "France" in Peterson, R. B., Managers and National Culture—A Global Perspective, Westport, Conn. Quorum Books, 1993.

12) As noted by Charles, C., "Histoire Sociale de la France au XIX° Siécle", Paris, Seuil, 1991, p. 42. See also the very interesting account of Chevalier, L., Classes laborieuses et classes dangereuses, Paris, Plon, 1958.

class, with the enduring and bitter opposition which was its result, and the analysis by Tocqueville of a very similar phenomenon occuring earlier, under the "Ancien Régime", before the French revolution of 1789, between the aristocracy and the "bourgeoisie" of the times, although withthe respective positions inverted. Tocqueville[13] draws a comparision between the French and British Aristocracy and demonstrates how the former one, bent upon keeping at all costs its formal privileges, at the same time left the reality of power escape towardsthe centralized royal authority and insisted on maintaining the most visibly possible barrier between the conditions ofthose belonging to the nobility and allothers. At the same time the British aristocracy merged, within a range of related and combined conditions, with the British Bourgeoisie.

This indeed constitutes another example of the same model.

ELEMENTS OF "SPONTANEOUS" WORKER'S ORGANIZATIONS IDEOLOGIES.

It is meant by spontaneous that they are not traced to philosophical or economic doctrines but that they appeared by themselves among unionists as they become manifest in demands and worker's expression of the times, without any prior influence of theoreticians, even though certain leaders later formalized them. We see them as a mix of three separate elements.

---

13) Tocqueville, A. de, "L'ancien Régime et la Révolution", Euvres Complétes, Tome 2, Paris, Gallimard, 1985, originally 1856.

ELEMENTS OF "SPONTANEOUS" WORKER'S ORGANIZATIONS IDEOLOGIES.

Uprising against the ruling elite

French urban people has demonstrated a spontaneous tradition of bloody uprising: for instance, the 1789 revolution, of course, but also in the violent strikes of Lyon in 1831, 1834 (when strikers took over the city for a period before been defeated by the army) and 1840, the Paris uprisings of 1830 and 1848 and the Commune of 1871, as well as "insurrectional" strikes notably in the North. In all those cases, collective action was more spontaneous than planned. Of course, leaders emerged and theoreticians appeared, but who joined the movement rather having organized it. In most cases, the insurgents were defeated and submitted to bloody repression. Interestingly, Benoit Malon, originally member of the Bakouninist anarchist "Federation du Jure", later a builder of French socialism, counts 1871 as the third defeat of the French Proletariat after June 1848 and Lyon, 1831-1834[14]. Characteristically, he does not include either 1789 or 1830, considered as "bourgeois" events and not proletarians uprisings. In the later cases the actors initially involed in the revolutionary action were not part of the industrial proletariat, but mostly artisans and handicraftsmen, together with elements of more wealthy bourgeoisie[15].

Equality

Whereas, as noted above, employers came to favor "lib-

---

14) Malon, B., La troisiéme défaite du prolétariat français, quoted by Lefranc, G., Le mouvement socialiste sous la troisiéme république, Paris, Payot 1977, T 1, p. 16.

15) As noted notably by Lorwin, op. cit. pp. 4 et 9.

erty" over "fraternity and equality", workers by themselves privileged "equality". Spontaneously, the revolutionary crowds of Paris in 1789 (the "sans-culottes") while not demanding the abolishment of private property (although regulated for the common good, whereas it was sovereign and with unlimited rights for the bourgeoisie for which it constituted the "natural right" enshrined later by the Napoleonic civil code) reflected a strong and powerful egalitarian ideology, present in the French society of the times, resulting in a view of a society made up of small proprietors. S. Lieberman[16] makes the point that this vision of an egalitarian society was appealing both to the small bourgeoisie and to a lower Class largely made of "artisans, craftsmen, shopkeepers and peasants who constituted the bulk of French society in the days of the revolution and the empire". It found its expression notably in the Acts selling the "national properties", holdings seized from the clergy and the nobility. The persistence of such a social structure instead of the massive apparition of a proletarian homogeneous Working Class, as described above, may help explain that a large segment of the labor movement accepted the principle of private property, and insisted upon equality in its allocation. Thus, instead of collectivism, private property remained an active principle in some worker's ideologies with the accent put on its equal distribution rather than on the advocacy of its replacement by collective ownership of the means of production.

---

16) op. cit., p. 227.

ELEMENTS OF "SPONTANEOUS" WORKER'S ORGANIZATIONS IDEOLOGIES.

Social improvement or corporatist unionism.

The first title which we give it is drawn from the work of Goetz-Girey"[17], who himself prefers to call it "doctrineless unionism", because it arose from a pragmatic non theoretical grassroots based process. The second one relates to our interpretation of this current of thought in more modern terms. During the period of suppression of unionism and labor movements, from 1791 to 1864 (or 1884 in legal if not de facto terms) some workers' organizations were nevertheless created under various guises, recognized by law or secretly constituted: survivors of "compagnonnage" (rival societies of craftsman organized on a national basis, and banned by the law), mutual help societies (with the purpose of gathering dues to pay members unemployment compensation and retirement pension in the face of the absence of any social security in the times, which were lawful under certain conditions) and "résistance sociétés" (adding to the protection against the former risks the one of granting pay during strikes, and therefore banned). These organizations had in common to be centered around corporatist concerns for an occupation. The chambres syndicales created after the 1864 "de facto" acceptance of unions, which will not be legally "de jure" authorized before 1884, by the liberal phase of the II° Empire, organize around similar concerns. Drawing on the remnants of these earlier organizations, after the commune

---

17) Goetz-Girey, R., La pensée syndicale française: militants et théoriciens, Cahiers de la fondation nationale des Sciences politiques n° 5, Paris, Armand Colin, 1948.

of Paris, Jules Barberet organizes first in 1872 a "union syndicale", immediately forbidden by the authorities, then the first workers' congress of Paris, in 1876 was tolerated, and will be followed by several others (Lyon in 1878 and Marseilles in 1879, discussed further below). It adopts a program characterized by three major trends. First is an insistence on practical and pragmatic goals, making it a forerunner of reformism. The (more ideologically and theoretically oriented) "bourgeois utopists" were condemned and a platform of immediate concrete reforms demanded (including 8 hours work day for women, pensions for workers administered by unions, free occupational education, freedom of unionism, labor courts, help for producers cooperatives). The strike if considered sometimes necessary was nevertheless deemed dangerous and the tactical accent was put on worker's education and studies and constructive propositions.

Second is an opposition to collective ownership and the recognition of individual property. Third is a strong accent put on the autonomy of the labor movement. It is to be made exclusively of workers and run by workers. Barberet, himself a journalist, has had even problems gaining entrance to the congress he was instrumental in organizing[18]. The grassroots home grown idea apparent in these principles of organization is that the labor movement should stand by itself, of itself. It does not need outside help either from theories and thoreticians or from "allies" drawn from outside the workers. On the one hand, what

---

18) Goetz-Girey, op. cit.

it must support is strictly occupational demands and not political change. On the other hand, it can face the power of capital alone and not only does not need the support of the State and/or of political parties but must be strictly separated from them. The idea of the autonomy of the labor movement from any foreign ideology or theory and of its capacity to free the working class by itself and to insure alone all the satisfaction of the needs of the workers is thus early apparent. It will play later a strong influence and will appear as tracing a deep dividing line between ideologies, notably against Marxism.

THE COMMUNIST INFLUENCE.

Babeuf

Early communism is marked by Gracchus Babeuf[19], probably the inventor of the term itself, beheaded, despite his earlier suicide, under the Directoire and whose "conspiration des égaux"(name both of his conspiracy and of the book later posthumously published and allegedly describing his ideas) was later popularized by one of the surviving members Michelangelo Buonarotti. Three elements appear important in his doctrine: absolute equality which combined here with the abolition of private property and was completed by the strategy of the seizure of power by the means of a conspiracy led by a society made of "an active minority". The latter will inspire notably Blanqui and his followers. Also, its legacy include the constitution of secret

---

19) who, in a spirit of republicanism had changed the first names in his family to ones found in the roman republic times.

societies as a means to prepare the grasp for power (Saisons, Droits de l'Homme), including workers, which will be then active in uprisings[20].

Marx

Indeed, Marx did write in the preamble to the By-Laws of the First International Workingmen Association that the liberation of the workers must be the work of the workers themselves. However, they were not supposed to achieve it alone and this statement must be qualified by the reading of some others of his writings.

In the annex B 7 to wage labour and capital[21] Marx writes specifically about workers associations: "...The aim of associations is to suppress competition and replace with union among workers...All these objections raised by bourgeois economists are, as we have already stated, correct, but only from their point of view. If the associations were only what they appear to be—i.e. concerned with fixing salaries, if the relationship between labor and capital were eternal, these coalitions would fail, powerless in the face of the reality of things. But they are of use to the unification of the working Class, to the preparation to the overthrow of the old society with all its Class antagonisms. And from this point of view the workers rightly pay no

---

20) On the latter point, Branciard, M., <u>Société Française et lutte de classes</u>, T 1, 1789/1914, Lyon, Chronique sociale de France, 1967, p. 46.

21) Editions en langues étrangéres, Pékin, 1976, translation from the French by the author.

attention to the conning bourgeois pedants who quote the cost of this civil war in dead, wounded and money. If you are going to do battle with your enemy you do not go and discuss the costs of war with him. And what proves the generosity of the workers to the economists themselves is the fact that it is the better-paid factory workers who form the coalitions and that the workers use all the money that they can save from their own salaries to create political and industrial associations and meet the costs of these movements. And if these bourgeois...are kind enough to allow the minimum increase in salary... it must seem as shameful as it is incomprehensible to them to see the workers using a portion of this pittance to finance the war against the bourgeoisie, and finding that their revolutionary activity gives them more pleasure than anything else".

Also, and even more significantly, in Wages, Price and Profit[22], he adds: "...is this saying that the working Class ought to renounce their resistance against the encroachments of capital and abandon their attempts at making the best of occasional chances for their temporary improvement? If they did, they would be degraded to one level mass of broken wretches past salvation... By cowardly giving way in their every day conflict with capital they would certainly disqualify themselves for the initiating of any larger movement. At the same time, and quite apart of the general servitude involved in the wages system, the

---

22) Foreign Language Press, Peking, 1975, p. 76.

working Class ought not to exaggerate to themselves the ultimate working of these every day struggles. They ought not to forget that they are fighting with effects, not with the causes of these effects. They ought to understand that with all the miseries it imposes upon them, the present system simultaneously engenders the material conditions and the social forms necessary for an economical reconstruction of society......Trade-unions work well as centers of resistance against the encroachments of capital. They fail partially from an injudicious use of their power. They fail generally from limiting themselves to a guerrilla war against the effects of the existing system, instead of simultaneously trying to change it, instead of using their organized forces as a lever for the final emancipation of the working Class, that is to say, the ultimate abolition of the wage system".

Thus, Marxism clearly inscribes immediately itself in full contradiction to the ideas just described of the spontaneous early French unionism, as it is obvious from the above quotations.

Guedism.

French communism is marked by the figure of Jules Guesde (1845-1922), an anarchist turned marxist who looked for (and obtained) the endorsement of the program of his party by Marx and Engels, from London, in 1880. At the third workers congress, in 1879, in Marseilles (mentionned above), Guesde will succeed in having it endorse a platform of collectivization of private property. He immediately creates the Fédération du Parti des Travailleurs de France, a political party, out of this worker's congress. In his understanding and reading of Marx, simplified and "personalized"[23] he privileges, beyond the promotion of collectivism and revolutionary action, the postulate that everything must pass through the seizure of power by the proletariat. This compulsorily happens with the Class political party which represents it. The rest is illusion. Thus is derived the conception of a strictly disciplined and organized party and the secondary, subordinate and submissive role of the union towards the Party. This concept will be extremely influential, positively and negatively, in the organization of French unions. Guesdists will for a brief time dominate the nascent union movement. The Fédération national des syndicats created in 1886 and inheritor of the tradition of the earlier socialists workers congresses, will initially fall under the Guesdists guidance[24]. However, the labor movement, later, will define itself against the principles of Guedism in the 1906 Charter of Amiens (which claims the independence of the labor movement from the State, Political Partires, Sects, etc...). However, starting then originating with Guesde, and later strenghtened, a powerful communist trend will be a permanent feature within the central umbrella union organization, to be later created.

---

23) as pointed by Lefranc, op. cit.

24) Winock, M., among others summarizes the process, Le socialisme en Frence et en Europe, Paris, Editions du Seuil, 1992, pp 75-76.

Lenin

In "What is to be done", Lenin formalizes the idea of the exteriority of class consciousness and of the role of the vanguard of the proletariat in the emancipation of the working class, unable to proceed to it by itself:

"We have said that there could not yet be Social-democratic consciousness among the workers. It could only be brought to them from without. The history of all countries shows that the working class, exclusively by its own effort, is able to develop only trade union consciousness, i. e. the conviction that it is necessary to combine in unions, fight the employers and strive to compel the government to pass necessary labor legislation, etc... The theory of socialism however, grew out of the philosophic, historical and economic theories that were elaborated by the educated representatives ofthe properied classes, the intellectuals"[25],..." "Everyone agrees" that it is necessary to develop the political consciousness of the working class. The question is how is that to be done and what is required to do it? The economic struggle merely "brings home" to the workers questions concerning the attitude of the government towards the working class. Consequently, however much we may try to "lend the economic struggle itself a political character" we shall never be able to develop the political consciousness of the workers (to the level of Social Democratic political consciousness) by keeping within the framework of economic struggle, for that framework is

---

25) Lenin, W. I., What is to be done, Foreign Language Press, Peking, 1975, p. 37 (initially written in 1905).

too narrow...Class political consciousness can be brought to the workers only from without, that is from outside of the economic struggle, from outside of the sphere of relations between workers and employers. The sphere from which alone it is possible to obtain this knowledge is the sphere of relationships between all the classes and strata and the state and the government, the sphere of the interrelations between all the classes[26].

He adds later[27] "In its work, the Party relies directly on the trade-unions...which are formally non-party. Actually all the directing bodies of the vast majority of the unions... consists of communists and carry out the directives of the Party. Thus on the whole, we have a formally non-Communist, flexible and relatively very powerful proletarian apparatus, by means of which the Party is closely linked up with the class and with the masses, and by means of which, under the leadership of the party the dictatorship of the class is exercised"

The union centre umbrella organization split of 1920-1921

The consequences of the implementation of these combined elements of doctrine in the development of French unionism are obvious. At the Tours Congress of the SFIO (French Socialist Party reconstituted as discussed below), the question of the adhesion to the Third International (communist) is raised. At the Union Congress in the fol-

---

26) id. pp. 97-98.
27) "Left-Wing Communism, an Infantile Disorder" Peking, Foreign Language Press, 1975, p. 38.

lowing year the debate spills over. Two of the twenty one conditions to be fulfilled for the adhesion concern the unions. The ninth foresees that within the unions it is necessary to create communist cores which, by a ceaseless and tenacious activity must gain these groups to the communist cause. These communist cores must be completely subordinated to the party. The tenth provides for international union activity "the duty to drive a stubborn fight against the "international" of the yellow unions of Amsterdam", to support "by all means the nascent international union of red unions which joined the communist international"[28]. Minority communists in the then reformist majority union center form revolutionary communist committees (CSR) which try to build influence and attempt to take over the union. It will end in both cases by a split in the party and in the union center. However, a strong legacy of a communist led union will be established, as well as a virulent anti communism in other parts of the labor movement.

OTHER SOCIALIST INFLUENCES.

Guedism is probably the forerunner of a political party of the left in the modern sense. Republicans and radicals parties of the times were more like loosely assembled gathering of individualities sharing a set of common ideas. Whilst upholding the objectives of political democracy they also remained, in practice, when they came to power, at-

---

[28] Branciard, M., <u>Syndicats et partis</u>, Paris, Syros, 1982, T. I, p. 89.

tached to the preeminence of private property, liberalism as a dogma in economic policy and individual freedom over collective rights. However, some "independent" socialists, had been elected in elections at various levels, including municipalities and parliament. On the one hand, they did not share much of the doctrines of the theoreticians of the times and stayed outside of the 5 socialist parties then existing (to be outlined below). On the other hand they did put forward their social concerns in economic areas and the pursuit of collective aims. Powerful influences will come from their ranks, such as Jaurés, Millerand, Viviani, Briand. An earlier attempt to create an independent socialist republican alliance in the 1880's (ASR), by survivors of the Paris Commune, had failed after one year.

The inheritors of the social improvement or corporatist unionism ideas will gather with other ideological currents in the ranks of the reformist unions. Here, one can count several distincs strands. On the one hand are the supporters of the revisionist socialism of Arthur Bernstein, promoting gradual improvement of the worker's condition within the existing liberal and capitalist system, by which it will finally spontaneously transform itself. On the other hand more intrinsically French currents of ideas are also influent. This is the case notably for positivists, followers of the doctrine of the philosopher August Comte which reserved a special place in his system for the proletariat as a guide in the transition towards the "sociocratic" society. Keufer, for instance who for more than 40 years headed the powerful union of the printers and "book workers" was also a dignitary in the international positivist society and the leader of the reformist trend within the central umbrella union organiation[29].

On the other hand, after the failure of the Paris Commune, the nascent revolutionary socialist movement was beheaded, until the pardon of 1880 and the return of the convicts, exiles and banned. In its reconstitution 5 socialist political parties will co-exist in between the repression of the commune and the (temporary) merger of 1905[30].

As discussed above, in 1879 the Marseilles worker's congress under the Guesdists influence gives birth to a political party, approving the version of Marxism, then adopted and adapted, by Guesde, in deciding upon the collective appropriation of the means of production. The FTST (Fédération des Travailleurs Socialistes de France) is thus created. In 1880 at the Le Havre Congress, the corporatists leave the Party, the following year the anarchists leave also. In 1881, after the return from the exiles of the Commune the Blanquists create their own Comité Révolutionnaire Central (CRC), under the leadership of Blanqui (who will have passed 36 years of his life in jail), and around his newspaper "Neither god nor master". It later will be headed by Edouard Vaillant, which will transforms it into the PSR (Parti Socialiste Révolutionnaire) in 1898. The Blanquists advocate the role of "active minorities" and

---

29) Dubief, op. cit., p. 21.
30) Their very complex history is simply outlined below.

secret societies in preparing and running the revolution. At the 1882's congress, under the leadership of Paul Brousse, the authoritarianism of Guesde is exposed. He leaves and creates the POF (Parti ouvrier français), whilst the FTSF under Brousse and the Broussistes adopts a "possibilist"(electoralist and reformist) stance. Another scission will take place in 1890, the Allemanistes under Jean Allemane, reproaching the broussists their compromissions with the radical political parti, then in power, leave to create the Party Ouvrier Socialiste Révolutionnnaire (POSR), which subordinates the political fight to the union fight, and represents revolutionary socialism, the political arm of revolutionary unionism, discussed below. After the elections of 1892 the socialists among the various appellations briefly recalled above have 50 seats in parliament and are dominant in town councils (municipalities). Some of the "parliamentary socialists", after the "Millerand" case try to integrate the labor movement within the State (Millerand, Jaurés, Poincaré). This will fail because of a dual opposition: the influence of the anti state tradition which prevents the union leadership to accept it[31] by condemning the integration of the labor movement into society (under the influence of a mixture of the ideologies of early corporatism and anarcho syndicalism, discussed above), and the opposition of the Guesdists and other socialists opposed in participation into "bourgeois" governments. In 1901, the socialist parties more to the left (POF, PSR and the Communist Alliance), split from the

---

31) Goetz-Girey, op. cit. p. 38.

POSR and join into the PSDF (Parti Socialiste de France), while the FTST and the independants socialists join in the PSF (Parti Socialiste Français) in 1902. The two will merge in 1905, together with the POSR, which even though with revolutionary aims has closer links to the PSF by opposition to the Guesdists, into the SFIO ("Section Frençaise de L'Internationale Ouvriére: Franch Chapter of the (second) International Workingmen Association). The merger is not easy. It takes place after multiple arguments, under the pressure of the International and finally in an uneasy compromise around the definition of the party as a class and revolutionary organization.

However, as electoral successes accumulate and as Jaurès becomes the dominant influence, among multiple debate, several divisions into rival internal factions and sometimes defections, the daily practice becomes more reformist. The Guesdists move gradually towards reformism also. Jules Guesde becomes a Minister in a war government of 1914 and looses any grip over the labor movement, which under the influence of revolutionary unionism, discussed immediately below and the unfortunate experience with divided political parties, constitutes itself then as against all political parties of which it fears the attempts towards control and which it despises for their rivalries and inefficiency.

Both World War I, and the victory of the bolchviks in Russia in 1917 will deeply change the situation within the socialists parties and the unions.

OTHER THEORETICIANS AND IDEOLOGUES.

Several could be quoted, often gathered under the generic category of "utopic socialists", such as Cabet, Fourrier, Enfantin and many others. Some left a practical as well as theoretical heritage, such as workers, cooperatives some of which established in the United States under Cabet's guidelines. However, a choice had to be made and two seemed particularly influent, through the intellectual pervasiveness of their work, although belonging to two very separate time periods and currents of thought:

Saint-Simon (1760-1825)

Durkheim sees in Saint-Simon the founder of socialism[32]. It is interesting to note that he served under Washington in the war of independence and then was deeply impressed by the characteristics of a society of producers which he found in the United States of the times[33] In his doctrine, he advocates the ruling of society by the best qualified, i. e. by what we would call today the technocracy. In an extremely amusing illustration, his parable, he opposes the consequences of the possible disappearance of the 30000 most important members of the court and dignitaries of the kingdom, starting with the Brother of the King, which would deeply pain the French, "for they are kind people", but which would leave the power and might

---

32) Durkheim, E. Le socialisme, Paris, Retz, 1978. (orig. P. U. F., Paris, 1928)
33) Desanti, D., Les socialistes de l'utopie, Paris, Payot, 1970.

of the Nation intact, to the situation where the 3000 most important scientists, artists, industrialists, traders and the like would disappear, which would bring France to a subordinate state among Nations. His system is not democratic either. Leaders are not elected, but appointed. That legacy, whether its source is recognized and acknowledged or not is very much alive in the French unions structure and organization today. It is demonstrated everyday in the recruitment of the elites, and, combined with the tradition of "the aristocracy of the working class" described below, explains why union leaders are most often called from the top, by those already in place and not elected and promoted from the bottom up by the rank and file.

Sorel (1847-1922)

He will be influential, notably through his famous and widely quoted "Réflexions sur la violence."(Reflexions on violence). His ideas are consonant, in general, with the main themes of revolutionary unionism. He starts from the point that the proletariat must live in its own moral world, that it must have values which are its own, different from the ones of the rest of society. Its purest expression, the union, must absorb first socialism and then the state. He advocates a specific and unique position in the means of action that he proposes to be used. On the one hand, the first of these means is the general strike. However it is understood, not as the practical tool considered by revolutionary unionism activists, but as a myth. Whether it ever takes place or not is irrelevant. Its strenght rests in distinguishing the proletariat from all other forces in society, in isolating and separating it from anything else, in dividing society into two camps and two camps only, which face each other. It makes all other mediations or interventions (intellectuals, political parties, etc...) irrelevant. All incidents, conflicts, local strike must be inscribed in the perspective of the social war in which there can be no armistice. The idea of the general strike gives a revolutionary perspective to all events referring to it. On the other hand, is his conception of violence. He opposes it to simple strength, which can merely impose a given social order dominated by a minority, for it has a different object: to destroy all social order and thus create a free society. This concept of pure violence does not compulsorily implies brute force or the use of revolutionary tactics (secret committees, beheadings and the like). It is closer to war and has the value of an exemple. Proletarian violence has the value of military demonstrations which imply neither hate nor revenge, but operate as much by dissuasion as by actual operations. It also marks the separation of the proletariat from the rest of society. It does not know compromise. Sorel advises the "blackest ingratitude" towards those who want to protect workers, to oppose insults to the advocacy of human fraternity and to answer by blows to the promoters of social peace. As aptly commented by Furet[34] "Violence for Sorel...aims to tear the veil of lies which covers society and to give back to individuals their moral dignity, together with the meaning

---

34) Furet, F. Le passé d'une illusion : Essai sur l'idée communiste au XX° siécle, Paris, Robert Laffont, 1995.

of their collective existence. It allows, as in Nietzsche, to ground again the greatness of man, beyond the universal smallness of the democratic times. The bourgeois lives within hypocrisy; the class struggle brings back virtue on the public scene, to the benefit of the proletarian. It gives violence an ethic finality and assimilates the revolutionary activist to the hero".

REVOLUTIONARY UNIONISM.

Direct influences
Proudhon 1809-1864

Proud'hon exemplifies the mix of the spirit of handicraft's man with working class aspirations. His social origin and his career place him into the class of craftsmen/ petty proprietors/minor civil servants discussed above. He has also a talent for expression and a gift for finding the most striking wording. He is the author of the slogan "property is theft", often since used out of context, although his system does not abolish totally private property, (ownership and patrimony remain) but aims only to limit its abusive use. He is also a prodigiously productive writer, publishing more than 40 books and countless articles in newspapers, including his own. His system embraces all aspects of human problems : economy, philosophy, morals, metaphysic, politics, religion.

He claims himself an anarchist, maybe the first one, even though he is opposed to revolutionary violence, and even to the use of the strike, as an abuse over others' dignity and freedom. He also, and he is maybe the first one to do so, points out the indelible complexity of social issues and he evidences the "contradictions" due to most things having a "double face" and thus prohibiting simple easy solutions, as ill fit to complex problems.

The central impact of his theories on the labor movement rests around the idea of justice, as the recognition in the other of a person equal to ours. It is the spontaneous and reciprocally guaranteed respect of human dignity in everyone and under any circumstance. It rests on equality and individual freedom. The link between individuals is horizontal, between equals and not hierarchical from superior to inferior, from governor to govened. Thus justice is opposed to power, property, state, government, authority (except the sacred one of the father upon the family and of the husband upon the wife).

His system is federalism, resting on the political side on self-administration by autonomous basic political groups articulated from the bottom up, and on the economic side on mutualist association of individual properties into cooperatives at various levels. Mutualism and federalism imply that the contracts into which individuals enter are totally free. To the difference of the "social contract" of Rousseau or Hobbes for instance, no individual abdicates anything to anyone. The contracts are besides always subject to revision, since circumstances change. Anyone must receive as much than he gives. No one can be forced into them against his will, and they are to change as things change. The system implies free credit. The multiplicity of contracts results in Federalism, which replaces the State. An equilibrium is perpetually secured by always modified and ever changing groupings.

Anarcho-syndicalism.

Some historians oppose the use sometimes made indifferently of anarcho-syndicalism and revolutionary unionism to cover the same phenomenon, because of the controversial and subjective meanings attached to the former[35]. However, many anarchists joined the labor movement, some, as discussed below, in order to influence it towards their own political aims, some others became convinced and influential unionists and union leaders, and still some others to which the two pursuits seemed fully compatible. It seems, thus, that a brief description of anarcho-syndicalism is justified, as a component of the more varied and encompassing concept of revolutionary unionism.

Also, in France, in common use, "anarchism" is considered as an equivalent of "libertarianism". Actually, among other definitions of "libertarian", the Robert dictionary offers "anarchist". In American use, the term "libertarian" seems, albeit coming from the same roots, to have taken a slightly different meaning. While advocating the absolute supremacy of individual freedom and the denial of any limitation to it, it appears also to be linked with 19th century indigenous transcendentalism, promoting an idealistic system of thought based on a belief of the essential unity of all creation, the innate goodness of man and the supremacy of insight over logic and experience for the

---

35) Notably Dubief, op. cit. p. 6.

revelation of truth, driving to a protest of the then established order[36]. Thoreau extended these ideas from the political and religious sphere into social and personal life, upholding the right to a life shaped by inner principle, whatever the dominant values and ideas of society around the individual, up to civil disobedience. Although based also in individualism, this type of libertarianism is definitely different from the one practiced by the French anarchists. It uphelds the right of man to defend, go by and obey his own values, what he deeply, individually feels to be true, be they in contradiction with the social dictae then prevailing, even if the latter are legally compulsory. However, apart of this power to assert oneself by oneself, it leaves social order alone. To the contrary the French anarchists of the times aim to suppress society as it is.

Etymologically, anarchy means without master, or without government. It has come to promote a society without government[37]. However, anarchism rests on two tenets[38]. Kropotkin holds that man is naturally social, if not good, as Rousseau provided. Bakunin illustrates the primacy of the individual, the autonomy, the independence of everyone. Society should be grounded in the voluntary cooperation of individuals for the fulfillment of their social and economic needs. Thus, organization from outside voluntary groups implying a degree of compulsion, in general, and

---

36) "trancendantalism", in the Encyclopedia Britannica.
37) G. Woodcock, (ed.), Introduction, The Anarchist Reader, Glasgow, Fontana, 1977.
38) Id.

by government in particular, is not only unnecessary, it is foremostly oppressive and harmful.

It is at first glance surprising that a movement which has for goal the suppression of society, of hierarchy, of all kind organization aligns itself with unionism, which is precisely the very organization of workers into an active force in order to make their demands prevail. At second glance, however, it appears that the two concepts have many common interests. Anarchism is federalist, that is. anti-centralism, anti-state (oppressive by definition), anti-democratic (it recommends non-voting, for to vote is to delegate one's own individual powers, to adibcate one's voice). Thus the state must be destroyed, with its values, its structures (church, government, employers, army), as well as not only those who proclaim and defend them, but also those who submit to them. The first method to be used is revolutionary violence. It includes individual "restitution" (i.e. theft, forgery) and propaganda by the deed (hopeless mini revolutions, terrorist acts hitting as much society as its voluntary slaves, in order to awaken the masses to the necessary revolution). The names of Ravachol and Bonnot illustrate this strategy. It resulted into a bloody failure. A second strategy passes through the unions, for political parties, which want to take over, instead of abolishing, the state as it should be the case, are useless. The advantages of the union from the point of view of the anarchists are well illustrated by Malatesta, in his debate with Monatte and others at the Congress of Amsterdam in 1907. "Syndicalism, or rather the workers movement (the workers' movement is a fact that nobody can ignore, whereas syndicalism is a doctrine, a system, and we must avoid to confuse the two) has always found in me a defender, staunch but not blind. It is because I have seen in it a particularly fertile ground for our revolutionary propaganda as well as a point of contact between the masses and us...... I want, today as yesterday, that anarchists join the labor movement. I am, today like yesterday a syndicalist in the sense that I am in favor of unions. I do not demand anarchist unions, which would immediately legitimate social-democratic, republican royalist... unions...... It is necessary that anarchists go into workers unions. First to make the anarchist propaganda, then because it is the only means for us to have to our disposal, on the day that they will be needed, groups able to take over the direction of production ... finally to react against this detestable state of mind which bring unions to defend only particular interests"[39].

It is not only a strategy of "entrism" to describe it in more modern terms, in order to use the channel of the unions to awaken its members to the need to pass from resistance (to employers) to revolt (against the government), but more in depth it illustrates at the times a commonality, at least partial, of objectives. Let us recall from earlier developments that the spontaneous organization of the first unions was, for part, oriented towards producers cooperatives, free associations of producers,

---

[39] "Amsterdam, 1907, le débat syndical", Spartacus, série B, n° 97, Sept.-Oct 1978, p. 25 ff.

which are fully compatible with the anarchist ideal of voluntary cooperation. Besides the unionists of the times and the anarchists have common foes. They are both opposed to the employers (even though for different reasons: very practical against somewhat theoretical); to the state, which systematically sides with the employers and arrests anarchists, but also fears the always potentially dangerous working class which it has failed to integrate; to the Church, which in the France of the times has long ago sided with the employers also and which, for the anarchists is an instrument of the state doctrine. Also, they both share, against the Guesdists and the Marxists, the idea that the proletariat owns in itself the means of his emancipation, of its liberation, that it does not need that a leadership be brought from outside to free it. Finally, they are both anti-parliamantarian and opposed to political parties, by doctrine for the anarchists, by having witnessed the ravages of political quarrels among socialists parties for the unions leaders.

Revolutionary unionism or syndicalism.

A pragmatic movement

It is sometimes called direct action unionism, because of the importance devoted by it to direct action, as discussed below. It is to some extent a product of its times, that is somewhat the result, positive or negative, of the many influences reviewed above, but it is not the inheritor of a deliberately thought out process or strategy. Delesalle, in

1910, states that "what characterizes the French union movement is its constant evolution... Revolutionary unionism does not come from out of the brain of a theoretician. It is a practice which is in search of a doctrine in order to grow and multiply"[40]. Julliard[41] will later insist on this point. More than a doctrine existing a priori, it is an ex-post theoretization of a grass roots movement, a field invented and practice honed set of moves and thoughts, born from day-to-day union work. All of it was then understood and interpreted in the light of the influence of what its practitioners knew of the work of social reformers and theoreticians. That element of doctrine was often self taught and often came from the readings and discussions of self educated activists,

The men

It gathers among its leaders men from different origins: corporatists, reformists, former guesdists, former blanquists, anarchists and former anarchists. Among the main leaders will be Pelloutier, Griffuelles, Pouget. Leaders and activists are issued from the numerous group (discussed above and born because of the slow rate industrialization) of handicraftsmen, self-employed, petty proprietors, low ranking civil servants, of autonomous, if however sometimes employed, highly skilled and skilled craftsmen, masters of

---

40) Spartacus, op. cit.
41) Julliard, J., Fernand Pelloutier et les origines du syndicalisme d'action directe, Paris, Le Seuil, 1971.

their trade, but slowly forced into the growing working class as victims of the many economic recessions[42]. The legacy of the repression of the Commune is also influent in terms of its ideological weight[43].

Workers aristocracy

It is a worker's movement limited in size[44], but voluntarily so, and which does not look for its development into a mass movement. It considers itself a working class aristocracy: belonging to the union is exclusive: it expresses the will of conscious men, against the uncounsciousness of the masses, drives to an ethical and exemplary behavior (made notably of solidarity).

"Unionism has for its goal to improve the moral (as well as) economic level of workers... it would be useless to recruit thousands of comrades if they simply pay the organization their dues... they would not be useful unionists"[45]. The union leader is seen and sees himself as a role model.

Notable characteristics.

---

42) A condition deplored but acknowledged in the authorized his tory of the CGT, see Bruhat, J., Piolot, M., Esquisse d'une histoire de la C. G. T., Paris, Centre Confédéral d'Education Ouvriére, Confédération Générale du Travail, 1966, p 35.
43) Dubief, op. cit., p. 18.
44) Bruhat, op. cit., p. 21.
45) Dubief, op. cit., p. 276.

It considers that unionism is self-sufficient. Economic and political action cannot be separated and are merged into union activity, which remains the only one necessary to transform society.

Revolutionary unionism is anti-political, anti parlementarian and opposed to political parties: the corporatists because they resent the political parties goals to use them to other ends than their own corporatist economic aims, the anarcho-syndicalists by doctrine and because they ridicule the centralism and authorianism of the Guedists, the reformists because the doctrine of the transmission belt assigns to the union a subordinate goal to the one of the party. Also, the quarrels and divisions of the socialists between 1871 and 1905 gives them little credibility in unionists eyes. Maybe, also the unions collect dues, and the parties are pennyless, the use of the money becomes a stake[46]. Besides, freedom and autonomy stand against the principle of authority of which democracy is the latest expression[47].

It is also anti religious, opposed to the nascent catholic unionism under the influence of the Encyclica Rerum Novarum and considers that just as the political parties, the Catholic Church aims to keep the workers in a subordinate position. It is of course anti government, which is

---

46) The dialectic of the Union-Party relationship in Europe, as time elapses, is interestingly analyzed in Kassalov, E., <u>Trade Unions and Industrial Relations: An International Comparison</u>, New-York, Random House, 1969, Chap. II and III.

47) Pouget, quoted by Dubief, <u>op. cit.,</u> p. 181.

merely the care taker of the oppressors. Finally it is antimilitaristic, with degrees. Generally speaking, the Army, "watchdog of capital" has many times opened fire on strikers. However, there is much discussion whether this should or not become anti-patriotic[48]. For certain factions, there is no doubt in the matter. Gustave Hervé, for instance, claims that the rightful place for the national French flag is to be stuck in a pile of manure. Ironically, he will become an ardent supporter of the "sacred union" against Germany in 1914. He also should be remembered as the author of the expression "le citoyen browning" (citizen Browning), where one will recognize the ancestor of the "comrade P 38" of the Italian leftists during the hot autumn of 1969, and of Mademoiselle Cisaille[49] (Miss Shears) for sabotage.

Workers as a separate class

Proud'hon, Bakunin and revolutionary unionism have in common with marxism to assert the specific condition in society of the proletariat and of the worker in industry. Proud'hon differs because he is not a revolutionary (despite his provocative discourse). He advocates federalism and mutuellism. However, revolutionary unionists differ from Marxists because they believe in the capacity of the proletariat to free itself, by its own devices. This stands

---

[48] Julliard, J. La CGT devant la Guerre, Le mouvement social, oct-déc 1964.

[49] recalled by Jouhaux, Griffhuelles et autres, quoted by Dubief, op. cit., p. 218.

against the doctrine of the party, vanguard of the working class and Marx doctrine of the exteriority of the emancipation of the proletariat. This is a common point with the Anarchists, but also an autonomous idea, held together with the early corporatists unionists, as recalled above. One of its consequences can be seen in the organization and federation of the "Labor exchanges" under the influence of Pelloutier, originally organizing workers locally, independently of political parties but also industrial unions, in order to create a control on the supply of labor.

Thus, both Marxism and revolutionary unionism share the idea of the specificity of the worker in industry: the proletariat. Both consider the worker as a separate class. However they draw different conclusions from it. This specificity of a class, also brings some segments of revolutionary unionism to consider the proletariat as a separate society. Despised, feared and kept at a distance by the dominant forces in society, it must create its own separate social institutions. In that light the union will set up several ones, such as educational, in which much hope is put, or providing services to the members, "viaticum", meals, etc...

This will be sometimes linked with a moral view of the working class (honest, decent) as opposed to the corrupt, vicious, sinful (particularly sexually) bourgeoisie. The sober "moral" mores of the working class are opposed it to the degenerate (as well as expensive and wasteful) ways of the dominant classes. A part of the literature of the times (see for instance the Journal d'une femme de chambre, by Octave Mirbeau) witnesses to this peculiar aspect of a society with its own, including moral, characteristics.

Sometimes, this conception of "moral" borders on prudishness and has some unfortunate aspects, particularly regarding sexual discrimination. Whilst some quarters of unionism protest the exploitation of women, some other assign the women a more than traditional rôle, and are clearly anti-feminist such as Proudhon, for instance. Dubief[50], reports that in Lyon, in 1913, an activist was excluded from the union because he had authorized his wife to work, and she, adding insult to injury, had the gall to try to join a union. Among the reformists, the same applies, and the traditional hostility to women joining their ranks from the part of the printers is well-known. It was deplored by Griffuelhes already at the times. It has changed little in some quarters, for recently, in the printing shop of a Paris evening newspaper a women manager was whistled out when she dared show up!

Means of action

They are well exposed by Griffhuelles and Pouget[51]. They are set in the framework of direct action. Direct action as a principle is of such importance that revolutionary unionism has sometimes been called "direct action" unionism. It is important on several levels, theoretical as well as practical, and in the latter sense it has a dual

---

50) op. cit., p. 147.
51) notably quoted in Dubief and Spartacus, op. cit.

meaning. On the one hand, it includes all the means of action which are at at the disposal of the worker, and only the means of action which are exclusively the worker's ones. It is defined as any demonstration, spontaneous or planned of the workers's will, carried out by them only and alone. On the other hand, workers must learn to master their means of action, and direct action means also conflict as training, as much for itself as for specific results and as well as propaganda, education of others, etc. The working class does not expect anything from men, powers or forces exterior to it, but creates its own conditions of power and gathers from within itself its own means of action. Direct action covers four activities in practice : sabotage, boycott, label and strike for Pouget. For Griffuelhes it includes the strike, the most natural weapon because it affirms the denial of recognition of the employers' authority, as well as it inflicting damages on him. It also consist of sabotage, under two guises : bad work for bad pay, but foremostly, working differently (sometimes favoring the end user or customer against the employer's interests) in support of demands. Finally there is the General strike. The complete stoppage of production by which the proletariat affirms its will of total conquest and will end the present society. However it is not a myth or an utopia. If it has failed repeatedly, it should certainly not be kept in reserve for the days where the conditions will be ripe, probably never to happen by themselves. Successive unsuccessful trials of general strikes must be considered as training and learning opportunities.

CATHOLIC UNIONISM

To be completed, this description should contain also a brief evocation of catholic unionism. It developed however late and slowly as a separate and autonomous trend, without much involvement in the currents discussed above. The revolution of 1848 and the Commune having aligned the Church and the State against the working class ideologies, Catholics remain apart of the nascent labor movement. It will later be marked by the influence of thinkers such as de Mun, La Tour du Pin, Sangnier. Its first significant emergence, by itself, is among white collar employees in Paris, in 1887. Threatened by the ideas of some catholic social thinkers of the times who advocate "mixed" unions, gathering employees and employers (later taken up by the Vichy regime), it will be reinforced by the Encyclica Rerum Novarum, issued by Leo XIII in 1891 which recognizes the legitimacy of autonomous workers organizations (without using the word "unions" per se though). A Christian Confederation will be created in 1919.

CONCLUSION

The school of thought of revolutionary unionism will come to dominate the newly born CGT in its early years, after its birth in 1895 and consolidation in 1902, until the years before World War II. It will find an expression in the famous Charter of Amiens, in 1906. Disappeared since, with the advent of the industrial and post industrial society, it has nevertheless left deep traces in the French labor ideology, however. Aas well as in present union statements, it can be traced together with the other ideologies described above within the multiple divisions and splits which scanse (always in the name of unity) the history of the French unions.

REFERENCES

Branciard, M., Société Française et lutte de classes, 3 Tomes, Lyon, Chronique sociale de France, 1967.

Branciard, M., Syndicats et partis, Paris, Syros, 1982.

Brécy, R., La grève générale en France, Paris, E. D. I., 1969.

Bruhat, J., Piolot, M., Esquisse d'une histoire de la C.G.T., Paris, Centre Confédéral d'Education Ouvriére, Confédération Générale du Travail, 1966.

Charles, C., "Histoire Sociale de la France au XIX° Siécle", Paris, Seuil, 1991.

Chevalier, L., Classes laborieuses et classes dangereuses, Paris, Plon, 1958.

Crozier, M., Le phénoméne bureaucratique, Paris, Le Seuil, 1956.

Desanti, D., Les socialistes de l'utopie, Paris, Payot, 1970.

Dolléans, A., et G. Dehove, Histoire du travail en France, Paris, Domat-Montchrestien, 1953.

Dolléans, A., Histoire du mouvement ouvrier, Paris, Armand Colin, 1953.

Dubief, H., Le Syndicalisme Révolutionnaire, Paris, Armand Colin, 1969.

Durkheirm, E. Le socialisme, Paris, Retz, 1978 (orig. P.U.F., Paris, 1928).

Furet, F. Le passé d'une illusion : Essai sur l'idée communiste au XX° siécle, Paris, Robert Laffont, 1995.

Goetz-Girey, R., La pensée syndicale française : militants et théoriciens, Cahiers de la fondation nationale des Sciences politiques n° 5, Paris, Armand Colin, 1948.

Hobshawn, E., L'ère des révolutions, Paris, Fayard, 1969.

Julliard, J. La CGT devant la Guerre, Le mouvement social, oct-déc

1964.

Julliard, J., *Fernand Pelloutier et les originrs du syndicalisme d'action directe*, Paris, Le Seuil, 1971.

Kassalov, E., *Trade Unions and Industrial Relations: An International Comparison*, New-York, Random House, 1969.

Labrousse, E., *Le mouvement ouvrier et les théories sociales en France au XIX° siécle*, Paris, CDU, 1952.

Lefranc, G., Histoire du travail et des travailleurs, Paris, Flammarion, 1957.

Lefranc, G., *Le mouvement socialiste sous la troisiéme république*, Paris, Payot 1977.

Lenin, W. I., *What is to be done*, Foreign Language Press, Peking, 1975, p. 37 (initially written in 1905).

Lenin, V. I., "*Left-Wing Communism, an Infantile Disorder*" Peking, Foreign Language Press, 1975.

Lieberman, S., *Labor Movements and Labor Thought—Spain, France, Germany and the United States*, New-York, Praeger, 1986, p. 184.

Lorwin, Val R., *The French Labor Movement*, Cambridge, Harvard University Press, 1954.

Marx, K., Wages, Labour and Capital, Foreign Language Press, Peking, 1975.

Marx, K., *Travail salarié, Prix et Profit* Editions en langues étrangéres, Péking, 1976.

Montreuil, J., *Histoire du mouvement ouvrier en France des origines à nos jours, Paris*, Aubier, 1947.

Noiriel, G., *Les ouvriers dans la société française-XIX°-XX° siécle*, Paris, Editions du Seuil, 1986.

Reynaud, J.-D., *Les syndicats en France*, Paris, Le Seuil, 1974.

Rojot, J. "The Development of French Employers' Policies towards Unions", *Labour and Society*, vol. 11, n° 1, Jan. 1986.

Rojot, J., "France" in Peterson, R. B., Managers and National Culture—*A Global Perspective*, Westport, Conn. Quorum Books, 1993.

Rojot, J., "France" in R. Pieper (ed.), *Human Resource Manage-*

ment : An International Comparison, Berlin, De Gruyter, 1990.

Rojot, J., "France", in M. J. Roomkin (ed.), Managers as employees, Oxford, Oxford University Press, 1989; "Human Resource Management in France".

Sellier, F., La confrontation sociale en France-1936-1981, Paris, P. U. F., 1984.

Winock, M., Le socialisme en France et en Europe, Paris, Editions du Seuil, 1992.

Woodcock, G., (ed.), Introduction, The Anarchist Reader, Glasgow, Fontana, 1977.

The Social Dumping Debate

Bob HEPPLE

Tadashi Hanami has played a major role in promoting international labour standards, so I should like in this contribution in his honour to consider a controversial question which is the source of much confusion in the attempts to establish a new international framework to regulate labour markets in the age of globalisation. This is whether a "social clause" in international trade and investment agreements can be justified on the grounds that it is necessary to avoid "social dumping", and to ask whether there is a better approach.

LIBERALISATION SEEN FROM NORTH[1] AND SOUTH

According to the theory of liberalisation the gains from international trade and foreign direct investment (FDI) depend upon the differences in factor endowments among nations. On the assumption that markets are efficient these differences reflect themselves in different costs and prices, so allowing countries to make use of comparative advantage. Countries with low labour costs are able to at-

---

1) I use "North", although not entirely accurate, to denote the richer industrialised nations.

tract investment. This in turn may lead to greater demand for labour, higher real wages and improved living and working conditions in those countries.

However, some argue that when labour costs rise in this way, companies will be tempted to relocate to countries where the costs of labour are lower and regulations are thought to be more "flexible". This leads to downward pressures on wage costs and labour standards in other countries. Workers in the richer countries are forced to accept reduced wages and labour standards in order to compete with workers who have inferior standards in poorer countries. According to this argument, the dilemma which free trade and FDI pose for nation states is that the more comprehensive and effective labour legislation is, the more likely it is that TNCs will wish to relocate. This in turn will destroy the very jobs which national labour law is designed to protect—a "race to the bottom" in which firms adopt short-term cost-cutting strategies rather than productivity improvements. While workers in the richer North have a head start in this race, they can stay ahead only if their employers improve investment in their workplaces; and it a race without end. This leads them to conclude that liberalisation poses a threat to labour and social standards in the North.

There is a different perspective from the developing countries of the South. These states are under immense pressure to compete among themselves for FDI and access to world markets. At the same time, most of these countries - at least those which are democracies—want to enhance and improve living and working conditions; in particular they are paying increasing attention to workers in the vast, heterogeneous, and still growing informal sector. The ILO's *World Labour Report 1997-98* notes that this "constitutes an important, if not central, aspect of the economic and social dynamics" of these countries (p. 176). The informal sector includes a wide variety of activities ranging from petty trade, service repairs and domestic work to transport, construction and manufacturing. It rarely involves a clear-cut employer-employee relationship. The diversity of jobs and employment status make it difficult for informal sector workers to organise themselves into unions; moreover patriarchal family and ethnic loyalties may count for more than solidarity between workers. The ILO Report points out that informal sector units "operate on the fringe, if not outside, the legal and administrative framework", with many ignoring or paying scant attention to regulations concerning safety, health, and working conditions.

In the past few years a number of trade unions and NGOs around the world have supported initiatives to help informal sector workers in the developing countries. However, the ILO Report concludes that "the State has a major role to play in helping informal sector workers overcome their disadvantages". This makes it a priority of national policy to establish and enforce a regulatory framework in which "the right of informal sector workers to join or create representative associations of their choosing, as well as state recognition of their role as interlocutors and/or partners in policy-making or programme implementation are...key enabling factors".

One threat to these essential national policies comes from the neo-liberal creed espoused, by, among others, the IMF, World Bank and other sources of capital, who make loans and assistance dependent upon the creation of so-called "flexible" and "deregulated" labour markets. Their aim is to ease the movement of capital, and at the same time restrict those kinds of solidarity which might increase their bargaining power with investors. Developing countries believe that they are being denied their sovereign right to determine their own labour standards.

SOCIAL CLAUSES IN TRADE AGREEMENTS

Another threat to the developing countries comes from attempts to impose protectionist "social clauses" in trade agreements. Pressure for adding "unfair labour standards", beyond those in Art. XX of GATT (which, inter alia, allows restrictions on the products of prison and forced labour) to international trade rules originated in the 1940s and 1950 s in the American and British trade unions, as a response to alleged social dumping. In 1959 the ICFTU proposed a labour standards provision. The Trade Union Advisory Committee (TUAC) of the OECD also repeatedly called for a social clause in GATT, linking participation in the multilateral trading system with the observance of minimum labour standards. At governmental level the United States and Canada together with France, Austria, Sweden and Norway were the most outspoken in promoting a social clause in the GATT. It was argued that a multilateral approach would avoid the inefficiencies and trade-diversionary effects of unco-ordinated unilateral approaches. The essential rationale for a social clause was that this was necessary in order to protect national labour and social standards against unfair comparative advantage of countries whose low costs were based on social oppression. These pressures were strongly resisted by most of the developing countries, which regarded them as protectionist. In Anderson's words:

> "What kindles the suspicion of many developing countries is a perception of social imperialism on the part of OECD countries. Developing countries feel that they are being denied their national sovereignty. While they are not being targeted *per se*, the fact that developing countries are poorer, and that their comparative advantage tends to be in labor-, natural resource-, and pollution-intensive industries, means that they are particularly vulnerable to pressure for stricter standards and the prospect of less market access in stricter-standard countries. Furthermore, should the use of trade policy to harmonise standards upward lead to trade retaliation and counter-retaliation, it could weaken the multilateral trading system on which developing countries are becoming more dependent as they liberalise their economies"[2].

---

2) K. Anderson, "The Intrusion of Environmental and Labor Standards into Trade Policy" in W. Martin and L. A. Winter (eds.), *The Uruguay Round and the Developing Countries*, Cambridge: Cambridge University Press (1996), pp. 435-462 at p. 452.

The position of the developing countries was in effect accepted in the declaration in December 1996 by trade ministers meeting in Singapore at the first WTO Ministerial Conference, paragraph 4 of which stated:

> "We renew our commitment to the observance of internationally recognised core labour standards. The International Labour Organisation (ILO) is the competent body to set and deal with these standards, and we affirm our support for its work in promoting them. We believe that economic growth and development fostered by increased trade and further trade liberalisation contribute to these standards. We reject the use of labour standards for protectionist purposes, and agree that the comparative advantage of countries, particularly low-wage developing countries, must in no way be put into question. In this regard we note that the WTO and ILO secretariats will continue their existing collaboration."

There were several reasons for regarding the ILO as a more appropriate body than the WTO to deal with employment and social issues. First, the WTO is a specialised organisation on trade where trade ministers serve as representatives, while the strength of the ILO, which has nearly 80 years' experience of labour and social matters, lies in its tripartite composition (governments, employers and workers' representatives). Secondly, decision-making in the WTO normally requires consensus, while the International Labour Conference can act by majority decision.

Thirdly, it would be extremely difficult to utilise WTO enforcement mechanisms. For example, quantitative restrictions against countries which abuse core labour standards could not be applied in a manner which constituted arbitrary or unjustifiable discrimination between countries where the same conditions prevail. This would involve an evaluation of labour standards of the whole membership of the WTO (including the country imposing the restriction) and assumes agreement on the criteria for such an evaluation. Moreover, the derogation from free trade would have to satisfy the test of proportionality, e. g. all imports could not be banned in order to prevent some products of child labour.

AN ALTERNATIVE: THE 1998 ILO DECLARATION

The Singapore Ministerial Declaration, by reaffirming the ILO's competence, strengthened the efforts initiated in the Director-General's Report to the 81st session (1994) of the ILO for ensuring a commitment by all 174 ILO Member States to the fundamental rights at work enshrined in seven "core" ILO Conventions: freedom of association and collective bargaining (1949, No. 87 and 1949. No. 98), forced labour (1930 No. 29 and 1957, No. 105), non-discrimination (1951, No. 100 and 1958, No. 111) and the minimum age in employment (1973, No. 138). An OECD Report (1996) suggested that improved enforcement of non-discrimination standards, and the elimination of forced and child labour might raise economic efficiency, and stated that concerns of developing countries that core standards, such as freedom of association and the right to collective bargaining, would negatively affect their economic performance or international competitive position are unfounded.

A campaign to encourage states which have not already done so to ratify the seven core Conventions brought the total number of ratifications by 31 December 1997 to 853, still requiring 356 ratifications before there would be universal coverage[3]. On 18June 1998, at the 86th session of the International Labour Conference, a Declaration of Fundamental Principles and Rights at Work was adopted by 273 votes in favour, 0 against, and 43 abstentions.

The basic obligations are set out in paragraph 2 in which it is declared that-

> "all Members, even if they have not ratified the Conventions in question, have an obligation arising from the very fact of membership in the Organisation, to respect, to promote and to realise, in good faith and in accordance with the Constitution, the principles concerning the fundamental rights which are the subject of those Conventions, namely:
>
> (a) freedom of association and the effective recognition of the right to collective bargaining;
> (b) the elimination of all forms of forced or compul-

---

[3] Only 37 countries have ratified all seven Conventions, while five countries have ratified none.

sory labour;

(c) the effective abolition of child labour;

(d) the elimination of discrimination in respect of employment and occupation."

The ILO Legal Adviser explained that the Declaration is a "political statement of a non-binding character." It does not impose any new legal obligations on Members beyond those set out in the ILO Constitution and the Declaration of Philadelphia 1944. Nor does it impose any obligation to observe the detailed requirements of any Convention which a Member State has not ratified, nor is a Member obliged to ratify any of the seven "core" Conventions. The Declaration simply sets out general "principles concerning fundamental rights"; it is purely promotional and not punitive or complaints-based.

The promotional follow-up mechanism (ILO, 1998b, Annex) is based on existing ILO procedures. Article 19(5)(e) of the ILO Constitution states that when the competent authorities have not consented to ratification "no further obligation shall rest upon the Member, except that it shall report...at appropriate intervals as requested by the Governing Body...". Since 1995, the Governing Body has required a four-yearly reports regarding fundamental rights. This will now be replaced by an annual report from governments which have not ratified one or more of the fundamental Conventions on any changes which may have taken place in their law and practice. These reports will be reviewed by the Governing Body with the help of an ad hoc group of experts. There will also be a global report, based on the annual reports and covering each year one of the four categories of fundamental principles and rights in turn. The Legal Adviser gave assurances that this procedure would not involve double jeopardy because the global report could not revisit the individual situation in each State, nor would it duplicate the supervisory system in relation to ratified Conventions or the work of the Committee on Freedom of Association, since it is concerned only the broad aims of the Conventions and not their detailed application.

The text of the Declaration is a compromise, the most contentious issues being the link between trade and labour standards (para. 5) and requirements by international financial institutions for compliance with labour standards (para. 3). Paragraph 5 of the Declaration, adopted by a significant majority of the Conference Committee -

> "stresses that labour standards should not be used for protectionist trade purposes, and that nothing in this Declaration and its follow-up shall be invoked or otherwise used for such purposes; in addition the comparative advantage of any country should in no way be called into question by this Declaration and its follow-up."

This is a very close paraphrase of the language used in the 1996 Singapore Declaration (above). It pleased the ILO Employers' Group and many of the governments of developing countries, but was a disappointment to a majority of the Workers' Group who argued that ensuring fundamental rights is not a form of protectionism.

Paragraph 3 of the Declaration recognises the obligation of the ILO to help Members attain the objectives in various ways. What proved to be contentious was the phrase which commits the ILO to "[encourage] other international organisations with which the ILO has established relations pursuant to Article 12 of the Constitution to support these efforts." The organisations with whom the ILO has concluded agreements under Article 12 include all members of the United Nations family, and the International Atomic Energy Authority, but no formal agreement has been made with the Bretton Woods institutions or the WTO. Despite this clarification, some developing country governments expressed the fear that paragraph 3 would be used to introduce labour standards as a condition for technical assistance by other organisations. The Egyptian Government spokesman, for example, stated that "it cannot agree to any new conditionality in international economic relations which would hinder national efforts to boost economic and social development and alleviate poverty"[4].

SOCIAL PROVISIONS IN INVESTMENT AGREEMENTS

A similar debate has been going on in relation to in-

---

4) Mr Elamawy, Discussion in Plenary on the Reports of the Committee on the Declaration of Principles, Geneva : ILO (1998).

vestment agreements. As yet there is no binding multilateral framework for international investment. The current network of nearly 2000 bilateral investment treaties only rarely refer specifically to employment and social issues, and these are mainly in United States practice requiring respect for "internationally recognised worker rights" without defining the phrase or imposing any sanctions for non-compliance. Sometimes these agreements require the enforcement of domestic labour laws.

Two distinct approaches to employment and social policy issues have emerged in the main regional multilateral treaties. The first is cross-border monitoring of domestic labour laws and employment practices. This is to be found in the North American Agreement on Labor Cooperation (NAALC), a side accord to the North American Free Trade Agreement (NAFTA), which came into operation in September 1993. This relies on cross-border monitoring to ensure that countries enforce their own domestic labour laws. The NAALC came into existence against the background of strong opposition from organised labour to the NAFTA because of the fear of "social dumping". Even though Mexican law specifies labour standards superior in many respects to those in the United States and Canada, it was alleged that those standards are poorly enforced. The NAALC commits each party to promote eleven basic principles[5] The three nations must promote these principles in accordance with their own laws, customs and history, similar to the treatment of the standards of the ILO. The agreement is administered by the Commission for Labor Cooperation, and contains a dispute resolution process. If a dispute related to the enforcement of labour laws cannot be resolved, nothing further can be done under the NAALC unless it relates to health and safety, child labour or minimum wages. In respect of those three issues a complaint may proceed to an arbitral tribunal. A panel finding in favour of the complainant may result in penalties including fines for Canada, and suspension from NAFTA's benefits for Mexico and the United States..

A second approach makes use of charters or declarations of fundamental rights of workers. The Social Chapter of the Treaty of the European Community, as amended by the Treaty of Amsterdam (1997), now refers specifically to the Community Charter of Fundamental Rights of Workers (1989) and to the European Social Charter (1961)[6] of the Council of Europe as the inspiration for Community social measures. However, Article 137(6) of the amended EC Treaty expressly excludes from the procedures for enacting Community law measures on pay, the right of association,

---

5) Freedom of association and protection of the right to organise, the right to bargain collectively, the right to strike, prohibition of forced labour, labour protections for children and young persons, minimum employment standards, elimination of employment discrimination, equal pay for women and men, prevention of occupational injuries and illnesses, compensation in cases of occupational injuries and illnesses, protection of migrant workers (NAALC, 1993, Annex 1).

6) The revised European Social Charter (1996) has not yet come into force.

the right to strike or to impose lock-outs. These matters remain within the exclusive legislative competence of the Member States. Although the European Works Council Directive 94/45/EC, requires large TNCs operating in more than one Member State of the EU to inform and consult the transnational works council, Community measures do not cover the fundamental rights to freedom of association and collective bargaining.

A weaker version of this approach seems to be emerging in the Mercado Comun del Sur (MERCOSUR). The Treaty of Asuncion (April 1991) between Argentina, Brazil, Paraguay and Uruguay establishing MERCOSUR referred to social issues only in its Preamble, which proclaims social justice as one of the fundamental objectives of integration and says that among the most difficult problems faced by the State Parties are unemployment and social, ethnic and cultural differences. In September 1991, trade unions suggested the adoption of a Charter of Social Rights. The social and labour aspects of integration were referred to a tripartite sub-working group (SWG No. 11) which proposed a minimum common framework of labour and social guarantees to reinforce the constitutionalised labour and social rights which exist in all four States. However, Brazil opposed the imposition of sanctions against any country breaking its own labour legislation, on the ground that there were adequate domestic mechanisms for this purpose. At the Second Summit of the Americas (Santiago, May 1998), the Heads of State and Government agreed a plan of action for the modernisation of the state in labour matters[7], for the exchange of information on their labour legislation and the promotion of core labour standards. The ILO was recognised as the competent body to set and deal with these standards.

A more far-reaching approach is to be found, in the OECD voluntary Guidelines for Multinational Enterprises (1976), which contain a chapter on Employment and Industrial Relations. These Guidelines have assumed particular importance under the OECD's Multilateral Agreement on Investment (MAI) which is currently being negotiated. This is to be a free-standing international treaty open to all OECD Members and the European Community, and to non-members willing and able to undertake its obligations. It aims to provide a comprehensive and stable framework for FDI which will give a new impetus to growth, employment and higher living standards.

In the course of negotiations for the MAI, a majority of governments appear to have accepted the following overall approach:

- an affirmation in the Preamble of their support for internationally recognised core labour stan-

---

[7] "Governments will...promote measures by their Ministries of Labour to provide high quality programmes and assistance for workers and employers, placing emphasis on greater decentralisation of their functions, the incorporation of new technologies, active labour market policies, better and more timely information regarding the labour market and improvement of safety and health conditions in the workplace."

dards, and that the ILO is the competent body to deal with these standards ;

· the annexing of the OECD Guidelines to the MAI Text, without changing their non-binding character ;

· a binding obligation on Contracting Parties not to waive or derogate from their domestic health, safety, environmental or labour measures as an encouragement to the establishment, acquisition, expansion, operation, management, maintenance, use, enjoyment and sale or other disposition of an investment of an investor (but this would not prevent governments from adjusting these measures for public policy reasons other than attracting foreign investment)[8].

In 1977 the ILO adopted a voluntary Tripartite Declaration on Multinational Enterprises and Social Policy, which parallels the OECD Guidelines and does not conflict with them. Although institutionally separate, the two instruments can be read together as laying down principles applicable to employment and social policy in relation to FDI.

There is also a wide variety of voluntary codes of conduct, drawn up TNCs themselves sometimes with specialist advice. The companies undertake to improve working

---

8) MAI Negotiating Text (as of 24 April 1998), Annex to Chairman's Proposals on environment and related matters and on labour, para. 4 ("not lowering measures").

and living conditions in the countries in which they operate on the basis of "best practice". These aim to influence local standards as well as keep the TNCs up to the mark. The weakness of these company codes is that the norms they uphold are not always consistent with the OECD or ILO standards (e. g. many do not include the right to effective collective bargaining) and they rely on self-enforcement, although some permit independent social audits.

TWO APPROACHES TO SECURING MINIMUM LABOUR STANDARDS

It should be clear from this account of the current debate that two distinct approaches have emerged in respect of minimum labour standards. The first is based on the notion of applying sanctions against "social dumping" in order to deter a "race to the bottom", the second seeks to encourage the development of processes within global production and distribution chains which favour the raising of labour standards, that is a "race to the top".

A definition of "social dumping" is suggested by Grossmann and Koopmann:

> "Unlike conventional dumping which means selling abroad below cost or at lower prices than charged in the home market, 'social dumping' refers to costs that are for their part depressed below a 'natural' level by means of 'social oppression' facilitating unfair pricing strategies against foreign competitors. Remedial action would either consist of the offending firms consenting

to raise their prices accordingly or failing that, imposing equivalent import restrictions."[9]

This approach depends on identifying those measures of "social oppression" which cause wage costs and labour standards to be unfairly depressed. Put in economic terms, the "social dumping" case for international labour regulation is that it is necessary to remove those distortions on competition which are not related to productivity. Such distortions occur when firms are able to utilise undervalued labour. By undervaluation is meant paying workers with comparable skills and productivity different wages simply by shifting demand for labour to a more disadvantaged group of workers who are unable to resist. Firms that can undervalue labour in this way can avoid more radical solutions to their competitive problems, such as by restructuring or investment in new technologies. Indeed, the availability of undervalued labour discourages innovation, and firms which are innovative face unfair competition from firms which are inefficient technically and managerially but are able to be profitable in the short-term by employing undervalued labour.

This argument was the justification given for including in the Treaty of Rome (1957) a provision (Art. 119) requiring equal remuneration for men and women doing the

---

[9] H. Grossmann and G. Koopmann, "Social Standards in International Trade" in H. Sander and A. Inotai *World Trade After the Uruguay Round*, London : Routledge (1996), p. 116.

same work. It was said by a group of experts that, "countries in which there are wage differentials by sex will pay relatively low wages in industries employing a large proportion of female labour and these industries will enjoy what might be called a special advantage over their competitors abroad where differentials according to security are smaller or non-existent"[10]. There are obviously greater opportunities for using undervalued labour in a system which discriminates on grounds of sex, race, or any other arbitrary basis. A similar argument justifies measures against other forms of social oppression such as forced and child labour.

It is doubtful, however, whether the concept of "social dumping" is adequate in itself to form the theoretical basis for a new approach to international labour regulation. First, it over-emphasises the likelihood of relocation. Enterprises are not likely to relocate to another state with lower *nominal* labour costs if those costs simply reflect lower productivity of workers in that state. This would mean that there is no net difference in unit labour costs. The basic point is that what matters is not the *nominal* level of wage costs in a firm or industry but the net unit labour costs, i. e. the costs of labour for each unit of production after taking productivity into account. If labour costs do not reflect the relative productivity in a particular state and enterprises do relocate to that state, the result

---

10) B. Ohlin, "Social Aspects of European Economic Co-operation" (1956) 74 *International Labour Review* 99-120 at p. 107.

would be to increase demand for labour with the likelihood of rising wage levels. This would cancel out the advantages of a relocation which was based purely on low labour costs. The *World Investment Report 1994*, concluded that "despite a few notable cases, TNCs do not often close down, on account of low labour cost considerations alone, production facilities in one country to re-establish them in another country;...Broader and more important macroeconomic and cyclical factors, technological change and labour market inflexibilities are the principal influences on the growth and distribution of employment"[11].

Secondly, there is no real evidence to establish that comparative advantage does in fact flow from "social dumping". An OECD study in 1996 pointed to empirical research which indicates that there is no correlation between aggregate real wage growth and the level of observance of core labour rights, such as freedom of association. Moreover, aggregate data on FDI suggests that the presence or absence of core labour rights are not significant determinants. Host states which observe core standards are not significantly worse in attracting FDI than those which systematically abuse those standards. On the contrary, raising labour standards may raise the motivation and health of workers so raising productivity and encouraging FDI[12]. A similar conclusion was reached by an Aus-

---

11) UNCTAD, *World Investment Report* 1994: *Transnational Corporatioins, Employment and the Workplace*, New York: United Nations (1994) p. xxvii.

tralian report on labour standards in the Asia-Pacific region[13]. There are, of course, abuses of labour standards in particular countries, especially in export processing zones. But the worst abuses usually occur in domestic, non-trade sectors against which restrictions on exports or FDI would have no direct effect.

The alternative to the "social dumping" approach to international labour regulation starts with an identification of those processes in global production and distribution chains which favour the raising of labour standards. The internal labour markets of TNCs usually provide better wages, conditions of work and social security benefits than those prevailing in domestic firms, due to the fact that they tend to be concentrated in industries which utilise high skills, are capital-intensive, and have superior managerial and organisational techniques. Indirectly, there may be a spillover of the best practices of these TNCs to domestic firms. The global commodity chains dominated by TNCs generate employment through various linkages with enterprises in home and host countries. The *World Investment Report* 1994 reported that "as a general rule, for each job directly generated by a TNC, one or two may result indirectly from backward and forward linkages"."

---

12) OECD, *Trade, Employment and Labour Standards-A Study of Core Workers' Rights and International Trade*, Paris : OECD (1996).

13) Commonwealth of Australia, *Report on Labour Standards in the Asia-Pacific Region*, Tripartite Committee on Labour Standards (Chair : Michael Duffy), Canberra : AGPS (1996).

Whether or not the quality of employment is raised throughout the global chain of production and distribution depends largely on corporate integration strategies. In the emerging model of complex integration - that is regionally or globally integrated production and distribution networks within function, product or process specialisation - there is likely to be a convergence in the employment conditions of parent and foreign affiliates in order to maximise the global efficiency of the TNC, and the TNC will increasingly rely on workforce quality in the host country, with positive effects on labour conditions throughout the global commodity chain.

THE TASK AHEAD

The task, therefore, is to create an international regulatory framework which encourages and develops the potential of TNCs to raise the labour standards of economically and socially disadvantaged groups of workers and producers, particularly in the informal sector. At national level, the application and elaboration of this framework has to take account of specific local cultural, social and economic features. We must, therefore, utilise those emerging methods of international labour regulation which have the greatest potential for the dissemination of "best practices". These include requirements for disclosure of information and consultation and other forms of participation; the mutual monitoring of the enforcement of domestic labour laws; and the imposition of international sanctions for the non-enforcement of "core" standards; compensation through additional preferences, structural funds and the like for social measures which aid development; and the stregthening of collective complaints-based procedures for the enforcement of agreed standards.

年　譜

1930年　東京都文京区に生まれる（勝治郎・静子次男）
1942年　東京女子師範学校（現学芸大学）付属小学校卒業
1946年　県立静岡中学校（現静岡高等学校）4年修了
1949年　旧静岡高等学校（現静岡大学）卒業
1953年　東京大学法学部法律学科卒業
　　　　東京大学法学部特別研究生（1958年まで）
1957年　神奈川大学講師（1959年まで）
1958年　日本労働学会研究員（1965年まで，以後非常勤研究員1984年まで）
1959年　フンボルト財団研究員としてケルン大学留学（9月—1961年まで）
1961年　東京工業大学講師（1964年まで）
　　　　法学博士（東京大学より）
1962年　上智大学講師（1962年まで）
1964年　フルブライト研究員としてコーネル大学留学（9月—1965年8月まで）
1965年　上智大学法学部教授（1999年まで）
　　　　日本労働法学会報告「アメリカ官公労働者の労働基本権」
1968年　東京都労働委員会公益委員会（10月—1979年まで）
1970年　司法試験考査委員（1982年まで）
　　　　文部省特定研究「産業構造の変革」傘下共同研究「産業構造の変化と労働法」事務局（1973年まで）
　9月　国際労使関係協会世界大会（ジュネーブ），国際労働法社会保障学会世界大会（ワルソー）出席・報告「社会保障における過失」，途上モスコー，レニングラード，ヘルシンキ，ミラノなどを訪れる。
1971年
　1月　Law Asia 大会（マニラ）出席・報告，帰途シンガポール，マレーシア，バンコク，香港を訪れる。
　5月　ILO 労働問題研究所シンポジウム「労使関係の将来」（ジュネーブ）出席・報告，サセックス大学にて講演「日本労使関係における

年　譜

　　　　　法の役割」,帰途イスラエルを訪れる。
1972年
　9月　欧州3カ国(英・独・伊)労働時間労使関係調査団団長,帰途ストレザ,ウィーンなどを訪れる。
1973年
　9月　国際労使関係協会世界大会(ロンドン)出席・報告「多国籍企業と労使関係」帰途ボン,ケルン,チューリヒなどを訪れる。
1975年
　3・9月　カリフォルニア大学(バークレー校)客員研究員,この間スタンフォード,ブランダイス大学などで講演
1976年
　8月　ナイジェリア日本企業労使関係調査団団長,途上ロンドン,サセックス,バーミンガム各大学で予備調査,帰途ナイロビを経て,ジュネーブ,ニューヨーク,サンフランシスコなどを訪れる。
1977年
　8月　研究プロジェクト「日本における紛争」企画会議(シアトル)
　　　　ルーヴァン大学法学部客員教授(9月―1978年1月まで)担当講義「日本労働法」,この間ランデン大学,フランクフルト大学などで講演
1979年　上智大学法学部長(1月―1982年末まで)
　3月　研究プロジェクト「日本における紛争」研究会議(ハワイ)
　4月　研究会議「労働組合における婦人」(ベッラジオ)
　9月　国際労使関係協会世界大会(パリ)出席
　10月　ILO専門家会議(シンガポール)「経済発展と労使関係」
　12月　アメリカの年齢差別法について現地調査(ワシントンD.C.,ニューヨーク)
1980年　上智大学法学部に国際関係法学科新設,学科長兼任(4月―1982年3月まで),Labor Relations in Japan Today で日本放送協会より国際出版文化賞受賞,フォード財団プロジェクト「労使紛争処理の比較研究」主宰(1983年まで)
　1月　トライラテラル・コミッション「労働市場」プロジェクト研究会議

　　　　　　（ワシントン D. C.）出席
　　3 月　同年次大会（ロンドン）
　　8 月　アスペン・インスティテュート・日本セミナー出席（アスペン・コロラド）
1981年
　　2 月　韓国使用者連盟，韓国労働法学会にて講演（ソウル）
　　5 月　国際交流基金派遣講演旅行（デンマーク，フィンランド，西ドイツ，イギリス）
1982年　労働基準法研究会・第 2 部会座長（5 月―1960年12月まで）
　　2 月　Comparative Labour Law & Industrial Relations 編集企画会議（フォンテンブロー）
　　9 月　国際労働法社会保障法学会世界大会（ワシントン D. C.）出席，オーストラリア労使関係学会，講演「労使関係の日本モデル」（ゴールド・コースト）
1983年
　　3 月　フォード財団研究プロジェクト「労使紛争処理の比較研究」研究会議（東京）主催，国際労使関係協会世界大会（京都）ゼネラル・ラポルトゥアー「労使関係の日本モデル」
　　8 月　OECD・IME 委員会視察（パリ）
1984年　日本労使関係研究協会常任理事（現）
　　　　ハーヴァード・ロー・スクール客員教授（9 月―1985年 6 月まで）担当講義「日本労働法」及びセミナー「比較紛争処理」この間コーネル大学，MIT，コロンビア大学，ウィスコンシン大学，全米仲裁協会年次大会などで講演，ニューヨークのジャパン・ソサイアテー主催のジャパン・キャラバンでサウス・カロライナ，バーミンガムなどで講演と討論
1985年
　　9 月　国際労働法社会保障学会世界大会（カラカス）出席（パネリスト「比較研究の方法」），帰途ボストン，ロス・アンゼルスなどを訪問
　　12月　ルーヴァン大学より名誉法学博士を授与され，授与式に出席，記念講演「日本的労使関係と労働法」，帰途ミュンヘンに遊ぶ。

年　譜

1986年　国際労使関係協会（IIRA）理事（現）
　　　　労基準法研究会（労災補償関係）座長（10月—1988年8月）
　4/5月　労働省「海外勤務の実態と法理」実態調査（ブラッセル, パリ, ロンドン, ボン, フランクフルト）
　8/9月　国際労使関係協会世界大会（ハンブルグ）出席・報告「労働者参加の現状」
1987年　統計研究会「外国人労働者実態調査委員会」委員長（1989年まで）
　　　　国際商業仲裁センター・仲裁・調停人委員会委員（現）
　2月　テラヴィヴ大学「日本の紛争」セミナー出席・報告, 国際労働法社会保障学会, 国際労使関係協会アジア地域会議（シンガポール）出席（パネリスト）, 帰途バリ島にて「労使紛争処理の比較研究」編集作業
　6月　太平洋地域労使関係会議（ヴァンクーヴァー）出席・報告「公共部門労使関係」
　9-12月　NHK教育テレビ市民大学「雇用と労働」
　10月　モントリオール大学労使関係学部創立10周年記念講演「労使関係の日本モデル—神話と現実」（モントリオール）
1988年　中央労働基準審議会会長（1988年3月まで）, 労働省「外国人労働問題に関する調査研究のための懇談会」受入制度に関するワーキング・パーティー座長（5月—12月）
　5月　エーベルト財団「比較労使関係」セミナー（ソウル）出席・報告
　8月　シンポジウム「西洋法の日本化」出席・報告（チュービンゲン）
　10月　太平洋圏経済発展会議（メキシコ）出席・報告
　12月　中華経済研究院・労工問題与経済発展国際研討会（台北）出席・報告
1989年　フロリダ大学法学部客員教授（2月）担当講義「比較労働法」
　3月　韓国労働研究院（ソウル）講演「労使紛争の処理」
　9月　国際労使関係学会世界大会（ブラッセル）出席
　10月　日経連—AFL—CIO定期協議（ニューヨーク）「在米日系企業労使関係ケーススタディー」ディスカッサント
1990年　ルーヴァン大学・欧日産業法研究所理事（現）, ハーヴァード・ロー・スクール客員教授（2月—5月）担当講義「日本労働法」

年　譜

　　3月　国際労働法社会保障学会アジア地域会議（東京）ゼネラル・ラポルトゥアー「アジアにおける労使紛争処理」
1991年
　　2月　南アフリカ労働法グループのための日本労働法講義（ケープ・タウン，ヨハネスブルグ）
　　9月　国際労働法・社会保障学会世界大会出席（アテネ），国際労使関係協会ヨーロッパ地域会議出席（バリ，ナポリ）
　10月　欧日産業法研究所セミナー出席・報告（ルーヴァン）
　11月　EC日本労使関係会議出席・報告（ブラッセル），南アフリカ労働法グループのための日本労働法講義（ヨハネスブルグ）
1992年　中央労働委員会公益委員（現）
　　2月　在米日系企業雇用慣行調査（ロサンゼルス，ニューヨーク，ワシントンDC）
　　5月　欧日産業法研究所セミナー出席・報告（ルーヴァン），カリアリ大学（イタリー）講義
　　7月　IBM国際人事会議出席（ニューヨーク），在米日系企業雇用慣行調査（ニューヨーク，ワシントンDC）
　8‐9月　国際労使関係協会世界大会出席（シドニー）
　　9月　在米日系企業雇用慣行調査（ニューヨーク，ワシントンDC，ロサンゼルス）
1993年　ルーヴァン大学客員教授（10月—11月）
　　9月　IBM国際人事会議出席（ニューヨーク）
　　　　ニュージーランド使用者連盟講演（オークランド）
　10月　ルント大学講演（スウェーデン）
1994年　コロンビア大学客員教授（4月）
　10月　WAI・JIL日米雇用問題共同研究会議出席・報告
　11月　MIT・JIL外国人労働者問題研究会議出席・報告
1995年
　　6月　国際労使関係協会世界会議出席（ワシントンDC），同協会次期会長President-Electに選出される。
1996年　日本労働研究機構研究所長（現），中央労働委員会会長代理（1998

年　譜

　　　　年まで），労働省「持株会社と労使関係」研究会座長
　1月　イタリア労使関係協会年次大会出席（ボローニャ）
　6月　「持株会社と労使関係」調査（ワシントンDC，ニューヨーク）
　9月　世界法会議 Law in Motion 出席・報告（ブラッセル）
　10月　日本労働研究機構・イリノイ産業研究所研究会議出席（シカゴ）
　12月　デンマーク社会省「社会的一体性」に関するシンクタンク出席（コペンハーゲン）

1997年
　4月　欧日産業法研究所セミナー出席・報告（ルーヴァン）
　5月　イタリア労使関係協会年次大会出席・報告（ヴェニス）
　6月　日本労働研究機構日系企業セミナー（ロンドン），デンマーク社会省「社会的一体性」に関するシンクタンク出席（コペンハーゲン）
　8月　国際労使関係協会ヨーロッパ会議出席（ダブリン），国際労使関係協会幹部会議（ローマ）
　10月　デンマーク社会省「社会的一体性」に関する世界大会出席（コペンハーゲン），コロンビア大学・日米労働法研究プロジェクト打合わせ（ニューヨーク）

1998年　中央労働委員会会長（現），国際労使関係協会 President（2000年まで）
　1月　EU日本労使関係会議出席・報告（ブラッセル）
　3月　イタリア労使関係協会年次大会出席・報告，国際労使関係協会幹部会議（ローマ），欧日産業法研究所セミナー出席・報告（ルーヴァン）
　9月　国際労使関係協会世界会議出席（ボローニャ），同協会 President に就任

1999年　上智大学名誉教授
　1月　上智大学最終講義
　4月　国際労使関係協会幹部会議（ジュネーブ）
　5月　欧日産業法研究所セミナー（ルーヴァン）
　9月　日独労働法学会シンポジウム出席（ケルン），IIRAアメリカ地域会議出席（リマ），サン・マルティン・ド・ポレス大学（ペルー）よ

り名誉博士を授与される。記念講演「東と西——労働問題の比較研究」（リマ）
＊官庁の研究会その他の非公式諮問機関の委員（座長など責任者でないもの），各種団体評議員その他臨時的なものなどは省略

著作目録

凡　例

『　』	著書	労経速報	労働経済判例速報
英文イタリック	著書	労協	日本労働協会雑誌
※	共著, 共編	労旬	労働法律旬報
・	判例研究	労研	日本労働研究雑誌
季労	季刊労働法	J. L. Bulletin	Japan Labor Bulletin
討労	討論労働法	Japan	Quarterly Review of Anglo-Japanese Economic Institute
法協	法学協会雑誌		
労問	月刊労働問題		

1953	9	公務員の労働者権―アメリカ(1)―	討労・22
	10	公務員の労働者権―アメリカ(2)―	討労・23
1955	3	はり紙と器物毀損	季労・15
	5	経歴詐欺にもとづく解雇	討労・38
	6	・退職者同盟の団体交渉と住居侵入及び業務妨害罪	法協・72-4
	10	懲戒権と懲戒解雇	労旬・216
	12	日本における懲戒権の現実と法規則	季労・18
1956	1	・憲法28条の保障する団結権ないし団体行動権の範囲	法協・73-1
	4	解雇理由と不当労働行為	労旬・234
	5	懲戒権の法理	労働法・8
		アメリカにおける「経営権」(1)	討労・50
	6	アメリカにおける「経営権」(2)	討労・51
	7	※労働時間（講座『労働時間と労働法』5）	弘文堂
	8	整理解雇と不当労働行為	労旬・244
	9	カナダ・ゼネラル・モーターズ争議をめぐって	討労・54
	10	懲戒権の法的限界	労働法・9
		労働契約における労働者の義務の内容	討労・55
	12	・労働基準法79条における業務上の死亡の意	法協・73-5

		味	
		・争議行為を理由とする懲戒解雇と不当労働行為	季労・22
		労働時間法制に関する若干の考察(1)	討労・57
1957	1	労働時間法制に関する若干の考察(2)	討労・58
	2	※『判例回顧』1956年	日本評論社
	5	労働契約の無効・取消について	法協・74-2
	6	試用契約の法的性質	季労・24
	7	・下部組合の協約と上部組合の指令にもとづく争議	討労・64
	8	・価格統制に違反した農地の売買契約の効力	法協・74-3
	11	同情スト合法論に対する疑問	ジュリスト142
1958	4	※『判例回顧』1957年	日本評論社
	5	懲戒権（『労働法講座』5）	有斐閣
	6	最近の最賃論議をめぐって	ジュリスト157
	8	・有給休暇請求権の性質と懲戒解雇無効の場合の賃金請求権の存否	ジュリスト160
		・株主たる従業員の株主としての行為の就業規則に定める解雇事由該当性	ジュリスト161
	9	・いわゆるレッド・パージの効力	季労・29
	10	※サミュエルズ『英国労働組合法』	有斐閣
		・失業保険法53条に規定する犯罪の構成要件と期待可能性	ジュリスト164
	11	・解雇が正当な組合活動の故になされたと認められたが，退職の勧告が組合活動をきらってなされたとしても，退職の意思表示に瑕疵のない限り合意退職は無効にならないとした例	ジュリスト167
1959	1	・無届の就業規則の効力，懲戒解雇の不当労働行為該当性	ジュリスト170
	2	・経歴詐欺を理由とする解雇と不当労働行為	ジュリスト171

著作目録

	4	・失業保険法8条に基く認可の取消処分が適法と認められた事例	ジュリスト176
	6	消極的団結権の反省	労問・13
		ILOと消極的団結権(1)	労協・3
	7	ILOと消極的団結権(2)	労協・4
	8	『労使間における懲戒権の研究』	勁草書房
		公労法4条3項とILO98号条約	ジュリスト184
		組合保障措置の国際的動向	世界の労働1959-7
		・王子製糸　苫小牧・春日井工場事件	ジュリスト184
	10	懲戒解雇（『綜合判例研究叢書』労働法6）	有斐閣
		・解雇が不当労働行為と認められたが，右解雇後行われた和解による退職が有効なものと認められた例	ジュリスト187
	11	教育委員会の行った専従不承認処分の効力	ジュリスト189
	12	スイスの組合保障制度	労問・19
1960	1	ヨーロッパ社会主義の衰退	労協・10
		※『判例回顧』1958年	日本評論社
	3	ドイツにおける組合強制	労協・12
	7	西ドイツの婦人労働	労問・26
	8	Das System und der Character des Japanischen Arbeisrechts	Recht der Arbeit 1960 Heft 8/9
1961	6	西ドイツにおける労働争議の実態	季労・40
		ドイツ雑感	中央経済10-6
		・タクシー会社争議仮処分事件	ジュリスト227
	7	目黒製作所事件をめぐる仮処分	ジュリスト229
	8	・解雇の承認と効力	ジュリスト234
		ILO結社の自由委員会179号（日本）事件コメント	労協・29
	10	和教祖専従不承認処分の効力	法律のひろば14-10
		目黒製作所事件をめぐる二つの仮処分決定に	労経速報12-29

		ついて	
	12	労働法（年間回顧1961年）	ジュリスト240
1962	1	・組合役員に対する解雇と不当労働行為	ジュリスト241
		J. R. デンプシー，勤労権立法の機能	労協・35
		・就業規則違反の懲戒解雇	ジュリスト244
	3	ILO 批准，その遅延と国際体制の問題点	東洋経済新報3-31
		※『工業大事典』	平凡社
	6	カナダにおける組合保障	ジュリスト251
		・労働基本権（ジュリスト『労働判例百選』）	有斐閣
		・労働者の行政訴訟（ジュリスト『労働判例百選』）	有斐閣
		・組合員以外の者を就労させない旨の会社・組合間の協定の効力	ジュリスト252
	7	D. N. プリット『労働組合と法』	ダイヤモンド社
		ILO87号と40時間労働制の勧告をめぐって	労働法学研究会報495
	8	公労法17条と争議行為	法律のひろば
	11	※『西ドイツの労働裁判』	日本労働協会
		・解雇無効の組合における解雇以後の昇給分の賃金請求権の有無	ジュリスト261
1963	1	ショップ制（『労働法大系』1）	有斐閣
	3	『ILO と日本の団結権』	ダイヤモンド社
		ドイツにおける労働組合と政治(1)	労協・48
	4	ドイツにおける労働組合と政治(2)	労協・49
		労働協約と私的自治	労働法・21
	6	ストライキに対する賃金カットの合法性の限界	日労研資料578
		※『世界大百科事典』	平凡社
	7	Labor Movement and Political Parties in Japan	Bombay Labor Journal, July 1963

著作目録

	9	災害補償と民事責任（労働法大系）	有斐閣
	11	余暇と労働基準法	学習3
1964	2	B.ミレン『新興国における労働組合の政治的役割』	労協・59
	4	※『現代法学入門』	有斐閣
	5	国際労働機関（『労働事典』）	青林書院
	6	経営者の組合に対する言論の自由とその限界	日労研資料611
	9	・取引会社の圧力による解雇と不当労働行為	労経速報541
	11	※『現代思想事典』	講談社
		※『労働法教室』I	有斐閣
	12	※『ケース・ブック労働法』	有信堂
1965	1	※『労働者の財産づくり』	日本労働協会
	4	※『教材法学入門』	有斐閣
	9	『労働組合の政治的役割』	未来社
	10	和教組最高裁判決をめぐって	法律のひろば
		J.D.フーヴァー「アメリカ労働運動は輸出されるべきか」	労協・80
1966	1	アメリカ雑感	中央経済15-1
		Twenty Years of the Labor Relations Commission	J. L. Bulletin Vol. 5-No. 1
	2	・労働者の過失による不合格製品作り直しのための時間外労働振替，休日振替出勤日の無届欠勤を理由とする解雇	ジュリスト399
		セニオリティの法律問題(1)	労協・83
	3	セニオリティの法律問題(2)	労協・84
		※『自習労働法30問』	有斐閣
	4	アメリカの労働問題と労働法	日労研資料670
		企業合同と従業員の地位	経法ジャーナル8
		アメリカ官公労働者の労働基本権	労働法・27
		セニオリティの法律問題(3)	労協・85
	5	マーケット・リサーチと団体交渉	日労研資料674

著作目録

	6	今日の米国労働法規と主要労働問題	アメリカの労働問題1966.6
	7	ビラ貼り行為の限界と刑事責任	労働法学研究会報673
		・企業別組合の結んだショップ協定と合同労組員の地位	ジュリスト349
	8	ILO87号条約関係国内法改正	経法ジャーナル12
	9	組合活動と年次有給休暇の関係	労経速報579
		・東海電通局庁舎ビラ貼り事件	季労・61
	10	政府きめ手失う	読売新聞10-26夕
	11	『労働協約』	日本労働協会
		・争議行為に利用された有給休暇中の賃金請求権	ジュリスト358
	12	・全逓中央郵便局事件最高裁判決について	判例時報462
		上部組織と下部組織（『新労働法講座』2）	有斐閣
1967	1	公務員等労働法	ジュリスト361
	2	官公労働者の争議権	労協・95
	5	・年次有給休暇（ジュリスト『労働判例百選新版』）	有斐閣
		・災害補償と民事責任（ジュリスト『労働判例百選新版』）	有斐閣
	6	結婚退職制	ソフィア16-2
	7	労働問題研究の方法論的反省	労協・100
	9	※『西ドイツの労働政策』	日本労働協会
	10	欧米労組の職場活動	労問・114
		The Retirement Age System in Japan	J. L. Bulletin Vol. 6-No. 1
		年次有給休暇と組合活動	検察資料141
	11	・国鉄労組分会の徴収した組合費の帰属関係	判例時報495
		※『新材労働法入門』	有斐閣
	12	・企業組合の組合員の定年制	ジュリスト388

著作目録

		書評　大野雄二郎著『争議行為法概論』	日労研資料724
1968	1	賃金カットの時期と範囲	日労研資料725
		Retirement Age—One of the Labor Problems	Japan No. 25
	3	懲戒条項の適用・解釈	季労・67
		※『ハンドブック労働法』	有信堂
	4	Industrial Relations in Japan's Taxi Industry (1)	J. L. Bulletin Vol. 7-No. 4
	5	Industrial Relations in Japan's Taxi Industry (2)	J. L. Bulletin Vol. 7-No. 5
		労働組合（『会社法律大辞典』）	第一法規
		自動車事故と労使関係—タクシー業を中心として—	事故と災害
	6	服務規律，表彰，懲戒（石井照久編『就業規則の実証的研究』）	日本労働協会
		・年次有給休暇と争議行為	ジュリスト年鑑1968
		・公労法18条にもとづく解雇は公法的性格のものか	ジュリスト339
	7	・基礎疫病がある場合の労務上死亡に当たるか否かの判決	ジュリスト401
	8	懲戒に関する最近の判例について	労経速報644
		・懲戒解雇が懲戒権の濫用として無効とされた事例	ジュリスト404
		・職場結婚をした場合，夫婦のうちいずれかが退職する旨の誓約書にもとづく退職の効力	判例時報522
		施設管理権と組合活動	地方公務員月報61
	10	西ドイツの労働裁判とわが国の問題点	労働法・32
		労使関係と労働法	宮城労働21-8
	11	年次有給休暇と組合活動	労協・116

		差別と法	差別と偏見 5
1969	4	労使紛争と裁判	労協・121
	5	Women Workers and Retirement after Marriage	J. L. Bulletin Vol. 8-No. 5
		労働組合の選挙活動と統制権の限界	官公労働23-5
	6	共稼ぎと会社の人事権	日労研資料771
	7	・事業場における政治活動を禁止する就業規則の効力	判例タイムズ235
	9	せみなあ　法職課程　労働法	法学セミナー163
		※『労使関係の法律相談』	有斐閣
		・55才定年制を新たに定めた就業規則改正の効力	ジュリスト433
	10	Labor disputes and their settlement（R. J. Ballon（ed.）, *Japanese Employee*）	Sophia/Tuttle
	11	『労働基本権』	中央公論社
1970	4	技術革新と労働基準法	労働と福祉61号
	4・5	お店の法律相談10回	読売新聞，地方経済欄
	5	失対労務者の団体交渉権	判例時報587
		労使関係から見た大学紛争	上智法学論集13-2/3
		New Problems Facing the Protective Labor Law（I）	J. L. Bulletin Vol. 9-No. 5
	6	New Problems Facing the Protective Labor Law（II）	J. L. Bulletin Vol. 9-No. 6
		労働組合の内部問題―統括―	労協・135
	9	・不当労働行為意思があっても解雇は有効か	日労研資料810
	11	『労働協約』（通信講座）	日本労働協会
	12	王立委員会「英国労使関係報告書」(6)	労協・141
1971	3	The Role and Functions of Industrial Relations Centres in Japan	Sophia Law Review, XIV, No. 2

	※B・エーロン「西欧五ヵ月における紛争処理手続」	労協・144
4	アジア・西太平洋諸国の労働法と労使関係	海外商事法務106
	※ティロー・ラム「労働裁判例の構成と機能」	労協・145
5	配転をめぐる法律問題	日労研資料829
	※ジノ・ジューニー「労働紛争解決の公的規則と私的規則」	労協・146
	※ザビエル・ブランクージューバン「未組織労働者の地位」	労協・146
6	労働法の理論と現実	季労・80
	※フォルケ・シュミット「調整・司法・行政手続」	労協・147
7	The Role and Functions of Industrial Relations Centres in Japan	Indian Journal of Industrial Relations 6-4
	※ウェダーバーン「労働争議における権利争議と利益争議」	労協・148
	※The Role of the "Fault" in Social Security Legislation	Sophia Law Review, XIV, No. 3
8	わが国における労働紛争とその処理	労協・149
	The Political Orientation of Japanese Unions	J. L. Bulletin Vol. 10-No. 8
10	産業構造の変化と労働法の変貌	労協・151
11	労使紛争の特質とその解決過程	労協・152
	・発言者のタイポロジー	ジュリスト491
	The Political Orientation of Japanese Unions	AFL-CIO, Free Trade Union News 26-11
	Die Politische Orientierung der Japanischen Gewerkschaften	Freigewerkschafthiche Nachirichten, 26-11

著作目録

		L'orientation politique des syndicats japonais	Nouvelles du Mouvement Syndicas Libre, 26-11
	12	※『労使交渉』	ダイヤモンド社
1972	2	労働運動における理想主義と現実主義	官公労働26-2
	3	政治スト	ジュリスト500
		働きすぎと時間短縮	官公労働26-4
		ビラ貼りをめぐるもめごと	官公労働26-3
		The Characteristics of Labor Disputes in Japan (*Social and Cultural Background of Labor-Management Relations in Asian Countries*)	Japan Institute of Labour
		争いのルール―争議権の濫用―（伊藤・甲斐編『現代における権利とは何か』）	有斐閣
	5	公務員，公企体職員の争議行為	日労研資料862
		官公労の争議行為と最近の判例	公労委季報 No. 11
		婦人労働の保護と平等	官公労働26-5
	6	・公労法17条違反の争議行為と懲戒処分	判例タイムズ276
		春闘をめぐって	官公労働26-6
	7	日本労使関係のステレオタイプ	官公労働26-7
	8	使用者としての私	官公労働26-8
	9	イギリスのゼネスト回避	官公労働26-9
		・宮城県都城郵便局事件判決をめぐって	官公労働26-9
	10	労使紛争の解決過程（『法社会学講座』）	岩波書店
		腹をたてないこと	官公労働26-10
	11	法律のむつかしさ	官公労働26-11
	12	Working Hours in Japan	J. L. Bulletin Vol. 11-No. 12
		ヨーロッパ三大発見（？）	官公労働26-12

著作目録

		傾向経営（ジュリスト『労働法の判例』）	有斐閣
1973	3	『労働争議―労使関係にみる日本的風土』	日本経済新聞社
	4	週5日制の後に来るもの	労協・169
		フレックス・タイム―日本導入の問題点	週刊ダイヤモンド428
		※『産業構造の変化と労働法』ジュリスト増刊	有斐閣
	5	週休2日制の後に来るもの	日労研資料891
		Future Industrial Relations-Japan	IILS Bulletin No. 10
		有給休暇と争議行為	官公労働27-5
	6	官公労の争議権と最高裁判決	ジュリスト536
	7	Labor Relations in the Public Sector	J. L. Bulletin Vol. 12-No. 7
	8	フレックス導入の日本的背景	NOMAプレスサービス245
		・他の事業場における争議行為の応援と年次有給休暇の成否	ジュリスト540
	9	年次有給休暇と争議行為	日労研資料902
	11	※フレックスタイムの実態と法理(1)	ジュリスト547
	12	ヨーロッパの労使関係の変化とわが国の問題点	中央労働時報551
		The role of "fault" in social security legislation (*Actes des VII—eme Congres International de Droit du Travail et de la Securite Sociale, Volume II*)	Warzawa
		※フレックスタイムの実態と法理(2)	ジュリスト549
		※フレックスタイムの実態と法理(3)	ジュリスト550
		※『労働基準法50講』	有斐閣
1974	2	職場規律と組合活動　上	官公労働28-2
		思想の自由と雇用関係	ジュリスト553
		※フレックスタイムの実態と法理(4)	ジュリスト553

		※フレックスタイムの実態と法理(5)	ジュリスト554
	3	「不当労働行為」	日本労働協会
		職場規律と組合活動　下	官公労働28-3
	4	スト権闘争(1)―(4)	公明新聞4-20, 23, 27, 30
		労働組合と政党支持の自由	ジュリスト557
		※『銀行の労働法』	新実業出版社
	5	採用の自由と思想・信条の自由	日労研資料921
	7	採用の自由と基本権（『労働法の諸問題』）	勁草書房
	9	休憩時間中の政治活動（『労働判例百選』第3）	有斐閣
		第三者の強制（『労働判例百選』第3）	有斐閣
		The Characteristics of Labor Disputes and Their Settlement in Japan (International Conference on Industrial and Labor Relations)	Jerusalem Academic Press
	10	Is slimness BFOQ?	J. L. Bulletin Vol. 13-No. 10
		裁判官と女性の容姿	ジュリスト573
1975	1	高度産業社会の労使関係	ジュリスト578
		終身雇用制があるための組織活動の悩み	日本の経営文化5
		産業構造の変化と労働法の変貌（川野健二編『産業構造の変革』第一巻）	日本評論社
	2	・労働契約と思想・信条の自由	ジュリスト580
		※『フレックス・タイム―勤務時間の再検討』	日本経済新聞社
	10	日本における労働争議	現代のエスプリ No. 10
		学生を送る側の論理	朝日新聞10-11朝
		わが国の知的状況と労働法	労協・200, 201
	12	空虚なスト違法論	読売新聞12-7朝
		※『労災補償安全衛生50講』	有斐閣

著作目録

1976	2	いかがわしい場所	ジュリスト606
		大学の退廃	官公労働30-2
	3	シュール・バイシュピール	官公労働30-3
		The Multinational Corporations and Japanese Industrial Relations (D. Kujawa (ed.) International Labor and the Multinational Enterprise)	Praeger Pub. N. Y. 1975
		スト権―国民的合意への道	公明168号
		ロックアウトについて㈠	官公労働30-3
	4	ロックアウトについて㈡	官公労働30-4
		ひとりよがりの経営哲学	労働と経営14-4
		・近頃の明るいニュース	官公労働30-4
		・退職金と労基法24条1項(『最高裁判所労働判例批評民事篇』)	有斐閣
		・違法な時間外労働と割増賃金支払義務(『最高裁判所労働判例批評民事篇』)	有斐閣
	5	婦人労働研究のすすめ	官公労働30-5
	5-6	The Lifetime Employment System in Japan : Its Reality and Future	May-June 1976, Atlanta Economic Review
	6	労働金庫について	官公労働30-6
		「日本的」経営参加論の反省	労協・208
	7	あるあっせん事件	官公労働30-7
	8	ILOと国際政治	官公労働30-8
	9	短文の難しさ	官公労働30-9
		Japan, (C. S. Aronstein (ed.), International Handbook on Contracts of Employment)	Kluwer
	10	新しい国の発見	官公労働30-10
	11	発展途上国の労使関係	ジュリスト625
		賄賂について	官公労働30-11

著作目録

		労使関係の国際比較	中央労働時報595
	12	イギリスの性差別禁止法について（『労働法の解釈理論』）	有斐閣
		伝統産業と近代化	官公労働30-12
1977	1	Worker Participation in Japan	J. L. Bulletin Vol. 16-No. 1
		わが国海外進出企業における労働問題――ナイジェリア――	労協・214
	2	公務員の特殊性と労使関係	季刊人事行政 No. 3
		民間84労組の経営参加の実態	季刊中央公論経営問題春季号
		※『新労働基準実例百選』	別冊ジュリスト No. 54
	3	公共部門の紛争処理について	公企労研究30
	4	Worker Participation in Japan	Japan No. 61
	6	Worker Participation in Management Today	Japan Echo, 18, 2
	7	Worker Participation in Management Today（I）	J. L. Bulletin Vol. 16-No. 8
	8	Worker Participation in Management Today（II）	J. L. Bulletin Vol. 16-No. 9
		※『労働組合読本』	東洋経済新報社
		※『諸外国における労働時間短縮，週休2日制に関する研究』	労働省
	10	「労働法再入門」を読んで	書斎の窓268
		テニスと健康	月刊「健康」10月号
	11	紛争処理の枠組と実態（小宮隆太郎編『公共部門の争議権』）	東大出版会
1978	2	※『わが国海外進出企業の労働問題――ナイジェリア』	日本労働協会

著作目録

	6	具体的改善策示さず	読売新聞6-14
	9	EEC労使関係規制	ジュリスト672
		三度目の正直	季労・109
		公共企業体系基本問題会議答申をめぐって	公企労研究36
	10	公社・公務員の労使関係について	現代の労働14号
1979	1	労働問題の国際化	ジュリスト681
		OECDと多国籍企業の労働問題	日本労働協会
		新春雑感	官公労働33-1
	2	人員整理について	官公労働33-2
	3	江川問題と法律家	官公労働33-3
	4	*Labour Law and Industrial Relations in Japan*	Kluwer
		労働委員会を去るに当たって	官公労働33-4
	5	『労働の世界について考える』	講談社
		国際会議の意味	官公労働33-5
		チョーサーと神戸牛	上智大学通信5-23
		Labor Relations in Japan Today	Kodansha-International
	6	私の法学教育	ジュリスト692
		スト誹謗は名誉毀損か	官公労働33-6
		雇用闘争と労働組合（ジュリスト総合特集『企業と労働』)	有斐閣
		今日の国際法とカルステン博士	ソフィア110号
	7	警察権と国民の人権	朝日新聞7-12朝
		「時評」のその後	官公労働33-7
	8	翻訳の恐しさ	官公労働33-8
		働きすぎと時間短縮	中央公論9月号
		How to deal with Japanese Unions	The Journal of the American Chamber of Commerce Vol.

486

		※『ベルギー日系企業の労働関係』	16, No. 7 日本労働協会
		※Japanese Multinational and Labor Relations in Belgium	Bulletin of Comparative Labour Relations No. 10
	9	採用の自由（ジュリスト『労働法の争点』）	有斐閣
		定年延長と昇給ストップ	官公労働33-9
	10	Overwork, Working Hours Reduction	Look Japan, Oct. 10
		不当労働行為事件の処理について	中央労働時報639
		日本論の再ブーム	官公労働33-10
	11	アジアとILOと日本	官公労働33-10
	12	日本人の勤勉さについて	官公労働33-10
		Protection or Equality?	J. L. Bulletin Vol. 18-No. 12
1980	4	80年代の雇用問題	ジュリスト713
	5	アメリカの年令差別法にみるその影響	エルダー5月号
	6	大学の大衆化と大学教育	厚生補導169
		不当労働行為事件の取扱いの現状と問題点	現代の労働21号
		※『就業規則の法理と実務』	日本労働協会
	7	マリリン・マクロウィッツ著「働き中毒—その対処法」	労協・256
	10	日本における男女平等法	ジュリスト725
		The Settlement of Labor Disputes in Worldwide Perspective	International Social Science Journal XXXII. 3
	11	『アメリカの年令差別禁止法—施行状況と問題点』	高年齢者雇用開発協会
		胃の検査始末記	月刊「健康」80-12
	12	働き中毒のすすめ	中公・経営問題冬季

著作目録

		国際関係法学科の開設について	上智法学論集24巻特別号
1981	4	西独留学の頃(『石黒拓爾,無,遺稿と追想』)	
		※『労働法・要点とまとめ』	北樹出版
	7	・経歴詐欺を理由とする試用期間中の解雇	判例評論269
		国際化ばやり	法と政策 No. 1
		国際化に応える	月刊リクルート7月号
		男女差別問題を考える	法学教室 No. 10
	8	労働基本権の制限(ジュリスト『労働判例百選』(第4版))	有斐閣
	10	労働と法(沢井外編『法学部学生のための法律学概論』)	有斐閣
		ヨーロッパから見た日本の労使関係	世界の労働31-10
	11	Worker Motivation and the Japanese Industrial Relations System	Japan Society News Letter Vol. XXIX No. 4
	12	アメリカの年令差別禁止法の施行状況と問題点	労協・273
		The Influence of ILO Standard on Law and Practice in Japan	International Labor Review Vol. 120, No. 6
1982	2	Worker Motivation in Japan (I)	J. L. Bulletin Vol. 21-No. 2
	3	Worker Motivation in Japan (II)	J. L. Bulletin Vol. 21-No. 3
		・団体交渉の委任	判例評論277
	4	賃金差別と不当労働行為	中央労働時報681
		Updating of International Encyclopedia	Kluwer
	5	Japan (E. Yermin (ed.), *Work Force Reductions in Undertakings*)	ILO

	7	最高裁判事の高年齢化	法令ニュース Vol. 17, No. 7
		・リボン闘争の正当性	ジュリスト771
	9	Workers' Participation in the Workshop and the Enterprise (R. Blanpain (ed.), *Law and Industrial Relations*)	Kluwer
		教科書問題から学ぶこと	ジュリスト774
		※『変貌する国際社会』	有斐閣
	10	『労働争議』	講談社
	12	一週間の旅	月刊「健康」12-8
		感情論より大局的判断を	読売新聞12-6朝
1983	1	企業の海外活動と労使関係	ジュリスト781
	2	産業調整と雇用(『80年代の労使関係』)	日本労働協会
		Viability of the Japanese Model of Industrial Relations	IIRA, Sixth World Congress Vol. 5
	3	労働需給構造の変化とその対策	上智大学法学部25周年記念論集
	4	日本的労使関係の国際的普遍性	労協・228
	5	両性の平等(『基本法学』Ⅰ)	岩波書店
	6	Unfair Labor Practices—Law and Practices—	J. L. Bulletin Vol. 22-No. 6
		日本の国際的地位	労協・290
		※ R. ブランパン編『労働問題の国際比較』	日本労働協会
	8	・格付けの誤りによる本採用拒否の適法性	ジュリスト796
		International Effects of Japanese Industrial Relations (*International Issues in Industrial Relations*)	Industrial Relations Society of Australia
		The Function of the Law in Japanese Industrial Relations (T. Shirai (ed.), *Contemporary Industrial Relations in*	University of Wisconsin Press

		Japan)	
	9	日本における外資系企業の労使関係	労協・293
		書評 竹前栄治著「戦後労働の改革」	労協・294
	11	公労法上の仲裁裁定の取扱いと効力	公企労センター調査研究資料111
		『海外進出企業の労使関係』	日本経済新聞社
	12	最近の国際労働関係文献	労協・296
1984	1	Japan (A. Cook, Lorwin, & Daniels (ed.), *Women and Trade Unions in Eleven Industrialized Countries*)	Temple University Press, 1984
	4	黒船, 安保, 雇用平等	官公労働38-4
	5	ニコラス・バルティコス『国際労働基準とILO』(監修)	三省堂
	6	反対論者へ"法の常識"教えます	官公労働38-8
		※『便宜供与の実態と法律問題』	公企労センター調査研究資料118
		※*Industrial Conflict Resolution in Market Economies*	Kluwer
	9	公共部門の労使関係	公企労研究No. 60
		Conflict and It's Resolution in Industrial Relations and Labor Law (Rohlen & Steinoff (ed.), *Conflict in Japan*)	University of Hawaii Press
1985		※『労使紛争処理の国際比較』	日本労働協会
	1	*Labor Law and Industrial Relations in Japan* (2nd & revised ed.)	Kluwer
	7	Equality and Prohibition of Discrimination in Employment—Japan	Bulletin of Comparative Labor Relation No. 14
	9	Employee Participation in the Workshop, the Office and in the Enterprise (R. Blanpain (ed.), *Comparative Labor*	Kluwer

Law and Industrial Relations）

1986	3	※『わかりやすい男女雇用機会均等法』	有斐閣
	4	雇用機会均等法の成立・施行と今後の課題	労協・322
		『現代の雇用平等』	三省堂
		日系企業の直面するアメリカの労働問題	世界の労働36-4
	6	二つの旅	官公労働40-6
		※『女性と企業の新時代』	有斐閣
		※『労働組合読本』第2版	東洋経済新報社
		※*Fifty Years of Labor Law & Social Security*	Kluwer
	10	企業の国際化と労使関係	公労委季報109
	11	労働時間の短縮について	月刊社会保険労務士22-1
	12	La Loi sur l'egalite des conditions d'emploi des femmes	Notes de conjoncture sociale No. 257, 12-8
		※『労働基準実例百選（第三版）』	有斐閣
1987	1	世の中と平和に	日本経済新聞1-16夕
	2	公社民営化と労使関係の課題	公季労研究70
	3	労働時間の短縮―中基審建議をめぐって―	労協・332
		Tendances recentes du marche du travail	Notes de conjoncture sociale No. 264, 3-16
		※『海外勤務の実態と法理』	日本労働協会
	6	組織に埋もれた"女性人材"の発掘をはかれ	実業の日本6-1
		法文化論的にみた均等法（篠塚英子編『雇用均等法の影響と企業の対応』）	日経センター
	7	※『雇用均等時代の経営と労働』	東洋経済新報社
	8	米国進出企業と「労働摩擦」への対応	労働法研究会報38-29

著作目録

		9	アメリカ労使関係法と労使協力	海外労働時報125

		9	アメリカ労使関係法と労使協力	海外労働時報125
			NHK市民大学『雇用と労働』	NHK出版
		12	※*Industrial Conflict Resolution in Market Economy*, II.	Kluwer
1988	2	余暇社会における労働	RIRI流通産業20-2
	4	年のとり方	月刊「健康」88-4
		Japanese Model of Industrial Relations : Myth and Reality (*Nouveaux modeles de Relations du travail*)	Universite de Montreal, 1987
		※『改正労働基準実例百選』	有斐閣
	8	Labor Law-Social Security (CCH, *Japan Business Law Guide*)	CCH International
		21世紀の労働	賃金事情2001
	10	外国人労働者問題（経済教室）	日本経済新聞10-21
	11	在米日系企業の雇用・労働対策1	在外企業109号
		A Guide to Personnel Management in Japan—Law and Practice—Part I	Labour Issues Quarterly No. 1
	12	在米日系企業の雇用・労働対策2	在外企業110号
1989	1	在米日系企業の雇用・労働対策3	在外企業111号
	2	外国人労働者問題の政策的視点	労働時報89-2
	3	在米日系企業の雇用・労働対策4	在外企業112号
		A Guide to Personnel Management in Japan—Law and Practice—Part II	Labour Issues Quarterly No. 2
	4	在米日系企業の雇用・労働対策5	在外企業113号
	5	鎖国か開放か—外国人労働者の受入れ	50億 89-5
		在米日系企業の雇用・労働対策6	在外企業114号
		Co-operation and Conflict in Public Sector Labor Relations in Japan (Gladstone et. al. (ed), *Current Issues La-*	de Gryter : N. Y.

		bor Relation)	
	6	在米日系企業の雇用・労働対策 7	在外企業115号
		A Guide to Personnel Management in Japan—Law and Practice—Part III	Labour Issues Quarterly No. 3
		西洋労働法の日本化	ジュリスト934
		※『明日の隣人　外国人労働者』	東洋経済新報社
	7	在米日系企業の雇用・労働対策 8	在外企業116号
		※新版『労使関係の法律相談』	有斐閣
		※Industrial Conflict Resolution in Market Economies, 2nd Revised Ed.	Kluwer
	8	商社等日系企業の米国における労務管理上の諸問題	日本貿易会月報 No. 426
	9	A Guide to Personnel Management in Japan—Law and Practice—Part IV	Labour Issues Quarterly No. 4
		在米日系企業をめぐる労働問題	在外企業117号
		外国人労働問題（年報『日本の労使関係』）	日本労働協会
		Conflict Resolution in Industrial Relations in the U. S. and Japan (*Conference on Labor and Economic Development*)	Chung-Hua Institute for Economic Development
		Industrial Democracy (Ishida & Krauss (ed.), *Democracy in Japan*)	Univ. of Pittsburg Press
	10	A Guide to Personnel Management in Japan—Law and Practice—Part V	Labour Issues Quarterly No. 5
		外国人労働者問題を考える	労働かながわ89-10
1990	1	外国人労働者問題—1999年末ある日の「朝までテレビ」—	労研・364
		A Guide to Personnel Management in Japan—Law and Practice—Part VI	Labour Issues Quarterly No. 6
		Japanization of Western Labor Law (H.	J. C. B. Mohr

著作目録

		Coing et. al.(ed.), *Die Japanisierung des Westlichen Rechts*)	(Paul Siebeck)
	2	外国人労働者問題の政策的課題	世界と人口192号
		『不当労働行為』	日本労働研究機構
		A Guide to Personnel Management in Japan—Law and Practice—Part VII	Labour Issues Quarterly No. 7
	3	過労死について	月刊「健康」90-7
		※報告書「専門家派遣の法的側面に関する基礎的研究―国際協力事業団委託研究―」	日本労働研究機構
	4	A Guide to Personnel Management in Japan—Law and Practice—Part VIII	Labour Issues Quarterly No. 8
	10	5年目の均等法	月刊社会保険労務士26-10
		A Guide to Personnel Management in Japan—Law and Practice—Part IX	Labour Issues Quarterly No. 9
	11	均等待遇（ジュリスト増刊「労働法の争点」（新版））	有斐閣
		Cambio Tecnologico y el modelo japones de relaciones industriales（Alejandro Alvarez y John Borrego (ed.), *La insercion de Mexico en la Cuenca del Pacifico*, Volumen III, Facultad de Economia, Universidad National Autonoma de Mexico）	Universidad National Autonoma de Mexico
1991	1	外国人労働者―アメリカからなにを学ぶか	労研・375
	3	Japanese Management and U. S. Labor Relations（Industrial Union Department, AFL-CIO & Japan Federation of Employers' Associations, *Cooperation is Better*）	Nikkeiren
		日本の企業と米国労使関係（日経連・AFL-	日経連

		CIO産業別組合部「より良い労使関係を求めて」)	
	4	400時間の労働時間差の原因	週刊東洋経済4-27
	8	Managing Japanese Workers - Personnel Management—Law and Practice in Japan—	Japan Institute of Labour
	10	日本的差別の構造―均等法五年で問われる婦人行政	ジュリスト988
	11	雇用平等の復権	月刊社会保険労務士27-11
1992	1	雇用差別に鈍感な日本企業	The Global Citizenship 新春号
		雇用平等の国際的展開	労研・385
		均等法を廃止して差別禁止法を	エンプロイ1月号
	2	日本企業の雇用差別とアメリカの議会	海外労働時報184
		Workers' Participation : Influence on Management Decision-Making by Labor in Private Sector—Japan	Bulletin of Comparative Labor Relations, 23, 1992
		『労働政策と労働法』	日本労働研究機構
	4	差別禁止法の制定を	世界の労働4月号
		Discrimination in the U. S. and Japan—from a legal viewpoint—	The Journal of American and Canadian Studies No. 8
	5	外国人労働者に関する国の政策と国連条約	大原社会問題研究所402号
		外国人居住者問題を考える	月刊「自治フォーラム」391号
	6	提言 意義ある休暇とは何か	月刊 実業の日本 6月号

著作目録

		Employed or Self-Employed—Japan—	Bulletin of Comparative Labor Relations, 24, 1992
	8	世界で問われる日本の企業文化と法文化―アメリカの連邦議会と日系企業―	労研・392
	10	均等法を否定して差別禁止法の制定を	月刊社会保険労務士10月号
	12	Employment Discrimination in U. S.-based Japanese Companies	Economic Eye 13-4
1993	4	職場と煙草	地方公務員 安全と健康フォーラム 93-4
	6	アメリカの出入国管理政策（桑原靖夫編『国際労働力移動のフロンティア』）	日本労働研究機構
	7	日系企業の雇用差別にみる日米比較文化（上智大学アメリカ・カナダ研究所『アメリカと日本』）	彩流社
		※『雇用平等日米合同調査―中間報告書』	日本労働研究機構
		※*The Japan-U. S. Joint Research Project on Employment Discrimination（Interim Report）*	Japan Institute of Labour
	8	クリントン政権の労働政策	月刊社会保険労務士8月号
		General Report "Settlement of Labor Disputes in Asian Countries"（*5th Asian Regional Congress of Labor Law and Social Security*）	
	8	※『ECと日本企業―人事労務管理の国際的展開―』	日本労働研究機構
	9	WHO・ILOのエイズ対策	季労・168

	10	日本的差別の構造（加藤・坂本・瀬地山編「フェミニズム・コレクションI―制度と達成―」）	勁草書房
	11	企業・エイズ・社会	「ジェトロセンサー」11月号
		※Industrial Relations and Human Resource Management in Japanese Enterprises in Europe―Belgium, France, Germany, Italy, the Netherlands and the United Kingdom―	Nomos Verlaggesellschaft
		※『あなたの隣人　外国人労働者』	東洋経済新報社
1994	1	女の特等席	海外労働時報211
	2	平等法理と私的自治	海外労働時報212
	3	平等法理と非合理の世界	海外労働時報213
	4	40時間制の出発と今後の課題	労働時報47-4
		週40時間制と企業の課題	企業会計46-5
		不況下の時短をどう考えるか？	労働基準46-4
		労働争訟を考える―日本における労使関係紛争処理―	経営法曹研究会報第4号
	5	歯の手入れと余生	月刊「健康」413号
		※Employment Security―Law and Practice in Belgium, Bulgaria, France, Germany, Great Britain, Italy, Japan and the EC	Peeters
	6	管理職の地位と労働法	労働法学研究会報1968
	7	日本企業における女性	リクルート調査月報19-4
		Industrial Relations and the Future of the ILO : Changing Issues and Actors (ILO, Visions of the Future of Social	ILO, Geneva

著作目録

	Justice)	
8	協調的労使関係の命運	月刊社会保険労務士8月号
10	労使関係とILOの将来―問題とアクターの変化―（ILO『社会正義の将来展望』）	日本ILO協会
12	管理職の地位と労働法	中央労働時報883
	社会的基本権の発想から労働委員会制度をみると	月刊労季労協465号
	労働法学研究所を回顧して	労働法学研究会報2000
4	規制緩和と労働法制の再検討	書斎の窓433
	ILOと社会条項	世界の労働45-4
5	アジアの国々と西欧の「普遍的」理念	季労・174
6	グールメでダンディの東北人（『保原先生これからもよろしく』）	
7	雇用平等法制	ジュリスト1071
8	たばこと男女平等	月刊社会保険労務士8月号
9	HIV感染者に対する企業の配慮義務	ジュリスト1074
10	チェック・オフ―エッソ石油事件（ジュリスト『労働判例百選』第六版）	有斐閣
11	※『アメリカ日系企業と雇用平等』	日本労働研究機構
	※European Works Councils	Peeters
12	依存組合と不当労働行為について	中央労働時報900
	Employment Security in Japanese Labor-Management Relations from a Legal Perspective（WAI & JIL, *Employment Security : Changing Characteristics in U. S. and Japan―Background Papers―*）	WAI & JIL

| 1996 | 4 | 労働法と規制緩和 | 労働かながわNo. 538 |

	5	均等法一〇年の再検討	季労・178
		女性の優遇と平等	労研・433
		Japanese Policies on the Rights and Benefits Granted to Foreign Workers, Residents, Refugees and Illegals	Center for International Studies, MIT
	7	在米日系企業が留意すべき米国労働法	日外協 Monthly 186号
		宮本君の壮絶な死(『宮本光雄弁護士を偲ぶ』)	
	8	日系企業のセクハラ訴訟	官公労働50-7
		ハーフ・リタヤーの弁	月刊「健康」1996年8月号
		職場における喫煙	月刊社会保険労務士7月号
	10	三つの"inter"―研究所長に就任して―	JILリサーチ27号
		The Employment Contract and Human Resource Development in Japan (WAI & JIL, *Employer Training in the New Economy: U. S. and Japanese Perspective, 1996*)	WAI & JIL
1997	1	時代の変遷と座標軸―丸山先生の思い出―	中央労働時報916
	2	Globalization of Employment and Social Clauses	J. L. Bulletin Vol. 36-No. 2
	4	スト権スト	労研・443
		Globalization, Employment and Social Clauses (*International Encyclopedia of Laws―World Law Conference*)	Law in Motion
	9	職場の喫煙と規制緩和	月刊社会保険労務士9月号
	10	規制緩和と労働法例	月刊社会民主509号
		※『貿易と国際労働基準』	日本労働研究機構

		12	社会的一体性のための新しいパートナーシップ	労研・451
1998	1	変革期における人事労務管理――労働基準法改正にちなんで	月刊人事労務107号
	7	持ち株会社の使用者性	関西経協7月号
		・ユニオン・ショップ協定の履行としての解雇の効力――中央港運事件――	ジュリスト1137
	8	※*Temporary Workers or Future Citizens ―Japanese and U. S. Migration Policies*	Macmillan Press
	9	たばこと歯とバイアグラ	月刊社会保険労務士9月号
		Equal Employment Opportunity in Japan―the Crossroad of Japanese Legal Culture（C. Engels & M. Weiss (ed.), *Labour Law and Industrial Relations at the Turn of the Century―Liber Amicorum in Honor of Prof. Roger Blanpain*）	Kluwer
1999	1	21世紀の労働政策と労使関係を考える	週刊労働ニュース1790号
		年頭所感――新しい世紀にのぞむ労使関係の構築――	中央労働時報946
	3	新しいワーキングスタイルに対応する労働法制	労働時報608
		Japan（R. Blanpain (ed.), *Non-Standard Work and Industrial Relations*）	Kluwer
	7	規制緩和と労働法	郵便局経営7月号
		労働基準法改正の意義	季労・189
		21世紀の労使関係を議論するIIRA世界会議	月刊社会保険労務士9月号
	9	Fixed-term Work―Second Class or Sal-	International

vation? Journal of Comparative Labour Law and Industrial Relations, 15-2

※ 編 集 後 記

　本書の特色は，まず何と言っても海外の研究者から多数執筆陣に参加していただいたことである。当初呼びかけたこれら外国人教授のほとんどが執筆を快諾して下さり，しかも締切日を厳守される方がこれまたほとんどであったのには驚き，日頃の自己の執筆態度を改めて反省させられた。本書の刊行作業が，編集担当者として予想していたよりも順調に進んだのは，このように海外の先生方のご理解とご協力によるところが大きいが，それのみではもちろんない。海外寄稿者との間のコンタクト・パースンを務めて下さった成城大学奥山教授，同様に海外からの英字論文の校正を丹念に行ってくれた富山大学小畑助教授には感謝の言葉もない。ご両人とも，花見先生の薫陶を受けた人々であり，師弟愛を痛感した次第である。ともあれ，2000年2月15日の花見先生のお誕生日前に刊行できたことは望外の幸せであった。内外を問わず，ご執筆下さった諸先生方には，この場をお借りして深く感謝申し上げたい。花見忠先生，古稀おめでとう存じます（中嶋記）。

編者紹介─────
山口 浩一郎
　　　上智大学法学部教授
渡辺　　章
　　　筑波大学社会科学系教授
菅野 和夫
　　　東京大学法学部教授
中嶋 士元也
　　　上智大学法学部教授

花見忠先生古稀記念論集
労働関係法の国際的潮流

2000年（平成12年）1月1日　初版第1刷発行

編　者	花見忠先生古稀記念論集刊行委員会
発行者	今井　　貴 渡辺　左近
発行所	信山社出版株式会社 〔〒113-0033〕東京都文京区本郷 6-2-9-102 電　話　03（3818）1019 ＦＡＸ　03（3818）0344

Printed in Japan

Ⓒ花見忠先生古稀記念論集刊行委員会　2000.　印刷・製本／松澤印刷

ISBN 4-7972-2156-9 C3332

〈日本立法資料全集〉

256	労働基準法(1)(法案)	渡辺　章	43,689円
257	労働基準法(2)	渡辺　章	55,000円
258	労働基準法(3)上（議会審議録）	渡辺　章	35,000円
259	労働基準法(3)下（議会審議録）	渡辺　章	34,000円
260	労働基準法(4)（施行関係）		近刊
2141	労務指揮権の現代的展開	土田道夫	18,000円
4589	労働基準法解説	寺本廣作	25,000円
553	労働関係法の解釈基準（上）	中嶋士元也	9,709円
554	労働関係法の解釈基準（下）	中嶋士元也	12,621円
560	英米解雇法制の研究	小宮文人	13,592円

125	不当労働行為争訟法の研究	山川隆一	6,602円
161	労働組合統制処分論	鈴木芳明	3,398円
561	オーストリア労使関係法	下井隆史	5,825円
615	外国人労働者法	野川　忍	2,800円
617	ドイツ労働法　A．ハナウ・手塚和彰訳		12,000円
790	マレーシア労使関係法	香川孝三	6,500円
874	雇用形態の多様化と労働法	伊藤博義	11,000円
1587	就業規則論	宮島尚史	6,000円
2051	イギリス労働法入門	小宮文人	2,500円
2053	オーストラリア労働法の基軸と展開	長渕満男	6,796円
2066	労働法律関係の当事者	高島良一	12,000円
2102	労働契約の変更と解雇	野田　進	15,000円
2114	アメリカ労使関係法	岸井貞男	近刊

2117	フーゴ・ジンツハイマーとドイツ労働法		
		久保敬治	3,000円
5090	外国人の法的地位	畑野 勇	続刊
2128	世界の労使関係―民主主義と社会的安定		
		ILO著 菅野和夫監修	4,000円
2130	不当労働行為の行政救済法理	道幸哲也	10,000円
2132	組織強制の法理	鈴木芳明	3,800円
2139	国際労働関係の法理	山川隆一	7,000円
2143	雇用社会の道しるべ	野川 忍	2,800円
2142	国際社会法の研究	川口美貴	15,000円
2119	高齢化社会への途		
		フォン・マイデル・手塚和彰	9,000円